RED EAGLES

America's Secret MiGs

OSPREY
PUBLISHING

RED EAGLES

America's Secret MiGs

STEVE DAVIES

First published in Great Britain in 2008 by Osprey Publishing,
Midland House, West Way, Botley, Oxford, OX2 0PH, United Kingdom.
443 Park Avenue South, New York, NY 10016, USA.

Email: info@ospreypublishing.com

A CIP catalog record for this book is available from the British Library

ISBN: 978 1 84603 378 0

Page layout by Myriam Bell Design, France
Index by Alison Worthington
Typeset in Adobe Garamond
Originated by PDQ Digital Media Solutions, Ltd.
Printed in China through Bookbuilders

08 09 10 11 12   10 9 8 7 6 5 4 3 2 1

For a catalog of all books published by Osprey please contact:

NORTH AMERICA

Osprey Direct, c/o Random House Distribution Center
400 Hahn Road, Westminster, MD 21157, USA

E-mail: info@ospreydirect.com

ALL OTHER REGIONS

Osprey Direct UK, P.O. Box 140, Wellingborough, Northants, NN8 2FA, UK

E-mail: info@ospreydirect.co.uk

www.ospreypublishing.com

Osprey Publishing is supporting the Woodland Trust, the UK's leading woodland
conservation charity, by funding the dedication of trees.

Cover images © USAF via Steve Davies

CONTENTS

DEDICATION   6

ACKNOWLEDGMENTS   7

FOREWORD   10

INTRODUCTION   12

PART 1 ACQUIRING "THE ASSETS"   15
    Chapter 1: HAVE MiGs, 1968–69   16
    Chapter 2: A Genesis for the Red Eagles, 1972–77   21

PART 2 LAYING THE GROUND WORK   49
    Chapter 3: CONSTANT PEG and Tonopah, 1977–79   50
    Chapter 4: The Red Eagles' First Days and the Early MiGs   78
    Chapter 5: The "Flogger" Arrives, 1980   126
    Chapter 6: Gold Wings, 1981   138

PART 3 EXPANDED EXPOSURES AND RED FLAG, 1982–85   155
    Chapter 7: The Fatalists, 1982   156
    Chapter 8: Postai's Crash   176
    Chapter 9: Exposing the TAF, 1983   193
    Chapter 10: "The Air Force is Coming," 1984   221
    Chapter 11: From Black to Gray, 1985   256

PART 4 THE FINAL YEARS, 1986–88   275
    Chapter 12: Increasing Blue Air Exposures, 1986   276
    Chapter 13: "Red Country," 1987   293
    Chapter 14: Arrival Shows, 1988   318

POSTSCRIPT   327

ENDNOTES   330

APPENDICES   334

GLOSSARY   342

INDEX   346

DEDICATION

In memory of LtCdr Hugh "Bandit" Brown and Capt Mark
"Toast" Postai

ACKNOWLEDGMENTS

This is a story about the Red Eagles: a group of men, and a handful of women, who provided America's fighter pilots with a level of training that was the stuff of dreams. It was codenamed CONSTANT PEG.

In a departure from the books that I usually write, this story is not grounded in absolute historical certainties, but rather is an amalgamation of the memories of 31 of a total of 69 Red Eagle pilots whose names appear on the official pilot roster of the 4477th Test & Evaluation Squadron (TES), United States Air Force (USAF), between April 1977 and March 1988. In addition, I interviewed six maintainers and several other non-flying Red Eagles.

I would love to have had a range of contemporary documents for reference, but sadly many have been lost, others were deliberately shredded in 1988, and those few that were preserved for declassification were burned in a safe when a hijacked airliner hit the Pentagon on September 11, 2001. Simple arithmetic dictates that even the freshest memories were 20 years old when this book was written, and that the oldest have had more than 30 years to dim. This fact is important, because in the course of the 65 hours of taped interviews I conducted and transcribed, there were many contradictions and disagreements about what happened and when, at the hands of whom, and why. Throughout the text I have relied extensively on quotations taken from these interviews, which were conducted in person or over the telephone between January and September 2007.

Moreover, there are parts to this story that the USAF and US Navy have yet to declassify. It was always made clear to me that there were rules governing what people could and could not say when talking about this story. I was not going to be given information about MiG operations that pre-dated 1979; the source of the MiGs was off-limits; and a definite no-no was any discussion related to flying MiGs from locations other than Tonopah, the home of

CONSTANT PEG, situated in the remote Nellis Ranges of Nevada. These rules were enforced without compromise by those who still work for the Air Force, and in particular by Gail Peck and Earl Henderson.

I honored all of these restrictions, and never once pushed a line of questioning into prohibited areas. It was instinctive, however, to want to tell as much of the story about the MiGs, and the genesis for the Red Eagles, as I could. The declassified history of CONSTANT PEG would suggest that the MiGs appeared all of a sudden on July 17, 1979. This appearance is the aeronautical equivalent of a magician pulling a rabbit from his seemingly empty hat, but even a small child knows that somewhere within the hat's lid there must be a hidden compartment. In fact, the US MiGs have a secret genesis that extends back more than a decade to 1968. A lot of that genesis remains classified, even today.

With all these elements in mind, I wrote this book in a manner that I think gives the most complete and accurate picture of the tactical applications for America's MiGs from 1968 to 1988 – there's more than enough for another book about the technical exploitation of America's MiGs, but I will leave that for someone else to write. I *have* discussed what I believe to be the likely sources of the MiGs. I *have* discussed the programs that led to the creation of the Red Eagles in 1977. I *have* discussed the types of MiGs that I believe were in use. Furthermore, I have mentioned the other location that everybody knows about, but whose name no one says aloud. But I have based such discussions on my own deductions and understandings, providing more details in the form of endnotes where appropriate. There is the possibility that some of the facts may be wrong, but they are as accurate as I can gather.

While not everybody who reads this book is going to agree with its version of events, I have done my best to accommodate the many different views and recollections from over the years. This book is written "warts 'n all," but I stopped short of demonizing certain individuals, and of conveying some of the uglier politicking and disagreements that pervade any squadron from time to time. Instead, I preferred to try and tell a balanced story with an emphasis as much on the people who made it happen as on the actual MiGs.

Regrettably, the maintainers closed ranks on me early on, despite many agreeing to be interviewed. Some just did not bother turning up to pre-arranged interviews when I visited Nellis Air Force Base (AFB) in February 2007. They offered no excuse or apology. Others stopped responding to phone calls and email messages. At the time I thought it odd, but as the story of the squadron played out, this behavior became less than surprising.

The reality is that everything you read about in this book happened because of the extraordinary talent and dedication of these maintainers. This book should have given additional exposure to the expertise and sacrifices of the maintainers; since only a handful agreed to be interviewed, their collective role appears to be far less prominent in the text than it actually was.

There are lots of people to thank, but none more so than LtCol (ret.) Earl "Obi Wan" Henderson and Col (ret.) Mike "Scotty" Scott, who read numerous iterations of this manuscript and spent tens of hours proofing and offering suggestions. Earl was a stoic supporter of this book from the outset, and he provided me with his office (and car) when I visited Nellis AFB to conduct interviews that he had set up on my behalf. He also gave me his backing, and that helped open doors that had remained shut for decades. Earl's son, Neil, was also a fine host who helped smooth my visit to Vegas. LtCol (USMC ret.) Lenny Bucko, and Col (ret.) Paco Geisler were also prominent supporters who helped with my research and constantly answered questions without once complaining. I also thank Jerry Bickford, Rick Wagner, Rob Geer, and Brad Fisher, maintainers who lent me their individual support and expertise, but whose stories I was unable to incorporate into the text because of constraints in time and word count. Finally, I would like to thank Col (ret.) Jack Manclark, without whom the 4477th TES would never have been declassified. Jack also gave me his support, putting me in touch with Earl early on, and lending this project a seal of approval that also helped open doors.

In addition, I thank the following for contributing their time and energy in helping to make this book possible: Adm John Nathman, R/Adm (ret.) Jim Robb, LtGen (ret.) John Hall, Capt (USN ret.) Cary Silvers, Col (ret.) Phil White, Col (ret.) George Gennin, Col (ret.) Tom Gibbs, Col (ret.) Ted Thompson, Col (ret.) Sam Therrien, LtCol (ret.) Paul Stucky, Col (ret.) Mike Simmons, Col (ret.) Mike Press, Col (ret.) Denny Phelan, Col (ret.) Gail Peck, Col (ret.) Joe Oberle, LtCol (ret.) Bert Myers, Col (ret.) George Tullos, Cdr (USN ret.) Tom Morgenfeld, Col (ret.) "Kobe" Mayo, Col (ret.) John Mann, Col (ret.) Tom Boma, Tony Mahoney, Cdr (ret.) Marty Macy, LtCol (ret.) Jim Matheny, LtCol (ret.) Larry Shervanick, LtCol (ret.) Dud Larsen, Bob Sheffield, Maj (ret.) John Nelson, Maj (ret.) Dan Futryk, Maj (ret.) Bob Drabant, Doug Robinson, Chico Noriega, Linda Jung, Linda Hughes, Thomas Newdick, Tom Cooper, Peter Merlin, and my good friend, Col (ret.) Doug Dildy, who proofread my manuscript and told me what a great guy Mark Postai had been.

If you would like to learn more about the Red Eagles, or would like to interact with some of the Red Eagles' pilots and maintainers, please visit: www.constantpeg.com.

FOREWORD

The names are legendary among generations of fighter pilots: HAVE DOUGHNUT, HAVE DRILL, CONSTANT PEG, Red Hats, Red Eagles, and the 4477th. The people are also legends: Frick, Peck, Iverson, Oberle, Manclark, McCloud, Nathman, Ellis. These programs and people, and many more revealed in the following pages, were part of the revolution in tactical thinking that took place in the years between the Vietnam War and the first Gulf War of 1991.

In the winter of 1969 I began pilot training in the F-4 Phantom; it was a low point in fighter training. I remember a cover of the Air Force safety magazine that highlighted 44 F-4 accidents due to "Loss-of-Control" during maneuvering flight. This was before computer-aided flight controls, and the venerable Phantom needed careful handling at high angles of attack. Rather than address the problem by properly training for high AoA maneuvering, air-to-air training was stopped for F-4 crews in the pipeline for Vietnam. While this policy reversed the mishap rate, it also produced a generation of Phantom pilots who could not learn the basics of roll, turn, acceleration, aspect angle, angle off and closure before going to war.

In the following pages you will learn about the loss of focus on air superiority training, the impact it had on our early performance over North Vietnam, and the effective programs adopted by the Air Force and the Navy to overcome these deficiencies. The most compelling programs to emerge from the tough lessons of the Vietnam years exposed later generations of Air Force and Navy pilots and crews to a level of realistic training we never dared dream would be possible.

My first exposure to our MiG program was as an instructor in the Fighter Weapons School, the 414th Fighter Weapons Squadron, 1974–77. It was a magical time. My fellow instructors included Dick Myers, later Chairman of the Joint Chiefs of Staff; Ron Keys, who later commanded Air Combat Command; Dick Anderegg, now the Air Force Historian and author of *Sierra Hotel*; and Joe Bob Philips, who fathered many formations and tactics that replaced the Korean War era tactics of Vietnam. These were the formative years of the Aggressor programs, Red Flag, the F-15, F-16, and the A-10. One highlight of my career was flying in the first Red Flag in 1975 and later, as the commander of Air Combat Command, in the 25th Anniversary Red Flag. It's hard to describe the dramatic improvements in combat capability and professional execution that occurred in those 25 years, many prompted by technology. The introduction of video tape recorders and Air Combat Maneuvering Instrumentation took the guesswork out of recreating complex aerial engagements. No longer could the first guy with the chalk get to the board and claim feats of airmanship defying the laws of physics. The "Briefing Room Rules" evolved: you showed your tape, you validated your shots, you debriefed the good and bad, and you paid five bucks for bad shots or breaking the rules – even if you were the wing commander. You laid it all on the debriefing room table, milking every lesson possible from that time in the air.

The Aggressor programs, Red Flag and the Weapons Schools played a part in the tactical transformation that gave the air combat excellence seen in Operation *Desert Storm* in 1991, Operation *Allied Force* in 1999, and beyond. But nothing contributed more than those classified programs of the 1970s and 1980s, exposing generations of young pilots to the naked reality of the first merge with the real thing. Even grizzled veterans' minds would go to mush as they gazed transfixed at the dart shape of the tiny MiG-21 canopy to canopy, only to realize that they had lost the first 20 degrees of turn advantage that was hard to recover in the F-4. My F-4 Weapons School class motto, "Why can't I think?" was coined for such occasions.

I need to make special mention of the maintainers associated with these classified programs. It's impossible to describe the miracles they performed. In many, probably most, cases, they started with hulks resembling flying machines and a pile of parts, and made them fly with reliability rates beyond anything the original owners could imagine. The ingenuity, dedication, and sweat equity of these NCOs made these programs progress beyond engineering testing and evaluations to the training world that required sortie generation and reliability. No other maintainers could have done what they did. America owes them more than it can ever repay.

Steve Davies does a superb job of telling the story of this magical era. Not surprisingly, you will see that success has many fathers, and memories vary among the many strong personalities who built these programs from virtually nothing. But we can all agree on one thing: among the people in this book are some of the greatest aviators and maintainers that ever lived. We salute them all.

General (ret.) John P. Jumper,
Chief of Staff of the United States Air Force, 2001–05

INTRODUCTION

"The morning brief stated only, 'Today you will be flying against an unknown threat.' We were to attack, identify the threat, and use what the TOPGUN instructors had taught us to engage and destroy the enemy," recalled retired two-star admiral, Jim "Rookie" Robb. "This put a great air of anticipation in the flight and as I manned the aircraft I felt an unusual level of tension, anticipation, and anxiety." Concerned that his F-14 Tomcat might develop a mechanical fault that would prevent him from flying the sortie, Robb patted the nose of the big fighter jet. "I told it that if it broke on me now, we were through for sure." It was the summer of 1976, and Robb was one of the first two pilots to attend the prestigious TOPGUN Navy Fighter Weapons School (FWS) in the F-14, the Navy's hottest and newest jet fighter.[1]

Robb and his wingman took off one at a time from Nellis AFB's single runway, and were vectored by ground control intercept (GCI) officers to fly 30 miles northwest – straight towards Groom Lake, an air base so secret that, save for the red hash-marked square that covered it on aeronautical charts, it did not officially exist. Pushing the throttles forward to command more thrust from the F-14's two big TF30 afterburning turbofans, Robb accelerated the Navy's new fleet defender to 400 knots – perhaps a little slow for the air combat that was about to happen, but not so fast that the experience would be over too quickly.

"The tension built as the mile markers ticked down. At about eight miles I could see a single spec of black through the windscreen. I was struggling to identify the dot from its outline; it was still too small." Robb was at a clear disadvantage, as even with the wings swept all the way back, his Tomcat had a 34ft wingspan. It also had a bulbous front cross section, and the sizeable 61,000lb jet could be spotted by a trained fighter pilot's eye as far away as ten miles. By contrast, his opponent was a diminutive little kite that weighed only 13,000lb fully loaded, and had a pencil-thin fuselage just big enough to accommodate a man and a motor.

Robb was entering a visual fight with his opponent, something that the Tomcat had not been designed for, and which his training at TOPGUN had taught him was a last-ditch measure. At three miles, he could just discern his opponent's high "T" tail. "I knew then that it was not one of ours."

The two jets now pointed directly at one another, and when one turned slightly to create some offset in heading, the other would adjust so that he kept pointing directly at him. It was what is known as "hot nosing."

> We continued to hot nose each other, finally passing left-to-left at about 2,000ft. It was a camouflage-painted MiG-17 "Fresco" and it was all mine. I was mesmerized by the sight of it and was determined not to lose it against the desert floor. I turned hard across his tail at 7Gs, half stunned and half trying to see what he was going to do. Bleeding energy quickly as I tried to equal his turn, it became clear that I had committed to a slow speed "knife-fight" with the MiG; not the school solution to be sure. Despite my best effort to get the best turn out of the Tomcat, the MiG continued to swing behind my wing line, headed for my six.

With the Fresco sliding easily behind the Tomcat's wing line – the defining point behind which an enemy fighter can control the fight and employ a heat-seeking missile – the TOPGUN student knew he was in trouble.

> I began maneuvering defensively with all we had, but the MiG stayed glued to my turn as if it was on a piece of string attached to my jet. Soon, I heard the words, "We are at the hard deck [altitude limit]. Knock it off!" The words coming out in English broke the magic of the moment and a deep sense of disappointment fell over me like coming to the end of a great ride at the amusement park. At least I didn't have to live with the words "Guns kill on the F-14" over the air, even though he could have probably made the case.

Robb could not believe how poorly he had flown. He had "committed several deadly sins," and knew that when he got back to Nellis he was going to have to account for each and every one in excruciating detail. He had entered the fight without a game plan or strategy; he had flown "arcing" turns that followed the predictably flat horizon; and worst of all, against all the academic advice from his instructors, he had entered a slow turning fight with a MiG-17. To top it all off, he had lost track of the hard deck.

He put it best: "My brain had clearly left my body soon after the initial vector from GCI." What he had experienced was "Buck Fever," a debilitating state of mind that in wartime cost fighter pilots their lives. Fortunately for Robb, the Russian-built MiG-17 had been flown not by the enemy, but by another US pilot.

Robb was no pushover: he'd got his call sign "Rookie" because in 1975, at the age of only 23, he became the first Navy pilot to fly the Tomcat straight from flight school – the others in his squadron were grizzled old salts who had been entrusted with the Tomcat because they were great pilots with many years of flying experience under their belts. "Rookie" had been selected to fly the new jet solely because he was a supremely gifted aviator who stood out from his peers.

The MiG-17 pilot called him over the radio and invited him to formate on him for close visual inspection, following which the two set up for another fight. Scribing imaginary circles in the sky, this time Robb entered a "two circle" fight, turning continuously through 720 degrees with the MiG, forcing it to bleed off speed before he suddenly fire-walled his throttles and used the Tomcat's superior thrust-to-weight ratio to "explode into the vertical." The MiG struggled to follow and just as Robb started to press home his advantage, both aircraft hit "bingo" fuel (a pre-arranged fuel limit) and disentangled themselves from the fight to head home. The MiG went north, back to Groom Lake, the Tomcat south, to Nellis. Although the ending had been inconclusive, Robb knew that the day would have been his had they just been able to continue for another couple of turns.

Flying home, the realization hit him: "The enemy was just another airplane. It was just another airplane that could be beaten … if you kept your cool." This realization was the basis for an entire USAF program. It was called CONSTANT PEG.

PART 1

ACQUIRING "THE ASSETS"

CHAPTER 1

HAVE MIGS, 1968–69

"[A Soviet MiG-21 fighter jet] was secretly brought to the US last spring and flight tested by USAF pilots to learn first-hand its capabilities and design characteristics," reported the February 17, 1969 issue of *Aviation Week & Space Technology* magazine. The report shocked many in the aviation world, and it also shocked the USAF Fighter Weapons School (FWS, also known as the Fighter Weapons Instructor Course, FWIC) and US Navy TOPGUN instructor pilots (IPs), albeit for very different reasons. Many of them were well aware that the Air Force was leading an exploitation program involving MiGs flown from a secret air base in the Nevada desert, known invariably as "Groom Lake," "The Container," "The Box," or "The Ranch." What surprised them was that the exploitation was considered so secret that they had been told that they would "disappear" if they ever leaked word of it. In fact, the USAF would wait until March 1998 before even acknowledging that the effort ever existed.

Surrounded on every side by mountain ranges, Groom Lake, about 90 miles north of Las Vegas, is a test airfield, part of the expansive Tonopah and Nellis Test Ranges. Its airspace is labeled as "Area 51" on tactical pilotage charts, leading many simply to refer to it as Area 51. The site, which covers an approximate area of 6 by 10 miles, had originally been identified by the Central Intelligence Agency (CIA) as a suitable location for testing secret projects and was remote enough that flying could be undertaken with little risk of compromise. It became home in the 1950s and 1960s to the U-2 and A-12 spy planes.

Groom Lake was America's testing ground for "black" aerospace projects – those that were so highly classified, so important to national security, that they did not officially exist and were funded by hidden pots of "black" money. Although the program was officially a USAF-led project, flying MiGs out of Groom Lake was always going to be a joint effort, with both Air Force and US Navy leaders keen to exploit the assets. The three main programs between 1968 and 1969 were HAVE DOUGHNUT, HAVE DRILL, and HAVE FERRY.

The story began on August 16, 1966, when Iraqi Air Force captain Monir Radfa strapped into the ejection seat of his Soviet-built MiG-21F-13 "Fishbed E" jet fighter and defected to Israel. Taking off from Rashid Air Base near Baghdad on what was ostensibly a navigation exercise, he headed southwest. Making a dash for freedom, he crossed the Jordanian border at such height and speed that Royal Jordanian Air Force Hawker Hunter fighters scrambled to intercept him were unable even to get close. He was soon intercepted by two Mirage III jet fighters in Israeli markings, and he responded by lowering his undercarriage and waggling his wings enthusiastically: the universally accepted signal that a pilot posed no threat and was attempting to defect. He landed at Hatzor Air Base, Israel, and was duly granted asylum.

Israel put in over 100 hours of flight testing on the MiG-21 over the next 12 months, learning how to beat it in air combat with the prolific, French-built, Mirage III fighter, and familiarizing its fighter pilots with the MiG's strengths and weaknesses. Tense relations between Israel and the Soviet Union gave Israel cause to refrain from immediately sharing its findings with America, although later that year a secret agreement negotiated by the US Defense Intelligence Agency (DIA) was reached. Israel would loan its MiG-21F-13 to the US on condition that America's F-4 Phantom II jet fighter was made available for sale to the Israeli Air Force (IAF).

The F-13 version of the MiG-21 – that supplied by Russia to some of her allies – not only posed a threat to Israel in the hands of its Arab neighbors, but also to American fighters in the skies of Vietnam in the hands of the North Vietnamese Air Force (NVAF). The DIA spun an intricate web to hide the source of the silver jet, numbered "007" by Israel in humorous reference to the fictional James Bond character, before handing it over to the USAF in 1968. It was flown from Israel to Groom Lake in the back of a C-5 Galaxy strategic airlifter, and was then reassembled for flight.

Responsibility for testing and evaluating foreign aircraft lay with the USAF's Foreign Technology Division (FTD) based at Wright-Patterson AFB, and came under the ownership of Air Force Systems Command (AFSC). AFSC used the identifier "HAVE" for all of its test programs, including those that exploited foreign technologies. In the case of the MiG-21 from Israel, it was to be evaluated under the program name HAVE DOUGHNUT.

HAVE DOUGHNUT

The exploitation took the form of two main types of flying. The first was to evaluate the aircraft's performance, its engineering and metallurgical strengths and weaknesses, and its pilot interface – the so-called technical, or engineering, exploitation. The second was to evaluate it in an operational capacity. It would be flown in mock dogfights against the US-built fighters it would encounter in times of real war; this part of the program was known as operational exploitation.

AFSC's focus on technical and engineering exploitation of HAVE DOUGHNUT left little room for flying against America's frontline tactical fighter pilots. AFSC recruited its pilots from the Air Force Flight Test Center (AFFTC), and that meant that they were typically graduates of various test pilot schools. By contrast, Tactical Air Command (TAC) was interested in operational testing, looking at the needs of the war fighter and working out the best way to turn the enemy into teeth, blood, and eyeballs. These pilots were usually Weapons School graduates and groundbreaking tactical thinkers.

HAVE DOUGHNUT undertook its first flight in America in January 1968 and by the time the final sortie was flown in April, the MiG-21 was far less of an enigma. It had even been flown in very precise profiles to see how easily it could be detected by radar, infrared (IR) missiles, and tracking devices, including optical tracking systems. It also flew against the nuclear bombers of Strategic Air Command (SAC) to see how well their electronic systems could detect its presence and jam its radar. The IR signature tests involved a T-39A Sabreliner, a small, militarized business jet equipped with a device that could simulate the heat-seeking sensor of various missiles, including America's latest IR missile, the AIM-9 Sidewinder, which was in widespread use in Vietnam. By flying the MiG at different speeds, altitudes, and power settings, the Air Force was able to determine which parts of its flight envelope left the Fishbed most vulnerable to a missile attack.

For three short months, HAVE DOUGHNUT provided the Navy and Air Force with its first real look at a MiG-21, following which the jet was ferried back to Israel as quietly as it had arrived. (TAC had flown 33 sorties and the Navy 25, out of a total of 102.) So far in 1968, the USAF and Navy's fighter pilots had been frequently humbled by the MiG-21 over North Vietnam. DOUGHNUT's findings would prove invaluable in helping rectify that situation, arriving not a minute too soon.

HAVE DRILL AND HAVE FERRY

On August 12, 1968, some four months after the completion of HAVE DOUGHNUT, the Israel Defense Forces (IDF) were once again the beneficiary of a fortuitous event. Two Syrian Air Force MiG-17F Fresco C fighters had been flying a navigation exercise when they became lost. Syrian 1st lieutenants Walid Adham and Radfan Rifai were at the controls of the MiGs when they landed inadvertently at Beset Landing Field, northern Israel.

Once again, acquisition of the MiG-17s was of paramount importance to America, because the NVAF used not only the MiG-21, but also the smaller, more nimble, Fresco. Indeed, many of North Vietnam's best pilots were qualified to fly both. The MiG-17 was an improvement over its predecessor the MiG-15, and although lacking the supersonic performance of the MiG-21, it was more agile than anything else over Vietnam's skies. Twisting and turning, in experienced hands it could run rings around the lumbering fighters used by the US Navy, Marines, and Air Force.

Adham and Rifai's Frescos were turned over to the US after Israel had conducted its own brief testing. By now, the US Navy was establishing the TOPGUN school in a bid to stem the tide of losses to NVAF MiGs.

The first MiG-17 flew under the codename HAVE DRILL in January 1969. The second MiG, codenamed HAVE FERRY, arrived a little later on in March. Both wore their original Syrian camouflage and markings, but also carried two-color identification stripes added by the Israelis, and, of course, the US "stars and bars" markings common to all US-operated fighters. One MiG had the original Syrian serial number 055 and the other had 002 in red, along each side of the nose.

In June 1969, the HAVE DRILL and HAVE FERRY programs wound down and the findings, along with those of HAVE DOUGHNUT, were made available to the TOPGUN instructors and students. They were also disseminated to USAF instructors at the Air Force FWS. Nevertheless, the effort to continue testing MiGs carried on unabated. Around 17 months later, on November 25, 1970, the United States sent a delegation from the FTD to inspect a Cambodian Air Force MiG-17 under the codename HAVE PRIVILEGE. Col Wendell Shawler, who had been the FTD's project officer for HAVE DRILL and HAVE FERRY, was selected as project pilot. A Khmer Air Force pilot flew the Chinese copy of the MiG-17F, the J-5A, to Phu Cat Air Base, Vietnam, where Shawler and Col William W. Gilbert made five evaluation flights to establish the facsimile Fresco's handling qualities and performance characteristics. When the tests were completed, the Cambodian pilot flew the aircraft back to Phnom Penh.

DOUGHNUT, DRILL, AND FERRY DECLASSIFIED

In 1989, a Pentagon official confirmed that tactics used by two US Navy Grumman F-14 Tomcats to down two Libyan Air Force jet fighters were developed in "mock combat tests" with US-operated Soviet fighters. It was the first official confirmation from the US government that it had been funding and supporting the testing of secretly acquired foreign jet fighters. The timing of the confirmation coincided closely with the declassification of the HAVE DOUGHNUT, HAVE DRILL, and HAVE FERRY programs of the late 1960s. What the Pentagon was not saying was that the tactics used by the Navy F-14s had been refined and honed using an altogether different program that, by no small coincidence, had just been disbanded. This program was of a scope and scale that dwarfed HAVE DOUGHNUT, HAVE DRILL, and HAVE FERRY, and was to remain black for almost another two decades.

CHAPTER 2

A GENESIS FOR THE RED EAGLES, 1972–77

RE-EVALUATIONS

When the USAF began its phased withdrawal from the Vietnam conflict in the early 1970s, it did so knowing that it had significantly underperformed. Both during and after the air war in Vietnam it had become clear that the standard of air-to-air combat training Air Force pilots received fell far below that which was required; their tactics were outdated and their weapons had not been as effective as had been forecast.

Joe "Jose" Oberle, a USAF captain with the 433rd Tactical Fighter Squadron (TFS), "Satan's Angels," Ubon Air Base, Thailand, in 1967, had flown the McDonnell F-4 Phantom II against North Vietnam's MiGs many times. "All my missions were up in the Hanoi area and we would encounter the MiGs on a frequent basis. They would use decoy tactics to get the strike force to drop their bombs so that they could try to defend themselves, and that's all the MiGs needed to do. The MiGs would occasionally come up from behind going really fast, take a shot or two, and then they'd duck away." Under the leadership of the legendary World War II fighter ace Col Robin Olds, Oberle and his squadron mates had done their best to counter the NVAF, but despite isolated successes of the likes of Operation *Bolo*,[2] the USAF was often hamstrung in the air combat arena.

Several cultural issues and technological factors influenced the poor standard of training and slow development of tactics, but it would be fair to summarize that TAC's fighter community, and even its elite FWS – responsible for determining the tactics that the frontline fighter pilots should be using – had not moved with the times. FWS was based at Nellis AFB on the northern tip of Las Vegas, Nevada, and was the school to which TAC sent its best fighter pilots to learn in excruciating detail how to employ their aircraft and weapons systems. The FWS course was six months long and relentless, and it taught the strengths and weaknesses of the enemy to the nth degree. Its IPs were widely viewed as being the best tacticians, weapons experts, and stick-and-rudder pilots that the USAF had to offer.

In fact, Nellis itself was the fighter pilot's Mecca. Many fighter pilots made it a professional ambition to go through the Weapons School, but comparatively few – perhaps only the top 5 percent – ever would. Successful completion of the Fighter Weapons Instructor Course (FWIC) would result in being awarded the coveted Weapons School graduate patch, and the best were invited back to be IPs at the FWIC. The invitation was the ultimate accolade and amounted to the professional apogee of a tactical fighter pilot's career.

Being an FWS graduate was all about responsibility, and at Nellis a huge weight sat on the collective shoulders of the tactical fighter community. The air war over Vietnam had shown with little room for doubt that the Korean War-era tactics used by TAC, where one aircraft is defined as "the shooter" while the others flew cover in rigid formation 1,500ft away, were inappropriate for modern air combat where the primary offensive weapon had shifted to the air-to-air missile (AAM). The fact that America's newest fighter, the Phantom II, was purchased without a gun was also a costly mistake. Oberle reflected:

> A lot of people decided since we had air-to-air missiles there was no need for a gun in the fighters. The Navy took the gun out of the F-4B that they had built. The Air Force adapted the Navy F-4 and made the F-4C and it didn't have a gun, so they decided they didn't need a gun. And so we went to war in these big interceptors against the small, difficult to see, MiG-17 and MiG-21. We often ended up in gun range and too close for missiles. The MiGs could outturn our airplanes, and while they also carried missiles, their main armament was the guns they used to close in and kill us with.

To complicate matters, America's rules of engagement limited its pilots' ability to employ radar-guided AIM-7 Sparrow missiles at their optimum range. "Why?" Oberle asked rhetorically. "Because you might shoot down a friendly aircraft. The rules were you had to have a visual identification on the plane before you could use a missile. To get a visual identification against a guy coming towards you, you'd be inside the minimum range of the Sparrow missile before you could see the other guy's airplane. Then you would get into a turning fight and you didn't have a gun to use."

Some engagements over Vietnam started with USAF F-4 Phantoms tackling an inferior number of MiGs, but ended with the F-4s still unable to take advantage of the situation. On one occasion, one Phantom accidentally shot down another with an AIM-9 Sidewinder that indiscriminately homed in on the hottest heat source it could find – friend *or* foe. But oftentimes, it was the USAF's "Fluid Four" formation that was to blame for the poor combat performance. This formation allowed only the lead aircraft to bring his weapons to bear. Numbers 2, 3, and 4 in the flight, each carrying eight AAMs of their own, simply tried to stay in formation – they never became the "engaged" fighter, and were prohibited from shooting their weapons at the enemy. In fact, they spent more time trying to stay in formation than anything else. Oberle recalled the frustration this created: "Get into a fight with a couple of MiG-17s that are in a turning dervish, and you've got six or eight F-4s all turning against two MiG-17s! As a wingman you are welded to number 1 or number 3, and unable to take a shot. Our employment effectiveness and our tactics at that time were not so good."

So little trust was given to wingmen in the 1960s that it was often joked that they were permitted to say only three things on the radio: "Two," to confirm an instruction or check in on the radio; "Lead, you're on fire!"; and "I'll take the fat one," which was reserved for the bar. The reality was that if the USAF was to do better against the communist NVAF, it had to start employing its aircraft more effectively, and it had to give wingmen the opportunity to engage the enemy directly as and when they saw him.

Those returning from tours in Vietnam knew as much, and it became the quest of some at Nellis to rectify the matter. Many a potential USAF leader sacrificed his career pursuing this goal, it is claimed. These men could do little to alter the rules of engagement as defined by the politicians in Washington, and had no control over the reliability and effectiveness of the underwhelming AIM-7 and AIM-9 missiles, but they were damned if they were going to continue to see their fellow aviators perish over North Vietnam because their tactics were antiquated.

Yet the FWS remained vehemently opposed to changing tactics in Vietnam until right at the very end. Perhaps it was because of inter- and intra-service rivalry: the US Navy and the USAF's Air Defense Command (ADC) were already using more progressive formations, and the FWS might lose face if it admitted it had got things so very wrong. It was a classic example of the "not invented here" mentality that prevailed at the time.

Eventually, common sense intervened – the archaic Fluid Four formation had to go. In its place, TAC introduced the "Fluid Two" formation, giving the wingman much more flexibility to cover the engaged fighter. Fluid Two meant that the wingman and leader provided each other with mutual protection, and should the lead pilot experience a weapons malfunction, or if the wingman spotted the enemy first, the tactical lead could be transferred and the wingman could become the engaged fighter.

THE RED BARON REPORTS

While the FWS at Nellis looked at tactics in Vietnam, fundamental changes that would shape the future of the dusty air base had already taken place. One of them was the metamorphosis under the leadership of Gen Ralph G. "Zack" Taylor of the 4520th Combat Crew Training Wing into the Tactical Fighter Weapons Center (TFWC) on September 1, 1966. Taylor, a World War II ace with six enemy fighter kills to his credit, had recognized that the 12,000 square miles of largely uninhabited land that stretched north of the base was ideal as a training range. Over the course of the next three years, he saw to it that his vision was realized and in doing so provided the playground for America's finest fighter pilots. The TFWC was a critical development that allowed some of the seeds of modern air combat's most impressive programs to germinate.

Increasingly, fighter pilots gravitated to the TFWC as it matured into a think tank of tactical fighter aviation. Soon, it had become the hub of all the operations that went on at Nellis, and it had fast became a central node for USAF fighter pilots the world over. Most famously, the TFWC was deeply involved with producing the "Red Baron" reports. There was a wealth of data and information that could be collected, collated, and analyzed from America's MiG encounters over North Vietnam, and since October 1966 the Department of Defense (DoD) Weapon Systems Evaluation Group (WSEG) had been analyzing 320 individual MiG encounters that involved F-4 Phantoms and Vought F-8 Crusaders up until July 1967. These were incorporated into Volume I; Volumes II and III covered another 259 MiG encounters by F-105s and other US aircraft, completing the Red Baron I reports. After completing this first look, the WSEG recommended a follow-on study be conducted by the military services. Thus in 1969, Red Baron II was implemented at the TFWC to study the air war from where Red Baron I left off and the termination of air operations over North Vietnam on November 1, 1968. Red Baron II identified and reconstructed 625 air-to-air encounters that occurred in this period. Later, Red Baron III wrapped things up and completed the study.

The reports were based on interviews with every crew that was involved in any kind of MiG engagement, and they were designed to provide America's combat aviators with a tool from which to learn for the future. A key figure at Nellis, and the man credited with starting Red Baron, was Maj Lloyd "Boots" Boothby, a man Oberle judged simply, "a classic."

I investigated Boothby and found a remarkable quote that seemed to sum up not only him, but also many of the men he served with at the time. He is reported to have once said, "I'd hate to see an epitaph on a fighter pilot's tombstone that says, 'I told you I needed training.' How do you train for the most dangerous game in the world by being as safe as possible? When you don't let a guy train because it's dangerous, you're saying, 'Go fight those lions with your bare hands in that arena, because we can't teach you to learn how to use a spear. If we do, you might cut your finger while you're learning.' And that's just about the same as murder."

Boothby was a man of great character who had mastered the age-old fighter pilot technique of re-enacting a dogfight with his hands. He would spew lighter fluid from his mouth onto a lit lighter in his left hand as he demonstrated the pitfalls of one wrong move in air combat maneuvering: as he brought his left hand – the "Bandit" – in front of his right – the US fighter – the lighter would erupt in flame as though gunned by invisible bullets or a phantom missile. The effect was startling for the student standing in front of him, but the lesson was clear.

The scope of the Red Baron reports was exhaustive, as Oberle testified: "Where were you when you first saw the bogeys? What tactics were they using? What was the set-up of the engagement? What were the outcomes of the engagement? What were the altitudes, the speeds? All those kind of things that went into the reports. It was a classified accumulation of data." The preliminary data told Boothby and his colleagues in the FWS something crucial: many of America's fighter pilots were simply not familiar enough with fighting other, dissimilar, aircraft. They desperately needed to start receiving so-called Dissimilar Air Combat Training, or DACT.

In fact, Red Baron's recommendations went further than that: they went on to ask the Air Force to give its fighter pilots realistic training "through the study of, and actual engagements with, possessed enemy aircraft or realistic substitutes."

THE AGGRESSORS

The Red Baron reports highlighted the limitations of flying basic fighter maneuvers during training against the same type of aircraft. Indeed, this was at the heart of the Air Force's lackluster performance. At this time, TAC was not doing any DACT, so F-4s would fight other F-4s, and F-105s would engage in mock air combat against other F-105s; none of these pilots could learn how to fight against an opponent whose aircraft had flying characteristics and capabilities similar to those of the MiGs. Boothby and fellow instructors Maj Richard "Moody" Suter, Maj Randy O'Neill, and Capt Roger G. Wells had a solution – they called it the "Aggressors."

O'Neill and Wells had flown the Israeli-supplied MiGs as part of their job running the air-to-air flight within the 414th TFS, otherwise known as the F-4 Phantom's FWS. As for Suter, he was an acknowledged genius whose thinking would turn out to be decades ahead of his time. The concept behind the Aggressors was simple: to create a squadron or more of aircraft and pilots whose sole objective was to immerse themselves in Soviet fighter doctrine and tactics, and then to replicate all of this in the air with maximum fidelity. Instead of one F-4 pilot always fighting against another F-4, he would now fly against a different jet fighter that handled more like a MiG, and was flown by a man who thought and flew like a Soviet pilot.

In order to succeed, the Aggressors would need money and high-level support. But with Boothby still busy traveling the length and breadth of the country interviewing and collecting Red Baron data, Wells' and Suter's attempts to get the concept exposure fell largely on deaf ears in Washington, where the Air Force's leadership was based.

As luck would have it, however, there were some who were listening. One of them was Maj John Corder, who was assigned to the Fighter Tactics Branch of the Tactical Division in the Air Staff at the Pentagon. Having worked at the TFWC in the Fighter Concepts and Doctrine Division between 1968 and 1970, Corder knew about the DOUGHNUT, DRILL, and FERRY MiGs and the exploits of the Air Force's FTD at Wright-Patterson. He started his USAF career as a navigator on the lumbering B-52 Stratofortress bombers, but had later earned a slot in pilot training and was soon flying combat in the F-4D in Vietnam. Now at the Pentagon and in a position of influence, he and his boss, Col William Kirk, agreed with the Nellis-based aviators that the Red Baron reports were irrefutable evidence that DACT was needed in order to prepare Air Force pilots for engagements with the enemy, and also agreed that the Aggressors idea was the way to deliver the solution.

Corder knew that Israel had permanently loaned America HAVE FERRY, and that there was a chance that HAVE DOUGHNUT and DRILL might return to Groom Lake once more. Accordingly, his first proposal was for TAC to use the MiGs as adversary tactics trainers. But that plan was not well received, perhaps because these "assets" were so few and so secret that they could have little impact on the overall training effort across the Air Force. Unperturbed, Corder pitched a second proposal, involving the use of the supersonic Northrop T-38A Talon, which the Air Force operated as an advanced jet trainer and which was in plentiful supply. This time, USAF Chief of Staff Gen John Ryan was more receptive; he agreed to the idea in principle. The MiGs as Aggressors would have been great, but the T-38s were certainly better than nothing.

In time-honored fashion, Nellis' fighter pilots were attacking the problem from multiple directions near simultaneously. While Corder worked the Pentagon angle, the Aggressor concept was surreptitiously pitched by Wells to the head of TAC, Gen William "Spike" Momyer, during a visit to Nellis in 1972. Momyer's staff had intransigently filtered out requests to brief their boss during his visit by Gen Bill Chairisell, the new TFWC commander, but upon hearing the plan during Wells' impromptu briefing, Momyer embraced it totally.

Wells was a lynchpin in the start-up of the Aggressor program. He had arrived at the FWS as an IP in the air-to-air flight. He had started in the Air Force as an enlisted C-130 crew chief. With his previous enlisted time and "hard-charging, hard-drinking living" he was much older than his rank. "So he had an 'old face' much like Suter," Earl Henderson recalled (for more on Henderson, see below):

> Roger had a deep baritone voice and a dramatic stage presence, which made him a captivating briefer. While assigned to the air-to-air flight in the 414th FWS, Roger was one of the first USAF fighter pilots to get security access to intelligence information on Soviet aircraft and training, and he traveled to all of the US intelligence agencies collecting data. Based on this "deep access" he was able to put together a set of comprehensive briefings on the Soviet air-to-air threat, especially the Soviet fighter pilot. In 1971 and 1972 he traveled all over the world giving his briefings. It was Roger's briefing to Gen Momyer in the summer of 1972 that launched the Aggressor program. The briefing was focused on requesting enough T-38s to form an adversary group (maybe six aircraft) that would be attached to the air-to-air flight of the 414th. Momyer liked the concept so much he said "Make it a squadron."

Suter, O'Neill, and Wells set to work putting the Aggressors together. And so the first Aggressor squadron was stood up: the 64th Fighter Weapons Squadron (64th FWS) was formed at Nellis in the summer of 1972, and fell under the purview of the 57th Fighter Weapons Wing (57th FWW), itself a subordinate unit of the TFWC. The first Aggressor pilots were assigned to the unit in the fall of the same year. Boothby, principal author of the Red Baron reports, became the squadron's first commander, and O'Neill became his operations officer (ops officer). But there was one remarkable omission. Wells was not selected to join the new unit. Henderson later disclosed: "As the 64th Aggressor Squadron pilots were being selected, Roger Wells was not chosen, even though he was one of the most obvious choices. Maj Randy O'Neill was the assistant ops officer of the 414th and the only FWS instructor allowed to go to the 64th. The 414th commander and ops officer were adamant that they would not be picked clean to man up the Aggressor squadron. Roger was devastated by being left behind and requested an immediate assignment out of the 414th to the TFWC headquarters."

The Aggressor squadron would fly against frontline TAC fighter units. This oppositional structure would allow America's fighter pilots and back-seat Weapons Systems Officers (WSOs) not only to see exactly how a formation of Soviet fighters would behave, but also to employ their own tactics and doctrine against a realistic threat. The Aggressors operated under the moniker "Red Air" because of their role as Soviet emulators, while friendly US fighters were termed "Blue Air."

The Aggressors were to be the kings of Soviet emulation, but there was a sting in their tail: whereas the Soviets initiated and executed their tactics without necessarily knowing what ranges and timings they should use to exploit the weaknesses of US fighters, the Aggressors would know these instinctively. The range at which an AIM-7 Sparrow AAM could be launched; where a US jet fighter's radar would be least effective; when a flight of US jets would "sort" their targets, dividing up the enemy radar contacts so that each entered the fight knowing which opponent he was responsible for engaging – these were all things the Red Air pilots would know well. With this in mind, the Aggressors, still faithfully following Soviet tactics, would be able to initiate and execute their tactics at the worst possible moment for Blue Air. And one other thing: when Red Air met Blue Air at the merge – the point at which they were visual with each other – the "handcuffs" of Soviet emulation came off and the Aggressor would do his darndest to win.

RECRUITING

In the winter of 1972, Boothby handed over control of the Red Baron project to LtCol Glenn "Pappy" Frick. Frick, known as Pappy because he was old for his rank, was another pilot who had flown the Air Force's MiGs, and was instrumental in the success of a number of Nellis-based programs – black and white – that would follow. He had begun his career in 1954 as an enlisted engine maintainer. By 1957 he had been awarded his commission and earned his pilot wings, making him an "old" 2nd lieutenant. He'd gone on to fly the F-4 during three combat tours in Southeast Asia.

Among the initial cadre of 64th FWS pilots hired by Boothby was Capt Earl Henderson. Henderson had earned the legendary "100 Missions North" patch following a tour in the Republic F-105 Thunderchief over North Vietnam from August 1967 to March 1968, and had been decorated with no fewer than six Distinguished Flying Crosses (DFCs) and a Silver Star in the process. Originally an Air Defense Command (ADC) interceptor pilot, he'd been assigned to the F-105 for his Vietnam tour before being released back to ADC on his return.

ADC had sent him back to the Convair F-106 Delta Dagger supersonic interceptor at Oxnard AFB, near Los Angeles, California. Within a year he'd applied and been accepted to the USAF's test pilot school at Edwards AFB, California, but as luck would have it he was simultaneously offered a slot at ADC's interceptor Weapons School at Tyndall AFB, Florida. Since the Weapons School was offering him the chance to complete the program and then stay on as an instructor, he made the decision to go to Florida. It was a decision that would shape the rest of his career, and by the time his three-year tour at Tyndall was up, he had accumulated 1,500 hours in the F-106.

While 1,500 hours flying the F-106 under radar control was not the same as 1,500 hours flying a tactical fighter like the F-4, a significant clump of Henderson's hours had actually been spent flying DACT. "The Navy and Air Defense Command both had dissimilar air combat training programs," Henderson explained. "The F-106s were flying DACT, and although the TAC people were certainly doing air-to-air and they had some talented pilots at the Weapons School at Nellis teaching it, they were only allowed to fight each other: F-4 against F-4." So important was this DACT, Henderson elucidated, that "Randy Cunningham, the Navy ace from Vietnam, gave testimony to the Senate Armed Services Committee about air combat training. He discussed the Navy's TOPGUN school and the DACT they flew, but he also put a plug in for ADC and our program, called 'COLLEGE DART,' which was an ADC air-to-air exercise."

COLLEGE DART gave visiting pilots 12 rides of dissimilar air-to-air training, with Red Air provided by the US Navy, since TAC did not permit DACT. "Out of Cunningham's testimony, TAC was ordered to look at the ADC command program, and so the top F-4 guys from the Weapons School came down to our program and flew with us at Tyndall in August 1972 to observe and figure out whether it was worthy of adoption. During that visit, they briefed us on a lot of different programs, and one of them was that they had just received permission to start up the Aggressors. That got my attention, and I thought, 'Now, *that's* what I want to do!'"

Henderson called, harassed, and politicked influential figures at Nellis and at TAC HQ until he was finally accepted into the Aggressor program: "To be candid, it was my three years' worth of dissimilar air combat experience in the F-106 that got me in." He became one of the initial cadre of pilots in November 1972. It was a perfect assignment for him: "I was a terrible bomber pilot; I hit the ground every time, but that's about all I can say!" His passion lay in the swirling, high-G art of dogfighting, and he would spend the next three years at Nellis, until the spring of 1975, doing exactly that.

Henderson's transfer to TAC raised hell with ADC, but no one within TAC could have cared less since pilots acquired from ADC were considered "freebees." No fighter wing in TAC was safe from being pillaged of its best pilots by the Aggressors, and soon wing commanders running fighter squadrons around the world were making noises about losing their jet jockeys to the new, Nellis-based outfit.

Oberle, who had also completed 100 missions over Vietnam, was another initial cadre Aggressor whose timing was similarly perfect. He was almost at the end of a tour flying the diminutive Douglas A-4 Skyhawk with the Navy's VF-121 Adversary training squadron at Naval Air Station Miramar, San Diego, when he'd been hired by Boothby. The Navy, seemingly always one step ahead of the Air Force in the fighter tactics arena, flew its A-4s to simulate the MiG-17s, and Oberle had spent two years on an exchange tour with them. He recalled: "The Navy had been doing this dissimilar air combat training and they were learning how to employ a big airplane like the F-4, which did not have a gun but which carried heat-seeking AIM-9 and radar-guided AIM-7 missiles, against airplanes that could out-turn them, like the MiG-17 and MiG-21."

Oberle was ready to leave VF-121 and was looking for a new Air Force assignment just as the Aggressors were being formed. "So, I scheduled an appointment with the Tactical Fighter Weapons Center's vice commander, flew a Navy T-28 back to Nellis, put on my Class A uniform, went to my appointment and said, 'Look, I'm coming out of a two-year Navy exchange tour; I've got all this experience, and I want to come to Nellis.' The vice commander, Col Martinez, said, 'Funny you should walk in, because we're just starting this Aggressor training program; you're exactly what we're looking for.'" And as quickly as that, Oberle was hired.

GATHERING INTELLIGENCE

Although the Navy's Adversary squadron at Miramar had been the first to provide a dedicated opponent for DACT, the Air Force's Aggressor unit was destined to be far more involved and sophisticated. "The Navy had just been flying the low wing-loaded A-4 against the F-4 to fly the dissimilar combat and work on their tactics," Oberle pointed out. The USAF was about to add several layers of complexity and depth to that service, as Oberle clarifies: "The first one was to use the intelligence communities in the US – the Defense Intelligence Agency, Central Intelligence Agency, and the Air Force Intelligence Agency [AFIA] – which were all what's called 'compartmentalized.' They were fighting for budget in the intelligence world, and they were very 'close hold' on their information: they did not share. They all did their own parallel collection efforts and analysis. They didn't put it to any joint use activity." Yet intelligence was the lifeblood of Boothby's synthetic adversaries, and gathering it from America's closeted intelligence agencies required approval at the highest levels. These intelligence agencies jealously protected their databases of secrets, but the Aggressors gained enough high-level support that they were able to break down the doors to each. Getting data from the Air Force's intelligence agency about its own Foreign Military Exploitation (FME) programs was also a challenge, but O'Neill and Frick were ideally placed to facilitate the effort, since both had black contacts in the classified worlds of the FTD and AFSC. These carefully fostered relationships would ultimately pay dividends.

The initial cadre of Aggressor pilots each undertook fact-finding missions so that they could pull all of the compartmentalized information together. Oberle revealed the extent of the access:

We got all the top secret clearances which allowed us to go to all these top secret intelligence vaults and spend weeks in there poring over their information, trying to learn about the threat. The threat at the time was the Soviet Union, and the satellites of the Soviet Union that purchased Russian equipment for use by their air forces. We would study the tactics, and we developed briefings on "the Man": How does a Soviet fighter pilot get to be a Soviet fighter pilot? What path does he take? How do they go through their training from youth to growing up into their "PVO Strani," which was their equivalent of Air Defense Command? Along with categorizing the airplanes we had in-depth briefings on the MiG-17 and the MiG-21. We knew all about the systems, the avionics, the capabilities, the fuel fractions for how much time they could stay and engage …

Once we had the clearances and we had the higher headquarters request for access, it was just a case of looking across all of the intelligence information and putting it together to decide what the real picture was. We ended up with a clearer picture of air-to-air combat, training, and the Man than any of the intelligence agencies had on their own.

The Aggressors put together a holistic package that far exceeded in depth and fidelity anything that had been done before. "Then we added another dimension," Oberle confided. "This was the Russians' complete reliance on ground control intercept for their missions. So, we added a section of GCI controllers. We would go and study the Russian formations that were flown and understand how they were directed and employed by the Russian ground-controlled intercept areas."

Henderson flew to West Germany and visited Wiesbaden Air Base, home to American intelligence in Germany.[3] Here he collected information that had been gathered by an electronic listening post – Templehof Air Station, West Berlin – that monitored Soviet fighter communications and observed their maneuvers on radar. Oberle explained that Henderson talked to the American GCI controllers tasked with monitoring the East German pilots:

The information that he got was an example of how we put the Aggressors together. Earl asked the guys who were sitting monitoring East Germany: "Do you see airplanes come up?" "Yes, of course. That's our job; we sit and we watch them," they told him. "OK. Do they separate – one goes to one corner while another goes to another area about 30 miles apart? And then do they fly towards each other?" Earl asked them. "Yeah, they do that often." Next, he asked them, "When they come together, what happens?" They explained, "The two radar blips merge and flare up as one blip for a second." So, Earl asks them, "Do you count 1001, 1002, 1003, and then all of sudden they come apart again going in opposite directions? Or do they stay in this one little area for 90 seconds, two minutes, three minutes – where they're kind of all together?" Well, the controller said to Earl with a blank stare, "We've never looked at that aspect. Why's that important?" Earl explained: "Here's the difference: If they're coming in and they merge together for three or four seconds and then they separate, then they're just flying intercepts and they're flying through to the other end. But, if they stop and they stay in that one area then they're doing a dynamic air-to-air engagement. That shows where the focus of their training is and that's the kind of data we need you to provide to us so we can assess how much of this air-to-air training they're doing versus intercept training."

Gathering of intelligence ran concurrently with actually being taught how to be an Aggressor. The checkout process was tough, Henderson said. "It was pure air-to-air, and our instructors – five or six guys – were very exacting and demanding about what we did."

Being an Aggressor was not just going to be about good stick-and-rudder skills and being a great air-to-air tactician. In order for the Aggressor program to be effective other units had to learn from the experience. That, Henderson stated bluntly:

> … required a lot of emphasis on personality and temperament. And that's still an issue to this day for people in that mission. Why? Because if you don't have the right guy he gets a big head. If you fly air-to-air every day and you were pretty good to begin with, you can go up and kick anybody's ass any day of the week. If you get a big head, and you come back after the mission and rub the guy's nose in it, then there's a very negative learning outcome that will result. It's offensive.
>
> So, what they had to do is go up there and hold their punches – tie one arm behind their back and not kick his ass – so that it became an experience that people can learn from. That's a real challenge, because people want to win. It takes a special person to tolerate this and accept it. So, we had a motto in our early history: "Be humble, you cool fucker!"

The motto was a veiled warning. Had the Aggressors antagonized every pilot in every unit they flew against, the program would almost certainly have been culled.

ROAD SHOWS

With the basic premise of the Aggressors working well, the second part of the concept – that the Aggressors should tour – was put into action. The "road shows" were born.

"Road shows," said Oberle, "were when we would go to the different bases and we'd spend two weeks there and we'd start out by giving academic presentations about the Man, their aircraft, and their tactics. Then we would go out and let them get some experience with higher wing-loaded aircraft against lower wing-loaded aircraft."

Wing-loading is the term applied to an aircraft based on the ratio between the wing area and the weight it must carry – it is one of the fundamental aerodynamic measurements that influences how differently one aircraft performs in air combat compared to another. Flying two aircraft with different wing-loading is the basis for DACT because they maneuver differently in a dogfight, and each has strengths and weaknesses.

Oberle continued:

> We'd fly offensive set-ups and defensive set-ups, and let them get the appreciation of how difficult the T-38 was to see, especially since its motors did not leave smoke trails. In the latter part of the two-week deployment we would get into the tactics phase, where a GCI controller would set us up on separate frequencies and we would fly the Russian formations and adhere to Russian tactics so the Americans could see it on their radar. The objective was not to just try to go out and beat Blue Air, but to try to give them a realistic scrimmage so they could train against the threat and be successful if they encountered it in a combat situation.

As it was, the "safety first" mindset that had dogged TAC in the last decade still prevailed. Initially, when the Aggressors showed up for road shows, some wing commanders refused to let their squadrons fly against them. At the time it was characteristic for the Air Force to fire a wing commander who lost a jet, and that paralyzed many into exercising extreme caution – there was no way they were going to lose their jobs because an overzealous Aggressor pilot might cause a mid-air collision, loss of aircraft control, or similar mishap. Ordinarily such cautiousness was to be applauded, but since the Aggressors had the explicit backing of the USAF Chief of Staff, a call to the wing commander from TAC HQ at Langley AFB, Virginia, was all it took to get him to cooperate fully.

RED FLAG

While the Aggressors developed rapidly into a highly effective training tool, Suter was pondering an even more progressive training concept. One evening he told majors Ed "Fast Eddie" Cobleigh and Gaillard "Evil" Peck, who worked for him as IPs at the 414th FWS, that he had a vision for a large-scale training exercise that would increase survival rates of young pilots who had never seen combat.

Peck had been a first-assignment IP whose plans to fly fighters in Vietnam had initially been thwarted when he graduated from flight school and was immediately posted to a job that saw him teaching brand new students how to fly Lockheed T-33 Shooting Stars and T-38s. He had eventually got his wish, and had flown the F-4 with the 8th Tactical Fighter Wing (TFW), 433rd TFS in Thailand – the same squadron to which Oberle and Cobleigh had been assigned. He'd flown 163 combat missions over Vietnam and Laos, 100 of them at night. He had also accompanied Henderson to West Germany to interview a defecting East German pilot in 1973. Cobleigh had flown the F-4 in Vietnam on two tours.

The two men had first attended the F-4 FWS at Nellis as students before being invited back to become instructors working for Suter in the summer of 1972. Peck had been made the head of the F-4 Air-to-Air section, and had watched the Aggressors closely as they spun up their first squadron, spending much of his time "selling" the 64th FWS, and explaining to other units how the concept would work.

It was late in the evening at the "724 Delta Bar" in Peck's backyard, and the three men were surrounded by half-empty bottles of Scotch whisky and comatose carcasses of their FWS brethren as they wrung out the details. They knew about the disproportionately low life expectancy of new fighter pilots in Vietnam, and that Air Force studies had demonstrated that the majority of combat losses occurred within a new pilot's first ten combat missions. Suter knew that if that new pilot could accrue the experience of these first ten missions without getting shot down or killed, his chances of survival jumped dramatically from mission 11 onwards. His vision was to recreate the first ten missions synthetically in a relatively safe training environment at Nellis. "We said, let's get these guys, bring them to Nellis and put them together in a team and let's really train these people," Peck recalled.

Suter's large-scale combat training operation would teach a new fighter pilot in peacetime many of the lessons that he would have to learn in real combat. In doing so, not only would his life expectancy increase, but so too would his overall accuracy in the air-to-ground bombing arena (which was another major Air Force concern). If this could be accomplished, the USAF's fighter pilots would leave for Vietnam having in effect already survived their first ten missions.

The three men agreed that the biggest hurdle was going to be convincing a TAC leadership infatuated with safety (to the detriment of almost everything else) that such an exercise could be accomplished without losing aircraft and pilots. There was no way of totally avoiding mishaps in the inherently dangerous world of tactical fast jet flying, but Suter wanted the opportunity to try to convince TAC's commander that such losses would be far outweighed by the reduction in losses that would be experienced in the combat zone and at the hands of the enemy.

Peck and Cobleigh encouraged Suter to take his concept to the leadership, and in May 1975 he briefed TAC commander, Gen Robert J. Dixon, and his senior staff. Dixon approved the idea and instructed the current TFWC commander, MajGen James A. Knight Jr, to establish "Red Flag" at Nellis within six months.

Suter quickly set to work formulating Red Flag and briefing key individuals at Nellis. Assisting him was a team that included majors Tom Christie and Pierre Sprey, who conducted research into the exact nature of the first ten missions that Red Flag was to duplicate. To make the Red Flag environment as realistic as possible, Suter arranged for as many of the components of an air war as possible to be represented. That meant he would invite the airborne tankers and the stand-off electronic jammers as well as the bombers, fighters, and tactical recce force. On the ground he arranged for Soviet radar systems, some of which were real examples captured from Soviet customers in the Middle East, to transmit their electrons across the range and in doing so create an integrated missile and antiaircraft artillery (AAA) umbrella similar to that which had been faced by America in Vietnam, and by Israel during the 1973 Yom Kippur War with Syria and Egypt. Finally, what he really wanted was a squadron of MiGs, flown by a dedicated unit, to be dissimilar air combat trainers; but for now he would settle for the Aggressors and their T-38s.

Right on schedule, Red Flag 1 started on November 29, 1975, and hosted 37 aircraft and 561 people for a tally of some 552 sorties flown. Focused on air-to-ground bombing training, it was a huge success. Although basic by today's standards, the first Red Flags were an eye opener to the rigors of combat.

Suter was not content to stop at Red Flag. He wanted the young pilots to undergo the most comprehensive exposure to Soviet tactics and equipment possible. One of the first to benefit from that driving force was a young F-4E pilot, Lt Larry "Shy" Shervanick. Shervanick had attended the next Red Flag and had been highly impressed by it. Yet the most impressive thing he saw was not at Nellis, but at a location 83 miles northwest of it. He was one of a select group who were secretly invited to Groom Lake to view the HAVE FERRY

MiG-17. Most interestingly, the little Fresco was clearly still in flyable condition. For Shervanick, the MiG was a source of fascination. His 1975 encounter was just the start of his association with America's secret MiGs.

CLARK, ALCONBURY, AND ANOTHER NELLIS AGGRESSOR SQUADRON

With three years' worth of operations under their belts, the 64th FWS Aggressors could consider themselves hugely successful. They were so well received that TAC ordered a second squadron to stand up at Nellis in 1975: the 65th FWS was born. This squadron, according to Oberle, who was now ready to depart Nellis for a one-year tour in the F-4 in Thailand, "was born out of the need to cover all the requests for deployments and road shows that the 64th FWS was receiving. The 64th was simultaneously flying as the adversary air during Red Flag – there just were not enough bodies and airframes to cover the road show activity and be the adversary air for the Red Flag exercise. So, the 65th FWS came along to share the workload."

After Wells had transferred from the F-4 FWS in protest against his commander's decision not to release him to the 64th FWS, he had moved to the TFWC and begun forming up the concept of an Aggressor squadron for the USAF's Pacific Air Force (PACAF). He then took an assignment to Clark AB, Philippines, and began briefing his idea around the PACAF command. They liked it, and on August 31, 1975, the 26th Tactical Fighter Training Squadron (TFTS) was formed, flying T-38s (the name was changed in 1983 to 26th Aggressor Squadron). He became the first ops officer from 1975 to 1977. During the same period, USAF Europe (USAFE) formed an Aggressor squadron and based it at RAF Alconbury, an air base in England.

Henderson made major early and was promoted to ops officer at the 64th FWS. Next, in April 1976, he was assigned to the Philippines as the T-38 Standardization & Evaluation (STAN/EVAL) check pilot for the Thirteenth Air Force. While at Clark, he was pivotal in the creation of "Cope Thunder," PACAF's version of Red Flag, which involved Japan and South Korea among others. He was attached to the 26th TFTS, where he came to know one of its new officers, a young captain by the name of Mike "Scotty" Scott.

Scott had gone through pilot training in 1971 and had shown up at Clark, minus his wife and two small children, in March 1975. He was flying F-4s with the 90th TFS at Clark when Wells had arrived in the Philippines to sell the Aggressor concept to PACAF and to recruit pilots for the outfit's initial cadre. The young captain had volunteered right away: "I couldn't get back to him fast enough. I was still a lieutenant at the time and I had a couple of my mentors, who were now majors, saying, 'Hey! You don't want to do that, that's regressing, you're going back to flying T-38s when you could be flying F-4s.'" Scott was unphased:

> I said, "No, I want in on this Aggressor thing." I was sent up for an interview with Roger Wells and I said: "You know what, Roger? If you hire me for this squadron I will extend over here on a consecutive overseas tour and I'll bring my family over here." Why was I so enamored and wanted to be an Aggressor? Why did he hire me? Because of my time flying the F-4E at Seymour Johnson AFB between 1973 and 1975, I had done six months of pure air-to-air and I had been exposed to the Aggressors. I liked their mission, I liked what they did, I didn't care what airplane I was flying: it was the mission that I was interested in.

Scott became one of the youngest recruits into the Aggressors, and by September was back at Nellis being put through the second formal Aggressor training course with the new 65th FWS.

The Aggressor squadrons at Nellis transitioned from the T-38s to F-5Es while Henderson was in the Philippines in 1975, and the Clark-based squadron followed suit in 1977. The single-seat Northrop F-5E Tiger II was an improved version of the F-5A Freedom Fighter on which the T-38 was based. Four of the two-seat T-38s were retained to augment the F-5Es. Henderson explained: "When Vietnam fell, there was a surplus of F-5s that were owned by the US State Department and which were intended to be sent to bolster the Saigon government as part of a Military Assistance Program. Well, we've got all of these F-5s already bought and paid for straight off the assembly line, plus the ones flown out of Vietnam into Thailand. There was 100 and something airplanes, so out of these we created four squadrons: the two here at Nellis, one at RAF Alconbury, England, and one at Clark AB in the Philippines."

In fact, Henderson had long maintained that the T-38 was ill suited to the Aggressor role because in certain negative and zero G flight conditions its main undercarriage gear doors would delaminate and then be sucked open. The result was that the main gear doors would be pulled out into the slipstream and ripped away. The main gear door would then impact the aft fuselage belly, slicing through control cables and causing total loss of control of the aircraft. As many as four such incidents had occurred, claiming the lives of at least six pilots, before one lucky soul managed to recover a stricken T-38 back to base at Clark and lived to tell the tale.

Henderson had battled over the T-38 issue with his close friend, Maj David "DL" Smith, who was at TAC HQ and planning a fifth squadron made up of T-38s:

Between 1976 and 1977, DL Smith was working long and hard at the TAC staff to form a fifth Aggressor squadron. Its mission would be to do all of the initial training of new Aggressor pilots and take the load off the 64th and 65th. He intended to use T-38s to equip that new squadron. I pleaded my case with DL, both from Clark and then from Nellis when I arrived back in June 1977, and asked that he kill the T-38 training squadron concept. He was highly resistant at first, especially since he had done such an extraordinary job selling it to the staff. But DL initiated his own research into the issue, poring over the T-38 safety records at Norton AFB. He found a common thread, with other units experiencing the same gear door problem. All of the units [that had suffered losses] had a high-Q [airspeed], unloaded flight profile in their mission: Edwards AFB test chase aircraft, USAF Thunderbirds, and the Aggressors. He did the smart thing and the fifth squadron never happened.

In April 1976 the 527th TFTS, equipped with F-5Es, was stood up at RAF Alconbury as the USAFE's own Aggressor element.

GCI

The new F-5E was a closer approximation of the Soviet MiG-21, and unless flown poorly it would outperform the older Phantoms. For the newer F-4E Phantom, which had a modified wing that gave it better handling at slow speeds, the chance of success against the F-5 was improved, but the "iddy biddy little F-5" as Henderson called it, was very nearly the perfect Fishbed simulator and could be an excellent adversary against even an FWS IP. Henderson painted the picture: "'Big ugly,' the Phantom, is out there against this small F-5 that he can't see, and meanwhile he's got these huge, coal-burning engines throwing out smoke. Little airplane sees big airplane and gets into position to kill him … 90 percent of the time he's going to win." Such was a routine scenario in Vietnam. The MiG-21 had such a small frontal cross section that it was extremely difficult to spot. If it was flying up behind the Phantom at Mach 1.6 in one of the NVAF's trademark, GCI-vectored slashing attacks, then the first indication it was there came when Phantoms started falling out of the sky.

The Aggressors mimicked the Soviet use of GCI in order to complete their re-enactment of Soviet fighter doctrine. According to Robert "Kobe" Mayo, then a major in the initial cadre of Aggressors back at the 64th FWS, Nellis:

> They were a fantastic asset. These guys flew with us, briefed with us, were part of the post-flight debriefing, and made it possible for us to do our mission. During our air-to-air engagements they were in there with us and we felt that they were as valuable as another wingman. I remember flying against a flight of two F-4s. During the debrief, I was playing my tape recording of the engagements and you could hear my GCI controller talking to me as if he were another fighter pilot participating in the fight. At one point in the fight I was engaged with one of the F-4s and "Stump," my GCI guy, was talking almost non-stop. "Kobe, you can press your fight ... the other F-4 is across the circle from you ... Kobe, you've got 40 seconds left before he's a threat ... Kobe, come off hard right. The other F-4 is at your 5 o'clock and 9,000ft, closing." I did break right, picked up the other F-4 and continued the fight. During the debrief when the F-4 guys heard my tape they were convinced that I had brought another wingman into the engagement. They said, "There is no way any GCI controller could have that much awareness of what's going on by looking at a radar screen. And he is not talking like a GCI controller, he's talking like the fighter pilot that he is!" They were really upset and I'm not sure to this day that I convinced them that I was the only T-38 in the fight. Our GCI controllers were absolutely fantastic.

After 15 months of developing Cope Thunder, Henderson returned once again to Nellis as the ops officer at the 64th Aggressor Squadron. There had been several distinct changes to the program, one being that while USAFE and PACAF still handpicked their Aggressor pilots for Alconbury and Clark respectively, TAC had dropped the bar and was now randomly assigning less experienced pilots to its two Nellis squadrons – TAC felt it simply could not continue to pillage its fighter units of their best sticks. The new criteria for a TAC Aggressor pilot was 750 hours' flying time and at least one fighter tour. "We paid the price and had an influx over several years of young kids who were very capable, but they didn't have the temperament. Maybe one in five did, but that was all," Henderson conceded. "We started having problems," he added, "and the operational unit would say, 'Hell, we don't want to deal with you.'"

Henderson also explained that the intensity of the missions had increased, particularly against the FWS. The Aggressors played Red Air for the students at the end of the six-month syllabus in what was known as the Ground Attack Tactics (GAT) phase. The mock war involved "very loose rules, and of such a high intensity that if you were not very sharp you'd get killed, literally," he explained. "When I came back from the Philippines it was at its most intense – the rules were the least stringent and allowed the most aggressive flying at low altitude, especially, of anything that I have seen before or since. There was some quasi-rule about not exceeding 90 degrees angle of bank at low altitude, but essentially it was a low-altitude flying contest and guys would kick up dust and scare themselves." It was a source of constant worry for an ops officer like Henderson. "We're doing what!?" he often exclaimed. Henderson explained his concerns:

> After my first GAT briefing, I went in to talk to the air-to-air flight commander, Maj Ron Keys, who later became the four-star commander of ACC [Air Combat Command]. I asked him where these new rules were written down and who approved them. Ron said they were in the GAT 5 and 6 phase briefings and that the TAC/DO [Director of Operations] had approved their entire syllabus. The catch was the phase briefings with the new rules did not make it before the eyes of any approval authority at TAC, only the syllabus. The 57th wing commander, Col William Strand, was fully aware of the rules and he was willing to take the high risk of losing an airplane and maybe a pilot to push the training envelope to the edge of combat. GAT 5 and 6 only happened twice each year, in May and in December, but the missions were so demanding on Aggressor pilots, young and old, we had to initiate a low-altitude training program so the pilots would feel "comfortable" flying at 100ft. At that altitude you had to spend the majority of the time watching for rocks and the rest of the time looking for the other aircraft. It was certainly a far cry from a swirling dogfight at 15,000ft. The lowest I have ever flown in a fighter was on those GAT 5 and 6 missions. Often, I found myself screaming across a dry lake bed at 100ft, hiding from Blue Air, and waiting to ambush the F-4s when they crossed the ridgeline. I would spot a flight of F-15s by seeing their twin tails just peeking over a rise in the terrain – just like shark fins cruising through the water. Many times, one of my young pilots would come back into the squadron from one of these missions ashen-faced and quiet – to this day I don't know what happened to them individually, but I am sure they each have a vivid memory that they still carry today.

The other obvious change Henderson could see was evolution of the so-called "Nellis freestyle." This had been prompted by the new McDonnell Douglas F-15 Eagle and General Dynamics F-16 Viper arriving on the scene. Their all-seeing radars and awesome maneuverability were too much for the Aggressor's Soviet tactics to spoof or defeat. Henderson elaborated: "Nellis freestyle was all about trick-tricky tactics to win the fight at the merge. Suddenly the F-15 comes along. He's got this radar that can see you almost anywhere, and he can maneuver like a son of a bitch to win the close-in fight; at least, if he's a good pilot. And then you go to the F-16, which is another little airplane with high-tech radar and weapons, so now the F-5 is losing the technology fight and getting outdated: surviving to the merge is becoming a real problem for the Aggressors."

Freestyle involved doing whifferdills (a rolling maneuver), F-5s hiding in very close formation underneath each other, and other non-traditional techniques. Henderson likens it to a scene in the Indiana Jones movie *Raiders of the Lost Ark*: "The guy confronts Indiana Jones ... with an impressive display of sword swinging; Indiana Jones pulls out his gun and just shoots him and walks away. Simplicity is the key to air combat success."

HAVE IDEA

While the Aggressors had been establishing themselves and Suter had been devising Red Flag, a very small cadre of Aggressor pilots had been pulled aside for special duties in a world that few knew existed. I was able to identify eight Aggressor pilots who were asked to conduct even more classified research from 1972 onwards. This research was so classified that not even their fellow Aggressors knew what they were doing.

Among the first to be picked was Capt Mike "Bat" Press: "Randy O'Neill just pulled me aside and said that he had an assignment for me to complete. If I wanted it then I couldn't tell anyone about it, and I couldn't tell anyone where I was going or what I was doing. It sounded like a great offer, so I accepted."

Press had been so keen to see combat action before the end of the Vietnam War that he'd pleaded with the Air Force's personnel center to assign him away from his F-4D unit in Europe to any combat unit in Vietnam that would take him. He'd got his wish and spent one year flying the turboprop OV-10 Bronco as an attached pilot to the US Army's special forces command on the Cambodian border. He'd flown 450 combat missions and earned two DFCs by the time his 12-month tour came to an end. From Vietnam he went on to become an air-to-air IP in the comparatively sedate world of the F-4 Phantom II school at MacDill, and it was while he was in his second year there that he was handpicked by O'Neill and Wells to join the initial cadre of Aggressors in 1972.

With the Aggressors still brand new, he had been tasked to write up the academics on the MiG-17 and MiG-21. Following his quiet talk with O'Neill, he found himself being sent "up range" to a location whose name could not be uttered aloud, where he was to fly aircraft that did not officially exist. Press was off to the ultra-secret Groom Lake to fly the MiG-17 and MiG-21.

Flying the MiGs gave Press the practical familiarity he would need to help write the academics and to instruct. Moreover, O'Neill knew that the lessons that could be learned from flying the real MiGs would underpin the Aggressors' use of the F-5E as a MiG-21 simulator. Press confirmed, "It showed me the differences between the MiG-21 and the F-5. There might have been some things that one could do but the other could not," but the only way to find that out and understand it was to fly both.

Another of the first pilots to be selected for the special duties was Capt Joe Lee Burns, an initial cadre 64th FWS pilot who was also a graduate of the F-4 Weapons School. He arrived at Nellis in the fall of 1972 fresh from a combat tour in F-4Ds and, he said, had opted for a job with the Aggressors over becoming a FWIC IP primarily because he so respected O'Neill. Unlike Press, Burns underwent a checkout in the Mach 2 Lockheed F-104 at Edwards AFB to familiarize himself with single engine fighter operations in preparation for the MiG-21.

Another of the selected pilots was "DL" Smith, Henderson's friend. Smith, who flew the MiG-17, was an initial cadre 64th FWS pilot. He had come to Nellis in the fall of 1972 from the 8th TFW, Ubon Air Base, Thailand, where he had forged a name for himself while leading the first laser-guided bombing mission on the Thanh Hoa Bridge in North Vietnam in May that year. "Thanh Hoa was an infamous, heavily defended bridge south of Hanoi that had withstood thousands of USAF and USN bombing sorties between 1965 and 1972 and was still standing," said Henderson. "I had the opportunity – misfortune – to attack it twice in 1967 in my F-105D, with zero effects. By early 1972 it had become a symbolic North Vietnamese 'triumph' because it had stood up to everything the US military could throw at it. DL Smith's successful four-ship LGB [laser-guided bomb] attack ended that 'triumph.' Shortly thereafter, DL led a flight against the Paul Doumer Bridge with the same result."

The exploitation of MiGs at Groom Lake was very much still alive. Following the 1968 and 1969 MiG exploitations, AFSC had continued to fly the solitary HAVE FERRY MiG-17, while HAVE DRILL and HAVE DOUGHNUT had been returned to Israel. According to aviation historian Peter Merlin:

Between mid-1969 and late 1972, Air Force Systems Command testing of MiGs was conducted by the 6512th Test Squadron of the Special Projects Branch, part of the Air Force Flight Test Center at Edwards Air Force Base. The original organization consisted of the HAVE FERRY MiG-17 and one test pilot, Major Norman L. Suits, and six maintenance personnel, and the MiG was a part-time or additional duty effort that took place at Groom Lake. But then the MiG-21 previously used in HAVE DOUGHNUT returned to the Test Site [Groom Lake] in 1972 when a new engine became available, and another pilot, Major Charles P. "Pete" Winters, was added.

The program grew slowly and the number of daily sorties increased to as many as four flights in a single day. A MiG-17PF [Fresco D] arrived around the same time, as did several more MiG-21 airframes, from which a single MiG-21 was made flyable using parts from all of them. The rest were kept as a source of spare parts. [The Air Force now had a total of two MiG-21F-13s Fishbed C/Es, and two MiG-17F Fresco C/Ds.]

The AFSC group called themselves the "Red Hats" and in 1973 they came up with a unit emblem. It featured a bear wearing a wide-brimmed red hat and surmounting a globe hemisphere, all against a yellow background. Six red stars arced over the top. Two tabs included the name, "RED HATS," and the motto, "MORE WITH LESS." The motto symbolized the team's ability to consistently produce useful data despite the challenges of operating from a remote location with a small cadre, and having to scrounge or make spare parts to keep their aircraft flyable.

All the while, the 57th FWW and the 414th TFS had been given access to the MiGs, which was how Frick (and probably Peck, Cobleigh, and others) had come to fly the assets. Their participation was kept secret even from their Aggressor brethren, such was the compartmentalization of this black program.

On May 30, 1973, AFSC consolidated the Air Force's MiG exploitations and initiated the blanket program HAVE IDEA. While the new program would leave AFSC maintaining overall operational control of the test assets and management of test activities, "It was intended to integrate test activity with participants from AFSC, TAC, and the Navy," says Merlin, adding: "The Red Hats' mission evolved to include project management for all phases of developmental [technical] test and evaluation, as well as some phases of operational test and evaluation of foreign aircraft, weapons, and radar systems."

More than one individual told me that O'Neill was highly influential not only in getting TAC pilots access to HAVE IDEA, but in getting HAVE IDEA started to begin with – he was still connected with the systems command guys and had been flying the MiGs following the completion of HAVE DOUGHNUT and DRILL. He was the only man who had the connections to get TAC pilots cleared into the program.

IDEA gave O'Neill the opportunity to get a greater degree of access to the MiGs, a process that was administratively done through Frick's Detachment 1

(Det 1), 57th FWW. Flying "the assets" was agreed between the Red Hats and the 57th FWW on a case-by-case basis. As Det 1 commander, Frick was the TAC point of contact responsible for these negotiations. While still a subordinate of the TFWC, writing the Red Baron reports and helping Suter establish Red Flag, Frick was responsible for putting together "test requirements" – formal requests to get some playtime with the MiGs – so that TAC could use them to evaluate tactics. TAC's involvement in IDEA had no name or identity, and was anything but formal.

Initially at least, only a single MiG – a MiG-21F-13 Fishbed C/E – had been made available to the TAC pilots and there was some consternation over flying it in case it broke or was lost in an accident. But eventually the other three MiGs were also incorporated. O'Neill had laid down the seeds of a program that would eventually develop into something much, much bigger.

For the time being, Press, Smith, and Burns were the first three TAC pilots formally to fly the MiGs "up range" at Groom Lake as part of HAVE IDEA. Then, in 1974 and 1975, the three were joined by fellow Aggressor Capt Alvin "Devil" Muller, and majors Ron Iverson and Robert "Kobe" Mayo. Iverson was another former "Satan's Angel" F-4C pilot who, like Oberle and Peck, had flown with the 433rd TFS between 1966 and 1967. He was also an Aggressor flight commander from November 1972 to August 1974. Mayo, another of the original Aggressors in 1972, was also the T-38A STAN/EVAL check pilot for the 57th FWW, to which the Aggressors reported. He had flown F-100 Super Sabres with the 35th TFW, flying against ground targets in South Vietnam and Laos, before returning for a second tour in the F-4 with the 49th TFW. A natural pick for the Aggressors because he had already accumulated 2,500 hours in the supersonic trainer T-38 as an IP, and had combat experience in the F-100 and F-4, in early 1972 he'd called O'Neill to tell him he wanted to be part of it. O'Neill had seen to it that he was.

Next, Aggressor captains Ed Clements and Gene Jackson each got one orientation ride in the MiG-17. Clements had flown more than 250 combat hours in the skies of Vietnam and Laos in the F-100 Super Sabre. He'd come to Nellis to be one of the Aggressors' initial cadre. Jackson had been similarly active in the years preceding the Aggressors. Between the two of them they played an important part in putting together course materials and intelligence for the 65th FWS that would be true and accurate to the last detail.

While O'Neill handpicked TAC's HAVE IDEA pilots, none of them had any idea that he was connected to the secret world of FME, or had previously flown MiGs. "That was all very secret," according to Mayo, who admitted that his time in the Aggressors had given him some idea that TAC had access to MiGs somewhere. That suspicion was not confirmed until Burns pulled him into a quiet room and told him he'd been invited to join the elite group of pilots flying them. It still came as quite some surprise: "It was like walking into the Air Force recruiter all those years ago and being asked if I wanted to fly. Shit hot! Of course I want to do that!"

Initially, the HAVE IDEA sorties were flown by TAC only in 1 v 1 mock combats against experienced FWS or Aggressor pilots. The set-ups alternated between the MiG and Air Force jet starting 1½ miles behind the other. But the sorties were infrequent, and there were months on end when shortages of spares and maintenance issues caused the assets to stay grounded. Despite this, the small band of Aggressor pilots developed the complexity of the exposures "very quickly," and engagements of 2 v 2 or more were being flown by 1975.

The six men appeared to all intents and purposes as "normal" Aggressor pilots and continued to spend most of their time flying the T-38s and F-5Es. One young Aggressor captain at the time was Paco Geisler. In 1975 he had been assigned as the first "slick wing" (relatively few total flight hours) captain to be sent to Aggressor training. He recalled that there were clearly some Aggressor pilots who were operating on the dark side. "There were rumors: you knew that the F-4 Weapons School was flying sorties with someone, somewhere, before they came and flew against us in the Aggressors. And when your Aggressor IP jumped on an airplane at Nellis and departed somewhere for a day or two, you wondered where he had gone. If you asked, they'd tell you to mind your own business. Pretty soon, they'd turn around and tell us they had new information on the MiGs, and that made you wonder whether they were flying them somewhere."

Once the new Aggressor had progressed far enough in skill and knowledge, he would be "read in" on HAVE IDEA. For Geisler, whose IP was Muller, that happened in 1975. "First, they showed me a MiG in a hangar [at Groom Lake], and then they had me exposed to one in the air. It was just after I had started teaching academics to the fighter squadrons, and they came to me and said they were going to give me a little more training. They told me I wasn't going to fly the next day. You get on an airplane, fly somewhere, get off an airplane, walk into a hangar and say, 'Holy shit!' They laugh and then tell you that if you tell anyone else they'll kill you. And then you went back."

NAVY EXPOSURES

TAC wasn't the only command getting playtime with the assets. The US Navy was also getting exposure to them. The Navy selected most of its MiG pilots from its test squadron, VX-4, based out of Point Mugu, California. VX-4 had been the source of the Navy's DRILL, FERRY, and DOUGHNUT pilots, who had established a reputation for being much more aggressive at exploiting the MiGs than their Air Force counterparts. VX-4's pilots were participating in HAVE IDEA in much the same way TAC was, and by now VX-4 was responsible for all areas of fighter operational test and evaluation for the Navy (having previously been largely focused on AAM development).

One VX-4 pilot at the time was LtCdr Tom Morgenfeld, a graduate of the British RAF's (Royal Air Force) Empire Test Pilots' School. Returning from England in 1976, Morgenfeld, whose Navy rank made him the equivalent of an Air Force major, had been sent straight to Point Mugu. He had at first been unhappy about his assignment to the test squadron, but when a friend of his told him that VX-4 was the only place where exciting things were happening, he soon brightened up.

His friend was not wrong. It quickly became apparent that there was flying to be had here that he could get nowhere else in the Navy. "I was soon running a number of classified programs that were concerned with Soviet tactics and hardware," Morgenfeld revealed, and he would come to know Iverson well. "I had had a good discourse with Ron to make sure that the Navy and Air Force were singing from the same hymn sheet insofar as our intelligence on Soviet tactics, weapons, and hardware was concerned. We would read the latest threat assessments to come out of the FTD and I would make sure that we were being consistent and correct about what we were doing."

Morgenfeld had always wanted to fly. While he was still an infant, his parents would drive him down to the local airfield on listless evenings; there, the penetrating drone of radial engines lulled him into deep sleep. Flying was all he could remember ever wanting to do. He got his chance when his local senator sponsored him into the Naval Academy, and he'd done well enough in flight training to be assigned to the VF-191 and the Vought F-8 Crusader. The Crusader was known as the "Last of the Gunfighters" because it was dependent on close-in cannon shots and rear aspect heat-seeking missiles. That he was going to fly this aircraft (and not the Navy's A-7 Corsair II or F-4 Phantom II) would have a significant impact on his career, mostly because the F-8 community were probably the best Basic Fighter Maneuvers (BFM) practitioners in the world, and that gave him a fine appreciation for the basics of air combat.

Although IDEA was gaining in momentum, sorties against the MiGs were still precious few. TAC was now beginning to allocate exposures to its FWIC students; the Navy similarly dedicated its playtime to training its TOPGUN students. One such lucky student had been then lieutenant Jim "Rookie" Robb.

THE INDONESIAN CONNECTION

A total of 8,435 miles away from Groom Lake, the CIA was continuing covert operations on the Asian archipelago of Indonesia. In 1970, the Indonesian Air Force had retired 30 MiG-17s, 10 MiG-19s, and 20 MiG-21s following the CIA-sponsored overthrow of the country's communist dictatorship. In response, Russia had swiftly withdrawn engineering and maintenance support for the MiGs. Naturally, the aircraft broke and could not be fixed, and the Indonesians left them outdoors in the monsoon rain, or pushed them unceremoniously into ditches and wetland.

All was not lost, though: under the Military Assistance Program started by the Kennedy administration in the 1960s, the US DoD supplied Indonesia with foreign military aid in the form of a multi-stage program to rebuild the country's once proud air force. Surplus USAF T-33 Shooting Star jet trainers and a number of UH-34D helicopters started arriving in the country in 1973, followed by the first batch of supersonic Northrop F-5E/F Tiger II jet fighters and turboprop OV-10 Broncos in 1976.

For Indonesia, all this material came at a modest price that included relinquishing ownership of its old MiGs – little more than a gesture considering that they were unflyable and represented very little value even as scrap. In fact, America had already transported four of Indonesia's MiG-21s to Groom Lake in 1973, and these were the source of the second HAVE IDEA Fishbed.

The Indonesian government would not have known that it held the key to allowing the USAF to develop its DACT beyond what had always been the Aggressors' limiting factor: that the F-5 was a great MiG simulator, but it was still just an F-5 nonetheless. Some at Nellis had dared to dream the impossible, Peck admitted. "The concept of a squadron of MiGs was a common item of discussion among the Weapons School instructors and senior Aggressors in the context of a dream that should, but may not ever, happen." HAVE IDEA had been the first step in making that dream come true.

PART 2

LAYING THE GROUND WORK

CHAPTER 3

CONSTANT PEG AND TONOPAH, 1977–79

Gail Peck's Pentagon assignment was in a sub-level of the five-sided building – in the fighter operations shop. He had taken the place of Suter, who'd been rewarded for his creation of Red Flag with promotion to lieutenant colonel and an assignment to Luke AFB to fly the new F-15 Eagle. Peck stepped into his shoes, and soon found that his friend's world had been very dark indeed.

Born in San Antonio to an Air Force officer and pilot, Peck was raised at Randolph AFB, Texas, and Eielson Air Base, Alaska, where the growl of the North American T-6 trainer's Wasp radial engine, and the P-51 Mustang fighter's supercharged V-12 Merlin engine, had made an indelible impression on him. He'd shown an interest in aviation for as long as he could remember, and his father did much to accommodate his son's fascination, even going as far as sneaking him into a firepower demonstration under a blanket at Eglin AFB, Florida, on one occasion. Not content simply to watch, Peck told how he once "dug a hole in the sand on the beach, and had little bottle caps and a stick to make myself a P-51 cockpit to fly in." Aviation was in his blood.

He'd gone on to enroll in the fourth class of the newly founded Air Force Academy (AFA), and while he "barely graduated" he went into overdrive at Undergraduate Pilot Training (UPT) and ranked first in his class. Whereas 89 percent of his fellow students were assigned to bombers and tankers, the only fighter assignments for him to choose from were two F-102s and a T-33 instructor slot. "I had nothing for [was disinterested in] the air defense interceptor mission that the F-102s did – I wanted to do air-to-air, shoot the guns and drop bombs," he recalled, and with a wife whose father was Chief of Staff of Air Training Command (ATC) – Doolittle raider Jack Hilger – and a new child to consider, Peck took the T-33 instructor assignment.

At Randolph AFB, Texas, the young IP found himself thrust into a social circle unique for a lieutenant, but one that would see him befriend the very man whom many years later would help make the Red Eagles possible: Capt Charles "Chuck" Donnelly Jr. Donnelly and Peck hit it off right away. James "Buster" Briggs was the commander of ATC, a three-star general who had been the superintendent of the AFA when Peck was a cadet there, and Donnelly was the general's aide-de-camp. It was while at the 25th reunion of the Doolittle raiders that Peck met the Air Force's chief of personnel, resulting in his being assigned to the F-4 and Vietnam. On his return he divorced his wife and was eventually posted to Nellis, where in the summer of 1975 he met and married one Peggy Hayes.

By the time Peck entered Suter's "dark world" in mid-1975, his friend from the early days, now one-star Gen Donnelly, was initially assigned to be the special assistant to the Deputy Chief of Staff (DCS) for Plans and Operations (AF/XO) at the Air Staff. As Peck's tenure at the Pentagon progressed, Donnelly was promoted to Deputy Director of Plans (Deputy XOX) for the AF/XO. Like so much about this story, Peck's assignment to the Pentagon, and Donnelly's most recent promotion, were perfect in their timing.

In late 1976 Indonesia had already received its first batches of F-5s and OV-10s, paving the way for the release of more of its MiGs to America.[4] Peck was aware of the acquisition of another batch of MiGs, and so he sat down with Gen Hoyt Vandenberg Jr, the "XOO," or Director of Operations and Readiness, and suggested to him that the MiGs be used to form an Aggressor squadron. To his delight, Vandenberg said, "Do it."

The idea was simple: take what the Aggressors were already doing with such great effect, only do it with MiGs. Whereas IDEA had been limited to exposing the assets to a tiny number of expert FWIC and Aggressor pilots, the new squadron would have a much broader remit that was similar to Red Flag: "We knew that when a man aimed his rifle at a deer for the first time he would experience 'Buck Fever.' We thought the same about air-to-air combat – that the first time you saw a MiG you were likely to experience the same thing," Peck explained. Those who had been exposed to IDEA, like Robb and Geisler, knew how effective even a single MiG could be at inducing the phenomenon: "The first time I saw a MiG-17 I just stopped flying the airplane," Geisler admitted. "I saw him from about 6,000ft away, but as he went past me close by, I didn't even make a standard radio call. I just transmitted, 'Shit! There he is!' Instead of using the vertical and speed, I tried to turn with him. He was like gum on my shoe; I couldn't shake him off. And then I went home and thought, 'Jeez. That sucked. I feel like a fool.' It was very humbling, but they told us that it happened to *everybody*."

Exposing pilots from the Tactical Air Forces to real MiGs was the only way to make sure that Buck Fever was something of the past by the time they came up against an enemy-flown MiG. "The idea was frequently discussed among those of us that worked classified programs. But, prior to that discussion with Vandenberg and the Pentagon discussions that followed, there was no concept of how to make it happen or where to locate the unit," Peck admitted.

Press had been involved in helping sow the seeds of such a program, giving briefings at the highest levels of the Air Force to push IDEA forward through the mid-1970s. "I helped Frick, Suter, and O'Neill present our plans for the assets to the generals. We wanted to wrestle them away from the Systems Command guys and put them under the control of the Tactical Air Command."

With the concept and scope of the program agreed by Vandenberg, himself the son of a former Air Force Chief of Staff, Peck was cleared to discuss the idea with his old friend Gen Donnelly, who was now the Deputy XOX at the Air Staff. A charismatic character with a can-do attitude, Donnelly's response to Peck's concept was priceless: "I can get you the MiGs if you can figure out how to build the airfield," Peck recalled him saying. "I didn't ask how, or where, or why or when he would be able to do that."[5]

He reported straight back to Vandenberg to communicate Donnelly's positive response. And as he turned to leave the room, he remembered the etiquette: all the programs run by the XOO took Vandenberg's call sign. "Sir, do you have a call sign?" Peck asked. "My call sign is Constant," Vandenberg replied. Peck walked down the corridors of the Pentagon half elated and half scared to death by the challenges that lay ahead. His thoughts turned to the comfort of his new wife, Peggy. "As I walked down the hallway to my office it dawned on me ... CONSTANT PEG. And so, that's how the program was named." In fewer than 12 months, it would go from concept to reality.

MAKE IT COME TRUE

Peck observed that "A previous XOO, Gen Billy Ellis, had tantalized his staff with cryptic notes. One was 'MICT.' Eventually, the action officers broke the code. MICT meant Make It Come True. Such was the task."

CONSTANT PEG gave TAC a way of consolidating its tactical exploitations, expanding the number of pilots that it could expose to the MiGs, going beyond the small clique of Aggressor IPs and FWS students and IPs to entire frontline squadrons. It also gave TAC a means of taking control of the "assets," which had long been an issue since AFSC had historically always been in charge. Donnelly's unflinching, but ambiguous, assurance to Peck, "If you can find an airfield, I can get you the MiGs," did not mean he was going to go out and find some MiGs, but rather that he could get the Indonesian MiGs assigned to CONSTANT PEG. Donnelly, it appears, was confident that all he had to do was stake his claim by pitching the concept, and the Indonesian MiGs would be his. As Deputy XOX, he worked for the DCS for Plans and Operations, a SAC three-star general named Andy Anderson, who was over both XOX and XOO directorates. While Anderson was not directly involved, Peck said, he was a great supporter.

The generals engaged in what were presumably their own high-level discussions on the matter of ownership and use, and Peck continued to refine the concept:

> I was one of what I like to call the "gang of three" worker bees who were the implementing cast: me; Maj David "DL" Smith, the head guy at Langley for TAC; and LtCol Glenn "Pappy" Frick, who was here at Nellis. These officers worked highly classified projects at Nellis and at TAC HQ [Smith provided support for MiG exploitations at TAC HQ]. Thus, we were colleagues in the black world. No one picked anyone in the "team forming" sense of the word. Frick had a group of Aggressor pilots at Nellis that helped him [the likes of Mayo, Muller, Iverson etc.], and Smith and I were engaged in individual one-man operations at our respective headquarters.

The three men worked together to plan and execute the formation of the squadron. "DL was the real conduit to TAC and to the generals down there at Langley. All three of us were Fighter Weapons School graduates, so that's the kind of people we had working this from the get-go." Frick was ideally placed to be the man on the ground at Nellis, not only because he had taken over the Red Baron reports from Boothby, but also because he was now flying with the 65th FWS as an attached pilot, according to Oberle. There was also, of course, the fact that Frick had flown the MiGs before.

HAVE BLUE

Only a handful of people knew exactly what Peck and his cohorts were up to, but for one AFSC colonel in the know, CONSTANT PEG represented a different kind of opportunity. The need to find a suitable remote airfield from which to operate the MiGs provided him with the opportunity to assist another, even more secret, program. His name was Col Bobby Bond.

Bond was an exemplary fighter pilot who'd flown combat in the North American F-86 Sabre in the Korean War and been an FWS IP and F-105 project test pilot. In 1963 he flew the "Thud" (the F-105) for his first tour in Vietnam, returning to Southeast Asia five years later and adding another 213 combat missions to his logbook, only this time in the F-4. His reward was a posting to be the first squadron commander of the USAF's new LVT A-7 strike fighter (the Air Force's version of the Navy's Corsair II) in 1970. Two years later he was back to Vietnam to try out the A-7 in combat.

He had returned from his third tour of Vietnam to be plunged in 1973 into the inky black abyss of the Air Force's Office of the Deputy Chief of Staff, Research and Development. He was no stranger to the goings on in AFSC, having flown HAVE DOUGHNUT, DRILL, and FERRY while he was the F-105 and General Dynamics F-111 Aardvark project officer in 1968–69, and now he was responsible for establishing and validating operational requirements and system modifications for tactical fighters. From his fourth floor Pentagon office he was running deeply classified black programs.

Bond's vantage point in the Pentagon allowed him to monitor CONSTANT PEG and he identified Peck as someone who could help him with one of his own projects. In fact, the two men already knew each other, having met on the Tactical Fighter Modernization Study Group – a group of fighter pilots assembled at Wright-Patterson in 1974 to look at operational derivatives of the Lightweight Fighter program (which eventually became the General Dynamics F-16 Fighting Falcon). He invited Peck to his office and told him to shut the door. "Then he opened a two-drawer safe and pulled out a folder. He said, 'Have a look at this,' and passed me the folder."

Peck was staggered – inside was a photograph of HAVE BLUE, an angular aircraft that defied conventional aerodynamic wisdom. It was like nothing he had seen before, but it would later become known the world over as the Lockheed F-117 Nighthawk – the stealth fighter.

He asked Bond what it was, to which the colonel responded simply: "Well, it has the radar cross section of a Sparrow. You need to figure out how to get yourself briefed in on this thing because I think that somehow this is going to figure in with your program." Peck immediately realized that HAVE BLUE could be located at the same remote airfield as CONSTANT PEG. TAC's black project could be used to hide AFSC's highly classified stealth design once it became operational.

Peck's security clearance, and his role in the inner sanctum of the Air Force's plans section, meant that he had up until this point been aware of the concept of HAVE BLUE – a stealthy jet fighter that could evade radar detection until the very last minute – but he had received no particular information and knew nothing of its pioneering shape. But now he actively sought an official "read in" on HAVE BLUE. "Reluctantly, they agreed," he said.

With that hurdle out of the way a strategy began to develop: AFSC would use CONSTANT PEG to find and develop a remote air base that would also eventually be home to the stealth jet fighter. The concept of a squadron of MiGs had just been significantly bolstered. "The advocacy that I put together in the Pentagon to make CONSTANT PEG happen was largely based on the ultimate need for somewhere to base what became known as the F-117. We were going to fly MiGs by day and stealth fighters by night, and that was the way it was going to be," Peck confirmed.

MAKING THE ASSETS AIRWORTHY

Peck ran tirelessly back and forth between political offices, as well as the various floors and sub-floors of the Pentagon, with a briefing folder under his arm, in order to keep the momentum and support for the program going. At Nellis, Frick had already been assigned custody of the two MiG-21s and two MiG-17s of the now-superseded HAVE IDEA, and was busy hiring maintainers to get CONSTANT PEG's other MiGs airworthy. "The task of finding guys that can fix airplanes without technical order to refer to was a challenge," Oberle confirmed. "We needed people that could take these assets apart. It's like rebuilding a vintage automobile; you take something apart and know how to put it back together instinctively, and if you don't have the right parts, you fabricate them. Finding guys that could do their specialties – like electronics guys, 'sparks'; hydraulics guys, 'bubble chasers'; avionics guys, 'beeps and tweaks' – became the priority."

The maintenance team was assembled and flown into Groom Lake. Each asset was assigned a crew chief and a team of specialists who would start the laborious process of taking it apart and rebuilding it. This was no small challenge since the assets were in varying states of disrepair. One pilot revealed: "One of the MiGs had been sitting in a water ditch up to the top canopy rails for four years before they brought it back, took it apart and did all the corrosion repair on it. Then they rebuilt it."

Peck used the analogy of a typical restoration project at any aviation museum with flyable warbirds to describe what they had to work with. "The MiGs were basically wreckage, and the maintainers were magicians who turned them from a mess into man-safe machines." For those MiGs that required rebuilding from scratch, it took around 18 months, and there were several such examples.

Heading all of this up was a supremely talented maintenance trooper, Senior (later, Chief) M/Sgt Robert O. "Bobby" Ellis. Ellis was a talented and well-respected maintainer who had been involved in black projects for a very long time. Of all the characters in the Red Eagles story, he is arguably the most highly revered. He had worked on the IDEA MiGs, as well as FTD exploitation programs (including DOUGHNUT/DRILL/FERRY). He knew MiGs better than any other Air Force maintainer, and had probably been out to Indonesia to select which MiGs were salvageable. Indeed, when Soviet pilot Victor Belenko defected in his MiG-25 "Foxbat" interceptor in September 1976, Ellis was handpicked to fly out to Hakodate, Japan, to dismantle and exploit the jet.

One of his strengths was his ability to think laterally. Bob Drabant, an Air Force analyst who later briefly worked on CONSTANT PEG, recalled: "One day, Ellis asked me where he could get a surveyor's transit [used to measure vertical and horizontal angles with great accuracy and down to extreme fractions of a unit]. I told him probably down at the civil engineering shop at Nellis. I then asked him what he needed one for. He told me that he thought a particular MiG-21 was bent and therefore flying crooked, so he wanted to shoot it with the transit to check the angles."

4477TH TEF INITIAL CADRE

On April 1, 1977, CONSTANT PEG took another step closer to becoming a reality when the 4477th Test & Evaluation Flight (TEF) was activated and assigned to the 57th FWW at Nellis by Special Order GA-19. The occasion was momentous because for the first time TAC would officially "own" the MiGs, and the days of going cap-in-hand to AFSC were formally at an end. The four-digit identifier (as opposed to the usual two- or three-digit number), as Peck recalls, came from the fact that all temporary or training squadrons/flights had to have four digits.

Since Frick was already the commander of Det 1, 57th FWW, the 4477th TEF's activation crystallized his role in the program and made him the official commander of the unit. Ron Iverson remained with the 57th FWW and would be responsible for the creation of training materials, while Mayo would become the first 4477th TEF ops officer,[6] and Alvin Muller would be the new unit's administrative officer and security officer. CONSTANT PEG was news to some of them: "We weren't privy to all that Peck was doing, and we didn't know exactly what was going to happen in the future," Mayo reflected. "Looking back, it seemed like all along we had been laying the foundations for CONSTANT PEG."

For Iverson, Mayo, and Muller, the activation of the 4477th TEF was a natural continuation of what they had been doing for years. For these men, it introduced no immediate change in their daily routines; it was as though one day there was no name for what they did, but the next day there was. The only tangible difference for them was that now they owned the MiGs, were looking for an airfield of their own, and the scale of the operation was about to be increased drastically.

By now, IDEA pilots Jackson and Press had been posted elsewhere on new assignments, and while Clements was still at Nellis, he was assigned to the initial cadre of the F-15 FWS and was no longer involved in flying the MiGs. The four remaining men were no longer required to work, cloak and dagger, from a small side room in the Aggressor squadron as they had during IDEA. They were now free to operate under cloak and dagger from their very own facility. They had identified a building at the northeast side of Nellis AFB that had a higher level of security – it was located on the site where Nellis' stash of nuclear weapons was stored – and afforded them the space they needed to get things moving while still maintaining the secrecy around the "need to know" CONSTANT PEG operation. Mayo recalled: "I was only the ops officer for about four months, but in that time we established a base of operations, got well into the process of hiring the right people and were well into planning for how we were going to operate as an official, but still highly classified, unit."

Prior to the momentous events on April 1, Frick had already made his first hires into CONSTANT PEG. The first was Oberle, who'd left the Aggressors after three years to return to Vietnam and had eventually been lined up to go to the brand new F-15 Eagle. Fortunately, as it turned out, a backlog in the Eagle Replacement Training Unit (RTU) school saw him go back to the far less glamorous Phantom instead. And then he got a call that changed everything.

It was Frick. "He talked around what the assignment was going to be. He couldn't tell me what it was. He just said, 'You won't believe what's happening up here. You're going to like this a lot. You're the guy I want, and I have a byname request that we can do it through TAC Headquarters. "DL" will work to make it happen. If you want it we'll have you out here right away.'" Oberle accepted the assignment knowing that Frick could be talking about only one thing. When he finally arrived at Nellis in January, Frick had made his second hire: Aggressor Major Gerry "Huffer" Huff. Huff had been an instructor at the 414th FWS at Nellis, and had also been the ops officer at the 26th TFTS at Clark AB. When Frick hired him, he was an Aggressor IP at Nellis. Frick kept up appearances at the TFWC to maintain an air of normality, and his five pilots for the moment continued to fly F-5 Aggressor sorties to mask their real mission.

The physical infrastructure for CONSTANT PEG was almost non-existent at this time, Oberle noted.

> Frick had one little room in the office over in the Tactical Fighter Weapons Center. He had a guy that worked with him on the Red Baron reports, but who was never a Red Eagle. That guy was as instrumental as anybody in getting the whole thing going. His name was Chuck Holden. Chuck had never been an Aggressor, but he was a former B-26 Air Commando and had combat tours in both the F-100 and the F-4, and he was the only one of us who knew how to fly light airplanes – and that turned out to be very important, as he helped Frick with all the necessary stuff to get the ball rolling on this.

In addition to the maintainers' efforts to get the MiGs ready for flight, Frick had to outsource several aspects of the process to US defense contractors (the Air Force had invited several contractors to view and examine the HAVE MiGs to help exploit them). Perhaps the most critical maintenance element of all was the MiGs' motors. General Electric (GE) was tasked with the responsibility of repairing and refurbishing the engines, a responsibility that it had already undertaken as part of its broader involvement in AFSC's FME programs.

The motors were particularly troubling, recalled Oberle. "The Russian strategy for engines is that they use them about 150 hours and then throw them away. They don't plan to do the overhaul and maintenance and keep them for 8,000 hours like we do. Taking an engine that was designed to be a throw-away engine and being able to make it robust enough to make many cycles was a major challenge. GE did a great job for us on that."

Safety underpinned all that was being done to get the jets airworthy, and Oberle was involved in a mission to reverse engineer the pyrotechnic charges that would blast the MiGs' ejection seats out of the aircraft if the pilot was left with no choice but to bail out. "You couldn't go buy them anywhere!" Oberle pointed out:

We had to go to the Naval Ordnance Lab up in the Washington D.C. area to have them reverse engineer the ejection seat cartridges. The ejection cartridges for any ejection seat have a shelf life, because the powder and chemicals that make the explosion degrade and revert, and do all the things that chemicals do over time. The metal cartridge and the explosive in it are designed so they can handle the intense heat and pressure of the explosion to make the seat travel up the rails. Plus, the charge has to burn and release its energy at a certain rate, otherwise it would create a shotgun blast that will break your back. This phased release starts an acceleration up the track to get the ejection seat clear of the vehicle. They had to reverse engineer the powder to get the seat up the rails in a safe manner, because we didn't have the exact same stuff.

The challenge here came not only from being able to mix the right cocktail of chemical powder in the right quantities and under the right conditions, but also from the cartridge itself. "The lab looked at their ejection cartridges, and concluded that the casing was of a different metal compound than what we have here in the US. So they also had to reverse engineer the metal casings to get something close to the original. If they had got it wrong, the cartridge would not have been able to withstand the pressure and the heat of the charge going off." It was all a bit like putting together a giant jigsaw puzzle, and this was one of the critical pieces.

THE BOSS

Mayo used words like "dynamo," "limitless energy," "enthusiasm," and "tenacity" to characterize Frick. "He so thoroughly enjoyed everything he did that even when he was upset he was happy. During the two or three years that I was working with or around Glenn, he had an active personal life which included totally restoring an old Ford Model A pickup truck. He did all the work himself. It was a real beauty and he loved it. He was also building a kit aeroplane in his garage. I could never figure out how he found time away from work to do those things and be a great husband and dad; he was at work all of the time."

Frick also had a finely honed sense of humor, Mayo judged:

Glenn and I used to go to one of the casino auditoriums downtown to watch our little girls perform in their ballet class. We would usually get there late and sit in the back rows but really get a kick out of watching the little ones perform. Pappy would say, "Wouldn't it be neat if we could sit back here, drink beer, yell 'Shit hot!' and roll our beer cans down the aisle?" And the thing is that he really did want to do that!

We once had a going-away party at Glenn's house for Mike Press and his wife, Rozy. Pappy was the proverbial prankster and he convinced me to help him in the prank he wanted to play on Rozy. I was gullible enough to do it. During his speech to Mike and Rozy, Pappy told them that we had gotten together and bought a beautiful Waterford Crystal punch bowl. He said, "Kobe, bring that up here." My part was to walk up, trip, fall flat on my face, and break the bowl into a thousand pieces. What they didn't know was that the bowl was really only a two-dollar glass bowl we had gotten at the "5 and Dime." Well, I did my part beautifully. However, because Pappy and I were the only ones who knew the truth, we got a lot of laughs at first but then all the wives said, "Kobe, how could you?" and "Poor Rozy!" Rozy wouldn't speak to me and I felt like a real jerk. So the next day I went down town and bought Rozy a real Waterford Crystal bowl and took it over to her house. She forgave me, but then my wife wanted to know where in the hell was her Waterford Crystal bowl? I'm still paying for hers.

Whether the decision to stand up the new flight on April Fools' Day was deliberate or not, it signaled the start of an individual and remarkable program whose crucial black world mission was underpinned by humor from day one. Oberle recalled that first day:

Gen Creech, TAC commander, was a stickler for professionalism and looking the part. The flight suit was an official uniform in the Air Force, and Tactical Air Command demanded that the zippers be zipped up and that you wore a scarf around your neck, wore your hat when you were outdoors, and had to have all the right insignia and rank and all the patches in the right place. Frick was not in that mold. Frick was a guy who had his sleeves pushed up, his zippers undone, his boots looked as if he had been ploughing a field with them, and he never wore his hat. To give you an idea of his personality, if he came up to a wall and there was a door there that was unlocked, rather than open the door and go through it, he would knock a hole through the wall just to make an entrance.

We're sitting over here in this little office in the Fighter Weapons Center on April 1. Frick comes in and he's got to go to the 57th Wing staff meetings and all of that sort of thing now he's the 4477th TEF commander. He comes in and gets his pad, then goes out the door with no scarf on, his zipper zipped down to his navel, and none of his other zippers zipped up. He immediately runs into a buzz saw over there! This full colonel and Director of Operations dresses him down right there about his standards!

So, Frick comes back hopping into the office digging into the drawers of his desk. "What are you looking for, Pappy?" "I've got a shoe brush and some shoe polish around here somewhere!" He's trying to polish his shoes. I guess the honeymoon's over on the first day of this thing; it was April Fools' Day that this operation got set up and Frick got hammered at his first staff meeting!

Frick's day was about to get worse, as Peck recounts:

My phone rang, and when I picked it up it was Frick out at Nellis. He said, "I have good news and bad news. The good news is that TAC has agreed to formulate the squadron. It's going to be the 4477th Test & Evaluation Flight." I said, "Two questions, Glenn. Where did 'forty-four, seventy-seven' come from, and why is it a flight and not a squadron?" He said, "4477th came right out of my ass; and it's going to be a flight instead of a squadron because we want to reduce the amount of attention that we might bring to ourselves if we are a full squadron instead of a flight." "So what is the bad news?" "The bad news is that I just made full colonel and they're already talking about shipping me off to Egypt."

I subsequently learned that Frick may have been inspired to pick those numbers because he was 44 years old and the year was 1977, but I was never able to substantiate the veracity of this account.

Frick had been earmarked for a job as air attaché to the US Embassy in Egypt, and with his imminent promotion to full colonel, he was likely to be leaving Nellis for Cairo sooner rather than later.

This was a potentially serious problem, explained Peck: "This whole thing could have come down around us like a pack of cards if either Frick or Smith left – these two guys were my black world contacts and I needed them both. I asked him what I could do about it, and he responded: 'I suggest you call the wing commander, Col Clements.' I was sitting there shaking my head in dismay that this thing might all fall apart because we might lose the personnel cohesion when the phone rang again. It was Col Clements, who I did not know. Well, he told me about Frick's promotion and told me that he wanted me to take command of the squadron." Naturally, Peck accepted and welcomed the offer with open arms.

EGYPTIAN MIGS

With his knowledge of MiG operations, it was probably no coincidence that the Air Force selected Frick to go to Egypt. Cairo had recently fallen out with Moscow with predictable results: less than one year after it started flying the Russian-supplied MiG-23 "Flogger" – a new and somewhat enigmatic supersonic interceptor that was greatly revered by US intelligence agencies – the Egyptian Air Force withdrew them from service as spare parts from the Motherland were withheld and their own stocks dried up.

The situation for Egypt's MiG-21s was marginally better, thanks to more plentiful stocks of spares, but even these would not last for too long. Cairo did the only thing it could and made its MiGs available to China and the United States in exchange for new hardware and hard currency.

America bought a large quantity of equipment from Egypt – MiGs, bombs, missiles, radars, surface-to-air missile (SAM) systems, and so on. But the jewel in the crown was the Flogger. Peter Merlin cited a former Red Hat commander as saying: "In the summer of 1977, the Red Hats acquired from Egypt 12 MiG-23MS 'Flogger E' interceptors and one MiG-23BN 'Flogger F' fighter-bomber.[7] They were shipped to the US in two C-5s, each carrying six airframes." AFSC took the first look at the two MiG-23 variants under the codename HAVE PAD. Soon, it would be TAC's turn.

LEARNING TO FLY MIGS

Mayo, Iverson, Muller, and Frick continued flying the Fishbeds and Frescos of Groom Lake, where the majority of MiG spares were located in "huge piles of junk and parts that sat in dirty, disorganized piles in a hangar." This would be the MiGs' home until the 4477th TEF could find an operating base. The maintenance effort was being concentrated on returning to flight four of the least decrepit Indonesian MiG-21s, and for the moment there was little emphasis on adding any more flyable MiG-17s to the unit's stock of assets.

For Oberle and Huff, who had never flown a MiG before, they relied on snippets of written notes, but mostly a healthy dose of advice from their four buddies. "Trying to fly airplanes that had no original parts, no markings in the cockpit that you could read, no flight manual of how you could fly them" was tough, Oberle recalled. "We had to go through and teach ourselves all of this stuff." There were some switches that they didn't have to know – such as those of the SIRENA radar warning system that alerted the MiG pilot when he was being swept or tracked by an enemy radar, but for the most part it was in their best interests to know the aircraft as thoroughly as possible.

In essence, not much had changed since FERRY, DOUGHNUT, or DRILL. A tradition of oratory – handing down the knowledge needed to fly the MiGs while at the bar – had persisted throughout IDEA; it was a rite of passage. "There was one book of notes," Mayo said. "You read the book really good.

Then you spent a long time and multiple briefings talking to the pilots who had already flown the airplanes. Then you flew the aircraft."

The then-classified Threat Training Facility (TTF) at Nellis, colloquially known as the "Petting Zoo," housed examples of the MiG-17 and MiG-21 for those with the appropriate security clearance to visit, and these jets provided Oberle and Huff, and later Peck, with a convenient means to familiarize themselves with the cockpit layouts without having to expend an entire day traveling to and from Groom Lake. There were also MiGs at Edwards AFB, California, and at Bolling Field, home of the National Air Intelligence Center in Washington. "Moody Suter's leadership philosophy was that we should expose our people to as much of this type of stuff as we could, and so these displays grew. We called them Warrior Prep[aration] Centers in Europe and Japan," Peck explained.

The DOUGHNUT pilots in 1968 had received a two-ride checkout process to get them qualified to fly the MiGs. Now, Morgenfeld, who had flown the IDEA MiG-21 as part of his job at VX-4, and Iverson were working to formalize the checkout process and to add a little more structure to getting the new MiG pilot ready to fly exposures and air combat.

With no two-seat trainer models available, actually learning to fly the MiGs was still a case of taking off and then gradually exploring the envelope by feel and intuition. Peck described the process thus:

> First you fly some gentle turns, then you make them more aggressive turns. Then you do some light aerobatics and lazy eights. Then you pull it up and make it stall; see how it falls off. Then put down the gear and flaps and fly a mock traffic pattern at altitude so that you can see how it feels in the pattern in slow flight. I tried to remember exactly what the pitch attitude was at the exact moment the MiG left the ground on take-off, because that's what you are looking for in the round-out as you come in to land.

There were other, less obvious things that had to be learned. Etiquette, for example. The etiquette of MiG operations had changed little in all those years. In 1975, when Mayo had first flown the MiG-21, he had walked out to the asset at Groom Lake [8] and started doing the usual exterior inspection to ensure there were no leaks or loose panels. "The crew chief, who had about a gazillion stripes on his arm, grabbed me by the collar and asked, 'Where in the hell do you think you're going, major?' I told him, 'I am doing the exterior inspection.' He ended it by saying, 'You fly it. I make sure it's ready to go.' As I strapped in, he added, 'Here's the deal: you can play with the shiny switches, but don't fuck with the red or rusty ones,' which sounded funny, but he was very serious."

Mayo elaborated further, with absolute sincerity: "You learn the airplane moment by moment. By that point in your career, it didn't really matter what you were flying. You pulled back on the pole and the trees got smaller; you pushed forward and they got bigger. In that sense, every airplane flies the same way."

When Peck visited Groom Lake[9] in 1978 to get his checkout in the MiG-17, he was immediately struck by how protective of the assets the maintainers were. He recalled that M/Sgt Don Lyons was typical in that he wasn't sure this experienced pilot would start the motor without exceeding its temperature limitations. Lyons would lean over the side and caution the lieutenant colonel about being over aggressive in advancing the throttle as the engine cranked over. While checking out in the MiG-21 later, Peck turned to him and confided: "Don, I don't think I'll ever be able to fly this airplane. I don't know what position any of these switches should be in." Lyons had responded dryly: "It's easy, Boss. They all either go up or forward!"

Within a couple of rides the new MiG pilot started learning how to employ the MiG as a weapon system – a death-dealing tool of destruction. But even with the first phase of formalization under way thanks to Morgenfeld and Iverson, there was still only a nominal number of sorties, around five to seven, put aside for this. Why? Because flying hours on the MiGs, despite the influx of additional assets from overseas, were still a precious commodity. An elongated checkout process would see the assets' useful training time reduced unacceptably.

At some point in the years that followed, the CONSTANT PEG program began retrospectively numbering the pilots that had flown the MiGs, with Mayo being administratively recorded as being the first of 69 fighter pilots who would eventually be assigned to, or attached to, the 4477th. He became "Bandit 1"; Iverson, "Bandit 2"; Muller, "Bandit 3"; Frick, "Bandit 4"; Oberle, "Bandit 5"; and Huff, "Bandit 6," all followed.[10]

THE FIRST TAC EXPOSURES

As the men of the 4477th TEF toiled to get the unit and CONSTANT PEG up and running, TAC continued to use the assets as it had during HAVE IDEA. These first 4477th TEF sorties were to form a very secret part of a Red Flag in the early summer of 1977. Mayo reflected fondly on this period:

It was without a doubt the most rewarding period of my time with the unit. Red Flag was in full swing, so visiting fighter wings were at Nellis a lot to participate in their "first ten days of the next war." The 4477th had been tasked to conduct an exercise with one of the visiting fighter wings and, as I recall, it was the 49th TFW from Holloman AFB. This was to be the first exposure of the MiG assets to an operational fighter wing and our excitement over this event was maximized. This is what we had wanted to do from day one! I was particularly excited because I was in the 417th TFS, 49th TFW, prior to joining the Aggressors and had flown in North Vietnam with the 49th.

I remember the day of our initial briefing with them at Nellis. The pilots were assembled in the briefing room not knowing exactly what we were going to be talking to them about; to the best of my knowledge they were not aware that they were going to have this opportunity. When I took the stage and said, "Congratulations! You guys are to be the first fighter wing in the Tactical Air Command to fly against the MiGs of the 4477th TEF," this audience of fighter pilots exploded. It took a full five minutes to get their minds back in their heads so we could outline the events of the next week or so. I have never in my life witnessed such a moment of exhilaration as on that day when these guys found out what was in store for them.

Mayo and his colleagues went on to brief the shocked Phantom pilots and WSOs thus: "Each fighter pilot was introduced to the MiGs with a 1 v 1 Basic Fighter Maneuvers [BFM] sortie; then 2 v 1 in Air Combat Maneuvers [ACM]; and then 2 v 2, with a MiG-17 and a MiG-21." By the standards of the immediate years that would follow, the number and complexity of these first exposures was impressive. So too was the actual flying. "For the first exposure, there were actually two F-4s airborne, and each would trade off with the other to allow both to fly against the two different MiG types. The next sortie, 2 v 1 ACM, saw the F-4s work as a team against a single MiG. Next was the 2 v 2, and we had either two MiG-21s against the Phantoms, or a mixed flight of a MiG-17 and a MiG-21. For a 'final go,' we flew 4 v 4 or a simulated strike flight with the F-4s flying ground attack and others flying MiG CAP [Combat Air Patrol]."

In the air, the learning curve was steep, just as it had been for Robb several years back. Importantly, there was more than enough Buck Fever to go around. Mayo said bluntly:

The first five minutes was all, "Oh my God! Holy shit! You gotta be shitting me!," sort of stuff. But once they got over the thrill of being five feet away from a MiG-21 in flight, the learning began. They were so appreciative you would have thought that we had guaranteed each of them 69 virgins in heaven.

We felt that we had made an unbelievably significant impact on the combat capability of every one of those pilots. When I was flying with the 49th over Hanoi

I saw MiGs and they held for me the fear of the unknown. They had that mystique that made them bigger than life. But for these guys we had just trained, they knew what it looked like up close, they knew how to pressure a MiG into making fatal errors; there was no mystique, there was only a Bogie who would easily become a Bandit, then a target, and then a kill. It was a very generous exposure for the 49th.

THE FIRST NAVY PILOT

With Mayo's departure imminent, the 4477th TEF hired Tom Morgenfeld, the Navy pilot from VX-4 who had been working with Iverson on Soviet tactics exploitation and IDEA. Morgenfeld was specifically recruited to be the 4477th TEF's MiG-21 "check pilot:" his job was to conduct the Fishbed conversion for new CONSTANT PEG pilots, but he would continue to be based at Point Mugu for the time being and would be "eased" into the unit over the course of a number of years. For the purposes of a cover story, he was instructed to tell anyone who asked that he was the Navy's liaison with the USAF's Aggressors.

Morgenfeld already had more MiG-21 hours than most, having done much flying of the IDEA jets against TOPGUN IPs and students. He had run a number of classified programs that focused on Soviet tactics: "I had tried to be the source for the squadron of everything that the Soviets were doing that was new. So, when the Navy was looking for someone who could fly unusual airplanes that were not mainstream US-developed aircraft, they looked at me and as I was a test school graduate felt a lot more comfortable about the whole thing." VX-4 also provided him with valuable experience, since not only had it focused on operational exploitation of friendly and enemy systems, but it had also been responsible for the development and creation of tactics that would optimize and defeat, respectively, said systems. In particular, VX-4 had worked with the AWG-9 radar system installed in the new F-14 Tomcat.

Geographically separated from Frick and the others for the time being, Morgenfeld worked on aspects of the program that required little interaction with the others. One such task was the creation of documentation, and in particular the creation of the first of many iterations of a flight manual for the MiG-21. As a template, he used an original, but "crude," MiG-21 flight manual that had been translated into English by the Soviets for one of their customers. His focus was less on creating a document that would provide a complete step-by-step guide to flying and operating the MiG-21 – although the manual duly noted every switch in the cockpit and its function – and more about using his test pilot training to verify precisely "the basic numbers" of take-off, landing, and performance so that the MiG could be flown safely. Morgenfeld also worked, in coordination with Iverson, on putting together a flight training syllabus for later Bandits to follow.

Lt Chuck "Heater" Heatley, another Navy pilot, joined Morgenfeld at around the same time. By the end of August 1977, the Air Force had formally approved both men's status as qualified MiG pilots. Morgenfeld became "Bandit 7," and Heatley became "Bandit 8."

Less glamorous work continued unabated back at Groom Lake and Nellis. The Indonesian MiGs were being completely overhauled and required the customary functional check flight (FCF) before they could be certified ready for flight. The FCF was an important part of the maintenance process governing every military aircraft that was taken apart and then reassembled during planned depot maintenance, but it was particularly important for the once-dilapidated MiGs. Morgenfeld was given the responsibility for writing the 4477th TEF's MiG-21 FCF process.

Oberle became one of the pilots qualified to fly the FCF profile prescribed by Morgenfeld. Since many of the MiGs had arrived at Groom Lake in an exceptionally poor condition, the first FCF flight was always an exciting affair. Oberle recalled one particular Fishbed that had taken 18 months to make airworthy: "The MiG had been taken apart and rebuilt. It was a labor of love for the crew chief, and I was going to be the first pilot on it. We did all the operational ground checks – taxi; phased acceleration where you'd go to 50 knots; shut it down and get the crew chief to check it over; then do it again with afterburner, but abort at a slow enough speed that we could stop at the end of the runway. When all of those were OK, we'd do the first flight with a T-38 as safety chase." The T-38 Talon, borrowed from the Aggressors and used to fly up to Groom Lake, performed what were known as the "clean and dry" checks:

We'd get airborne, the T-38 would join underneath and see if we had any leaks, and then we'd check the flight controls overhead the field with the gear down so that we could land immediately. The T-38 chase would stay with us in position. If that went OK we'd come back and tell the crew chief if it needed better rigging because it was rolling left, or whatever. Then we'd take it up for one or two more flights like that before raising the gear. Safety chase checked that the doors were all up and locked, and then we'd do higher altitude and more aggressive maneuvering to make sure that the gear was going to stay up and to ensure that there were no leaks. Then, by about the fourth flight, I was ready to take it out for a supersonic flight. [Supersonic flight verified that the MiG-21's nose cone would operate properly.]

In the fully operational MiG-21 a computer is hooked up to an air data computer that gets information from the pitot-static system. The nose cone would protrude to move the supersonic shockwave and to keep the intake air subsonic as you went faster. Picture a boat in the water and the wake that it causes; the cone would retract to make for a blunter face that would make that wake go out wider than the intake. You could go up to Mach 1.3 with the cone as it was, and then there was a little switch that would retract the cone, allowing you to go up to 1.6 Mach. I'd fly the FCF out to 1.6 Mach. You'd feel rumbling, but it was a stable airplane.

We were learning that once supersonic you could pull the throttle back to mil [military] power and it would stay supersonic for a long time. It would almost supercruise, it was so clean. This is what we'd seen in tactics in Vietnam – the MiG-21 pilot would run away, climb to a higher altitude while supersonic, and then he could sit there for a long time without burning a lot of fuel. Normally, by the fifth flight, we were ready to put that jet on the schedule and send it out to fight.

As the newly prepared MiGs went through the FCF process, the Red Hats were conducting other maintenance and engineering tests to determine the long-term viability of operating the MiGs. Some of their MiGs underwent extensive ground-based study, including metallurgical examination and x-ray inspections in hangars at Edwards AFB's "North Base."

The FTD had never been busier, and the Red Hats' operations were reaching mammoth proportions, as Merlin expanded:

By the end of 1977 the Red Hats possessed 1,200 percent more total assets than they had in 1972, and managed a budget in excess of $670,000 per fiscal year. The cadre included two test pilots and 38 enlisted personnel for maintenance, operations, and administrative duties. They flew an average of 25 percent of all AFFTC sorties annually. Personnel now went TDY [temporary duty] to the Test Site on a continuous Monday-through-Friday basis, with occasional extra TDY when required to accomplish high-priority or special missions.

Because of the Special Projects Branch's diversified and expanded mission, the classified nature of its projects, its unique support requirements, and its geographic separation from its parent unit, AFFTC commander MajGen Thomas P. Stafford proposed elevating the organization to squadron status. The new unit was activated as the 6513th Test Squadron on December 1, 1977.

FINDING A LOCATION

Peck had compiled a shortlist of locations for the MiGs based on the suggestions of various colleagues. The objective was to find a location secure enough to allow the MiGs to operate without having people driving through or inadvertently flying into their airspace.

Suter had suggested the Gold Water Ranges south of Luke AFB, Arizona, which were roughly 20 miles wide by 120 miles long, extending from Yuma to approximately 25 miles east of Gila Bend, from Interstate Highway 8 south to the Cabeza Prieta National Wildlife Refuge. Also on the list was the Dugway Proving Grounds Range, which was 80 miles west-southwest of Salt Lake City, Utah, and was the testing ground for a number of nuclear, biological, and chemical weapons programs. Finally, there was the vast Tonopah Test Range (TTR), measuring a mammoth 625 square miles, and just a stone's throw from the Groom Lake test site 70 miles to the southeast.

Frick and Oberle leased a Cessna 207, N1592U, with Holden, Frick's Red Baron reports assistant, at the controls. They were to fly the initial recce flights ahead of a later visit by Peck. Oberle recalls looking at the Dugway Range:

> It was an army storage facility for chemical and biological weapons. It was highly classified, highly guarded, and it was in a secure area. And it had a little runway there. We flew up there and checked it out. Then we flew back into the ranges in the classified areas where the Atomic Energy Agency did their nuclear testing. We found a place up there in the Yuka Flats that had a little runway that was about 3,000ft. It was in a secure area, too. We did all of the pros and cons on site survey for that. Then we looked at the airstrip up in the northwest corner near Tonopah, Nevada, which was inside the range space so you had to have clearance to enter the range if you were in an airplane. It was also restricted from the ground because the Atomic Energy Commission owned this little site.

The Department of Energy [DoE] used the airfield at Tonopah to fly ballistics tests on nuclear weapon "shapes" and to test the release mechanisms for the atomic weapons. "They would do drogue deliveries from airplanes, and then check the ballistics and release conditions in case they had to use one of these for real," Oberle stated.

Of all the sites, Tonopah seemed like the most suitable location, Frick told Peck on the phone. Located about 30 miles southeast of the small town of Tonopah, the airfield was located on the northern fringe of the Nellis Range and was inaccessible to the public. Frick had told Peck that the town of Tonopah was "pretty sleepy," with only a mining museum and "a famous hotel" being of note. Peck flew into Nellis, jumped in the right seat of N1592U with Holden in the left and Frick in the back, and the three flew into Tonopah.

The remoteness of TTR lent itself well to the low profile that CONSTANT PEG would need if it were to survive, explained Peck: "Even though the airfield could be seen from high sites, I physically went out there with a pair of binoculars and found that there is so much thermal activity out there on the desert floor that you can't get a clear image of what you're looking at. I could never really visually see anything from any of the vantage points that I personally went to and surveyed."

Peck bought a commercial airline ticket and flew with Western Airlines down to Gila Bend to see the Gold Water Ranges. En route he sketched onto a Western Airlines napkin the current outline of the Tonopah runway, and then sketched in the improvements that it would need to host the MiGs. "My idea was to expand the runway, add turnaround areas at each end – we didn't need taxi ways – and then to build a compound. The compound would have three hangars: one for operations, one for maintenance, and one to store the airplanes. We would have a space outside for parking the jets and a POL [petroleum, oil, lubricant] for jet fuel, and that'd be it." Peck never made it to the Gold Water Ranges. On arrival at Gila Bend, he turned straight around, napkin in hand, and returned to the Pentagon.

Arriving back in Washington he announced: "We've found our site. We're going to go to Tonopah." He compiled a briefing book with the help of a Pentagon artist, Jerry Hansen, that outlined his plans and went to the top Air Force generals to get their "chop," or blessing, for CONSTANT PEG's basing arrangements. They approved them without delay. "The airfield actually belonged to the DoE and their Albuquerque operation. It was a general aviation-capable runway that could handle light airplanes, and they had a twin Convair. So, we approached Albuquerque [home of the DoE] and convinced them that if we could enhance their airfield, instead of bringing their people to work in these old twin-engine Convair prop jobs they could maybe bring jets in. They thought it was a good idea after that."

Smith worked along similar lines at TAC HQ, getting the program "top-lined" so that by the time Peck approached the Office of the Secretary of Defense (OSD) on the Pentagon's third floor for final approval, they would sign off on the program. Soon after, the US Navy was administratively brought onboard. By January 30, 1978, the Air Force had approved the CONSTANT PEG Concept of Operations: TAC would have control over the program, and the Air Force would pay 70 percent of the flight's funding, with the remaining 30 percent coming from the Navy. Less than two months later, on March 15, John Stetson, Secretary of the Air Force, approved CONSTANT PEG's Concept of Operations.

FINANCING CONSTANT PEG AND DEVELOPING TONOPAH

Getting money for the program that was not subject to close public scrutiny was critical if it was to retain its black status. "Gen Currie came up with the idea of financing this out of the Office of the Secretary of the Air Force's emergency construction fund," Peck grinned.

> He was the money guy. He knew how to spend money the right way without anyone going to jail. Col Dick Murray in the AF Controller's office set up a conduit directly from the Pentagon to Nellis. At the other end of that conduit was Mary Jane Smith. When I needed money for construction, I went to see her. So, we were able to spend money that was allocated to a line on the budget without actually asking Congress – we simply notified them. I went across the river and I briefed the staffers for the Chairmen of the House and Senate Armed Services and Appropriations Committees. The project was embraced by Congress.

Likewise, at the Pentagon and everywhere else, Peck noted, "No one was recalcitrant, no one tried to block the path or cause problems. I would walk into a general's office, and more often than not they would greet me like a long lost friend. They'd walk around their desk and we'd sit in easy chairs, and they'd say, 'What have you got for me today? How can I help you?'" Peck holds nothing back in acknowledging the importance of such support. "Imagine that you had a football team that you had just formed, and then imagine that you took it to the Super Bowl in its first year. Now consider what the chances are of winning. Well, winning the Super Bowl with that team was the equivalent of what we were doing."

It wasn't all smooth sailing, but sometimes small hiccups would turn out for the best. Peck told me that one Saturday Vandenberg had been in a foul mood when he'd learned that his usual secretary was unavailable to prepare correspondence on CONSTANT PEG. As he began venting at Peck that it was incredible that no one knew a secretary available on Saturday with a Top Secret clearance, Peck calmly responded that he did know someone with the necessary clearance: his wife, Peggy. "Vandenberg said, 'Get her in here,' so I did. We briefed her there and then and so she knew about the program from the get-go."

In May 1978, the Deputy Secretary of Defense, Charles Duncan Jr, approved $7 million to fund Phase I of the modifications to Tonopah Test Range first sketched by Peck on the back of his napkin. While $7 million had been released, Peck recalled that he had authority for as much as $10 million. He used his new DoE connections to arrange for the Phase I improvements of architectural and engineering aspects of the airfield, and the DoE also assisted him in sourcing contractors to undertake construction work "in order to get the airfield actually built to our standards."

"More interesting," Peck divulged, "was how we actually built the airfield. We did it by using an old law from the Depression days – the Economic Recovery Act of 1932 – and what that does is authorize one government agency to transfer money to another government agency. We courted the DoE both at the site [Tonopah] and their host [or chain of command, Albuquerque], advocating this project and getting to know them." The DoE had sole source contracting authority at the Tonopah site that allowed the Air Force to transfer the funds for construction to their coffers, and they in turn contracted Reynolds Engineering & Electrical Company (REECo), the on-scene contractor, and Holmes & Narver (H&N) to conduct the architectural and engineering work. REECo was the engineering firm that did all of the construction work across the Nevada test site, and H&N would design the CONSTANT PEG facility.

The deal was a good one for the DoE – Phase I would see the Air Force pay for the runway to be extended and widened. Huff had taken Peck's napkin and used a contractor to create a "project book" that could be presented to H&N to allow them to draw up precise plans from which REECo could work. The project book did not include the giant, net-like, jet barriers nicknamed "Rabbit Catchers" that needed to be installed at each end of the runway to net any MiG with failed brakes before it ran off the end of the runway and into the dirt. The barriers came as an afterthought requirement. The project book did include the turnarounds; POL and parking area; and three hangars. Peck flew into Orange County, home of H&N's offices, and sat through a formal presentation of the proposed changes that was true to his original vision. An H&N executive asked Peck if they should execute the plans, and without first consulting the XOO in Washington Peck took the bold decision to respond unerringly: "Do it!"

While Huff coordinated with the construction firms at Tonopah, and Muller devised the program's security practices throughout 1978, Frick's small team at Nellis had changed. In August, Mayo had been offered the ops officer job with the 65th FWS squadron and had accepted it, seeing it as a good career move. For his final flight, he and Muller had flown two MiG-21s against a pair of FWS F-15s in a 21-mile ACM set-up. And who won? "We did, of course!" said Mayo. Oberle took his place as 4477th TEF ops officer. Ron Iverson had similarly departed to take a promotion to lieutenant colonel and an assignment back at TAC HQ that led to promotion to colonel.

It was Huff who did much of the engineering contract liaison work, and he worked closely with Dell Gaulker, the construction manager for REECo. The two worked closely to build the remote airstrip into something that could accommodate the MiGs, while Muller took care of the site's security arrangements.

Muller had been a former Chicago Bears halfback before joining the Air Force, and had flown in Vietnam as an F-100 "Misty" Forward Air Controller (FAC), during which he'd bailed out of the Super Sabre twice. He was now confronted with a paradox: keeping CONSTANT PEG under wraps involved not making obvious changes to the security arrangements at the site. The Tonopah Test Range already had its own chain link and barbed wire fence that spanned the length of its borders. Both the main gate and the immediate security of the airfield itself were staffed by civilian security patrolmen supplied by EG&G – the contractor responsible for site security for classified ranges and locations, including Groom Lake. None of this was changed, and rather than worrying about the physical security aspects of the program, Muller's task was primarily oriented around how people would access CONSTANT PEG, who would be briefed in on it, how the names of these people would be tracked, and similar administrative elements vital if the MiGs were to remain close hold.

Frick and Oberle started looking around Nellis for new temporary accommodation when the munitions storage area on the north side of the base became too inconvenient. Oberle noted: "We lived in that for three or four months. This thing had double barbed wire fence, guarded. You'd have to pull your vehicle in and they had to inspect with mirrors every time you went in and out of there. It got to be too cumbersome, and we left that. We finally had a little room in another building down at Nellis and eventually we got a trailer and set up down by 57th wing headquarters."

HAVE PAD

By the spring of 1978, TAC had become involved in HAVE PAD, the exploitation of the 12 MiG-23MS Flogger Es and solitary MiG-23BN Flogger F obtained from Egypt in summer 1977. It had been Iverson's responsibility to head TAC's HAVE PAD team as more of the Floggers were made flyable and the Red Hats started freeing them for operational exploitation. Part of the operational exploitation involved hiring an analyst, and Iverson hired Capt Bob Drabant. Drabant joined the 4477th TEF in April 1978.[11] Presumably, Iverson's team also represented a sort of advance party that would be able to analyze what logistics, support, and training would be needed when it was time for the 4477th TEF to incorporate the MiG-23 into CONSTANT PEG.

Drabant had earned the respect of the fighter community by working on the groundbreaking Energy Maneuverability (EM) theory as put forth by the highly controversial (but ultimately much-respected) Col Jon Boyd and civilian mathematician Tom Christie. He had turned the concept into a reality by creating performance graphs that the average fighter pilot could look at and understand. Between 1970 and 1974, he had conducted his EM work as an aero engineer at the Air Force Armament Lab's Weapon System Analysis Division, Eglin AFB, Florida.

The EM concept, and Drabant's graphs, provided the fighter pilot with a snap-shot overview of an aircraft's performance capability. By studying the EM graph of one aircraft, or by overlaying it on top of the EM graph of another, its relative strengths and weaknesses became clear. The EM graph showed how fast, how high, and how many sustained Gs a given fighter could achieve in any given area of the flight envelope.

Drabant had one foot planted in the white world and the other in the black world. He'd participated in Freedom Fighter Source Selection, resulting in the Northrop F-5E; and Lightweight Fighter Source Selection, the winners of which were the General Dynamics F-16A for the Air Force, and the Northrop F/A-18A for the Navy, at the same time. But on the dark side, he had created the MiG-17 and MiG-21 EM graphs during HAVE IDEA, using them as examples during the process of "transferring EM capability to AFSC and the FTD."[12]

By August, Drabant's work for Iverson[13] on HAVE PAD was complete and he turned his hand to assisting Huff at Tonopah, as he explains:

CONSTANT PEG was in a transition phase at that time. After I finished the work that Ron hired me for, I hung around to work on the CONSTANT PEG program. I really didn't do analytical work for the 4477th TEF, but what I did do was odd jobs trying to get Tonopah up and running so we could do MiG flight ops. My unofficial title was Deputy Base Commander of TTR, while the unofficial base commander was my friend and roommate, Maj Gerry "Huffer" Huff. One of my jobs was to run a ditch witch behind our three hangars so that we would be able to lay weather cables to both ends of the runway. The ditch witch is a small ditch-digging machine, and the weather cables were electrical cables that we were going to run to either end of the runway and attach to wind speed and direction equipment. They would then enable us to monitor this information in the operations section of the complex.

As work preparing Tonopah continued on schedule through the summer of 1978, the 4477th TEF pilots flew the first ever CONSTANT PEG exposures, but they were also flying technical evaluations that overlapped with the work more usually associated with the Red Hats. Under great secrecy, the 4477th TEF invited a contingent of six 49th TFW pilots to Nellis. The 49th TFW were now the proud operators of America's newest jet fighter, the F-15, which they had begun to receive in December 1977. The Eagle pilots deployed to Nellis for what they had been told were "advanced air-to-air tactics" sorties, but there was little other detail.

The Eagle drivers flew to Nellis on a Sunday afternoon and were briefed on CONSTANT PEG. Only then was the detail revealed: the 4477th TEF instructed the F-15 Eagles to focus on employing their AIM-9P Sidewinders against the MiGs to see how vulnerable the assets were. The tests of the AIM-9P would provide a baseline from which to establish how much more lethal the newest version of the Sidewinder missile, the AIM-9L, was. The FWS would be called upon by the 4477th TEF to conduct similar tests of the newer version of the missile.

To make the analysis realistic, the Holloman-based Eagle pilots were told: "There are no training rules. Just make sure you don't crash." For two to three weeks the Eagles flew 2 v 2 sorties against the MiGs several times a day. Occasionally, a "neutral" Aggressor T-38 would fly in among the assets to create a 3 v 2 scenario where the Eagle pilots had to be sure not to shoot the Talon. Likewise, the rules on when the Sidewinder could be employed throughout the tests were varied to further challenge the pilots.

With the radarless MiGs' heavy dependency on GCI apparent, the Eagles would fly in low to the ground and below the coverage of the GCI radars; since there was no minimum height restriction, this was perfectly legal. This tactic blinded the MiGs at long range, and forced the 4477th TEF pilots – Frick, Muller, Oberle, and Heatley – to rely on their Mk I eyeballs to pick up a visual on the Eagles. More often than not, the F-15s were already converting on the MiGs' sterns and locking their Sidewinders onto their hot jet pipes before they knew what was happening.

When the assets were flown in a mixed force of MiG-21s and MiG-17s, the Holloman flyers tried first to kill the faster Fishbed, which could accelerate almost as well as the dual-motor F-15. They avoided turning with the agile, but comparatively slow, Fresco.

MOVING INTO TONOPAH

By October 1978, the 4477th TEF was clearly in need of something bigger and better than the N1592U, and Oberle was tasked by Frick to source a replacement. "I leased a Cessna 404 from a company in Houston, Texas, and we kept it at Nellis. We would fly it back and forth to Tonopah every day." As the unit grew, the number of leased Cessna 404s increased correspondingly, and it would not be long until the 4477th TEF had four of the little transports.[14] The pilots then had to get their civilian multi-engine flying ratings so that they could legally pilot the twin-prop aircraft. "We went down to McCarran airport to get our licenses," Oberle recalled. Peck added: "The flight training was done by a company called 'Terra Training,' which was owned by a former Air Force fighter pilot, 'Mort' Mortenson."

Phase I work to complete the runway improvements at Tonopah was almost complete by the summer. So too were the flight's hangars. Accordingly, a heavy lifting team covertly transported examples of both the MiG-17 and MiG-21 to TTR in preparation for their use as sources of spare parts. These so-called Hangar Queens were those MiGs that had been damaged or had deteriorated to such a degree that Ellis and his maintainers could not return them to flight. Once at Tonopah, Oberle recalled, the forlorn MiGs were gradually dismantled to create a stockpile of parts ready for use when the flyable MiGs arrived.

Despite the black nature of the program and the fact that it was exempt from the usual administration and reporting typical of an Air Force fighter unit, the 4477th TEF could not escape the scrutiny of the Air Force's safety inspectorate. When the safety team started demanding an inspection of TTR and its facilities, Frick was forced to brief in one person. That person was the commander of the Air Force Safety Center, whom Frick already knew well. Oberle explained: "This colonel spends a few days looking around and interviewing the maintenance guys. Then, he walks into Frick's office and says, 'Glenn, I hate to tell you, but some of your maintenance procedures are not up to Air Force standards and I am going to have to go back and report that.' Glenn pushed back. He said: 'We'll try and straighten out whatever you tell us to, but we can't afford to have people come up here crawling all over us if you go back and write that up.'" Eventually, the two reached a deal and Frick was granted more time to rectify matters.

PECK TAKES OVER, SEPTEMBER 6, 1978

Peck's first stop on his way from flying a desk at the "Puzzle Palace" (the Pentagon) to commander-designee of the 4477th TEF, was Holloman AFB, New Mexico. "I had spent three years out of the cockpit, and the previous airplane I had flown was the F-4, but the next airplane I was going to fly was the F-5E with the Aggressors. So, I went for two rides in the T-38 with the Lead In Fighter Training course in order to get my jet wings going again." The wing commander at Holloman was a former Academy friend of Peck's, and he called him into to his office. "Brad said to me, 'I hear you got yourself a fat cat job?!' and then, 'That's a pretty high-risk job. I hope it goes well.'"

Peck arrived at Nellis and checked in with the 64th FWS. He would be attached to them while he waited for his own squadron to spin up, but in the meantime would undergo the exhaustive and extensive Aggressor checkout program. On September 6, 1978, Frick formally handed the 4477th over to him, and began preparations for his departure to Cairo. Later that month, Peck qualified to fly the MiG-17, officially becoming "Bandit 9."

The move to Tonopah was a milestone that was still ten months away, but it was close enough that Morgenfeld was finally ordered to relocate to Nellis. Up until that point, most of his liaison with the Air Force had taken place over secure telephone conversations from Point Mugu, but with MiG availability on the increase and with their relocation to TTR looming, it was time to move. In order to sustain the cover story that he was sharing information with the Air Force on the Aggressor squadrons, he went to TOPGUN to get checked out on the F-5 in November 1978, and shortly after went to Nellis to go through the Aggressor course with the 64th FWS. In doing so, Morgenfeld became the first Navy pilot to be a qualified Air Force Aggressor pilot.

CHAPTER 4

THE RED EAGLES' FIRST DAYS AND THE EARLY MIGS

With Frick departing for Egypt, Peck immediately began completing his team of players. The Navy was now fully integrated into the squadron, with Morgenfeld and Heatley forming much more than just "token squids" in the initial cadre of 4477th TEF MiG drivers. In January 1979, Morgenfeld and his wife finally packed up and moved from Point Mugu to Nellis: "It was all being made to look like I was there as part of a normal exchange tour," he explained.

The Department of the Navy was paying 30 percent of the program's costs, and its pilots would be responsible for the hands-on training with the Navy and Marine units that would eventually come to Tonopah to be exposed to the MiGs. Regarding the selection of the Navy pilots Oberle recalled: "The Navy would select the guys they wanted and send them to us, but we had a veto if we felt that they weren't the right person. Adm Gilchrist was the guy over at Miramar, head of the Navy input. He was very supportive of our operations over there. If we made one phone call back over there and said, 'Send somebody else,' they'd do it immediately."

It was a Navy pilot who is credited with naming the 4477th TEF. "Heatley came up with the Red Eagles," Peck told me. "He stuck to it like a frog on a June bug; he just wouldn't let it go. I said to him, 'Heater, that is just too provocative. We can't go putting on a Red Eagles patch – that's the Russian Fighter Weapons School or some damn thing!'" But Peck considered the name over the next few weeks, eventually deciding, "What the hell? Let's use it." And so the name became official. By then "DL" Smith was gearing up to lead the Air Force

Thunderbirds demonstration team, so his replacement at Langley, Joseph "CT" Wang, pushed its approval through the official channels at TAC.

While Peck and his team entered the final stages of preparation at Tonopah, the maintainers handpicked to work the MiGs remained at Groom Lake to continue preparing the assets for their move to the TTR. The maintainers made only limited changes to the MiGs to make them ready for flight. One such change was the installation of a tunable UHF radio, and another was a conventional pitot-static system for measuring airspeed and altitude, thus overcoming the pilots' unfamiliarity with the "kilometer per fortnight" scale, according to Peck. This translated into a new airspeed indicator (ASI) and a new altimeter. The G-suit valve, which supplies compressed air to inflate the pilot's G-suit and help prevent loss of consciousness during heavy maneuvering, was fitted with a converter to allow the Americans' G-suits to plug in; but other than that the MiGs' systems were left untouched.

March 1979 saw the Red Eagles' pilot roster grow. Capt David "Marshall" McCloud, an experienced F-4 pilot who, like Henderson, had previously flown the F-106 with ADC, was hired by Peck from the Aggressors. He'd been an F-5E instructor pilot, flight commander, chief of academics, and detachment commander for the 64th FWS and 65th FWS since October 1976. McCloud became "Bandit 10." He was followed in May 1979 by Karl "Harpo" Whittenberg, "Bandit 11."

But all was not well with Morgenfeld. "I never found out why, but it became apparent that I had been passed up for command of a Navy fighter squadron once my tour of the 4477th TEF was over. I couldn't understand why – I had a reasonable reputation in the F-8, had my Masters degree, and had graduated number one in my test pilot class, and I was now flying MiGs – so I had done everything right. So I elected to leave the Navy." Morgenfeld was the third 4477th TEF pilot to leave the unit before the program could bed down at Tonopah. Although administratively speaking he would remain a member of the unit until November, he had already started looking to his career outside the Navy and was lining up a job as a test pilot with the Lockheed "Skunk Works," the aerospace giant's black arm.

He suggested that he be replaced by Lt Hugh "Bandit" Brown, who was flying with VX-4. Morgenfeld had flown against, and with, Brown at Point Mugu, and knew the man well. "He was a very good pilot with a nice mentality: he wasn't all balls and no brains. He was a good pilot without being brash, and we just felt that we could not accept cowboys up there. We had no desire for the swashbuckler bravado thing. We also didn't want people who had a problem living in the dark, or were unable to do anything without taking the credit. Hugh was certainly not like that: a wonderfully warm man with a great sense of humor. He was a great guy to have on your team because he would always ask, 'What do you need me to do?'"

Morgenfeld's suggestion was endorsed and approved by the Navy. In April 1979 Brown and his wife Linda moved with their two young boys from Camarillo, California, to Nellis. In May 1979, he became "Bandit 12."

The squadron continued flying its leased 404s to Tonopah and back several times a day. For transit flights to and from the site, the 404s were parked close to Nellis' Base Operations building, and the maintainers would be flown out to Tonopah by one of the Red Eagle pilots as soon as ten or so of them were ready to depart. Throughout, the pilots maintained their fighter proficiency by flying F-5 Aggressor missions during the day, and many remained active participants in the Aggressor program itself.

Oberle characterized three distinct changes in the Red Eagles' integration with the Aggressors: "In the beginning [January 1977 to late summer 1977], when we were getting the runway fixed and we were working on the airplanes, I spent a lot of time flying with the Aggressors; two-thirds of my time with them, and a third of my time getting things up and running. Then [late summer 1977 to summer 1978], when we began to get things formalized – we had a runway and we were doing things 'up north' – 75 percent of my time was spent with the Red Eagles. When we finally became fully operational [1979 onwards], I spent almost 100 percent of my time with the Red Eagles."

Flying with the Aggressors, and the insistence that the highly skilled Navy TOPGUN pilots complete the Aggressor checkout, did more than just keep the pilots current: it was the cover for their presence at Nellis. To the outside world the Red Eagles would have appeared to have been normal Aggressor pilots.

INDIAN VILLAGE

One day, Ellis walked into Peck's office and declared: "Boss, we need a truck." Peck responded in the affirmative: "OK, what kind of truck do you need?" Ellis' response was priceless: "Actually, we already bought the truck, what we really need is a check." The whole scene must have been even more peculiar because the maintainers were not expected to conform to the Air Force's 35-10 dress regulations: to appear less conspicuous they dressed as civilians, they sported pork chop sideburns and even mustaches, and most wore jeans and tee-shirts.

When a sudden injection of cash was required, and for occasions like this, Peck would visit Mary Jane Smith at the Pentagon. She would duck behind her desk so as to be hidden when she saw him coming, and would always ask him: "Is this going to cost me tens, hundreds, tens of thousands, or hundreds of thousands today!?"

The 18-wheeler Kenworth truck allowed Ellis and his maintainers to haul spares and parts for the MiGs from all over the country. Oberle noted that: "Bobby was a phenomenal scrounge rat. He could go and get anything, and it was amazing the stuff we'd see that he had brought in here. Where he'd got it from we didn't know and didn't ask. He was phenomenal, and he attracted other guys like him from the enlisted ranks."

Ellis brought "junk" by the truckload, much of it salvaged from the DRMO (Defense Reutilization and Management Office) salvage yards that housed old military hardware suitable for recycling. One day the maintainers called Peck down to the Indian Village (the name given to a small maintenance area at Tonopah), and while hesitant because of the mud that permeated everything down there, he agreed to go. When he got there he saw three wheelless trailers arranged in a U shape, between which pierced steel planking (designed to be used for temporary runways) provided a solid floor. Overhead, a parachute canopy covered the three trailers and kept the elements at bay, and beneath that was a small assembly line. Astounded at their resourcefulness, Peck was witnessing his men assemble jeeps from scrap metal and DRMO-salvaged chassis. The men presented him with the first vehicle, the "command vehicle," and from then onwards he never had to walk at Tonopah.

"We quickly ran out of space," Peck recalled. "We were short-sighted in our planning, needing facilities for AGE [Aircraft Ground Equipment] and vehicle maintenance as well as storage. We ended up begging for some inflatable hangars from Holloman. They were from the Emergency War Reserves supply, and they didn't want to give them to us, but eventually we got them." A few hundred yards from the Indian Village was the apron and its three newly installed hangars. "There was no dedicated hangar for the MiG-17s and the MiG-21s; the airplanes were just worked on in whichever hangars they happened to be at the time," Peck said.

One of the more problematic issues that Peck had to deal with at Tonopah was certification and quality control of the squadron's POL tank, which sat on the southeastern corner of the small operating apron. Given the base's remoteness, this had to be built from scratch from the Phase I construction funds, and it took time to check the device to ensure that the fuel distributed was not contaminated.

As he concentrated on the actual base and its infrastructure, Peck instructed Oberle to look at the "TX course" – the type conversion syllabus – that future Red Eagle pilots would have to go through to qualify to fly the MiGs. Peck wanted future pilots to be armed with documentation, and to be put through an official TX course. "I actually harmonized the course, then formalized the checkout program to include grade books." It was a start, but time would show that it was not enough.

THE FIRST TONOPAH EXPOSURES

On July 17, 1979, MiG operations at Tonopah began. In the days before, six MiG-21s and two MiG-17s had been flown in from Groom Lake. Peck flew the first MiG-21 sortie from Tonopah, and Oberle the first MiG-17.

Coordinating the first operational squadron exposures flown out of Tonopah, Oberle remembered, was a matter of identifying units that were coming in to participate in Red Flag, or that were deployed in specifically for CONSTANT PEG. In the case of the former, a squadron would deploy to Nellis with absolutely no idea that they were going to do anything other than Red Flag. However, for the duration of the two-week exercise, two or three pilots per day would be taken off the flying schedule and told instead to report to another building on the Nellis compound for some unspecified training. In the case of the latter, the squadron would usually send a small cadre of six aircraft and as many as eight pilots.

The Blue Air pilots, no doubt mystified, would arrive at the 4477th TEF's plain white trailer vans located in the FWS parking lot, away from the main hub of flying operations. There they would be greeted by one or two unfamiliar pilots wearing the yellow and black checkered scarves of the Nellis elite beneath the collars of their flight suits, and on their left shoulders a circular patch depicting a Soviet-styled red eagle with wings spreading either side of a white five-point star. In red at the bottom of the circle were the numbers and letters "4477th TEF." At the top was written "Red Eagles."

The Blue Air pilots would be seated in a small briefing room in the trailers, and were finally read into the CONSTANT PEG program. "They had the fear of God hammered into them," Peck said. "We left them in no doubt that any divulgence of the program's secrets would be dealt with in the most severe of ways." The Red Eagle pilots would brief them, usually in small groups of two or four, about what they were going to see the next day, how the sorties were going to be sequenced, and what would be demonstrated while airborne.

The next morning the Red Eagle pilots left Nellis early, arriving at TTR in the Cessna or a borrowed Aggressor T-38. As the first two Blue Air pilots briefed the sortie at Nellis and stepped to their jets for take-off, the two Bandit pilots would be getting ready to man the MiGs. Approaching the airfield at a prearranged time, and broadcasting their position on the Red Eagles' radio frequency, the Blue Air pilots would announce their imminent arrival. Oberle explained: "We'd be in the cockpit, and as soon as we heard them check in, we'd crank and taxi out to the end of the runway. When they got overhead we'd take off and they would join up with us to get their first look at an airborne asset."

A record of each pilot to undergo exposure to the MiGs was filed at Tonopah, allowing the 4477th TEF to determine who had received what training, and against which aircraft, for future reference. This was critical because not only was it desired that the Red Eagles expose as many frontline fighter pilots as possible, but also that each pilot participate in three different types of exposure with each MiG type during the course of his career.

The three-stage exposure program now differed in its overall aggression and tone from that which had been flown prior to the arrival of the MiGs at Tonopah. Whereas the exposures prior to September 1979 had essentially gone straight for the kill, with dogfighting on the first sortie and 2 v 2 or even 4 v 2 on the third sortie, the new regime took a more gradual approach. Stage one, the first exposure, incorporated a performance profile (PP), followed by a brief stint of BFM at the end if fuel allowed. The PP constituted the new, more gentle introduction to the MiGs and would often start with an interception using the visiting pilot's radar, followed by a visual join up. "You'd be there in this little biddy MiG-17, with your head sticking out above the canopy rail, and the guy's eyes would just about pop out of his head as he joined up with you in formation," Peck chuckled.

The PP had actually been devised in late 1967 by Maj Duke Johnston, the chief of air-to-air at the F-4 FWS at the time, and the man who had been selected by TAC to be the project pilot for operational exploitation of HAVE DOUGHNUT. Johnston had devised the profile around key criteria that would demonstrate how one aircraft performed compared to another, and it was a scripted precursor to engaging the DOUGHNUT MiG in unscripted dogfights. It had since been adopted by test pilot schools and follow-on foreign military exploitation (FME) programs alike.

The PP started with the Red Eagle instructing his adversary to take up various formations, according to the pre-briefed flow, so that he could show the MiG's strengths and weaknesses in direct comparison to the visitor's mount. "I'd tell him to look at me from various angles, and then I'd tell him that we were going to have a race," Peck remembered. In order to demonstrate the relative differences in acceleration, both aircraft would go to afterburner and accelerate to 500 knots. Then the PP would become more involved. Against an F-4 pilot, for example: "We would have him fly formation with us and then tell him we were about to do our best sustained turn. His job was to follow us. Well, he couldn't, because the turn circle in the F-4 would just puke through. The lesson there for the F-4 guy is that if he wants to fight a MiG-17, he can't turn with him. If the MiG-17 turns, then he has to go up to become like a stitch in a sewing machine, riding his turn circle every time the MiG starts to turn. Maneuvering into the vertical to stay within the same plane (arc) as the MiG's turn was the only way to do it."

There were of course rules, but these were standard Air Force training rules, according to Oberle: "We had a 5,000ft floor AGL [Above Ground Level], a 1,000ft bubble around each airplane that you weren't to penetrate, and the idea was not to get into a slow-speed rat race but to try to learn to maintain your energy and fly the strength of your airplane against the weakness of the MiGs." Teaching pilots who'd never flown against the MiG-17 was an exciting experience for Peck, and it wouldn't take long for the Phantom driver to truly recognize that the excess thrust he had in comparison to the tiny MiG could be used to counter the Fresco's exceptional turn capability.

Sortie number two saw a continuation of BFM. The Red Eagle pilot would invite the visitor to "take up a perch," which is to position themselves a set distance (usually 6,000ft) away so that they could do some basic BFM. As the opposition pilot's proficiency increased, the MiG would be flown in a correspondingly tighter turn to challenge them and get them used to it. That would be followed by a defensive perch, said Peck: "He would go out in front and we would show him how difficult it was to see a MiG at your six while pulling 5G." For Peck this lesson was one of the most valuable: "We were used to looking at the gigantic planforms with smoking engines, and suddenly we're teaching these guys to look for canopy glints and things like that. If a MiG is converting to your 6 o'clock, a canopy glint may be all that you see because he's pointing at you the whole time and his visual cross section is tiny."

By the time the visiting pilot was receiving his third exposure, he would be told to execute "butterfly" set-ups – where the two fighters would line up side-by-side and then turn into each other and pass canopy to canopy; they then fought to see who could gain the tactical advantage. After this, more tactical radar intercepts would be flown, provided there was enough gas remaining. The intercepts allowed the pilots to see the ranges that the Soviet jets would appear at on radar, and to see what the electronic indications that the MiGs' own range-only gun radar would look like and sound like on a radar warning receiver.

For the Red Eagle pilot, a typical day would produce two MiG sorties, following which he flew back down to Nellis to individually debrief the men he had flown against. As more pilots qualified to fly the MiGs, a rota system was developed to allow a pilot to spend one day at Nellis debriefing the visiting pilots he had flown against the day before, then briefing the pilots he was to fly against the next day. That night, or early the next morning, he would fly up to Tonopah and spend the whole day there. The next day the process would repeat.

Although two types of MiG and three sorties per MiG resulted in the maximum number of sorties per Blue Air pilot being limited to just six, few actually experienced that many. For a pilot attending Red Flag, he would be fortunate to fly three sorties against the MiGs on the day he had been taken off the normal flying schedule. The next day he was back onto the Red Flag schedule and two other pilots from his squadron would be whisked away for the day. There were exceptions to that rule, and some squadrons visiting Red Flag would use their two-seat trainers to make sure that as many pilots as possible got exposed to the program before their visit to Nellis was over.

In reality, it took two or three days to get a single pilot through the entire exposure program, and weather aborts and maintenance aborts by either party would mean that that sortie was lost forever – it was not rescheduled, it was tough luck.

A number of factors influenced the small number of sorties available. The first was that the fuel fraction of the MiGs – the amount of time they could remain airborne – was exceptionally short and this limited the amount of "playtime" that each MiG would have; and the second was that with the almost certain shock of Buck Fever that the visiting pilots would experience on first sighting the MiGs, the first exposure would be spent helping them to pull their jaws from the depths of the cockpit floor. CONSTANT PEG would work along similar lines to Red Flag, allowing the pilots, astonished by what they were seeing, the luxury of becoming accustomed to the MiGs before they finally realized that there was nothing magical about them – they were simply other jets.

CONTINUED GROWTH

Because neither the Fishbed C/E nor Fresco had any air intercept radar, Peck hired his own GCI controllers. Jim "Bluto" Keys and Bud "Chops" Horan were brought in to work the radars at Nellis. Their job was to be the MiGs' eyes until they came within visual range of their quarry. With no table of allowance assigned to the flight, Peck wasn't exactly sure what level of manpower he was allowed to accrue, so administratively he was in a state of limbo. More pressing was that despite the experience of the Red Hats and HAVE IDEA with the Tumansky R-11F-300 motor of the MiG-21F-13 Fishbed C/E and the VK-1F of the MiG-17 Fresco C/D, no one really knew how long they were going to last. In the end, Peck said, "We just ran them until they didn't work any more."

Meanwhile, former Apollo astronaut and the creator of the Red Hats, three-star general Tom Stafford, turned up at Tonopah, ostensibly for a tour of the facilities and a look-see at the security arrangements. In actual fact, Stafford was there to do a site survey for the F-117 program. Stafford was now the DCS of Research and Development at the Pentagon, and was Bobby Bond's boss.

What he found at Tonopah impressed him. But there was an aspect of the Red Eagles' facility at Tonopah that would need to be looked at: as a money-saving measure, they had not concreted the entire apron, "and that caused us a lot of grief, because the jet fuel mixing with the asphalt just turned it into a load of goo. That was one thing which I wish I had done differently," Peck admitted. Regardless, it was something that could be remedied with ease when the F-117 money arrived. Thus, the wheels had been set in motion for a second phase of construction that would start readying the airfield for the eventual arrival of the stealth fighter.

"BANDIT" BROWN'S MISHAP, AUGUST 23, 1979

On August 23, 1979, "Bandit 12," Hugh Brown, was fighting a Navy F-5 adversary in his MiG-17F when he pulled back on the stick and the Fresco entered a spin. Accounts of what followed differ from one person to the next, but it is agreed that he had recovered only partially from the spin when, as the ground rushed up towards him at an alarming rate, he entered a new spin. This second spin was unrecoverable.

Brown made no attempt to bail out from his MiG, and the aircraft impacted the ground and disintegrated into a deep hole. He could have attempted ejection, but Morgenfeld believes that, like so many did, he would have felt "a tremendous sense of responsibility for flying what were vital national assets. He was going to do his very best to bring it back, and I think that he just stayed at it too long and worked too hard to do that." Because of the MiG-17's severely limited fuel fraction, most of the exposures that it participated in took place over, or very near to, the Tonopah airfield. Thus, when the crash occurred, Brown had been right over the airfield boundary. Help was on hand quickly, but there was nothing that could be done. The impact had been at high vertical speed, and Brown had died instantly.

It was a tragic and shocking loss, all the more so because he was a family man who left behind a wife, Linda, and their two sons, Brady, three years old, and Brian, 11 months old. Linda told me: "Hugh was so proud when Brady was born that he had a special squadron name tag made for the occasion. It read, 'I am a Daddy.' He had a great smile and was very intelligent; his love of life and music was intoxicating, and he could dance like James Brown!" Brown had come from a family with a history in the US Navy, she said. "He was born May 21, 1948, in Roanoke, Virginia, and was the eldest of three siblings. His dad, Melvin Crocket Brown, was a chief in the Navy who had retired after 30 years of service. Hugh's given name at birth was Melvin Hugh Brown, after his father. He never liked Melvin, so he signed everything 'M. Hugh Brown.' Being a Navy brat gave Hugh the insight into Navy life and reinforced his patriotism, and by high school he already knew that he wanted to fly Navy jets."

Following graduation from the Naval Academy in June 1970 and until a slot opened up for him to begin pilot training, Brown was sent on a brief exchange to the Air Force's Eglin AFB, Florida. It was here that he met his soon-to-be wife:

We met in June 1970. Folks kept saying, "Have I got a guy for you!" and "Have I got a girl for you!" We saw each other across the room and he smiled at me. I was 18 and he was 21, and he stood out from the Air Force officers as his uniform was khaki.

Hugh was also a tall, handsome guy with curly brown hair and brown eyes that smiled at you. In August 1970, he asked me out for my 19th birthday; we had dinner at the Officers' Beach Club at a table next to the Thunderbirds. We dated for two years as he worked his way through flight training in Naval Air Station, Pensacola, Florida, and got his Masters in Aeronautical Engineering at the University of North West Florida. We were engaged April 1972, and in July that year he earned his wings of gold. In September we were married, and then we drove across country to San Diego, California, for our first duty station at NAS Miramar.

Brown's first assignment was to the Pacific Fleet Adversary Squadron, VF-126, which had been flying A-4 Skyhawks as "Bandits" for the Navy's West Coast fighter squadrons since April 1967. He amassed 1,000 hours in the squadron's TA-4J Skyhawks before being assigned to an operational tour on the F-4N

Phantom with VF-21. Next he joined VF-121, the Pacific Coast Replacement Air Group, as an instructor pilot. In 1976, Brown spent six months on board the USS *Ranger*, and then went to TOPGUN. And that's probably when this "loving and sentimental husband, good cook, and an awesome dad" of a fighter pilot was exposed for the first time to the MiGs of HAVE IDEA. Following his successful completion of TOPGUN he was assigned to VX-4.

For Linda, August 23, 1979, started like any other Thursday. But it would end very differently:

> Our alarm clock rang. Our baby boy cried for his bottle. And the sun rose over the horizon. After breakfast, I kissed Hugh goodbye and off he went to work. I was home preparing dinner when the doorbell rang at approximately 1730. Gail Peck, his wife, Peggy, and the chaplain were standing there. At first, I kiddingly told them they were just in time for dinner. Then, I realized that something terrible had happened. The chaplain and Gail walked me to the sofa in the living room as Peggy went into the family room with the boys. Gail spoke softly and said, "We've lost Hugh." Those words will never be erased from my mind. The tears came uncontrollably, realizing that life as we knew it would never be the same.

Brown's death that day changed many people's lives forever. For Linda the impact was brutal: "They said Hugh was flying a test in an F-5 and it was very confidential, so I had very little detail." The Air Force told Linda Brown nothing more, but local papers quoted an Air Force press release that was surprisingly candid: it talked about "a specially modified test aircraft," code for a MiG, and was specific enough about the location ("90 miles northwest of Las Vegas") that even a casual observer would notice that Tonopah's airfield was very close by. But Linda had no reason to be overly suspicious, and believed that her husband was simply a Navy pilot on exchange with the Air Force's Aggressors – a cover story reinforced by the fact that he never wore a Red Eagles patch, instead opting for the Aggressor patch.

For the maintainers out at Tonopah, the grim job of recovery that Thursday afternoon would be imprinted on their minds for the rest of their days. The small unit had no dedicated accident investigation resources, and the program was so secret that it was simply impossible to convene a full-scale, trained, mishap board without jeopardizing the whole effort. Instead, the maintainers and pilots found themselves tasked with the grisly and grim responsibility of photographing the scene of the crash, recovering Brown's remains, and burying what remained of the MiG to keep it from prying eyes. The MiG had made a hole in the desert floor, and the men took it in turns to dig out the remains. They could each manage only about ten minutes at a time, according to Oberle, who was one of the recovery team. They were doing a job for which they had not been trained, and one which Air Force maintainers in no other unit would have been asked to do. "It was one of the most difficult things I have done," said Oberle.

As Linda sat in shock, Peck called her parents in Florida. They came to Las Vegas the following day. That evening, Peggy Peck stayed the night and offered sedatives to help Linda sleep. For others, Brown's death invoked a sense of guilt. Morgenfeld was on vacation in New York with his wife Norma when he got a call that afternoon from Heatley. "He told me that Hugh had gone down and that he hadn't got out. Even though he couldn't say anything more over the unsecure line, he didn't need to say anything else. I was stunned, and I went out and sat down on the front porch by myself trying to get my thoughts together. I felt a sense of responsibility because I had picked him to go out there. Chuck was pretty broken up, bless his heart. He had been one of the first to arrive at the scene."

Linda recalled: "Hugh always spoke highly of the team he worked with, especially the non-commissioned officers. I had never met the men that Hugh spoke of until his death, when they all attended a memorial service to show their support. It was very touching." Linda acted decisively and as best as she knew how:

> I sold the house and left Las Vegas, never looking back. I took Brady and Brian to my parents' home in Destin, Florida. There I was able to grieve and take care of matters. That time was very difficult for us all. My parents had always been there for me and they loved Hugh as their son. I was home for six weeks when I decided to return to San Diego where we had started our life. It was a good decision. I joined a support group for Navy widows, which was invaluable, and I returned to work part-time at the school at which I was employed before Hugh and I had had our children.
>
> As Brady and Brian grew up, I told them about their dad being a brave fighter pilot and how he was the best of the best and he was on a secret mission when he was killed and I did not know any more information. I always told them that I was hopeful that we would someday know.[15]

RAMIFICATIONS

Henderson was the ops officer, and a lieutenant colonel, at the 64th FWS squadron at Nellis when he received a call late one evening. "It was from my wing commander, one-star general Tom Swalm, and he told me that I was to go and meet with two-star general Robert Kelley, the Tactical Fighter Weapons Center commander, the next morning. He said a couple of things, but one of them was that I could not talk to anybody. I knew at that moment that it was probably going to be Gail getting fired, and that I was probably going to get the squadron."

It was while working Cope Thunder at Clark AB in the Philippines in 1977 that Henderson first heard that a squadron of MiGs would be forming. "I wanted to be a part of that outfit: the MiG was the ultimate Aggressor and it couldn't get any more accurate than that. But when I called Glenn Frick at Nellis to throw my hat into the ring, they had already chosen their people. One of the guys I roomed with, Gerry Huff, had already gone back [to Nellis] to be a part of the group."

Some squadron commanders in the late 1970s survived losing a jet without being fired, but Peck would not. Kelley, who was administratively directly responsible for the 4477th TEF, took less than two weeks to fire him. Kelley was "a tough-as-nails kind of commander," Henderson said, "and he was very uncomfortable with Gail and all that he was doing outside of the Nellis community, as it was so different from a normal fighter squadron. Gail had no choice but to deal directly with the Air Staff, the logistics people, and other organizations." Kelley probably based his decision not only on the fact that a jet had been lost and Brown killed, but also on the revelation that Brown had previously spun the Fresco in similar circumstances, but had allegedly failed to inform Peck.

When Henderson met the TFWC commander the next day, his fears were immediately confirmed. "He told me again: 'Don't tell anybody. We're going to meet with Gen Creech and get him to approve you as commander.' So, I go to the airport the next day and I see Jose Oberle, and he's on the same flight. When he sees me he knows what's going on – he's devastated because he knows that Gail's going to be fired." Kelley, Henderson, and Oberle boarded the same flight and headed to Langley AFB.

Oberle was to brief Creech on the mishap as a subject matter expert on the MiG-17 – he was required to explain to the general how the MiG would stall violently even when flying fast. Oberle's presence was required despite the fact that an accident investigation had been hastily convened and executed. There were photographs of the site that had been taken by the maintainers, but the investigation was close hold and its scope and purpose were limited by the usual standards. It was better to have Oberle personally brief the general based on what he had managed to find out about the mishap. Once that briefing was over, Kelley wanted to introduce Henderson to the TAC commander for his blessing as the new Red Eagles commander. Henderson reflected: "It was a tragedy for Gail, and a situation where we were very good friends before that, and now we are again, but at the time it was incredibly difficult for him to adjust to that slam. He'd been so involved, and they were barely started, barely off the ground and he just gets pulled right out of there."

It was a bittersweet moment for Henderson, and one made all the more ironic because, he confessed: "The week before, Gail was in my office and somehow the subject came up about what I wanted to do next. I told him, 'I want your job!' Oh, it was very untimely! I thought that I might succeed him a year or two later, but I had no inkling."

On the flight to Langley, Oberle and Henderson sat separately from Gen Kelley. Oberle briefed Henderson extensively on how the outfit had been formed and what the outfit had just been through, including the horrific trauma of recovering the remains of a close friend and squadron member at the crash site very close to the airfield. "Jose gave me a complete thumbnail of what had been going on because I didn't know a lot of these things. They were going through a lot of traumas; there are problems when you're that secretive," Henderson explained.

It was only after arriving at the officers' quarters at Langley and Gen Kelley had departed for his own room that Oberle was permitted to pick the phone up and call his boss. That Peck learned of his dismissal not from his immediate superior, Kelley, but from a subordinate was a final insult. It was, according to Henderson, "a very brutal and cruel way to do things."

"Risk assessment wasn't a common thought at that time," Peck told me, "and by the time we were flying the MiGs we had complete confidence in them." And there was every reason to do so. HAVE IDEA had not resulted in a single write-off or fatal mishap, and the FTD's exploitations before that had been noteworthy for their excellent safety record in this regard.

"It was a pretty hard pill to swallow," Peck admitted. "You go from being the superstar and the darling of the world to being an outcast. From that moment on, the iron doors of CONSTANT PEG shut on me. I was told nothing more about the program. I was completely shut out." Peck was dying by the sword, just as he had lived by it – the security arrangements that Muller had designed, and Peck had approved, were now being applied to the former commander.

"OBI WAN" TAKES COMMAND

Henderson took charge of the 4477th TEF on September 6, 1979. He became "Bandit 13" that month. "There was no magic solution when I came into the squadron. Jose had said to me: 'The first person you have to sit down with is Bobby [Ellis]. You have to get him on your side.' So, that's what I did."

When Henderson took over the flight, it consisted of only 30 people. "I walked into the squadron and I called a meeting of everyone. I explained how the events of the past 48 hours had unfolded and what guidance I had received from Gen Creech and Gen Kelley. I then asked for a private meeting with Bobby Ellis where I requested that he work with me to get past the turbulence of a sudden change of command."

Ellis was businesslike, but flustered by the proceedings of recent days. "He probably viewed that squadron as being his own. He was wary of me and appeared to be suspicious of what impact I might have upon 'his world.' He wanted to let me know that he was in charge, not me. We ended the meeting with him sort of loaning me the squadron to do what I needed to do with it. Over the next nine months he delivered on that promise and we developed a harmonious working relationship and the job got done."

The presence of a number of characters in the Red Eagles helped break the inevitable tension that followed Peck's sudden departure. When Henderson first arrived at Tonopah to take over the squadron, he was taking in the scenery at the remote airfield – "very austere, high desert, 5,500ft above sea level" – when an incongruous vision presented itself:

It was one of our vehicle maintenance guys. His name was Billy Lightfoot. He's got this Fu Manchu beard and, and he drives up in his "vehicle." I use that term very loosely: it is a chassis with a seat and a steering column and an engine, and that's what he comes driving up in. He made it out of parts that he got God knows from where. More than once I was left with trying to explain to my DO or the TFWC commander why I needed a vehicle that had only an engine, a chassis, a steering wheel and a seat ... and who was that tiny man driving the vehicle who looked like Yosemite Sam, full beard, unkempt hair and all.

When the squadron was activated at Tonopah in 1979, it was envisioned that the maintenance men would live in the town of Tonopah and the pilots would fly to TTR from Nellis and back each day in the Cessna 404. Part of the cover story was that the maintenance men were civilian contractors and not active duty personnel. They were told to wear civilian clothes, let their hair grow out, and everyone went by first names or call signs. It did not take long for them to acquire the "civilian look." Some simply let their hair grow to where it touched their ears, some grew handlebar mustaches – Bobby Ellis always had a buzz cut. The senior officers in my chain of command were less than thrilled with the "look" but went along reluctantly.

The maintainers came from an enormous pool of candidates:

> The pool was probably five to ten times larger than the pilot pool. Many of the crew chiefs and various specialists were drawn from the test community, with strong ties to Edwards AFB. Edwards was a filter similar to the FWS filter for the pilots at Nellis, in that there was a vetting that occurred before they ever got assigned to Edwards. The maintenance personnel there were always tasked to work on a variety of systems, including some foreign systems, and had to be creative and flexible. The small Edwards community was easy to track and reputations were well known, both good and bad.
>
> When it came to hiring from outside of the test community, it meant searching a database and choosing potential candidates. All enlisted personnel worldwide were in a microfiche database, which was updated several times a year. Bobby Ellis would search the database, identify potential candidates, check up on the unknown candidates by calling a trusted agent who knew the candidate or worked with the candidate. Then, if the candidate looked promising, Bobby would fly to his base and interview him. If it were a fit, he would start the reassignment process. The military personnel center would put a special code on each of the 4477th enlisted men's records. This prevented reassignment sooner than six years, with additional years to be negotiated down the road. This was, most commanders believed, essential if the maintainers were ever going to become truly skilled at maintaining the enigmatic MiGs.

DEVELOPING TTR

Henderson was now responsible for the continued development of TTR and he was soon attending meetings with contractors accordingly:

> Because the initial budget was so small it was envisioned that it would be a bare-base operation with a radio-equipped jeep for air traffic control, a single runway with no parallel taxiway, and three very small hangars. We envisioned an operation more like a forward airfield in France in World War II – Quonset huts and all. When VIPs started visiting, which was almost immediately, things started to change dramatically. The local generals, Kelley and Swalm, could not stand the bare-base look at Tonopah. The maintenance men had to wear white coveralls, we had to have nice china to serve coffee and carpet in the hallway and all of the offices. We needed much larger hangars for the MiG-23s that we were told we would be receiving, and so the three little hangars housing our "17s" and "21s" were to be supplemented by two very large hangars that were probably two or three times larger.

While only at planning stage at this time, the addition of the MiG-23 hangars would also require that the small ramp (parking area in front of the three MiG hangars) be extended as well, and all of this was going to draw attention from unwanted quarters, as was the engineering effort that was needed to level out the terrain to the north of the Red Eagles' small pan and hangars. This situation was another planning issue on which Henderson had to focus his attentions: "Our ramp was kind of on a small bump, so before we could extend the ramp northwards, we needed to smooth the incline and descent to and from the pan so that we weren't going to be taxiing the MiGs up and down a hill."

Ellis was integral to the process and heavily involved throughout, as Henderson observed: "Bobby had boundless energy and always seemed to be working ten issues simultaneously. He was everywhere throughout the flying day – on the line watching and correcting crew chiefs if necessary, in the supply hangar helping design a parts stocking inventory system, in the fuel pit trying to figure out why our brand new POL tank was leaking, looking at blueprints for the new MiG-23 hangars to ensure the correct three-phase power was in the right location. It was mind-boggling the depth of knowledge he had on so many subjects."

Keeping the Red Eagles "low profile" was becoming more of a challenge. "We were trying to blend in," Henderson recalled, "but I had to ask myself, 'Who are we fooling?'" The daily influx of military pilots into what was once a quiet DoE airfield, and the construction planned to start in 12 to 18 months, was something that the Soviets were likely to pick up on. At least the civilian-looking maintainers, who blended in while they stayed at Tonopah Monday through Thursday, were far less obvious.

Some maintenance challenges were too complex for the Red Eagles' talented maintainers to address, or required specialist facilities to rectify. One such task was the refurbishment of the MiG-21's Tumansky turbojet engines, which were by now beginning to yield more of their secrets ... like how many hours they were good for. "Most of the downtime we had on the jets was engine-related – for an extended refurbishment after only 125–75 hours of engine running time, it took GE six months and a million bucks before they handed the engine back to us," Henderson revealed. Ellis and his crew had fashioned a dolly for the motors, and transported them direct to GE on the 18-wheeler Kenworth, which was now painted fire engine red with gold eagle motifs on the doors, and christened "Big Red."

CONSOLIDATION

The short engine life cycle was so expensive to fix that it sucked a huge proportion of what little funds remained in the 4477th TEF's coffers, and left everything else having to be done on a shoe-string budget. One victim of this was the TX course, the USAF's conversion course that transitioned experienced fighter pilots into new or different aircraft. Although Oberle had been working on the course, and Morgenfeld and Iverson had started from scratch putting together limited manuals, Peck had not been in his job as the Red Eagles' commander for long enough truly to formalize this process. So, while the squadron remained grounded awaiting the findings of the mishap report into Brown's accident, Henderson looked to consolidate matters.

He started by reviewing the publications used by new pilots to learn how to fly the Soviet jets, and ordered that what currently amounted to hand-me-down notes and very basic written instructions take on a more structured format. He then looked closely at the TX course. "The problem was that we could not afford to give the new pilots a big spin-up on the jets. Every flight hour on these national assets was precious and we could only give them a few rides before they were expected to go up there and fly full air combat in the airplane."

By the time Brown had arrived at the Red Eagles, the TX course had evolved significantly from the days of HAVE IDEA and even the earliest 4477th TEF operations of 1977, but by how much is a matter of contention. Oberle was adamant that "Hugh had gone through a checkout consisting of basic formation flying and aerobatics integrated into a syllabus of about nine or ten rides, each supervised and documented in grade sheets. Then he had flown controlled, graded, BFM flights against the T-38. Hugh was very aggressive and wanted to do well." But Oberle is alone in this recollection, with most pilots of the time remembering that the course was substantially shorter – in the order of only five sorties. Indeed, a declassified list of CONSTANT PEG pilots (Appendix B) shows that Brown had been killed on only his ninth MiG-17 sortie with the unit, which contradicts Oberle's assurance that the Navy pilot had received a checkout that consisted of nine or ten rides. And Peck deflected attention from the matter by stating that his recollection was that Brown came to the 4477th TEF already fully qualified to fly the MiG-17 by VX-4.

Henderson believes that the expedited TX course was possibly one of the things that killed Brown:

> The MiG-17 can depart at high speed, and it's a very violent out of control experience, but you're still flying at 300 miles per hour. The stick was very high, so

you'd go through the pebbles and the boulders – buffet that gives you indication that you maybe ought to let up on the stick – you had to put the stick forward to get all of the positive G-forces off the jet: only then would it recover. Brown departed like this, obviously not all that high, but only partially recovered. All of the pilots assigned to the 4477th were highly experienced aviators when they came on board and the checkout was kept to a minimum because of the aircraft being a limited, critical asset. I was one of those, and I checked out in the MiG-17 for a total of four or five rides. That number of rides to get checked out in a "new" aircraft, including air-to-air, is a very short syllabus. I had a lot of faith in the maintenance men to give me the best possible machine, but I would have been all thumbs in an emergency in that early phase.

The month that Brown was killed, the Red Eagles had hired a new pilot who helped to document both the flying manuals and the TX course. He was a former Clark Aggressor who had been hired by Peck in July 1979, direct from the Philippines. It was Capt Mike "Scotty" Scott. Having spent almost four years as an Aggressor in the Philippines "I was slapping myself because I was doing the same thing, day-in, day-out. Sure, I had my family with me, I didn't have to fly at night, and life was good." But it was time for a change, and his time with the 26th TFTS was at an end. Scott had so impressed his superiors that they had offered him a choice of assignments. He could go and fly the F-15, the F-16, or return to Nellis as an IP at one of the Aggressor squadrons there.

In the end, the decision was made for him when, in the spring of 1979, he received a message via an old friend, Tom Hood, who had been his first flight commander when the Clark Aggressors were formed. "Tom told me that his old buddy from the 414th FWS, Gerry Huff, had been in touch to say that something was being formed and that he wanted me to apply for it." Since Scott had worked for Huff in the Philippines, Huff was now sponsoring his application to the secret unit. The now-familiar catch was that he couldn't say anything about the job. "Tom told to me to write a résumé, so I just wrote a two-page letter putting down my qualifications and saying that I was interested. I didn't put it in a folder, or type it, I just put it in a letter and sent it to Tom Hood. Hood told me, 'I'll get this to Huffer.'"

Scott received orders for the 64th Aggressor Squadron at Nellis, arriving in the summer and reporting in to his new commander, LtCol Rich Graham. "But Richie Graham said to me: 'You're not going to be an Aggressor. I want you to walk down the street to a trailer house with a sign outside that says 4477th TEF, and go in there and ask for Gail Peck.' I knew who Peck was because my squadron commander at Clark had told me and had given me some idea of what he had been planning, just not the extent or where it was going."

Scott had walked into the trailer to the sight of Peck, Heatley, Oberle, and Morgenfeld fulfilling various administrative functions. Huff, the only man in the unit that he knew, was out of town. "Oh, it was exciting. And to be honest, it was an ego-fulfilling moment: I had been chosen out of all these young captains that these guys had eyes on out here at Nellis, yet I had still been picked from Clark Air Base in the Philippines. It told me that people thought I had something to offer." What Scott did not know was that this day would start an affiliation for him with the Red Eagles that lasted until the squadron finally closed its doors. From now on, he would be directly associated with the unit in one capacity or another for almost every day until its demise. He became "Bandit 14"[16] in August, simultaneously becoming the first new Red Eagle pilot to go straight to the MiG-21.

Scott says that the decision to hire him was in part due to the fact that he had a current rating as an IP, FCF, and STAN/EVAL pilot on the T-38A and F-5E. The Red Eagles had borrowed one Aggressor T-38 for chase duties in the months before Peck's departure,[17] and on August 24, 1979, had been permanently loaned two Talons by the 49th TFW at Holloman. Scott could check out the other Red Eagle pilots on the T-38 if need be, and so too could McCloud, who later also qualified as a T-38 IP.

Prior to the arrival of the Holloman Talons, one or two Aggressor F-5s were flown up to TTR early each morning. Henderson said that the loaned T-38s were far more appropriate because the Aggressor squadrons didn't like losing their F-5s to Tonopah each day. Plus, the two-seat T-38 finally allowed them to fly some photo chase sorties. The T-38s were swapped out with "new" examples at Holloman about every nine months, with basic maintenance on them being done on the ramp outside Base Operations at Nellis.

TAC'S INFLUENCE

By October 31, Henderson had formalized and structured the CONSTANT PEG program to the satisfaction of the TAC commander. Until then, Scott said, "We had handwritten or crudely typed 'Dash 1' pilots' manuals. And the TX course had been written down, but the problem was that it wasn't spelt out in 'TACese' – the language and format that TAC required." Predictably, the formalization process changed nothing about how the unit operated, or how the pilots flew the MiGs, Scott added, but the important thing for TAC was that it now more closely conformed to its minimum standards.

Scott was vital to this process. His first job had been to put the program into "Air Force mode." He worked hard to document formal manuals, and would actually spend the next four years on the squadron in overall charge of writing and refining manuals – a cyclical process that was never ending. The actual process involved several members of the squadron being given responsibility for a section of the manual, which was the best way forward given that the unit was somewhat undermanned at that time. Scott was also tasked with formalizing the T-38 checkout process, as well as securing the necessary TAC approvals to allow the Red Eagles' pilots to be dual qualified in the T-38 and the F-5. "We had to work some paperwork to get the T-38 and F-5 designated as the same airplane; that way we were effectively qualified in just one type."

While the formalization appeased Gen Creech somewhat, he had developed cold feet about the *modus operandi* of the Red Eagles, and Henderson was now left to fight the TAC commander for the survival of CONSTANT PEG in the format that Peck had originally envisioned only three years before. "Creech wanted the MiGs to be a simple, static flying tool that didn't maneuver at all," Henderson summarized. The earlier loss of Brown and his MiG-17 had given the TAC commander pause for thought, and the idea of another mishap was worrying enough for him to rein in the squadron's flying program to mitigate the chances of that happening. "He told us: 'You're not out there to fight! The Soviets don't fight that aggressively.'"

It was frustrating that TAC still had such a risk-averse attitude, but Scott believed there was more to it than met the eye. He had watched the Aggressors start conservatively in the early 1970s, before gradually increasing the complexity of the training and the sophistication of the scenarios. Then it all changed. In 1977 the Air Force and Navy jointly ran the Air Intercept Missile Evaluation (AIMVAL) and Air Combat Evaluations (ACEVAL) tests against Navy F-14s and Air Force F-15s to develop tactics and the next generation of weapons, a program on which Drabant had been an analyst. Over the course of more than 2,300 sorties, tactics and other factors were evaluated by Aggressor pilots and Navy adversary pilots flying Red Air F-5Es against Blue Air F-15s and F-14s. The evaluations provided some great data, but they brought out the worst in the "Type A" personalities on both sides. By the end of the evaluation, trickery and underhanded techniques were being used to help win an engagement at any cost. It went against everything the Aggressors stood for.

"This type of attitude was starting to become more common within Aggressors by this time, and they therefore developed a reputation for winning at all costs as opposed to training other fighter pilots to improve," Scott said.

The Aggressors' mantra, "Be humble, you cool fucker," was going out of the window, and Creech knew it. "He did not want this attitude to spill over into the Red Eagles. Hence his keenness to keep our exposures simple, with very scripted profiles. In Creech's view, our program was going to be a training mission, but one that operated in a scripted exposure mode."

One month later, on the night of Halloween, Henderson returned to Langley to sell Creech on the changes that would keep CONSTANT PEG viable. "There was not a lot I could change, but I was following Heatley's suggestion and working with the Navy on getting a spin orientation program started up. One of the real hang-ups about the MiG-17 mishap was that Hugh had departed the airplane on a previous mission, but he had not reported it adequately. So I introduced a very formal and structured manner of reporting spins and departures: you had to report them immediately."

Creech was satisfied with what he saw, and Henderson left the meeting having managed to reach something of a compromise with the general. Scott recalled that one compromise was a limitation that prohibited the Red Eagle pilot from turning the MiG through more than 360 degrees before calling "Knock it off!" the radio transmission that terminated the fight. It was not ideal, but it was much better than flying around in gentle turns as Creech had earlier suggested.

There was no immediate effort made to replace Brown's MiG-17. Patty 002 had some history – it was actually HAVE FERRY, and had been flown by America since 1969. For now, the Red Eagles made do with just one Fresco, but another MiG-17F would arrive within a year.

FLYING THE MIG-17

The Fresco was an amazing little aircraft. Throughout the 255 sorties that HAVE DRILL flew in 1969, it experienced not a single mechanical fault that would cause it to be removed from the flying schedule. As with the MiG-21, its construction was sturdy yet simple, and it featured some very basic systems that made it less likely to fail in the air. And when there were maintenance issues, Henderson divulged, there was a massive stockpile of spares available for the Fresco, certainly far more than was the case for the Fishbed. Ignoring the upkeep and refurbishment of the VK-1F motor, keeping the MiG-17 airworthy was quite straightforward.

Back in 1949, the Mikoyan-Gurevich (MiG) design bureau had been ordered to create a successor to its highly successful MiG-15 "Faggot." MiG retained the basic design of the Faggot, but added a wing with a 45-degree sweep instead of the original 35 degrees, and stretched the fuselage by 3ft. The vertical tail was also enlarged. Two pre-production aircraft were built and flown in 1951, and the new fighter was designated the MiG-17. By 1952, the first production machines – featuring larger airbrakes, an updated avionics suite, and an electrical engine self-starting system – were rolling off the production lines.

The MiG-17 soon entered service with the Voenno-Vozdushnye Sily (VVS), the Soviet Air Force, and was given the NATO codename "Fresco." The MiG-17 was small by anyone's standards: its vertical tail was only 12ft tall, and its wings spanned just 32ft. From nose to tail, the Fresco was just 37ft long.

The version of the MiG-17 acquired by America from Israel was the re-engined MiG-17F, Fresco C. It boasted the VK-1F motor, which was a copy of the British Rolls-Royce Nene and offered just under 7,500lb of thrust. The aircraft had an empty weight of 8,646lb, and its afterburner improved climb performance if not acceleration and maximum speed, the latter of which was placarded (officially limited) at 700 miles per hour at 10,000ft. The 1952 C-model Fresco featured a number of small improvements over the original MiG-17, including an SRD-1 radar gunsight and a revised fuel system. Externally, it was distinct from the previous model in having bigger speed brakes, a revised exhaust nozzle to cater for the afterburner of the F-model of the VK-1, and a rear-view mirror mounted on the canopy.

The most immediate and obvious difference between the MiG-17 and American jet fighters became apparent before even taking off. When it came to taxiing, Henderson explained, "They had a totally different way of doing it. They used air pressure, applied by a lever on the stick grip to the brakes. You squeezed the lever and then you moved the rudder pedal differentially to steer the aircraft. It was not a natural act! We dedicated an entire TX ride to taxiing; start engines, taxi down the taxi way, and then come back." The MiG-21 used exactly the same system.

Oberle expounded further:

Taxiing the airplanes was a bit of a trick. If you wanted to turn right, you pushed the left rudder bar in and you pulsed this lever on the control stick. That dumped the pneumatic pressure to the brake on the left wheel and transferred it to the right wheel. You would get the free-swinging nose wheel to start to turn to the right, and then as you got ready to come out of that turn you'd have to push the left rudder bar past neutral and you'd have to start pumping the little paddle again to get the power back on the left wheel, to get the nose to straighten out so you could taxi straight!

It was like a snake taxiing out down the taxiway until you got more familiar with it. Once you learned it, you could taxi fairly comfortably.

Henderson said the MiG-17 was easy to fly for the most part, but reminded him of an old tractor. "It had bumps and crap all over the exterior surface. It was crude. The cockpit visibility was terrible and the cockpit had valves – faucets, literally – to turn things on and off." Oberle agreed completely: "It was designed by an apprentice plumber to be flown by an orangutan. There were hydraulic, oil, and pneumatic valves running through the cockpit that you had to reach around behind your elbow to operate during various emergency procedures."

Henderson's first attempt at starting the MiG-17s VK-1F engine had resulted in a false start. "After the first start attempt, I had inadvertently left one valve open so that fuel was continuing to pour into the tailpipe. When I started the engine a second time there was a huge fireball that came out of the tailpipe. That spectacular sight was pretty interesting to see, and I was impressing the hell out of my maintenance guys! They must have been thinking, 'Oh my God. Is this our commander?'"

The VK-1F was slow to respond to movements of the throttle, and it took in the region of 15 seconds for it to go from idle thrust to "military" thrust power setting (the maximum non-afterburning thrust available). Oberle observed: "This slow engine response was a characteristic of the old engines. If you kept the power up above 80 percent you had pretty good engine response, but if you ever pulled it back to idle and then pushed the power up to accelerate, it would take forever for the engine to spool back up to the 80 percent range where you finally started getting power. My technique was I never went below 80 percent. If I needed more deceleration I kept at 80 percent and put speed brakes out; I wasn't sitting there waiting for the engine to spool up."

Peck noted that the elevator trim switch – used to keep the aircraft flying straight and level as airspeed changed – was located not on the stick as was traditional in contemporary US aircraft, but took the form of a wheel mounted on the cockpit side below the canopy rail, an antiquated approach that dated the Fresco and had long since been superseded in Western fighters. "There were also no landing gear indicators in the cockpit of either MiG, and so when the gear came down a little barber pole stuck up on the upper surface of the wing and on the nose of the fuselage forward of the cockpit."

Adding to the Fresco pilot's woes, its ejection seat could not be adjusted in height, so it became an important life support issue to go out to the jet and be measured for seat pads that positioned the pilot at the optimum sitting height. "People protected their pads carefully," Peck said candidly, "because everyone has a slightly different seating position and you didn't want to be too low or too high." Too low and visibility from the cockpit was further restricted, and too high and the pilot's head rattled against the canopy and periscope. Further, the pilot could be knocked unconscious, or worse, killed during ejection.

The antiquated and industrial nature of the Fresco's systems and cockpits made for a different set of cockpit tasks than most of the Red Eagles were used to. Oberle elucidated: "When you took off, you raised the landing gear handle until the gear came up and locked, and then you had to put the gear handle back in the neutral position to take the pressure off the top of the gear, otherwise you kept the hydraulic system running. Putting it to neutral turned it off until you were ready to come back and land."

Oberle had one particularly serious In Flight Emergency (IFE) in the Fresco:

I had an IFE on take-off. We had wing tanks on it because we were trying to get longer sorties on it. I am rolling down the runway, and as I lift off the afterburner blows out. I was too fast and too far down the runway to catch the rabbit catcher, so I called mobile control and asked them to drop the barricade. I had flying speed, but barely lifted off by the end of the runway. I had to leave the gear and flaps down as it continued to accelerate against the rising terrain. As it eventually did that, I raised the gear and flaps and milked as much out of it as I could.

He made it, but it was a close thing. "It was one of those situations where you had to decide on whether to take the barricade, or to rely on your skills. Relying on my skills paid off."

"The MiG-17 was so forgiving in the landing pattern," Oberle continued:

You could flare and hold it off until you gently greased the wheels onto the runway. The -17 was not too different from the Air Force's T-37B Tweet: it could flare and you could hold it off. You always had the speed brakes out when you landed. The technique would be to come in, put the gear and the flaps down coming off the base turn. You pulled the power back until you got slowed down, then you kept the power up in the 80 percent range as you came in on finals to land. When the landing was assured, and by that I mean you've come in over the runway overrun area and you know you're not going to go around, you could go ahead and close the throttle off to idle and flare until it touched down. On finals, you could keep the power in 80 percent range and modulate speed brakes to keep it the speed where you wanted it. Then, if you needed to go around, you closed the speed brakes, increased the power, raised your nose for the climb out, and raised the gear and flaps.

Since the VK-1F centrifugal compressor motor generated only 6,000lb of thrust without afterburner, and the Fresco C had a fighting weight of just under 12,000lb, the motor's RPM gauge was one instrument that everybody got to know well. In fact, the MiG-17 did not have a nozzle position indicator to inform the pilot that the afterburner had lit, and instead he relied on a peanut-sized boost gauge that indicated whether the raw fuel pouring into the exhaust nozzle had lit off. Such indications were normally felt by a push in the back as the augmentation kicked into life, but the Fresco was underpowered enough that the additional thrust of its afterburner was imperceptible. Because the fuel fraction in the MiG-17 was so small, the Red Eagles flew their Frescos with external wing fuel tanks that increased their sortie duration, but added more aerodynamic drag. That made them even "sportier" on take-off.

As part of Henderson's formalization of the TX course, one of the first rides required the student to depart the aircraft deliberately from controlled flight so that the spin characteristics, and more importantly, recovery technique, could be experienced and practiced under a controlled and safe environment. Oberle explained the feedback that the MiG-17 gave the pilot as he demanded a tighter and tighter turn or pitch-up: "If you were loading it up with Gs you'd begin to get an onset buffet. This told you that you were losing some lift and approaching an accelerated stall. If you pulled in a little tighter the airplane would begin to wing rock a bit, which was telling you were getting into an accelerated stall. If you continued to pull through those characteristics it would snap roll on you, very violently so you'd bang your head on the canopy. It was as well to have a helmet on, otherwise you would be dazed."

On his first flight in the Fresco, as per his newly approved TX course syllabus, Henderson was required to put the aircraft into an accelerated high-speed stall under the watchful eye of McCloud, now a major. McCloud, the assistant ops officer and Henderson's IP, was flying as chase in the T-38. Henderson takes up the story: "Dave said, 'OK, get your speed up, get into the turn and get your nose position set.' So, I did all that, went through the pebbles and boulders, and then the airplane departed. It was very violent – a continuous snap role. I put the stick forward, but the MiG didn't recover. Holy shit! I was totally amazed that it did not recover and I am looking right down at the airfield thinking: 'This is going to be spectacular.'" As the Fresco twisted violently through the air, Henderson was experiencing the shock of his life, and was baffled as to the Fresco's refusal to recover. "That's when I really put the stick on the white line painted on the instrument panel. Only then did it recover. Pushing the stick forward when you're going fast creates lots of negative Gs, so it threw me up and out of the seat."

Since Henderson had failed, initially at least, to recover from the spin, he respected the reporting system he had just briefed to Gen Creech following Brown's mishap, and went straight to the 57th FWW Director of Operations at Nellis and told him what had happened. It was the first incident of mandatory reporting of unplanned departure from controlled flight by 4477th pilots.

The sort of training that McCloud had just given Henderson was an order of magnitude more structured than the IDEA pilots had ever had. They had joked among themselves, according to Mayo, "Damn, those Russian pilots must really be stupid to have to have that white line there." His experience was typical of the pre-CONSTANT PEG days. "The first time I tried to do a high-G reversal with aileron against an F-4, I knew immediately what that line was for, and all of a sudden it was really smart. I had lost about 150 knots and I had no idea which direction my airplane had tumbled, rolled, or whatever. It went so quickly that I just fought to get the stick up against that white line. It was actually very clever, and it also served to remind you the rest of the time that this airplane has some flight characteristics that will bite you in the ass."

FIGHTING THE MIG-17

If there was one rule to observe when fighting against the Fresco, Henderson said, it was: "You absolutely could not get slow with it. You had to hit the Fresco high-speed, go away and then come back round and hit it again. When someone got slow with us, you'd think, 'Alright! I've got him now.'" Lack of speed and acceleration, and vicious accelerated stall characteristics, were just a few of the Fresco's weaknesses. Another was its instability in yaw: its nose hunted from side to side and required the pilot to use rudder to correct. "This made it very difficult to hold a steady tracking shot," a problem made worse by a lack of cine camera to record the engagement, Peck confirmed.

Peck had evolved the Fresco's snap roll from an accelerated stall into a tactical maneuver. "I spent a lot of time in that airplane intentionally out of control," he counseled. "Why? Because you could reef and sneef and pull real hard in that airplane, and it would do this outside rolling departure that would put you in the perfect position to shoot someone who had just overshot but hadn't been smart enough to go into the vertical." This was exactly the kind of training that

A young Capt Earl Henderson cradles his flight helmet prior to a sortie over North Vietnam. Henderson would go on complete his '100 Missions North' in the F-105, earning six Distinguished Flying Crosses and a Silver Star in the process. (Earl Henderson via Steve Davies)

LtCol Fred Cuthill, of AFSC, straps into the HAVE DOUGHNUT MiG-21 at Groom Lake in 1969 with the assistance of TAC pilot Maj Jerry Larsen. At the time, Larsen was assigned to the 1137th Special Activities Squadron, based at the Pentagon. (US DoD)

Lt Bob "Kobe" Mayo poses before a combat mission over Vietnam in his F-100 Super Sabre in 1969. Mayo would eventually become a TAC HAVE IDEA pilot. (Kobe Mayo via Steve Davies)

Maj Ed Clements had flown the F-100 Super Sabre in Vietnam, and would go on to become one of the initial cadre of the F-15 FWIC. He was allotted a single HAVE IDEA sortie in the MiG-17. (USAF via Earl Henderson)

LtCol Lloyd "Boots" Boothby, the father of the Aggressors, photographed in the summer of 1972 while he headed up the Red Baron reports. (Joyce Boothby via Earl Henderson)

Maj David "DL" Smith photographed at Nellis AFB in 1974 during his time with the 64th FWS. Smith, who had made a name for himself in Vietnam, became one of the first three TAC HAVE IDEA pilots, and was instrumental in the creation of CONSTANT PEG. (USAF via Earl Henderson)

Maj Phil "Hound Dog" White, ops officer of 65th FWS Aggressors in 1979. White took command of the 4477th TES in August 1984. (USAF via Earl Henderson)

LtCol Earl Henderson hosts a party at the Mizpah Hotel Bar, Tonopah, in spring 1980. From left to right: Bill McHenry, a MiG-17 crew chief; Henderson; and Tommy Karnes, a MiG-21 crew chief. (Earl Henderson via Steve Davies)

LtCol Earl "Obi Wan" Henderson, the ops officer for the 64th FWS Aggressors, photographed in the summer of 1979. Months later he would become the third commander of the Red Eagles. (Earl Henderson via Steve Davies)

From left to right: Maj Gerry "Huffer" Huff; Dell Gaulker, REECo's construction manager responsible for Tonopah; and LtCol Gail "Evil" Peck, the incoming 4477th TEF commander, at the Mizpah Hotel Bar in the spring of 1979. (Earl Henderson via Steve Davies)

64th FWS Aggressor Maj Ronald Iverson in 1978. This photo was taken at around the same time that he was secretly heading the Foreign Military Exploitation of the ex-Egyptian Air Force MiG-23 Floggers under codename HAVE PAD. (USAF via Earl Henderson)

Maj Dave "Marshall" McCloud, complete with beard, following a successful TDY to collect MiG parts "in a foreign country" in December 1979. (Earl Henderson via Steve Davies)

Master Sergeant Robert "Bobby" Ellis at the Mizpah Hotel Bar in spring 1979. Ellis, who was also known as "Daddy," always sported a buzz cut hairstyle. (Earl Henderson via Steve Davies)

Maj Joe Lee Burns, who had successfully ejected from a crippled F-4 Phantom off the coast of Vietnam, was one of the first pilots selected by TAC to fly MiGs as part of HAVE IDEA. This close-up, dating to 1974, was extracted from the 64th FWS squadron group photo. (USAF via Earl Henderson)

Maj Alvin "Devil" Muller photographed in 1974 during his stint with the 64th FWS. At this time, Muller was secretly flying the HAVE IDEA MiGs, and would eventually join the 4477th TEF where he would become responsible for planning the security arrangements surrounding CONSTANT PEG. (USAF via Earl Henderson)

The 64th FWS Aggressors of 1974 photographed in front of a T-38 Talon. Those who went on to be Red Eagles or flew the HAVE IDEA MiGs are: Back row, left to right – Mike Press, Earl Henderson, and (fifth along) Ed Clements; Front row, left to right – (fourth along) DL Smith, Gene Jackson, and (far right) Joe Lee Burns. (USAF via Earl Henderson)

LtCol Joe "Jose" Oberle sits in the cockpit of his F-16 Viper in the fall of 1980. So secret was CONSTANT PEG at the time that Oberle's squadron commander had no idea that his new pilot had come from a tour flying MiGs. (Earl Henderson via Steve Davies)

LtCol Joe "Jose" Oberle holds a falcon bird of prey – the namesake of the Air Force's official title for the F-16 – at McDill AFB in 1980. (USAF via Earl Henderson)

Maj Karl "Harpo" Whittenberg, "Bandit 11," relaxes beer in hand at one of Henderson's frequent parties in 1980. (Earl Henderson via Steve Davies)

Maj Chuck "Chuckles" Corder in relaxed surroundings in 1980. Corder became a well-respected operations officer for the Red Eagles. (Earl Henderson via Steve Davies)

LtCdr Tom Morgenfeld, photographed in the spring of 1980 just prior to his retirement from the Navy, had first flown the HAVE IDEA MiGs with VX-4 at Point Mugu. He was hired by the 4477th TEF to teach new pilots to fly the MiG-21. (Earl Henderson via Steve Davies)

With the aid of Henderson's swimming pool and some willing volunteers, LtCol Tom Gibbs undergoes recurrency training in water survival in July 1980 prior to taking command of the 4477th TES from Henderson. (Earl Henderson via Steve Davies)

Maj Joe "Jose" Oberle in his Volkswagen Beetle: "Glenn Frick and I acquired two used 20mm gun barrels, cut holes in the hood and then welded the barrels in. We then painted it to look like an Aggressor F-5, and I drove this around Las Vegas during my time in CONSTANT PEG." (Joe Oberle via Steve Davies)

Ike Crawley, a Red Eagles engine maintainer, and Ralph Payne, one of Tonopah's small cadre of firemen. (Earl Henderson via Steve Davies)

LtCdr Keith Shean reads an announcement outside the MiG hangars at Tonopah. Shean acquired the call sign "Soxs" because he never wore any. (USAF via Steve Davies)

Maj Mike "Bat" Press and LtCol Joe "Jose" Oberle swap "There I Was" stories in June 1980. Press had been secretly flying MiGs in the US and abroad for many years before he joined the 4477th TES. (Earl Henderson via Steve Davies)

LtCol Tom Gibbs, life vest inflated, completes his refresher water survival training in Henderson's pool. He has been tethered to a rope and dragged through the water to simulate being dragged along by his parachute. (Earl Henderson via Steve Davies)

The 4477th TES maintainers, resplendent in white coveralls and red and white Red Eagles baseball caps, stand at ease on Tonopah's ramp under the watchful eye of Maj Chuck Corder (looking back). The occasion was the change of command ceremony between Henderson and Gibbs in summer 1980. (Lenny Bucko via Steve Davies)

Lenny Bucko took on the role of events organizer upon being selected to join the 4477th TES. A Marine aviator with a passion for scuba diving and water sports, he is seen here in the middle of the back row following a white water rafting trip. Chuck Corder is in the blue tee-shirt to the far right, and Burt Myers is second from left in the yellow tee-shirt. (Lenny Bucko via Steve Davies)

Photographed in front of the MiG hangars at Tonopah; (left to right) Myers, Corder, Bucko, Postai, Scott, (bottom row) Laughter, and Green receive their cash advances for expenses prior to setting off to Houston, Texas, to qualify for their FAA multi-engine rating. As is clear, the men approached the trip with deadly seriousness. (Lenny Bucko via Steve Davies)

LtCol Earl Henderson (left) salutes incoming commander, Lt Col Tom Gibbs, at Tonopah during the June 1980 handover ceremony. Henderson's flying career had been cut short by the discovery of heart disease during a routine flight physical examination. (Lenny Bucko via Steve Davies)

LtCol Earl "Obi Wan" Henderson and Captain Herbert "Hawk" Carlisle during an intelligence-gathering trip to East Berlin in 1988. Carlisle had not long before ejected from an out-of-control MiG-23 over the Tonopah Test Range. (Earl Henderson via Steve Davies)

Maj Rick "Caz" Cazessus photographed in around 1990 as a 64th FWS Aggressor pilot. Cazessus went to the Aggressors following the shut down of the 4477th TES in 1988. (USAF via Earl Henderson)

Lloyd "Boots" Boothby and Randy O'Neill talk during the 1992 Aggressor reunion at Nellis AFB. O'Neill, who had deep-rooted black world contacts, is widely regarded as the driving force behind HAVE IDEA. (Earl Henderson via Steve Davies)

Col Glenn "Pappy" Frick during the 1992 Aggressor reunion at Nellis. Frick was the Red Eagles' first commander. (Earl Henderson via Steve Davies)

Earl Henderson (left) and Chuck Holden at the Nellis Officers' Club, Nellis AFB, in January 2008. Holden had flown Frick, Oberle, and Peck around during the search for an operating location for CONSTANT PEG. (Earl Henderson via Steve Davies)

Commonly referred to as "the HAVE DOUGHNUT article" by those involved in its exploitation, the MIG-21F-13 is seen here having test instrumentation installed inside a hangar at Groom Lake in 1968. (US DoD)

HAVE DOUGHNUT was flown only by US Navy and US Air Force Systems Command pilots during its 1968 exploitation (one of whom, LtCol Joe Jordan, was seconded to TAC for the evaluation). Only later would TAC pilots be allowed to take the controls. (US DoD)

HAVE FERRY was the second of the two MiG-17F Frescos loaned to the United States by Israel in 1969. It was this exact aircraft, 002, in which Navy LtCdr Hugh "Bandit" Brown would lose his life in August 1979. (US DoD)

HAVE DRILL was used for the majority of the early MiG-17 exploitations, while HAVE FERRY acted as a spare. (US DoD)

An unidentified Red Eagle marks the small cabin used initially by the 4477th TEF as its operations room in 1979. (USAF via Steve Davies)

The MiG-21 cockpit was a jumbled assortment of switches and dials, and was quite confined by the standard of most Western fighters. In later years, English placards were eventually added by the ever-resourceful Red Eagles maintainers to help the pilots in their cockpit checks. (USAF via Steve Davies)

The charter members of the 4477th TEF maintenance contingent show off their new 18-wheel Kenworth truck. Ellis (far left) used the truck to transport secret shipments of MiG parts and spares around the country. (Earl Henderson via Steve Davies)

One of the first challenges a US MiG pilot had to master was the pneumatic braking system, activated via a lever on the stick (seen here being demonstrated by a 4477th TES pilot sitting in a MiG-21F-13). (USAF via Steve Davies)

A still image, taken from a long-list movie reel, of a MiG-17F Fresco C taxiing back to the newly laid ramp at Tonopah. The date is probably late 1979. (USAF via Steve Davies)

The view ahead in the MiG-21 was marred by a large 8mm gun camera (right), and various other instruments. Some aircraft featured printed checklists below the gunsight, as in the case of this 4477th TES MiG-21F-13. (USAF via Steve Davies)

only CONSTANT PEG could provide; no other Aggressor simulator could even approximate that level of training.

While the MiG had plenty of elevator authority to control pitch (raise and lower the nose) at slow and moderate speeds, when flown too fast it quickly became difficult to maneuver as the airflow over the elevator increased and the control stick became very difficult to move. This, Oberle recalled, was a key point for pilots being exposed to the MiG-17 to learn.

> We had to teach them that if they could – as a defender in an American airplane – get the MiG-17 into the 450-knot regime, and then start to turn, then the MiG pilot would have to overcome this huge aerodynamic load on the tail without any hydraulic assistance. He may have had the potential to pull 7Gs, but he could probably pull no more than 2Gs because he simply didn't have the physical strength to overcome the loads on the tail. In order to get into the best turn, the MiG-17 pilot had to decelerate into the 300–330-knot regime, that was ideal for the MiG-17. And when you got into that you could go into 7Gs and pretty much maintain that at 300–330 knots in a fight. It was a ferocious little competitor at that regime. Out at 450 knots it was more of a lead sled.

The Mikoyan-Gurevich bureau had positioned the Fresco's control stick high up in the cockpit to help the pilot gain leverage against these heavy aerodynamic loads, but the only solution to the problem was to install hydraulically boosted controls and that never happened.

The positioning of the stick – unusually high by American standards – may also have been a factor in Brown's second departure. The added elevation sometimes resulted in over-controlling in pitch and a resultant accelerated stall, and that was what many believed had killed the Navy pilot.

One of the Red Eagles' MiG-17s was a PF variant, NATO reporting name Fresco D. It had a primitive Izumrud radar that sometimes worked. The radar was linked into the Fresco's aiming device – an illuminated gun sight reticle projected onto a combining glass in front of the pilot's face. Oberle explained the operation of the two systems: "The radar was a range-only system. You set a manual distance for the wingspan of the airplane you were engaging via the throttle, and when you were locked on to your opponent the reticle would tell you that you were in range to fire when the airplane filled its span. You'd also get some lead computing for guns." This meant that the reticle would show the approximate fall of rounds fired from the Fresco's 37mm Nudelman N-37 cannon and its two 23mm Nudelman-Rikhter NR-23 cannons. The gunsight, however, was flawed. "It buried itself out of sight as soon as you put 2.5G to 3G on the airplane," Peck revealed. Validating simulated gun kills during the Fresco's CONSTANT PEG exposures therefore relied on some degree of posturing and bravado. "We were in position, but since we weren't shooting real bullets, who really knows whether it was a kill?" he added. While Soviet jet fighters were not renowned for their visibility to the rear, the so-called 6 o'clock position in aviation speak, the MiG-17 had an excellent periscope that was focused at infinity and provided the pilot with a very clear view behind him. "It took a little training to get used to it, but it was useful," Peck judged.

Although Scott became the first pilot to go straight to the MiG-21, he later also qualified to fly the MiG-17. He recalled:

> The worst airplane we'd fight was an F-16 with a Fighter Weapons School instructor in it. He would do one hard break, go vertical and be behind you before you did a 360-degree turn. The MiG-17 was a very fun airplane to fly. I'm now a pilot for Southwest Airlines and there's another pilot for Southwest Airlines that I regularly meet on the line. He will come up and tell me: "I'll never forget the day I flew against you when they were building the F-16 Fighter Weapons School." As part of their checkout program, he flew against me. I was flying a MiG-17. And this guy was well known for patting himself on the back as being a really good fighter pilot, and he was. But he got into the area that he should not have gotten into: what we call "the telephone booth." He slowed down and got into a little turn and burn fight with me. You could stop a MiG-17 on a dime and just move the nose around and point right at him; he could never do anything. He learned his lesson and went home … The next day he came back and he had to repeat that ride because he didn't kill me. I'll tell you that I don't think I lasted 30 seconds the next time. The lesson had been learned: don't get in *this* arena with *that* airplane and you're going to be just fine. But until you actually do it, sometimes the lesson isn't learned.

Since the MiG-17's fuel fractions were small, timing was a key element in the exposures of Blue Air pilots to the Fresco. Henderson concluded: "The guys would take off from either Fallon Naval Air Station or Nellis, 100 to 125 miles away, so we wouldn't even go out to the airplane until after they'd taken off. We'd walk out, trusting the crew chiefs to make the assets ready, and then would strap on the airplane and wait until the Blue Air guy called up our fight frequency, which meant he was within maybe 20 miles of the base. Our missions were only 15 to 20 minutes long."

GREAT HORNED LARKS

In November 1979, Morgenfeld finally left the Red Eagles and the US Navy. 'What we accomplished as a group would have taken the mainstream Navy or Air Force years to pull off, and I take very little credit for any of that. But the Red Eagles had prepared me well for the Skunk Works: we were a small close-knit team, and we were used to making important decisions ourselves.'

CONSTANT PEG was grounded once again throughout October and November of 1979, but for an altogether unexpected reason: birds of the feathered variety.

"We had the great horned lark visit us – the fattest, dumbest little bird you ever could imagine," explained Henderson. "They invaded our world up there. Our runway was flat and pitted, so whenever any rain fell the water collected in the pits. Tumbleweeds would roll across the runway, dropping their seeds into these wet pits; the birds would then nestle on the runway and put their little bodies up against that black asphalt: they had water, they had seeds, and they had warmth! They were there by the thousands, and it was a major problem."

The great horned larks were less of a concern for the pilots flying the three recently leased Cessna 404 support aircraft, which were now shuttling back and forth between Nellis and Tonopah several times daily. "We'd rattle down the runway in the Cessnas and you'd hear 'bump, bump, bump' as they flew into the windshield," Henderson admitted. The Cessnas were one thing, but if a MiG sucked one of the birds into its engine on take-off, another fatal mishap could follow within seconds. Before long, the Red Eagles commander sat asking himself: "What the fuck are we going to do?"

As an interim measure, he gave permission for his pilots and maintainers to patrol the runway armed with shotguns. "They blasted away at these damned birds, and we even put fake owls out there, but these stupid birds always came back." He eventually managed to get approval to recruit an Air Force sergeant who he'd heard on the grape vine was a qualified falconer. "That's a career field that is not in the Air Force, so we had to go out and find this guy. Sure enough [on December 6] he came in and went out there about half an hour before we flew, and this falcon flew around and scared away the birds."

How effective the falconer was in the long run is debatable, but neither Henderson nor the commanders that followed were ever really satisfied with the results. "It was just too much trouble, with uneven results, and there were probably less involved ways of fixing the problem. We could not chance MiG operations with them on the runway. It took forever to get it fully implemented, because the falconer we hired had to capture a baby falcon and spend months training it." The peregrine falcon he brought with him initially in December was only on loan, and he soon had to return it to its owner.

The birds never left Tonopah. "I personally think the invasion of 1979 was unusually heavy, and the following years were not nearly as bad," Henderson explained. 'I know that in the late 1980s [the Red Eagles] made clearing the birds a sport – driving up and down the runway before launch, and right before recovery, awarding points for kills, etc. The environmentalists would probably cringe, but it got the job done."

In November 1979, the squadron hired Maj Charles "Chuck" Corder, "Bandit 15," as assistant ops officer. Corder was an F-4 Weapons School graduate, and had flown combat in the F-4 in Vietnam as a young lieutenant. Assigned to the TFWC as a planner on Red Flag when he was selected for the 4477th TEF, he had gone through the Aggressor course in spring of that year prior to reporting to the Red Eagles. Whittenberg described him as "a very likeable guy; always up for a good time and a fine aviator," while Oberle said, 'He was always laughing and smiling. He was a gentle giant. The kind you would like to have on your wing in combat or in a bar."

By December, Huff was getting ready to leave the squadron and the Air Force. His departure also meant that a new pilot had to be recruited, and that man was Capt Robert "Catfish" Sheffield, "Bandit 16." Drabant was also preparing to leave the program to join the team performing Multinational Operational Test & Evaluation on the new General Dynamics F-16. Sheffield told me that Huff was disgusted by the way in which Peck had been treated, and resigned his commission in protest. He'd done so, says Sheffield, at great financial loss: "He must have been in the Air Force for 14 years by that time, but he just quit: no pension, no retirement benefits. Nothing." Huff had seen enough, and since he wasn't worried about possible disciplinary repercussions "he put on a pretty good show for his final flight," Scott said.

Sheffield had come from the F-4, via the 26th TFTS at Clark and then the 64th FWS at Nellis. He'd been an Aggressor IP at Nellis in January 1979 when he had first flown against the 4477th TEF's MiGs operating out of Groom Lake. He'd first heard of the Red Eagles during his checkout as an Aggressor in summer 1977, but he wouldn't be exposed to them until January during his checkout as an IP with the 64th FWS. Like Scott, he went straight to the MiG-21, explaining that he was not fazed by the brief checkout process: "You didn't get into the Red Eagles unless you were exceptionally good. Over the course of my time in the Air Force, I had had the opportunity to fly against many fighter pilots from a great number of the world's air forces. In my opinion, the guys in the Red Eagles were easily in the top 50 of all the fighter pilots I ever flew against. These were not guys who were going to go out and do something stupid. There was enough of a similarity between flying the F-5E and the MiG-21 that there was no emphasis on extensive flying handling training on the MiG."

At the close of 1979, CONSTANT PEG had made slow, but deliberate, progress. The Red Eagles had flown 87 sorties [18] with eight MiGs, exposing 68 Air Force pilots to the most realistic air combat training available anywhere in the world. Most of these early exposures had been flown against Air Force Aggressor pilots, with the Navy and Marines yet to fly against the 4477th TEF. Peck reasoned that this was because the program needed to be ramped up gradually; flying against colleagues in the 64th and 65th FWS at Nellis was beneficial and convenient to both parties, and was the best way to ease into the program.

CHAPTER 5

THE "FLOGGER" ARRIVES, 1980

SPIN TESTING

On January 14, 1980, Henderson, Oberle, Heatley, McCloud, Whittenberg, Scott, Sheffield, and newly hired Navy pilot Keith Shean, "Bandit 17," all flew to NAS Miramar to participate in a spin orientation program run by the US Navy's VF-126.

VF-126 was the Navy's West Coast (Pacific) Adversary Squadron, and had a number of T-2 Buckeye trainers in order to administer this special course. But there were two ironies about the event. The first was that this was a course initially identified by Peck, according to Henderson: "Gail had suggested T-2 training for his pilots to Gen Swalm, the 57th FWW commander, in May 1979. He had been told that it looked like another 4477th boondoggle, and Swalm promptly disapproved it. After Hugh Brown's accident the attitude was different. Heatley and Oberle reengaged the suggestion after I came on board and it was quickly approved by Swalm." Secondly, VF-126 was the same squadron that Hugh Brown had flown with on his first operational assignment and was also the Navy's out-of-control flight training school.

The T-2 was an excellent choice, Henderson stated. "You could be put into a spin, and then apply any spin recovery procedure known to man and it would recover. So, our MiG-21 pilots could apply their spin recovery procedure, and the MiG-17 guys theirs; and you could practice your procedures until you were completely familiar with them. They even took us up and did a Lumshavak – a sickening, disorientating, tumbling maneuver."

The ability to recover from a spin, or a departure from controlled flight of any sort, is a fundamental aspect of flying most aircraft, but for the MiGs it was particularly important because it represented an alternative to ejecting. "There was a lot of no-confidence in the ejection seats," according to Henderson. "The cartridges in the seats had a shelf life, and so there was lots of speculation about whether they would fire and whether the seat would actually come out of the airplane." Despite Oberle's best efforts to reverse engineer the cartridges, for the moment at least the pilots who flew the MiGs were content to try their luck at landing a stricken or damaged asset. It would be several years before a dedicated trial of the ejection cartridges was conducted.

WEAPONS SCHOOL INTRODUCTION

With Creech watching carefully, Henderson began to grow the Red Eagles' exposure program, gradually expanding it and increasing its sophistication. Henderson invited the FWS at Nellis to introduce one additional sortie to the end of its six-month Weapons School course. Up until now, only the occasional FWS student had been lucky enough to fly against a HAVE IDEA MiG, and CONSTANT PEG had thus far limited its formalized program of exposures to Aggressor IPs, a small number of Tactical Air Forces (TAF) units, and FWS IPs. The graduation ride took the student and let him fly a one-on-one, no-holds-barred sortie against a MiG. Henderson explained: "We didn't do an awful lot of emulation in the Red Eagles. Why? Because we've come all of this way and spent all of this money to get these MiGs flying, and now we're going to cut and run just like the Soviets would have? It was a little different from being an Aggressor – a cool, humble fucker – and you're now being really aggressive so that you can show the student the capabilities of the airplane."

Henderson's responsibilities at the helm of CONSTANT PEG were varied and many, and he had many plates to keep spinning. He approximates that he spent about 50 percent of his time conducting VIP tours. "The squadron was the number one stop for many of the VIPs visiting the western USA. Of course, it wasn't a bad thing for them that they would also be based out of Vegas for their stay. They would fly up in a Lear Jet and land, we'd greet them getting off the airplane, then show them the MiGs and our facilities, and finally give them a briefing on our activities." Over the course of CONSTANT PEG, over 450 VIPs would visit the unit, according to one official Air Force document.

There remained issues between TAC and the Red Eagles, though. Still holding down their cover jobs as Aggressors, the civilian multi-engine rating meant that many of their number were now qualified to fly four aircraft types: the Cessna 404, T-38, F-5E, and one of the MiGs. Due to operational necessity that included pilot shortages due to unexpected assignments, some of the pilots, like Scott, would move back and forth between the MiG-17 and the MiG-21, but officially were not qualified in both at the same time. Sheffield stated: "I was proud of the fact that I was checked out in so many different types and that some days I would fly them all. We would take off at first light in a Cessna 404, fly one sortie in an F-5E and then two in a MiG-21, and then fly home in a T-38 12 hours later. Looking back on it now it amazes me. We were also pushing the crew rest regulations that said we had to have 12 hours' uninterrupted rest between flying days."

It was all a "bone of contention," recalled Henderson, "and it was a battle that I had to fight several times during my time as commander of the unit. TAC wanted us to be qualified in only one type of airplane at a time, but I had to tell them that if that was the case we could not do our mission. The Cessnas were also a problem, but how else would we have gotten up there [Tonopah]?" TAC eventually relented. The Red Eagles had won the battle, for now at least.

The Red Eagles worked long, hard hours. There was nothing to do at Tonopah, and while the maintainers would spend Monday to Thursday at the bare-bones air base, the pilots enjoyed the luxury of returning home to Vegas and their families or girlfriends each night. The daily early morning trip to TTR each day gave the pilots ample opportunity to get up to mischief. "Whoever flew the Cessna up there, usually accompanied by a couple of other pilots and some maintainers, would open up the airfield when they arrived," Sheffield explained. "This guy would land, drive up the runway to make sure there was no debris to get sucked into the MiGs' motors, and then would head out to this lone little Runway Service Unit, RSU, that was alongside the runway." In the absence of an air traffic control tower at Tonopah at this time, the RSU was a sort of mini control tower on wheels. "Once he was in the RSU he was listening for follow-on radio calls from the next inbound flights – usually an F-5 or T-38. If you were flying one of these, you could have some fun. As the sun rose in the east, you could come flying towards this RSU at less than 50ft, with the sun behind you, just under the speed of sound. You'd barely miss it, and as you got to it you'd light the afterburner and pull straight up. You could do this at Tonopah because it was an uncontrolled airport and at that time TAC had no minimum altitude restriction."

In March 1980, Henderson was struck by a personal tragedy when he was diagnosed with heart disease. The diagnosis, at the young age of 39, immediately grounded him. So far, of the three commanders – Frick, Peck, and Henderson –

none had served a full two-year tenure. But life went on, and Henderson continued to lead the unit until a replacement was found. One month after the diagnosis, Heatley departed the Red Eagles and was replaced like-for-like by Navy pilot and "Bandit 18," Selvyn "Sel" Laughter, a US Navy test pilot.

Then, on May 1, the 4477th Test & Evaluation Flight became the 4477th Test & Evaluation Squadron (TES). The move made Henderson a squadron commander, and that gave him more influence. It is unclear exactly why the flight became a squadron, particularly considering Frick's reasons for keeping the Red Eagles as inconspicuous as possible only a few years before, but Henderson has a hunch: "The MiG-23s were going to be coming on board within the year – the large hangar for the MiG-23s was already in the works at Tonopah – plus we were getting more pilots and maintenance people, so a squadron was a more proper organization."

Henderson had been a popular leader for the short time that he was in the post, and he had been instrumental in keeping his team tight-knit against all the odds during the tumultuous months that had followed Brown's death and Peck's departure. He had even hosted the majority of the unit's parties at his house. "We had perhaps six or eight squadron parties during my command. The 4477th senior NCOs were crusty, hard partiers, and generally they and their wives all smoked and liked to drink good whisky. Immediately after I gave up the squadron I had to have my kitchen floor replaced, and the house completely re-carpeted, because of cigarette burns and spilled drink stains."

LTCOL TOM GIBBS TAKES COMMAND, JUNE 6, 1980

In June the squadron saw the arrival of three new pilots: Maj Burt "Buffalo" Myers, "Bandit 19"; Maj Michael "Bat" Press, previously of HAVE IDEA, "Bandit 20"; and LtCol Tom Gibbs, "Bandit 21." Gibbs, a combat pilot of considerable experience, had been hired to take over from Henderson, who was soon to undergo open heart surgery. Press joined the Red Eagles as the ops officer. He had left the Aggressors and HAVE IDEA in 1977 to go to school, and had then been assigned as the F-5 advisor to the Shah of Iran in 1978. Following the revolution and subsequent overthrow of the Shah in February 1979, he had been "left behind" and had hidden in a safe house in the capital, Tehran, as the revolutionaries closed all the borders. He was spared a clandestine hike to the safety of Turkey when the newly installed Iranian leader, Ayatollah Ruhollah Khomeini, granted safe passage to the 100 or so Americans still in the country. Press had then gone on a classified mission to fly MiGs with a foreign nation, before he returned to Nellis as an Aggressor IP in late 1979. That was when he'd received a call to report to Tonopah.

Myers' appointment to the squadron broke the mold because up until then, with the exception of Peck, every single USAF Red Eagle had been hired from the ranks of the Aggressors. That didn't make him any less qualified to join: he had flown the F-105 and the F-4, the latter in combat, and then moved on to the cutting-edge F-15. He was also a graduate of both the F-4 and F-15 FWS and was serving as an IP with the 433rd TFS, "Satan's Angels," which had been reactivated as the F-15 FWS at the time.

"I was brought into the program as an F-15 guy with the understanding that I would still teach in the F-15 FWIC," Myers explained. "I would fly the MiGs four days a week, and on Friday I would fly the F-15 as an instructor." It was an arrangement that would remain in place for the duration of his three years on the squadron. Given his large physical stature, hence the call sign "Buffalo," Myers was sent straight to the MiG-21. It was unlikely that he'd have fitted inside the tiny MiG-17, seat cushions or not.

Soon after Myers joined the 4477th TES, Geisler, the former Aggressor, was hired by the Satan's Angels from his assignment as an F-15 pilot with the 49th TFW at Holloman. He had gone through the 433rd FWS' second ever class in December, 1978, and had graduated with distinction. Now back at Nellis and going through the FWIC upgrade, he was once again being exposed to the MiGs. This time, though, he would fly against Myers: "It was clear that a lot had changed with the MiG training and that there had been growth, not necessarily in size, but in credibility; there were only seven Satan's Angels IPs, so the fact that one of us was getting to fly the MiGs was very impressive. He [Myers] could really give me a good exposure as a result – he could tell me while we were fighting, 'OK, this is all I got,' and that was very useful." By November, Geisler would be a fully qualified FWS IP, a process immeasurably assisted by Henderson's decision to hire Myers.

FINI FLIGHT

On the day of the squadron change of command, June 6, Henderson snuck into Tonopah to fulfill an Air Force tradition. His sudden diagnosis had meant that he'd missed out on an official "fini flight" to mark the end of his flying days, and that was not something that he would stand for. He awoke early and joined Oberle on a Cessna 404 for the short flight from Nellis to Tonopah before dawn.

He climbed into a MiG-17, fired it up, and took off into the sunrise. Oberle looked on, pleased that his boss would at least be able to see out his Air Force flying career with a little pizzazz, but simultaneously warning Henderson that he would deny ever taking part in the venture if the story got out.

Henderson flew the MiG fast and hard, making the most of his last flight at the controls of a high-performance fighter jet, and finished his fini flight with a few high-speed passes over Tonopah's stretched runway. Upon landing he taxied the small jet back to the hangar and unstrapped. Clutching his helmet under his arm, still wearing his G-suit, and with the imprint of his oxygen mask still visible on his face, he walked back into the squadron only to be confronted by the 57th wing vice commander, Col Tony Gardecki. Since he reported directly to Gardecki's boss, Gen Charles J. Cunningham Jr, Henderson thought he was going to end up being court martialed – why on earth would the colonel be here so early in the morning unless he'd heard of what was going on?

Bracing himself for the dressing down that was surely going to follow, he was surprised when Gardecki started apologizing to him. It turned out that the colonel had been giving a tour of the DoE nuclear test ranges north of Tonopah to a group of senior enlisted airmen when Henderson's MiG-17 had screamed over their heads at low level. Surprised that CONSTANT PEG operations had begun so early that morning, the colonel believed he was at fault for inadvertently exposing a group of airmen to the existence of the MiGs. If only he knew.

ROLL REVERSAL, OR ROLE REVERSAL?

When Gibbs arrived to take command of the squadron, the Red Eagles were still wrestling with a semantic issue with regards to their exposures. Incredibly, the debate waged over a rule that had never been documented, but was instead a "verbal transmission" that had come down through the echelons of TAC from the commander, Gen Creech.

Scott told me that this rule prohibited the Red Eagles from executing a roll/role reversal in a dogfight. The problem was that the term could be spelt both ways, each with very different meanings. Since it was a verbal command, there was no definitive way of knowing which. "It was one of those things where 'Hey! The general has spoken!' and we were all supposed to understand exactly what he'd said. No one was of a mind to ask him what he actually meant," Scott admitted. "One party interpreted it as r-o-l-l, roll reversal, which meant that in a defensive position if you caused the attacker to overshoot and you then reversed your direction of flight, you had to call, 'Knock it off!' Then there was the other interpretation – the correct one in my mind, and a little more liberal – r-o-l-e, role reversal, which was where the MiG started off defensive, caused an overshoot, rolled and reversed into the attacker, but you could still keep fighting so long as you didn't change your role from being defensive to offensive." What Creech was trying to do was prevent the Red Eagles from getting into close quarters, overly aggressive dogfights. "He didn't want us getting into scissors [a series of speed-sapping turns] fights, and we struggled with the interpretation of this and we spent many hours in the squadron discussing what it meant," Scott continued. Creech was a progressive leader who understood tactics. "I cannot believe in my mind today that he meant r-o-l-l." The TAC Director of Operations, two-star general Larry Welch, was keeping a close eye on the Red Eagles at that time, and used his wing commanders, who would fly against the Red Eagles, to keep him abreast of developments. Scott surmised that since the Red Eagle pilots adopted r-o-l-e as the "correct" interpretation without ever being chastised by higher headquarters, this must have been what Creech actually meant.

REORGANIZATION AND THE NEW BOSS

On July 1, 1980, the Red Eagles were given an $18 million fund in order to finance Phase II construction at Tonopah. The start date for construction was set for the middle of September. Phase II would consist of one additional hangar (Bldg 188), a new apron and taxiway, JP-4 fuel tanks, a warehouse, and support utilities.

Almost two months later, on August 25, the 4477th TES was assigned under the command and control of the Deputy Commander, Tactics & Test, 57th FWW's Director of Test (57FWW/DT). Previously, the squadron had moved from being under the direct control of the wing's commander (57FWW/CC) to its Director of Operations, (57FWW/DO), but DT was a new position that followed reorganization at Nellis. Administratively speaking, DT was directly under the DO. Oberle explained: "All of the squadron commanders at Nellis reported directly to the 57th FWW Director of Operations. They created another layer of supervision because there got to be so many commanders that one Director of Operations was unable to maintain watch over all of them." The Aggressors were similarly reassigned to the control of 57FWW/DT at the same time.

Meanwhile, the new Red Eagles commander was settling in rapidly. At only 24 years of age, Gibbs had become the first lieutenant to complete 100 F-105 missions over North Vietnam, in October 1966,[19] returning to fly the F-106 interceptor with ADC. In November 1969 he was selected to fly with the Air

Force's "Thunderbirds" demonstration team, and that was followed in early 1972 with an assignment to the F-4 FWS. He'd returned to Vietnam with the 13th TFS in the summer, flying another 275 combat missions in the F-4, and had participated in the Air Force's last mission over North Vietnam in February 1973.

Until now, he had been the STAN/EVAL chief for the 57th FWW, responsible for both Aggressor units and the Red Eagles. He had first learned about CONSTANT PEG in 1977, when he had arrived back at Nellis following one year at Command and Staff College and another three at the Air Force Academy. His return to Nellis and the cockpit had coincided with the creation of the 4477th TEF, but he had not been made aware of TAC's involvement in HAVE IDEA. "I knew that we had MiGs, but I thought that they were being flown by the Systems Command pilots."

As chief of STAN/EVAL for the Red Eagles' parent unit, he had been fortunate enough to be invited out to Tonopah one day in 1979 to observe their operations. He was impressed not only by the assets, but also by the set-up: "The squadron commander out there was more like a wing commander. He had the entire base to maintain; not only the airplanes, but the maintenance, fire department, motor pool, housing, and so on."

Unlike Henderson, Gibbs wasn't forced to visit Creech for personal approval, even though Gen Kelley (who had fired Peck and taken Henderson to Langley for approval) was still the TFWC commander at that time. Instead, Creech visited Nellis a few months later and was briefed by Gibbs in person on his progress with the Red Eagles.

He had first discovered that he was getting command of CONSTANT PEG when he was called to the office of Gen Cunningham, the TFWC commander. "I thought I was going to get the 414th FWS, but Buster Glosson got given that instead. I was therefore surprised to get the MiGs, but I was ready and excited about being the squadron commander."

"Once Gibbs took over it was kind of business as usual," Oberle stated. "I don't recall any dramatic changes. We continued to pursue the same tempo and the ops concept that we had been working to all along." The first port of call for Gibbs was predictable. "I went to talk to Bobby Ellis and took an inventory of what we had. We had the best maintenance guys in the world, and our MiGs were in excellent condition. I wanted to keep up the training that CONSTANT PEG had been providing, and to help the operation to grow."

It soon became apparent to Gibbs just how challenging the maintenance operation was: "We had a maintenance function that could reverse engineer parts that would have been the envy of any TAC fighter wing in the world.

There were some short cuts that could be taken: you could use the nose wheel tire from a T-38 on the MiG-21, and hydraulic pumps off the F-100 on them. They didn't go directly, the maintenance guys had to do a little re-tubing and install a different rack, but they did go." He had just under 100 maintainers working for him, which represented dramatic growth over a period of only nine months since Henderson had taken command of the unit. Not all of these men worked directly on the MiGs; some worked on the motor pool, fire trucks, and ground equipment for the MiGs.

Despite the maintainers' dedication and expertise, the arrival of the new commander heralded the start of a change that would have significant repercussions later. While he allowed the men to continue to dress casually, he began to tighten down the screws on some of the informality. "They wanted to call me Tom, but I told them my name was Boss. I wanted to maintain more of a hierarchy between the enlisted and the officers. That is not to say I did not admire and respect every one of them, just that we had to tighten things down a little bit." It was the first of many changes the next few years would bring.

At the end of September 1980, Oberle left CONSTANT PEG just as work began on Phase II. He'd flown 186 sorties in the MiG-17 and MiG-21 since he'd started flying the assets. His next move was to Hill AFB, Utah, where he became the ops officer of an F-16 squadron. When he arrived at the Utah base, his official service records showed that he had been a member of the Aggressors at Nellis for the last three years. Nowhere was there any indication of the true identity of his previous unit.

THE FLOGGER

On November 1, 1980, the first MiG-23 was flown by the 4477th TES at Tonopah when a single MiG-23BN Flogger F flew in from Groom Lake. Ellis, Henderson explained, had been crucial in preparing for the arrival of the Flogger. "The 4477th's budget never quite caught up with the exploding growth of the operation and the arrival of the MiG-23. We were always scrounging for makeshift solutions to storage, housing, supply, etc. Only Bobby knew the 'grand plan' and I was constantly being surprised by a new structure or vehicle at the complex at Tonopah. It looked like a shantytown and it was called Indian Village for very obvious reasons."

TAC had been flying the Flogger on and off since Iverson's team participated in HAVE PAD in spring 1978, but it is probably more than coincidental that the permanent acquisition of the first Flogger in November corresponded with the end of AFSC's HAVE LIGHTER and HAVE DOWN testing of "Type IIIB" aircraft by the Red Hats, according to Peter Merlin.

The MiG-23 was designed in the 1960s as a next-generation fighter for Russia's Frontovaya Aviatsiya (Frontal Aviation), a part of the VVS. FA was the equivalent of TAC, and it wanted a fighter with performance superior to the MiG-21, and the ability to operate from short airstrips. The prototype first flew in the summer of 1967; the first production model – the MiG-23S – followed in 1969. NATO called it the Flogger A. Improved Floggers had followed, and Russia was soon developing export variants for sale to its allies. For the least trusted of those, Russia offered the MiG-23MS Flogger E. It was based on the 1970s MiG-23M Flogger B that was operated by the VVS, but had a less sophisticated Sapfir RP-22SM radar, known to NATO as the "Jaybird," and a very basic avionics suite that severely limited its effectiveness as a beyond-visual-range interceptor. When Russia developed a dedicated air-to-ground variant, the MiG-23B Flogger F, they deleted the radar and completely revised the nose profile to allow the pilot better visibility out front. This too was made available in the form of the MiG-23BN Flogger F.

The Flogger used variable geometry ("swing") wings similar to those found on the General Dynamics F-111 and F-14. The wings were manually set to 16 degrees for take-offs, landings, or low-speed cruise; 45 degrees for high-speed cruise; and 72 degrees for supersonic flight. Each wing featured trailing-edge flaps to improve low-speed handling, and spoilers on the top that popped up to generate roll, working in unison with the two large horizontal "tailerons" at the back of the fuselage. The vertical stabilizer – the "tail plane" – had a long strake that ran along the fuselage, and a ventral fin under the tail helped maintain high-speed directional stability. A fairing at the back of the vertical stabilizer housed a brake parachute to reduce landing distance.

The Flogger had a GSh-23L twin-barreled 23mm cannon mounted flush with the underside of the fuselage, and there were two weapons pylons under the forward fuselage, and one under each wing glove. These could carry the R-3S (NATO designation, AA-2 "Atoll") IR AAMs, or the R-3R (AA-2-2 "Advanced Atoll") semi-active radar homing (radar-guided) derivative. The pilot sat on a Mikoyan-Gurevich KM-1 ejection seat that required a minimum speed of 70 knots in order for the parachute to deploy.

On paper, the Flogger was a decent design that, when used in conjunction with the Soviet doctrine of strength in numbers (as opposed to NATO's "quality versus quantity") could offer the VVS and the USSR's allies an effective interceptor capability. But it wasn't the air superiority fighter that the FA had wanted. More worryingly, the Flogger was plagued from the outset by design flaws, poor reliability, and an airframe that was easy to overstress. But the MiG-23 Floggers E and F were *fast*. There was no denying it. The Tumansky R-29-300 (R-29A) motor common to both would churn out 27,500lb of thrust, easily taking the Flogger to its placarded limit of Mach 2.4, or more than 1,500mph. In its early years, the Flogger's parachute had a propensity to deploy spontaneously in flight. While this would be startling, but not necessarily fatal, there were several handling issues with the MiG-23 that had, and continued to, kill its pilots. It did not like to be spun and was averse to the low-speed maneuvering flight that characterized the final stages of BFM – when two evenly pitted adversaries might be out of altitude and airspeed.

At the opposite end of the spectrum, the Flogger was unstable in yaw as it passed through the sound barrier, and then again as it exceeded Mach 2. Even in regular phases of flight – like take-off and landing – it was a handful. Its narrow landing gear would skid and slide on a damp, icy, or wet runway; and since its main landing gear was articulated to absorb the bumps and ruts of an unprepared surface, the jet sat low to the ground where its two intakes could suck up foreign objects.

Corder, the Red Eagles' assistant ops officer, must have known most of, if not all, of this as a result of HAVE PAD and other sources when he volunteered to be the first Red Eagle at Tonopah to fly the MiG-23. McCloud followed suit and became the second to check out in the Flogger, Scott recalls. "It was a new experience and we didn't know too much about the jet; it didn't come with the knowledge that the other countries operating it around the world took for granted," he added. As they learned each day, Corder got to work writing the Flogger's Dash 1.

With experience flying MiGs going back more than seven years, Press was soon selected to transition to the Flogger, becoming the third pilot in the unit to do so. But the Flogger immediately proved problematic: "On about my second or third sortie in it I was up with Dave McCloud flying chase in a T-38. It was basically an aircraft-handling sortie to investigate the envelope. Up at about 20,000ft, I pulled a little too hard on the stick with the wings swept back and the thing went out of control and entered a spin. McCloud was calling: 'You're on fire! Bail out!' I managed to get it out of the spin, but the engine shaft had warped from the motion of the spin." All was not well. The Flogger's engine intakes featured a system of louvers around the compressor section of the R-29A, and these were used to take surplus "bleed" air for use by the Flogger's environmental control system for cooling the avionics and the pilot. "The spin and warping had caused the compressor blades to tear out the louvers, and these had gone into the turbine section, causing turbine blades to break off and fly everywhere. That was the cause of the fire."

By now the fire had gone out, but he had no engine and was faced with either landing the 34,000lb fighter like a glider – known as a "deadstick" landing – or to eject. "I still had enough hydraulic power to get the wings forward, and the gear came down via pneumatics, so I decided to head back towards Tonopah. The thing was coming down like the space shuttle and McCloud kept telling me he didn't think I would be able to make it. I told him I could. I got the gear down and landed 500ft down the runway and rolled to a stop."

Press had inadvertently demonstrated that the Flogger's engine casing was the weak link during out-of-control maneuvers, and while intentionally spinning any of the MiGs was already against the rules, the MiG-23 pilots at Tonopah now understood exactly how dangerous the Flogger could be. It was an incredible baptism of fire, and the incident put Press in the history books as the only Red Eagle to deadstick a Flogger.

"There were other things that we had to find out for ourselves, one of which was structural," adds Scott. "The Flogger was never designed for the sort of high-G flying that we were putting it through, so we developed a modification to reinforce the 'wing carry-through box,' which held the sweeping wings in place. These were 'discovery' problems, the sorts of things that Tom Gibbs was having to deal with on a day-by-day basis as we learned new things about the jet." The addition of the third type of MiG created more pressure for Gibbs' men and complicated the issue of reverse engineering. "But we at least had a pretty good budget to deal with that, probably a little bit more than $1 million," Gibbs estimated.

As 1980 came to a close, 1,015 sorties had been accumulated, accounting for the exposure of the MiGs to some 372 Air Force and Navy pilots. CONSTANT PEG's first full year at Tonopah had been hugely successful, and at one point in 1980 the Red Eagles had flown five sorties a day for two straight weeks, including weekends, says Sheffield.

CHAPTER 6

GOLD WINGS, 1981

SIMULATED FLAMEOUT LANDINGS

For Mike Scott, 1981 started with just a little excitement when he experienced an engine failure in a MiG-21. Incredibly, he managed to deadstick the powerless jet to a successful landing. "I was out over Range 71 on a sortie against a 422nd Test & Evaluation Squadron F-16 from Nellis being flown by Don 'Doc' Kremple. We were on a 1 v 1 scenario and I was on the offensive. I attacked him and as he turned hard into me, and as I slid through his turn circle I got two or three loud bangs – compressor stalls. I pulled the throttle back to clear the stalls, but as I did so I realized that the engine had quit."

It was time for Scott to put to good use the simulated flameout (SFO) landings that all the pilots on the MiG-17 and MiG-21 practiced each time they returned to Tonopah. "I just said, 'OK, I have lost the motor,' and pointed towards Tonopah. This particular MiG-21 was one of the early vintage ones where we didn't really trust the ejection seats, and I was thinking to myself that I didn't have much of an intention of ejecting unless it became clear I wasn't going to make the field. I was going through the restart procedures, but it was becoming clear that it was not going to happen." *

In an incredible act of composure, Scott realized that he needed to get as much information out about what had happened in case he died in the ensuing moments: "I told Doc over the radio everything that I had seen and heard, so it would be recorded on his cockpit video recorder. The MiG-21 was not made to do flameout landings. The Soviet philosophy was that you punched out if you lost your engine. We did it because we had experience in single-engine fighters, and we trained for it by putting out our speed brakes to simulate the drag of the stalled engine, and flying certain parameters. I was now flying these parameters for real, one of which was to maintain at least 250 knots so that the engine would windmill and keep the hydraulics working." This was crucial: the hydraulics drove the MiG's flight control surfaces. Without the hydraulics the surfaces would freeze and cause Scott to lose control.

"The problem was that you couldn't touch down at 250 knots in that airplane. The drag chute was made for a maximum of 190 knots and the brakes weren't strong enough to stop you. As advertised, I popped the chute and it disintegrated or ripped itself out of the housing. That left the rabbit catcher, the netting that would catch the airplane and stop it." Scott duly became the first pilot to test the MiG-21 with the barrier at the end of the runway, thankfully with positive results – "The airplane flew again, I flew again, and we bought a new barrier!"

SOMALIA

In March 1981, and with only two weeks' notice, Press dispatched Scott and Sheffield on TDY to Somalia to fly the MiG-21 with the Somalia Air Corps in what was probably a CIA-led initiative. The two men took with them a single maintainer, Chico Noriega.[20] As Red Eagles ops officer, Press was now responsible for organizing such clandestine missions, and had himself flown MiGs with a third-world country between his return from Iran in 1979 and his arrival to the Aggressors later that year.

Somalia was at the end of a protracted conflict with Ethiopia, a conflict that had started in 1974 and ended with the destruction of the Somali insurgency just prior to the Red Eagles' TDY. Like many underdeveloped nations in Africa and across other continents, Somalia had embraced the Soviet Union briefly in the 1970s, but had then decided it no longer wanted Moscow's help. It ejected all of the Soviet advisors, but only once they had rebuilt the Somalia Air Corps' military infrastructure. This formation had around two squadrons of MiG-21MF Fishbed Js (and MiG-21UM Mongol trainers), as well as some MiG-17s and F-6s (Chinese-built MiG-19s). Only about half of the Fishbeds were airworthy by the early 1980s.

The three Red Eagles were there, Scott said, "to help generate favor with the country's government, but we were also able to determine the standard of their pilots and their training." Presumably, the defeat of the Somali insurgency was enough to prompt the CIA to engage the country's increasingly erratic dictator, Mohammed Siad Barre, in discussions about his future. It was better, they no doubt argued, for Somalia to become a US client state than it was for him to continue down his current path. Military training for his vagabond pilots was presumably just one of the carrots dangled in front of his face. Soon, the United Nations and Western aid agencies would join the chorus, but ultimately, none would be successful.

None of this mattered to Scott or Sheffield, of course. They were there to fly with the Somali pilots. "They weren't very good. We saw the product of the Soviet training system. It was bureaucratic, regimented, and not very effective," Sheffield observed. In contrast to a 1979 visit by representatives of the Red Hats to the Sudanese Air Force, the two Red Eagle pilots wore sanitized flight suits for their 1981 visit; they removed the patches that would indicate the squadron to which they belonged. The Somalis were tacitly led to believe that neither pilot had flown the Fishbed before now, but invariably they were going to wonder how it was that the enigmatic Americans could master the MiG-21 so quickly. Scott was candid about this:

> A part of the Aggressor job was to be an expert in the various Soviet Air Force subjects – tactics, training, "the Man," the aircraft, etc. During my years as an Aggressor, I had certified on all of the academic briefs at one time or another so I was able to converse on many aspects of Soviet Air Force training, including the operation of various MiG aircraft. At that time, I was also maintaining currency as an F-5 Aggressor.
>
> My cover story to the host as to why flying the MiGs came so "easily" simply combined those two aspects of the Aggressors – the knowledge of systems and operating procedures was a result of my academic "expertise" and the ease of flying was due to the similarity of F-5 and MiG-21 flying characteristics. Explaining my ability to taxi competently from the get-go required a different story. With the exception of the T-33, most USAF aircraft of my era had relatively easy-to-use steering technology; however, steering the MiG-17 and MiG-21's air release method was somewhat like the T-33, I was told. Since the MiG and T-33 taxiing required a different sort of hand–foot coordination which, in turn, necessitated a bit of practice before one could satisfactorily master the task of taxiing the aircraft without embarrassment, I simply fabricated an explanation that I had flown the T-33, thus my familiarity with the taxiing issues.

The Somalis checked out both pilots in the two-seat version of the MiG-21MF, known as the Mongol B, to satisfy themselves that the two could be trusted to fly what was a very limited and important national asset. Later the roles reversed, and the Red Eagles showed the Somali pilots how the MiGs should be flown properly. For Sheffield, that process turned out to be a little more exciting than he might have hoped for. On one particular day, he was instructing in a Mongol B from the back seat with the Somali squadron commander in the front:

> He became fixated on the guy we were fighting, which was Mike Scott and another pilot in the back of a similar aircraft. We were just spiraling towards the ground. Our agreed call to end maneuvering was "knock it off," which I said, but he continued spiraling into the ground.
>
> I managed to get his attention somehow, and then for the first time he stopped looking over his shoulder at the other aircraft and realized that we were not only low, but also slow, with probably only 250 knots. He literally buried the stick in my lap and we departed controlled flight. We did a snap roll to the right and were about to spin and crash into the ground. I forced the stick forward and stomped on the left rudder. He was pulling back to start with, but the nose dumping towards the ground scares him even more, so he starts fighting me for control.

Sheffield overpowered the other man and the jet began a gradual recovery. But it had been very, very close: "We came so close to the ground that our jet exhaust blew the straw roof off a hut on the ground. When we got back I literally kissed the ground, I was so fortunate still to be alive."

SEMPER FI

While Sheffield and Scott were busy in Africa, back at Tonopah an unexpected visitor had dropped by. It was Kobe Mayo. Now a lieutenant colonel, he was very pleased with how far the operation had come: "Wow! It was the fantasy come true. I met some of the guys, signed my name in the log and was really impressed by what I saw." Mayo's visit coincided with the arrival of the first ever Marine Corps pilot assigned to the Red Eagles. His name was Maj Lenny Bucko, and he became "Bandit 22."

Bucko had flown F-4Js with the US Marine Corps in Hawaii and Japan, and had also punched out of an F-4 in the Philippines when one of the "spoilers" – the device on the wing that makes it roll – popped up on take-off and became stuck, causing a rapid uncontrolled roll to the right. As he pushed on the left rudder with all his might, the 42,000lb "Rhino" had stopped rolling. He plugged in the afterburners to gain some height, but the F-4 became uncontrollable with the associated increase in speed, as Bucko recounts: "It did a snap roll at about 600ft above the sea. My radar intercept officer, Rob Stockus, initiated ejection and got out at about 600ft and 120 degrees angle of bank. I got out when the airplane was even lower and completely upside down."

The ejection broke several of the vertebrae in Stockus' back, ending his flying career. For Bucko, who walked away unscathed, death had been nanoseconds away. His parachute had not fully inflated when he hit the sea next to, and almost at the same time as, the malfunctioning Phantom. To the pilot of the F-4 taking off behind, it looked like he had ridden the Phantom into the ocean – he had transmitted "Bucko didn't make it out." But he had, and after a few nights in hospital for observation he went out and had "a week's worth of big boy drinks." On his very next flight in the F-4 he had experienced an engine fire on take-off, followed by an interesting single-engine landing.

The perils of tactical fast jet aviation were more than familiar to him, but so too were the perils of everyday life. He had gone to TOPGUN as a student in 1974, and had returned as an IP under less happy circumstances in 1979. He arrived in San Diego just before his eldest daughter, seven-year-old Jaime, died of cancer. She had battled the disease for 2½ years. Just prior to her death, his marriage had broken up. "It was the low point in my life, and the job at Miramar was a saving grace because I could plunge myself into it."

In the intervening years between the two TOPGUN assignments, Bucko had been selected to transition to the F-14, spending four months of training on the Tomcat before the Corps learned they were not going to operate the type after all. With the Tomcat destined only for the Navy, his skills as a fighter pilot were put to use teaching new Marine pilots how to fly the Phantom. He instructed for three years and then joined Marine Air Weapons Tactics Squadron 1 (MAWTS 1), which was the Marine equivalent of an Air Force FWS or Navy TOPGUN. He was based at El Toro, and part of his job at MAWTS 1 was to qualify as an Adversary pilot so that he could teach other Marine Corps units Air Combat Tactics Training. This was a program unique to the Marine Corps and utilized the A-4 Skyhawk, but was similar to the Aggressor road show concept in its purpose.

It was while at MAWTS 1 that he had gone through TOPGUN as a student. On his return to El Toro, which was a mere 100 miles or so from Miramar, Bucko had remained in contact with his instructors at TOPGUN and established a working relationship that would see a flight of four TOPGUN students and IPs fly up to MAWTS 1 each weekend to fight the Adversary A-4s. The IPs had stayed at his house each weekend, and bonds had been formed. Before long, he was invited to join their ranks as a TOPGUN instructor.

At Miramar in 1979, Bucko had become involved in coordinating what the Navy called "overland" ACM week, which involved CONSTANT PEG exposures and usually meant five days of flying out of Nellis. By this point, Bucko had read "everything that I could ever find out about Soviet fighters. I knew how to identify every model and make and version by antennae, intakes, ECM [electronic countermeasures] blisters, etc. When I came to TOPGUN I had several projects and lectures that I was in charge of. I gave a three-hour lecture on the Middle East, Israeli pilot training, and terrorism groups of the Middle East. I also gave a two-hour lecture on Soviet aircraft and how to identify them," he said. "As coordinator for overland ACM week, I set up the week of flying up at Tonopah by getting the class to Las Vegas, getting briefing rooms, organizing range times, setting up the briefings and debriefings, and leading flights onto the ranges and escorting them home." He'd got to fly against the assets, too, testing his skills against the likes of Oberle, Press, and McCloud. All three impressed him immensely.

In mid-1980, Henderson, who had seen what Bucko was doing and liked him, approached the big Marine. "He told me that they were going to make it a requirement that they had a Marine pilot on the squadron. He asked me what I thought the requirements should be. I said 'We need to make sure he has a lot of A-4 time, 1,000 hours of F-5 time, and 1,000 hours of F-4 time.' He said 'You know anyone like that?' and I said, 'Yeah, me!' So I got a set of orders sending me to Nellis." Bucko's Aggressor checkout was a walk in the park. Since he was already so experienced as both a fighter pilot and tactician, it amounted to "a bit of a joke. It was really just about maintaining the cover story." Bucko became the first pilot to hold all three Aggressor and Adversary ratings: Air Force, Marine, and Navy.

Spring and summer of 1981 saw lots of personnel changes in the Red Eagles. In May, LtCol Mike Press left the 4477th TES to take command of the 65th Aggressor Squadron. He was just a year shy of having been flying the MiGs on and off for a decade. His departure followed the earlier arrival in April of Navy pilot Lt Russell M. "Bud" Taylor, "Bandit 23." In July, two more new pilots joined. Maj Monroe Watley came from the F-4 FWS, the 414th TFS, and became "Bandit 24," and a young captain called Mark "Toast" Postai, "Bandit 25," arrived from Nellis' 65th Aggressor Squadron; he had previously flown F-4Ds with the 48th TFW at RAF Lakenheath, England. Like Myers, who maintained alternate currency with his old unit, the F-15 FWS, Watley continued to maintain F-4 currency with the 414th, and subsequently the 422nd Test Squadron. Neither Myers nor Watley flew the F-5E or the T-38 and, considering the extensive knowledge of the Soviet system(s) that they'd acquired in their previous jobs, were provided only some rudimentary "Aggressor" academics. Postai remained attached to the 65th and flew the F-5E/T-38 as his alternate aircraft.

As for Henderson, since his departure the year before, he had remained closely associated with the 4477th TES:

> After I relinquished command of the 4477th TES in June 1980, I worked as the executive officer for the 57th FWW commander, Gen Charles J. Cunningham. After about 60 days I went to work at the Range Group as the Red Czar, where I was in charge of coordinating the Aggressor air threat with the ground threats on the Nellis ranges. I hated the job and was looking for anything else that might be available. When I found out I was going to need heart bypass surgery in June 1981, I convinced my Range Group boss that I would not be coming back after surgery because of medical retirement. In the meantime, I had contacted Col Roger Sorenson [who was about to be the first commander of the 57th FWW Tactics & Test]. He promised me a job as head of special programs, which included foreign material testing, 3-1 tactics manual production [USAF tactics from the MCM 3-1 manual], and range ground threat systems testing. I also was tasked to work a few 4477th TES problems during the first few years. I would do the research and provide a report to the squadron and wing commanders.

GOLD WINGS

Bucko's influence on the Marine Corps' ability to participate in CONSTANT PEG in 1980 had been significant. "I had made it clear to the Navy and to the Air Force that if they had sorties against the MiGs that they had to cancel for whatever reason, the IPs from MAWTS 1 could be overhead at Tonopah with only 30 minutes' notice." The message, loud and clear, resulted in a fair number of ad hoc sorties going to the Marines, who were unencumbered by some of the bureaucracy that the Air Force and Navy units had to deal with when deploying to Nellis, which could result in the cancellation of sorties at the last minute.

Since the Red Eagles had grown from a flight into a squadron, the structure of the flying part of the organization had been broken up into three flights: A, B, and C. C Flight became known as "Gold Flight" because it was where the Navy pilots, who wore wings of gold (as opposed to the Air Force's wings of silver), were assigned and was also referred to as "Sea Flight," for obvious reasons. Since the Marines were administratively part of the Navy, and as they also wore wings of gold, Bucko entered C Flight accordingly, joining Navy pilots Laughter and Shean. Completing the quartet of "squids" was Taylor, who arrived on the flight a month after Bucko.

Now that the mustached Marine was at Tonopah and on the inside, he became the Corps' point of contact and would focus in particular on making sure that the guys at El Toro got as many exposures as possible. He also looked after them in other ways, bringing them life support items: flight suits, jackets, oxygen masks, and in particular anti-G suits that had failed the Air Force's inspections:

> The Marine Corps was at the end of the supply chain, but when I arrived at Nellis the amount of stuff the Air Force signed out to me made me feel like it was Christmas. I had worn the same G-suit in the Marine Corps for about eight years, but up there at Nellis I would get a new one every four months or so. The Air Force test was to inflate the G-suit and leave it overnight. In the morning, if it had deflated at all, it got thrown away. I would take a parachute bag and collect all this stuff that the Air Force wanted to throw away, and I would take it to the bros at El Toro. I was like their pawnbroker.

Although things were well in most respects, Bucko was encountering hostility from certain quarters. One evening at the bar in Nellis, two Aggressor pilots walked up to him and asked him whether he was as tough as the Marines made themselves out to be. They challenged him to a ritualistic contest to determine if he was: all three would consume a raw egg followed by a large shot of alcohol. The mix was almost guaranteed to turn all but the hardest stomach. Simultaneously, all three pilots downed the two ingredients. The two Aggressors almost immediately vomited the egg and alcohol mix back into their glasses. Bucko did not. Instead, he took both of their glasses and drank their vomit. He was not pestered at the bar again.

While such bar talk was intentionally provocative and par for the course for inter-service rivalry and fighter pilot ego, there was genuine hostility towards Bucko, most notably from some of the enlisted men who seemed to be increasingly losing respect for rank or chain of command. One, a big man named Paul, Bucko told me, openly put it about that he didn't know why the squadron needed a Marine pilot, and that actually, he didn't like Marines at all. Bucko became aware of the maintainer's views, as was no doubt intended. One evening he decided enough was enough – the big maintainer was staring at him while he played pool in the well-furnished recreation building behind the MiG hangars. Bucko takes up the story:

Some of these guys had been in black programs for many years, and you didn't really want to fuck with them because the MiGs were theirs. They had been there since they came out of the box, or since they went to some country and stole it or crated it up. You really respected them. I walked up to him and said, "Hey! Paul, let's be friends. OK?" to which he responded, "I dunno." But he put his hand out as if to shake hands. I responded by grabbing his face with both hands and kissing him square on the lips. The crowd went crazy and he was really pissed.

Paul had been put in his place, and the ice had been broken.

Other pressures on Bucko came from within his own mind. The pressure and stress of not wanting to fail weighed heavily on him in those early days. Failure would not only bring the rest of the Corps into disrepute, but it could also end the Marines' involvement in CONSTANT PEG for good. That realization was like a hammer blow, but there was also the simple understanding that these MiGs were nowhere near as safe as even the two Phantoms that had almost killed him on successive sorties in Japan. With absolute candidness, Bucko explained that he was so nervous before his first MiG-21 flight he vomited and urinated nervously. The night before, he'd sat in the corner of the bar at Tonopah going over the sortie with his IP, Myers, but despite Myers' wisdom and calming influence, the Marine was feeling the pressure. He was not alone.

CONSTANT PEG'S FIRST KILLS AND THE GULF OF SIDRA

In August 1981, America deployed two US Navy Carrier Battle Groups (CVBG) – the USS *Forrestal* (CV-59) and the USS *Nimitz* (CVN-68) – to the Mediterranean waters north of Libya. Libya's dictator, Col Muammar al-Gaddafi, had decreed that a stretch of water off the north coast of Libya, the Gulf of Sidra, was sovereign territory. America refused to acknowledge this assertion, insisting that the standard 12-mile territorial limit from a nation's shoreline meant that Gaddafi's "line of death" illegally dissected international waters. The deployment of the two carriers, each stuffed with jet fighters and supporting war planes, was a direct challenge to Gaddafi's authority.

The two carriers began exercises near the Gulf of Sidra on August 18, in response to which the Libyan Arab Republic Air Force (LARAF) forward deployed a squadron of MiG-25 Foxbat, MiG-23 Flogger, and Sukhoi Su-22 "Fitter" interceptors and fighter-bombers closer to the northern shoreline, and thus the US carriers. According to aviation historian Tom Cooper, in an email exchange with the author: "Early that morning, at least three MiG-25s approached the two US CVBGs, but all were escorted away by F-4s of VF-11 and VF-31 from the USS *Forrestal*, and F-14As of VF-41 and VF-84 from the USS *Nimitz*. In an attempt to try and establish the exact position of US carriers slightly better, later that day the LARAF dispatched no fewer than 35 pairs of MiG-23s, MiG-25s, Su-22s, and Mirage F1s into the area. These were all, one after the other, successively intercepted by a total of seven pairs of Tomcats and Phantoms."

The situation changed early the next morning, when a Grumman E-2C Hawkeye, with its far-reaching search radar, detected two Libyan fighters taking off. Two VF-41 "Black Aces" Tomcats were launched in response. The two pilots and two RIOs (Radar Intercept Officers), Lt Dave Venlet and Cdr Henry Kleeman (the commander of VF-41) in F-14 "Fast Eagle 107," and Lt Larry "Music" Muczynski and Lt James Anderson in F-14 "Fast Eagle 102," had all been through CONSTANT PEG.

As the two F-14s and the Libyan Su-22 Fitters passed by each other, the lead Libyan apparently fired a K-13M missile at one of the Tomcats. With Buck Fever something that both the Navy pilots and RIOs had experienced out over the Nellis ranges at the hands of the Red Eagles, all four men knew that it could kill them if they let it. The two pilots reacted instinctively, turning the Tomcats hard to position for AIM-9L Sidewinder shots from the optimum position behind the Fitters. Fast Eagle 102 downed the lead Fitter, followed seconds later by his wingman at the hands of Fast Eagle 107. CONSTANT PEG had just achieved its first kills.

HIRING OF A NEW SECRETARY AND THE ADMIRAL

Like any organization, the Red Eagles needed administrative support. For many years, that came from the unit's secretary, Eunice Warren. Warren was hired by Henderson in the aftermath of Peck's sudden departure. Henderson explained:

> With his sudden departure, not surprisingly, Gail left me with many incomplete tasks and issues, one of which was hiring a new secretary to replace the one who had just quit. The maintenance guys (and pilots) referred to the outgoing secretary as "Broom Hilda." Needless to say, she was not of their blood and she could not wait to get away from that weird group of individuals with the super-secret mission. And the squadron guys were equally happy to see her go.

The Nellis Red Eagle operations were conducted out of a white double-wide trailer in the parking lot south of the Fighter Weapons School. There simply was no privacy. The commander's office was a 10ft x 10ft room with an accordion door that would not even latch. As I interviewed new secretary candidates, everyone in the squadron could and did walk by to "check them out." They would individually give me a secret ballot vote with a thumbs up or thumbs down. I always had to make sure the new candidate was sitting in a chair where she could not see the men walking by in the hallway. I also had to work very hard to keep my sober game face on during the interview.

After about ten candidate interviews, in walks Eunice Warren. Eunice had just recently married Sgt David Warren, a maintenance technician on the USAF Thunderbirds. They had met when the team visited Wright-Patterson AFB. Eunice was a GS-11 executive secretary for one of the directorates in Air Force Systems Command. She moved to Nellis after marrying David and was looking for work as a secretary. She quickly found out that a senior GS-11 position was out of the question, and the best she could do was a GS-4. When she showed up at our trailers she was dressed very smartly, very business-like. She was very beautiful and had a very ample bosom. The commotion outside my office during the interview was exceedingly distracting. At least 50 men passed my door and there were only 30 men in total in my squadron. There were a lot of second and third looks and a unanimous thumbs up. She was hired.

Our daily routine was to gather at the trailers early in the morning, generally before dawn, sort out the day's schedule and figure out the transportation to Tonopah. Then we were off to Tonopah and a long day. Only one or two people were left behind – the secretary, an admin troop, and perhaps a supply guy. For the first six weeks, Eunice came to work dressed just as she had for the interview – a nice business suit. But she soon found out she was all dressed up with nowhere to go. At Wright-Patterson, she got a lot of coffee for visiting generals, flashed a pretty smile, and did a little typing. In the trailers she did a lot of typing and answering the phone, no coffee, no visiting generals, no need for a pretty smile.

There was a marked difference between working for a three-star general and dealing with a bunch of crusty old sergeants and bone-tired fighter pilots at the end of a long day. Soon Eunice was wearing blue jeans and a bulky sweater. The bulky sweater at least diverted the more obvious stares. She had a sweet personality and we almost ruined her with the coarse treatment. She somehow kept her sense of humor and figured out a way to give at least as much as she got. The result endeared her to all squadron members.

Underpinning the Red Eagles' operations was Maj John "Admiral" Nelson, a non-rated officer with a history of assignments in maintenance administration.

He'd progressed into procurement – "everybody needs to buy stuff, and I love to spend money" – and then logistics, when one day he was asked if he would like a special duty assignment. "I came down to Nellis in May 1980, interviewed with Obi, and got the job. I think Obi was after my ability to do what needed to be done without giving anything away or taking no for an answer." Nelson would spend the next five years with the Red Eagles, creating annual assessments of the squadron budget and equipment the unit needed. He would take this to the Air Staff for approval. Some of the money went on paying the 99th Range Group, which was based at Nellis and owned the ranges. Some of it went on buildings and facilities for the soon-to-arrive stealth fighter: "These guys would just turn up in my office and tell me what they needed," Nelson divulged: "we built it with our money and they reimbursed us later."

Nelson took care of all the unit's travel, procurement, and finances: "There was a lot to do, and things to buy. But you could take [invoices for] parts a, b, and c and put them together to learn about what we were doing." Nelson had quickly realized that having to go through the procurement office at the 57th FWW created a paper trail that led to the 4477th TES and then on to Tonopah. "That was not what you wanted. So, one day we had the TAC Logistics two-star general visit us. I explained it to him and he told me he would take care of it. Within a month I had a contracting warrant that allowed me to spend $100,000 on any single purchase without any questions asked. I went over to procurement and told them I wanted one hundred of these purchase orders. 'You can't have that!' they said. But they called a colonel in the TAC HQ and he ordered them to comply."

Nelson typed up every single purchase order (PO) himself. Nobody saw any of them. He could now place a single order for $100,000, and issue a PO number to the vendor, who would contact the 57th FWW finance office for payment. The 57th FWW had no idea what it was paying for, and the vendor had no idea who he was selling his products to. Secrecy was therefore maintained. Anything costing more than $100,000 would be purchased by a special projects division of the Air Force's Logistics Command, based in Utah.

Nelson's system worked well until an ambitious captain on the Air Force's Inspectorate General (IG) team discovered that the 57th FWW was missing "at least five hundred" PO numbers, said Nelson. "He said, 'Where are they?' They said, 'Admiral has them.' 'Well, where's Admiral and what is he doing with them?' he replied. 'He's over there in a trailer, and we have no idea,' they said. We briefed the Deputy of Procurement [at the 57th FWW], Pat Gill, in on the program, but she had played dumb with this captain. He came over to the office and told me he wanted to see the POs."

What followed was a debate about whether the IG had a need to know. Eventually, Nelson had had enough. "You don't have a need to know. You had better call your team leader and ask him. The captain said, 'I can't call him, he's with Gen Gregory.' I said, 'OK. That's even easier.' I picked up the phone and called Gen Gregory's office. I passed the phone to the captain. He said, 'Sir, I am over here at this office. This major will not let me see them … Yes, sir … No, sir … Yes, sir!' and that was it. He said, 'OK. I am out of here,' and he left just like that. We never saw him again and no one else ever came back."

To enable a degree of oversight, Nelson would occasionally invite Gill to review his POs, but the reality was that his position relied on his absolute integrity: "I was not about to cheat the government, and I wasn't going to let a businessman do it, either." The POs were kept for three years and were then buried by Silver Bow Lake at Tonopah, Nelson revealed. So, why not shred them? "Because we didn't have a shredder!"

Other administrative tasks included applying the Air Force's STAN/EVAL procedures to the squadron, a job for Scott and McCloud. Scott explained: "I did everything on a grease board – the guys' names were on there with a list of who needed what check rides and when. The STAN/EVAL guy for the F-5 and T-38 at TAC was an ex-Aggressor called Mike Tobin, and he knew about our MiG operations. He would come out and inspect us, and while he would sometimes tell us we were a little behind the rest of the Air Force with our documented training reports, the other side of the coin was that we couldn't send our documentation anywhere because of the classified nature of the program."

Henderson explained further:

> Like the rest of the Air Force, the pilots accomplished STAN/EVAL and instrument checks in their non-MiG aircraft; and they were administered on an annual basis by TAC-certified check pilots. The MiGs were a different story. During initial checkout, the grade slips were filled out by the instructor for each ride. Since the MiGs were only flown in day VFR [visual flight rules] weather, a STAN/EVAL program would have very limited things to "eval." The STAN/EVAL pilot could fly chase in the traffic pattern, maybe circle the fight during a 1 v 1 engagement, or be the wingman/chase during a two-ship engagement. Although none of these had very practical meanings, records were maintained in proper format – Form 8 – and included the in-house portion of the pilot's official USAF STAN/EVAL "847" record [the MiGs were coded as YF-110, YF-113, or YF-114, as applicable.] The pilot records and the program, which was TAC/DO approved, were inspected on an annual basis by Tobin.

Tragically, on September 8, 1981, "DL" Smith, by now a lieutenant colonel, was killed in a T-38A crash. Following the successful creation of CONSTANT PEG, Smith had left his black world assignment at TAC HQ in 1979 to become the commander and flight leader of the Air Force's aerobatic demonstration team, the Thunderbirds, for the 1980 display season.[21] While this post usually lasted only one year, TAC's commander, Creech, had personally requested that Smith stay in the role for the 1981 season, too. Smith agreed, but it was following a four-day weekend of displaying in Cleveland toward the end of the season that Smith perished. Sheffield was assigned to take part as the pilot member of the ensuing mishap board.

Taking off on the Tuesday morning with his crew chief in the back seat of the Talon, Smith had rotated smoothly off the runway as the white jet reached flying speed, and immediately ingested a flock of seagulls that had congregated near Lake Erie. Power loss had been instant, and ejection was the only choice. "Smith's backseater got a good 'chute, but 'DL' did not," Sheffield relayed. A lanyard to the parachute on Smith's back had been accidentally released during the ejection sequence, and that meant that his parachute had failed to deploy. Smith had been killed by "the oddest of chances of the ejection sequence going wrong in the oddest of ways."

On September 20, Sheffield was involved in an altercation in a Las Vegas casino. He was struck by a blow that knocked him to the floor, and as he landed he banged his head. The resultant trauma to his brain induced a coma. He was taken to hospital where he remained comatose for a period of several weeks. Eventually he started to return to consciousness, but in his dazed and confused state he started talking about the MiGs. This was clearly not deliberate on his part, but it was an alarming breach in security. Until he finally regained full control over his senses, one of the Red Eagles remained with him around the clock in a bid to keep him from revealing the secret that was CONSTANT PEG. When he did talk about the MiGs when doctors, nurses, and anyone else were within earshot, the Red Eagle pilot with him would smile and explain that Sheffield's delirium must have been worse than anyone had previously thought.

Sheffield's injury left him grounded for the remainder of his time with the Red Eagles (the Air Force categorizes such groundings as DNIF – Duties Not Including Flying), but as he convalesced he knew that his time in the active duty Air Force was over. "Gail Peck is one of the finest men I have ever known, and the way the Air Force treated him was just shitty. Having seen that, and then seen how they treated Richie Graham [the Aggressor commander], one of the best commanders I ever worked for, helped me make up my mind. It was a 'one mistake Air Force.' You could be the man who walked on water, but if someone else under your command screwed up indirectly, the first response of the senior Air Force leaders was to fire the commander." In the case of Graham, one of Sheffield's friends going through the Aggressor checkout had put an F-5E into an unrecoverable spin on his first flight with the squadron, having flown in a manner that he had been specifically instructed not to by the upgrading Aggressor IP. "He ejected, and Rich Graham was summarily fired." Sheffield handed in his papers to leave the Air Force.

While Sheffield recovered through September and the Air Force started working out a leaving date for him, his best friend, McCloud, was making preparations to leave the squadron for a three-year tour as Actions Officer and Program Element Monitor in the enigmatically titled "Special Projects Office" at the Pentagon. In fact, Sheffield called McCloud "Mr Black," on account of the fact that he was involved in many of the 4477th TES's most secret ancillary duties.

McCloud had been Sheffield's best man at his wedding and the two had first met when they were assigned to fly the F-4 at Kadena Air Base, on the Japanese island of Okinawa. When Sheffield arrived at Nellis to become an IP with the Aggressors in 1979, McCloud had conducted some of his checkout rides: "There is a basic maneuver called the high Yo-Yo, and most people would say that if your opponent is really committed to beat you, it's a pretty worthless maneuver: he's turning hard to get inside you, and you're pulling the nose up and then pirouetting to come back down. Well, they keep their lift vector on you throughout, and that negates the maneuver ... usually. He [McCloud] was the first guy that I ever saw execute a high Yo-Yo that actually worked. He called the shot and got the kill."

More than just a great stick, "he was most of all a great human being. If you met him you could spend an hour talking to him, but when you walked away you would know nothing about him and he would know everything about you. If you knew anything special, he would want to know everything about it. It wasn't manipulative; he genuinely wanted to know everything. If he met someone who had some knowledge, he was like a sponge sucking it out of them." Many others had similar levels of respect for McCloud, including Oberle: "He was on the fast track. He was a great officer who was level-headed and strong, and a great pilot who could tell you how to fly."

THE MU-2S

On October 3, the Red Eagles returned their leased Cessna 404 aircraft and replaced them with Mitsubishi MU-2s, but only after an extensive selection process and some legal wranglings that caused Nelson and Gibbs some headaches. Some of the pilots had taken to allowing their passengers to fly the Cessnas from the right seat, and competitions between the pilots had even begun to see who could land furthest down the runway in order to reduce the amount of taxi time required to get back to the parking apron. With such practices continuing in the Mitsubishis, Myers, the assistant ops officer at the time, cautioned his fellow Red Eagles not to become too casual, and to recognize the dangers of being rated in so many different aircraft:

> I would brief guys that when you were flying a MiG you had your hands on a national asset. Furthermore, you are a little bit of a test pilot, because these things are less common than an F-15 or F-16, and if anything out of the ordinary happens you need to get it back on the ground. You don't push things like a warning light just to get another engagement in. Likewise, when you flew the Mitsubishis, you were an airline pilot. You weren't there to dogfight; you flew shallow turns and were trying to think about the comfort of the guys in the back of the airplane. Lastly, when the guys flew as Aggressors, they were there as instructors, and when I flew against the F-15 in another F-15, I was there as an F-15 instructor pilot. I wanted to ensure that the guys did not transition between these three different hats while they were flying the wrong aircraft.

Myers and Corder had also been responsible for the acquisition of two $4,000 fax machines to allow the flying schedule to be transmitted between Tonopah and Nellis each morning. It was an expense for which Nelson was happy to shell out.

Later that month, according to Henderson, "a company called Information Management Inc. (IMI) submitted an unsolicited proposal to take over all [Red Eagles] maintenance functions with contractors. It was my job to conduct an evaluation of that proposal." He did so, forwarding the recommendation that the Air Force consider the proposal, but it would be more than six months before they would reply. Incredibly, IMI was owned by Gerry Huff, the Red Eagle who had so vehemently disassociated himself from the Air Force following Peck's firing.

For Gibbs the year had gone well, and he was pleased with the level of support he had received from both Gen Kelley and Gen Cunningham.

"Cunningham used to fly the F-5, land at Tonopah and come in and say 'Hi!' to everybody. In between my other responsibilities, I was still getting to fly as much as I wanted, 15 to 20 sorties per month, or thereabouts."

The year had had its moments for Gibbs too, Nelson revealed:

I brought a newspaper to Tonopah each morning. On one morning I arrived to find a visiting general standing alone in the squadron.[22] We started talking and he then asked me where the head was. I showed him and he grabbed the newspaper and walked off. A few minutes later, Tom Gibbs came in. His usual routine was to grab the paper and walk off into the head. He asks, "Where's the paper?" and I told him it was in the head. He went back to his office, did a couple of jobs and then walked to the head a few minutes later. He banged on the door, "Hey! You! Hurry up. I gotta go!" About this time, Dave Stringer, the maintenance officer, walks in. Tom again bangs on the door, and this time a voice calls back, "OK!" and the toilet flushes. The three of us are standing there at the coffee bar when the general comes out of the head. Tom immediately says, "OK, Stringer, you had to go so bad, get your butt in there!" It was one of those times that Tom was really quick on his feet.

As 1981 slipped into the past, the Red Eagles were operating three MiG-17F Fresco Cs, six MiG-21F-13 Fishbed C/Es, and one MiG-23BN Flogger F. In total, they had flown 1,340 sorties, providing 462 exposures to fellow American fighter aircrews.

PART 3

EXPANDED EXPOSURES AND RED FLAG, 1982–85

CHAPTER 7

THE FATALISTS, 1982

1982 was the start of what would prove to be a tumultuous time in the history of the 4477th TES. The year started well, with the completion of Phase II construction at TTR. The new hangar, "Building 188," and the new apron and taxiways were complemented by JP-4 fuel tanks, a warehouse, and other support utilities that signaled the transition of Tonopah from a bare base to a standard Air Force base.

The Air Force was preparing Tonopah for the arrival of the F-117, which by that time had been undergoing full-scale development testing at Groom Lake for 31 months. It had matured extensively since the days of the HAVE BLUE technology demonstrator that Peck had been briefed in on in 1977, and was now 40 percent larger and somewhat different in configuration, albeit still highly faceted and distinctly at odds with other aircraft designs. More importantly, Lockheed was shortly due to deliver the Air Force its first operational standard F-117. Additional testing would follow, but the F-117's arrival at TTR was drawing ever closer, and that was an event that was going to have a massive impact on the Red Eagles.

On January 13, 1982, Scott experienced his second serious IFE in a MiG. Scott had first flown the MiG-21, because it was more numerous than the MiG-17, when he joined the Red Eagles, but he had now added the MiG-17 to his logbook. At any one time he was only "officially" qualified in one of the types, but he transferred between both MiGs on two separate occasions. In reality, he was qualified to fly both, but never flew them concurrently. In fact, he had qualified as an IP and FCF pilot for both types, and it was on one such ride that his second IFE occurred:

We had just rebuilt a MiG-17 that we had acquired and I was in the process of doing the FCFs for it. There were certain things that you checked on the first day that the maintainers would fix for the second day. On this particular second day, I took off and the generator failed. The battery in the jet was only good for five or six minutes when the generator was not providing electricity. [The snag was that there was no warning light in the cockpit to show that the generator had failed. Scott had identified the problem only as a result of keeping a careful eye on the small battery gauge in the cockpit.] By the time you recognized that generator had failed, especially if you were in the throes of a mission, there was not going to be much time left on the battery. We preached for this emergency: "Don't use the radios, because that's the major battery drainer." Well, by the time I caught it, it was at a stage where if I used the radio at all, it was going to completely deplete the battery. I was left with a choice to make: I could use the radio and tell someone what had happened, or I could keep quiet and no one would ever know what had happened if the sortie ended in tragedy. As it turned out, it did not matter. By the time my mind had gone through that thought process, the battery was dead. You could tell that because the gas gauge didn't work any more.

Scott was not only unable to communicate with anyone, but he now had no idea how much gas he had remaining:

Even the back-up gas gauge, a little red light that came on when your fuel level reached a predetermined level, was reliant on the battery. My T-38 chase pilot, Karl Whittenberg, pulled up alongside, but the hand signals that we used to communicate were hard for him to interpret because the canopy in the MiG-17 was so small. For electrical problems you would put your fist to the top of the canopy and wait for the chase pilot to acknowledge. When he did, you then showed him one finger for hydraulics, two for electrics, three for fuel, four for oxygen, or five for engine. The canopy was so low that he never saw the fist, he just saw the two fingers I was holding up and thought that I wanted him to come up on channel two on the radio.

When I tried to put the gear handle down, nothing happened. The MiG-17 was dependent on electrics for a lot of things, including the gear, but it had mechanical back-ups for many of those. The mechanical back-up for the gear was to pull two handles attached to cables that were attached to the gear door locks. You pulled the handles, the gear doors unlocked, and the weight of the gear doors would make them extend. The left handle did the nose gear and the left main gear. The right handle just did the right main. The left handle worked fine, but when I pulled the right nothing happened; the cable had not been adjusted properly during the rebuild and the gear never came down. I didn't have time to jack around, so I was trying to shake the airplane to get the gear to come down.

No amount of abrupt maneuvering would budge the right gear, and Scott was now burning even more gas as the drag from his left main and nose gears forced the use of additional throttle to keep the jet in the air. Not knowing how much gas he had remaining, "I just made the decision to come on in and land it on the left main gear. I flew it on the runway for as long as I could until the right wing dipped, touched the runway and then dragged me off onto the desert floor. I got out to be greeted by the maintenance guys. They jacked it up, towed it back, and all they had to do was put on a new flap. I flew that airplane the very next day. It was a tribute to the MiG-17 – it was a very strong airplane."

Scott had twice now recovered a national asset that he could have abandoned without fear of repercussions. While his earlier MiG-21 deadstick landing had never been formally written up, Gibbs had this mishap documented and forwarded, along with an overview of the earlier MiG-21 incident, to TAC. Scott was recommended for a DFC, but since the write-up had been stripped of much of its classified information by the time it reached the board that convened annually to approve such requests, it was denied.

Five days later, the Thunderbirds suffered the worst mishap in the team's history when, on January 18 during pre-season training at Indian Springs, Thunderbirds commander Maj Bill Lowry flew his formation of four T-38s into the ground. The mishap became known as the "Diamond Crash," and it took the lives of Lowry and captains Willie Mays, Pete Peterson, and Mark Melancon. "I was at Tonopah the day of the Diamond Crash," Bucko told me. "As a result of that they took the seats out of our airplanes [MU-2s] and Chuck Corder and Buffalo Myers were sent to Indian Springs to pick up the body bags. It was a black day."

OVERHEAD TIMES

The overhead times of Russia's satellites were tracked daily by the Air Force's Space Command, and these governed the 4477th TEF's daily schedule. The Air Force believed that the Soviet cameras were not good enough to image an aircraft in flight, but any static or slow object on the ground was vulnerable to being photographed. As such, during the 22-minute window that constituted the overhead time, the MiGs had to be inside the hangar or airborne.

The Soviet satellites had always posed a problem, but the Air Force had done its best to mitigate the threat they posed to the secret: in June 1979, the month before the MiGs were flown into Tonopah, it had conducted a "reverse cover operation," as Henderson recalled. "This involved flying in a number of odd-looking aircraft, including the F-104, F-86, A-10, and F-14. The intent was to confuse the Soviet satellites – give them a real good look so if they later caught us in the open but only got a grainy low angle shot, they might automatically assume it was an F-104 and not a MiG-21."

The satellite overheads were usually simple enough to plan for, but emergencies sometimes put a spanner in the works. One such minor emergency was a brake failure that Sheffield suffered while taxiing his MiG-21 at the end of a sortie:

> They were getting a bunch of us down at the same time because there was a satellite about to come overhead. One of the things you were supposed to do was turn base leg of the landing and call, "Three green, and air check," which meant you had looked at your undercarriage indicators to show the gear was down, and that you had checked the air gauge so that you knew you would have brakes and steering capability. I remember well that I checked the gear and it was good.
>
> We landed to the north end, away from the hangar. I pulled into the taxi way and stopped next to a fire truck while two other guys landed and taxiied in behind me. We then got radio clearance to taxi back to the hangar. I released the brakes and as I did so I tried to steer but nothing happened. A leak had developed while I was sitting there waiting for the other two.

Sheffield's Fishbed ran straight into the fire truck: "It happened so fast that I didn't have time to get scared, but the boys in the fire truck were bailing out of that thing! The nose of the aircraft went past the front of the truck, and the right wing caught the truck, spinning the aircraft around. One minute I was looking at them from the left side of the truck, the next I was looking at them from the right side." Good fortune meant that no one was hurt and that the aircraft was soon returned to flight, and Sheffield himself was exonerated when tests showed that his Fishbed's air system leaked so long as the brake lever was depressed. By sitting there awaiting the arrival of the other two MiGs, the jet had stealthily exhausted its supply of pressurized air. As for the satellite coverage, Sheffield said, "I suspect we got our picture taken that day. We didn't get the MiG into the hangar in time."

In March 1982, Sheffield finally left the Air Force and the Red Eagles. Having logged 231 sorties, he ranked as the second most experienced MiG-21 pilot in the squadron's history at that time, second only to Scott. Originally destined to go and fly F-4s with the Louisiana Air National Guard, he instead joined the petroleum giant Shell. The month before, Air Force captain James W. "Wiley" Green, "Bandit 26," and James "Thug" Matheny, "Bandit 27," had joined the squadron and qualified to fly the assets. They were joined in April by Capt Larry "Shy" Shervanick, "Bandit 28," and Navy pilot John "Black" Nathman, "Bandit 29."

FRESH BLOOD

Matheny had left school at 16 years of age, and started his working life as an auto mechanic. By the time he was 17, he had already borrowed enough money to open his own shop. Looking for something more challenging, he'd taken a correspondence course on jet engines before the realization that he might be able to fly for a living dawned on him. He sold his business and went to the Reserve Officer Training College (ROTC) program at his local college in northern Ohio, and had maxed the academic tests to earn a flight in a Toledo Air National Guard F-100. He'd been violently airsick – an issue that would plague him throughout flight training – but he had been bitten by the flying bug. Auto mechanic he may have been, but he was wickedly smart with it.

His talent wasn't confined to the classroom, either. He was approaching 27 years old when he graduated top of his pilot training class in 1975 and went to F-4s. He was clearly a gifted aviator and became the first lieutenant IP in his F-4 squadron in Alaska between 1976 and 1979. Flying alert in Alaska had seen him intercept his fair share of the lumbering Tupolev Tu-95 "Bear" and Tu-16 "Badger" bomber planes sent to test ADC's response times, and Ilyushin Il-14 "Crate" recce planes sent to chart ice flows. These intercepts had not always been friendly: "The Crates would sometimes turn into you as you sat there all jacked up in the F-4 with no airspeed, no maneuverability and all kinds of angle of attack just trying to fly formation with them." When they did this, the Phantoms would accelerate away and then wheel around in afterburner to buzz the Russian crew at high speed. "We'd buzz them close enough that they were in our jet wash. We made it clear to them that we didn't like it when they did that." Matheny's mean look had resulted in his call sign "Thug," but in the air he treated his opponents with a great deal more refinement. He'd become an Aggressor in 1979 and had shone in the role, resulting in his selection for the Red Eagles.

Shervanick, who had attended the second ever Red Flag in 1975 and been exposed to HAVE FERRY, had had no trouble at all working out that he wanted to be a pilot in the Air Force. As a teenager he'd flown a small Piper aeroplane and instantly recognized that this was what he had been born to do. With the Vietnam War ongoing, he'd joined the Air Force straight out of college. Of 68 student pilots in his UPT (Undergraduate Pilot Training) class, Shervanick finished first. "You got your pick of airplanes for coming first, and I picked the F-4. I had done pretty well at the F-4 RTU (Replacement Training Unit) in 1973, and on graduation day the squadron commander asked me where I was going. At that time I was going to go to a unit at Moody, which had an air-to-ground commitment. He said, 'Why don't you go and fly air-to-air? You're good enough to do that.'" He agreed and went instead to the new F-4E at Seymour Johnson AFB.

At Seymour he'd flown under the guidance of a good number of Vietnam vets, and had impressed them enough to be promoted to a flight lead while he was still a lieutenant. A year flying the F-4E in the air-to-air role at Osan AB, Korea, had followed in 1976, and by the time he was done he had already been earmarked for the Aggressors. He'd spent four months qualifying with the 64th FWS before heading out to the Philippines to join the 26th TFTS in January 1978. Prior to leaving for the Philippines, he had once again been invited up range to Groom Lake, and this time had been exposed to both a Fresco and a Fishbed courtesy of the 4477th TEF.

Shervanick stayed at Clark for two years, flying both the T-38 and the F-5, and then returned to Nellis in January 1980 to continue his stint as an Aggressor with the 64th FWS. Here he became an IP teaching the Aggressor Tactics Instructor Course (ATIC), teaching other Aggressors who were bound for any of the other three Aggressor squadrons. Since he had twice before been to Groom Lake to see the MiGs, and was aware of HAVE IDEA from his time in the Aggressors, he was keen to be part of the team. "I let it be known that I was interested in flying the assets," he admitted. Word got around and as his tour with the 64th FWS approached completion, he was quietly tapped on the shoulder.

Nathman, like several of the Navy pilots before him, enjoyed a background that included being a TOPGUN IP and a test pilot graduate. He had attended the Air Force's test pilot school in 1976, graduating with distinction. With such a broad range of tactical and test flying experiences under his belt, he was not easily impressed. During his Aggressor checkout, he recalled that he spent quite a bit of time teaching the Aggressor IPs checking him out how to do things: "That's not to brag, but I had experience in several operational fighter squadrons and had much more air-to-air experience than these guys. I was at a much more advanced stage than their initial training for me was at." Once he got to Tonopah, however, it soon became apparent to him that his fellow pilots in the Red Eagles were the cream of the crop: "The stick-and-rudder skills in that squadron were immense. Up at Tonopah, the talent level was pretty much the same."

POSTAI'S FLAMEOUT

On April 8, 1982, Postai had an engine flameout on take-off as he crossed the threshold of the Tonopah runway in his MiG-17. Unwilling to take his chances with the ejection seat, he rode the powerless "tractor" as it bumped and bounced along the desert floor. Scott had since requalified in the MiG-17 and was Postai's instructor pilot. He and Postai were the only Air Force Fresco pilots and, since the investigation was to be conducted by the USAF, Scott was assigned as the investigating pilot officer of the mishap board that looked into the incident, and reported:

> The MiG-17's engine casing had cracked into the turbine on take-off. The turbine had spat some blades, cut some fuel lines, and set the motor on fire. The landing was initially successful, but before he could bring the MiG to a stop, he encountered an arroyo, a natural, ditch-like desert characteristic formed from water runoff, and he tried to "leap" it using the residual energy of his rollout. Although he cleared the deepest portion of the arroyo, his effort was unsuccessful in that the aircraft nosed into the far side. That impact caused one of the gun barrels located on the right forward underbelly to be pushed back into the fuel tanks. Then the fuel tank caught on fire and the aircraft was destroyed. During that early period of the program, our aircraft were always launched with a chase airplane to ensure everything was kosher after take-off – all gear up, no leaks, etc. On that occasion, Jim "Wiley" Green was the T-38 chase pilot who witnessed the entire sequence.
>
> The Red Eagle firemen and maintenance folks, led by Bobby Ellis, raced through the desert and reached the aircraft within minutes of the incident. When they arrived, the aft portion of the aircraft was burning and the entire aircraft was engulfed in the resultant smoke. Because of the smoke, the rescuers could not determine if Mark had escaped from the cockpit and Bobby Ellis, despite the fire, approached the plane and reached through the smoke only to find that the canopy was open and Mark was gone. At about that time, Mark gained their attention by waving and yelling from a vantage point about 100 yards away. Although he had hit his head and was not sure if he'd been knocked unconscious, he quickly regained his senses and egressed prior to the arrival of the rescuers. In their single-mindedness towards rescuing him from the burning MiG, they had not seen him off in the distance until he managed to gain their attention.

All this had been apparent to Matheny: "Chuck Corder and I launched in an MU-2 immediately after Toast went in. Circling the site, we saw him standing away from the aircraft waving his arms to let us know he was OK." Soon after the mishap, Postai told his friend from pilot training, Capt Doug Dildy, who had been read into CONSTANT PEG when his F-15 squadron visited Nellis, that as he stepped clear of the silver MiG its ejection seat fired all by itself and flames engulfed the fuselage. Matheny confirmed this: "After Mark had got out, the seat had fired. It had popped up just high enough to clear the cockpit frame, and then it had toppled over. Such was the condition of those seats." That evening the alcohol flowed freely. Secretly, the incident had shaken Postai, and though no one would ever admit it, it had given them all a reminder of their mortality.

Postai's deadstick landing onto the desert floor was the final straw for TAC. The incident resulted in the grounding of the MiG-17 indefinitely and with immediate effect. "The fact was that it was no longer a viable threat, and let's be honest, flying the thing was just a little bit dangerous," Henderson smiled. Scott concurred, saying, "When coupling the potential of encountering a MiG-17 in any conflict with the cost – safety and monetary – of maintaining them, it was decided that a more appropriate course of action was to concentrate on the MiG-21 and the emerging MiG-23 portions of the program." The irony was that spares for the Fresco continued to be available in great quantities. Had the VK-1F motor been more reliable the little jet could have continued to have been flown for quite some time.

FLOGGER FLIGHT

McCloud's departure late the year before had left Corder as the only Air Force pilot now flying the MiG-23. In fact, it was largely down to C Flight to operate the type, since by this time Corder and McCloud had converted Laughter and Shean to the Flogger, and Shean was now in the process of getting Bucko and Taylor type rated on it. The academics consisted of reading a handful of notes and talking to the maintainers, Bucko remembered: "The Flogger was like a graduation present for having mastered the MiG-21, although none of us wanted to fly it!"

The Navy pilots' familiarity with variable geometry wings may have been one of the reasons why they now formed the bulk of the Flogger cadre. Bucko explained both systems:

The F-14 allows you to put the wing sweep in "Auto": a computer gives you optimum wing sweep versus Mach, altitude, and all those things that are critical to safe flight. "Manual" would be used in certain situations; coming into the pitch you would put the wings manually at 45 degrees and fly at 350–400 knots to look good. As you break to fly to the downwind position you hit the wing control to Auto and the wings would go to the optimum position for the required airspeed. As you slowed down, the wings would automatically move to 16 degrees for the landing. The MiG-23 had a completely manual wing sweep control that required you to read a gauge that showed optimum wing position for the surrounding conditions, but you had to manually put the wings at that position to safely fly the airplane.

Flying the Flogger for the first time had elicited the same physical response in Bucko as had the Fishbed; he vomited once again before the sortie. The increased risks aside, the problem C Flight had with the Flogger was its lack of serviceability and reliability. "Whenever it experienced a hitch," Bucko explained, "we would end up grounded for a couple of weeks while they fixed it. In particular, the 23's motor was vibrating and so the blades on the fan were coming loose, plus we were having fuel problems. We would say to the Air Force guys, 'Hey, we're getting the short end of the stick here. While we are grounded and pulling runway duty, you're doing all the flying.'"

The problem lay in part with the fact that the Red Eagles now had too few MiG-21s (only six) and an excess of pilots. While Shean had been in the process of checking Bucko out in the MiG-17 earlier in the year, Postai's deadstick and the consequent grounding of the Fresco fleet meant that there was nothing else for the men with gold wings on their chests to fly.

But there were other factors that complicated matters. Senior pilots from other units (i.e. officers not assigned to the Red Eagles) would frequently visit Tonopah to fly the MiGs, Bucko said. "Lou Hoight, the TOPGUN commander and the pilot who was flying against Hugh Brown when he was killed, would turn up and fly the MiG-21 from time to time. It was frustrating to see because we flew hardly ever over a period of six months. These guys were coming in and flying the MiG-21 when I was stuck on the ground." Still, the flying had been great when Bucko arrived. "When I first got there, we were flying full-blown ACM in the MiG-17 and MiG-21. We fought to the death."

FLYING THE MIG-21

Much like the MiG-17, the Red Eagle pilots had found the Fishbed to be a real joy to fly. It was considered safer to fly than both the MiG-17 and the MiG-23. The MiG-21 had entered service in 1959, earning the NATO call sign

"Fishbed," and was a result of the lessons learned by Russian advisors during the Korean War. It was built as a Mach 2, lightweight fighter. What resulted was a design made mostly of aluminum alloy that boasted a slender fuselage with a circular intake in the nose. Inside the intake, a cone governed the airflow to the compressor blades of the Tumansky R-11 motor.

The R-11F-300 was the specific motor found in the MiG-21F-13 Fishbed C/Es that the Red Eagles were currently operating. It was actually a turbojet that produced 8,555lb of thrust at military power, and 12,655lb in afterburner. With a normal operating weight of around 15,000lb, that gave the Fishbed a decent thrust-to-weight ratio for the time.

The MiG-21 was an attractive design, with triangular delta wings swept at 57 degrees that were cropped at the tips and spanned 23ft. They were attached to a slender fuselage some 44ft in length. A swept tail plane raked sharply backwards at 60 degrees and, like the MiG-23 that followed, it had tailerons for roll and pitch control, a brake parachute fairing, and airbrakes under the fuselage. The Fishbed's ailerons were hydraulically boosted, while the tailerons relied completely on hydraulic power to function. Their tips were weighted with pod-like "mass balancers" to reduce vibration.

The little jet's cockpit was somewhat less spacious than that of the F-5, and in the Fishbed C/E the pilot sat on an SK-1 Canopy Capsule Seat. Above him was a one-piece "clamshell" canopy that opened up and forward, and hinged at the front. During ejection, the forward hinge bolt was withdrawn, and as the seat left the aircraft the canopy rotated forward on the seat's headrest and acted as a shield to protect the pilot from the windblast.

The MiG-21F-13 export model featured twin Nudelmann-Richter NR-30 30mm automatic cannons installed internally and below the cockpit. Each wing could carry a single weapons pylon for bombs or unguided rocket pods, and each pylon could also accommodate a single AA-2 Atoll, for which the basic SRD-5M Kvant radar in the nose generated range data on the target. An ASP-5ND gunsight featured a reticle projected onto a combining glass to allow the Fishbed's cannons to be aimed. Oberle's verdict on the aircraft was positive:

> The MiG-21 was a super airplane that flies as good as it looks. You can pull 7Gs in it, look over your shoulder and still be very comfortable. I didn't have any flameout landings, but we did have precautionary measures when we flew an SFO [simulated flameout approach] if it was making a noise we didn't like. The MiG-21 had a drag chute we could deploy with a little button, so it had a pretty good stopping distance, and it landed a lot like the F-5, so it was a pretty easy transition. Compared to the

MiG-17, it was faster, but still had a very similar cockpit picture – they both sit close to the runway and about the same distance to look out over the nose.

Peck explained that, like the MiG-17, the MiG-21's throttle grip could be twisted to change the span setting of the gunsight reticle. "It had a tall control stick and its rudder became effective from about 30 knots. On take-off the nose would lighten at 140 knots, you rotated the nose wheel off the ground at 170 knots, and then you climbed at 0.88 Mach."

There was nothing out of the ordinary about these figures. But the maneuver characteristics and slow-speed flight handling of the Fishbed were both compelling and absolutely out of the ordinary. The MiG-21 could fly maneuvers that contemporary US aircraft could not, at least not without their jet motors stalling and flaming out. Sheffield remembered: "You could actually do a hammerhead turn in it – go straight up to around 100 knots, at which point you start to lose control authority. You push the stick forward and add right aileron and full left rudder, and around she would come. You would never really want to get that slow in a dogfight, but it could be done."

Some of the early Indonesian Fishbed C/Es had arrived in the US in terrible condition, requiring complete rebuilds. In the very early years in particular, some of them were repaired and then reassembled slightly out of kilter. This meant that some would depart from control when the pilot pulled back on the stick aggressively. Scott also found that this could be used to great advantage:

> Since the MiG-21 turned so well anyway, all our [Blue Air] airplanes would inevitably overshoot, and all you had to do was put a little uncoordinated control into those things and it would depart. But it would depart in roll, usually through 180 degrees. That could be done either positively, so the canopy rolled towards the sky, or negatively, where the canopy rolled towards the ground. It was a great maneuver because you turned faster than you could move the airplane with the controls. All you did was release the controls and the airplane would enter controlled flight again. It was that forgiving to fly.

It later occurred to Scott that flying the MiGs in uncoordinated flight was not sensible. "It was pointed out to me by some of my more qualified colleagues that it wasn't really a very smart way to fly the airplane. In fact, once I found out that I was supposed to report any out-of-control situation, I stopped using that tactic."

Physically flying the MiG-21 was a little less comfortable than flying the F-5E, in Sheffield's opinion, for one simple reason: "You could fly the F-5 with your right hand on the stick and your right forearm resting comfortably against your right thigh. On the MiG-21, your arm was up in the air because the stick was a little longer."

FIGHTING THE MIG-21

The Fishbed was a formidable opponent in air combat when flown properly. "It was a very good point interceptor," said Myers. But it still had limitations that could be exploited and exposed.

Against the venerable F-4, "below 20,000" and above 400 knots, the MiG-21 was at a disadvantage. But the MiG-21 still had better "instantaneous G available than the Phantom and could snatch a bat turn on you," Peck had discovered. The F-4 would out-accelerate the Fishbed down low, but the MiG's wing generated enough lift to produce a climb at any airspeed above 250 knots, which the Phantom could not follow.

Sheffield had been pleasantly surprised by just how good the Fishbed was. His experiences in it led him to conclude: "If the North Vietnamese Air Force had been any good, they could have really kicked butt in Vietnam." In other words, as bad as things had got for Air Force and Navy fighter aircrews at various stages in that conflict, it could have been a lot worse had the NVAF pilots been trained properly.

"In the hands of a good pilot, versus the F-4, the MiG-21 wins every time," Sheffield stated. While he never used the hammerhead maneuver during dogfights with visiting pilots, he did use a similar technique. "I would go into the vertical and then at fairly low speed, around 150 knots, I would put in a boot load of right rudder and right aileron to really make that thing turn around. It was a fairly good maneuver not only to get someone off your six, but also to get behind someone who had fairly low energy."

"The biggest problem everyone had was seeing it, finding it, and tracking it," Peck said. "I remember being behind it in gun-tracking situations and thinking, "There's nothing to this thing. All I can see is the wing." Trying to acquire the MiG-21 visually was a learning experience in itself, Sheffield concurred. "Believe it or not, finding the MiG-21 visually the first time actually makes it easier to do it again the second time." Sheffield also warned that "perhaps the most important lesson on fighting the MiG-21 was that it was very maneuverable and that it was better to take care of it before you got into a tussle with it. The only aircraft that was more or less unbeatable against the MiG-21 was the F-16. It could sustain the energy [airspeed] and it could pull

9Gs. The MiG-21 could only pull 7.33Gs and bled energy. So, the F-16 can get inside the MiG's turn [and point his nose at me]. And if he's not running out of energy, he can still do something to me when he gets there."

Naturally, a lot depended on who was flying the Blue Air jet, as well as the jet type. Bucko later flew the F/A-18 Hornet against the MiG-21 on a number of occasions. "In all humility, since I had already flown the MiG-21, I knew that I could beat it every time in the Hornet."

The Red Eagle pilots who had flown the F-5E as a MiG-21 simulator soon came to realize just how even the two designs were, and therefore how good a choice the Tiger was for the Aggressors. Sheffield explained: "The MiG-21 had better low-speed nose authority, but the F-5E sustained energy just a little bit better. If you had put a clone of me in the F-5E, and another in the Fishbed C/Es that we flew, the F-5E would probably win most of the time, but only by a very slight margin." During BFM: "Head-on passes would invariably end up with someone going vertical to get behind the other. You'd end up between 150 and 300 knots in a vertical rolling scissors, or some other slow speed maneuver. If the F-5 didn't get a shot in before they started to get below 200 knots, then the MiG-21 would start to gain the upper hand." Much has been made of the blind spot behind the Fishbed created by its canopy that is flush with the fuselage, but Sheffield maintains that the F-5E's blind spot was actually worse.

SOCIAL LIVES

On May 18, Vice President George Bush Sr visited the Red Eagles and toured the squadron and the assets. As former head of the CIA, Bush no doubt knew more about the sources and intricacies of sourcing the MiGs than even they did, but getting to see them in operation must have been intriguing nonetheless.

The visit was preceded by an interesting incident, Matheny recounted:

George Bush Sr was to get a tour of the F-117 ops then come and get a tour of the MiGs. My job was to brief and give him a hands-on cockpit tour of the MiG-23 in our "show" hangar. Gen Creech decided that he would review our briefings and tour as a practice for the VP's visit. After the brief I took the general up the stand to view and brief him on the cockpit. The stand was like a miniature boarding ladder or walkway for an airliner. While we were looking into the cockpit, for some reason the stand's hydraulics failed and it collapsed. Some instinct triggered and I grabbed the general in a bear-hug to keep him from falling as the stand dropped about 8ft. Creech brushed himself off and said, "Somebody ought to fix that thing." His colonels looked on with bulging eyeballs, and one came up to me afterwards and asked, "Why did you catch him!?" Not surprisingly, the next day when I checked the stand I saw that a metal pipe had been welded onto the stand to ensure it could not collapse under any weight.

Later that month, Langley responded to Henderson's 1981 report on IMI's maintenance outsourcing proposal. TAC was going to defer a decision until its manpower department, of whom only a few were cleared on CONSTANT PEG, could take a look.

As Shean prepared to leave the Red Eagles for command of a training wing in Texas, CONSTANT PEG's sole Marine, Bucko, was rallying his colleagues and their families on the weekends. Despite the adrenalin-fueled day job of flying MiGs at Tonopah, Bucko helped some of the Red Eagles and their wives, girlfriends, and families maintain an equally exciting social life. With his passion for scuba diving and his status as a qualified diving instructor, the Marine had taken the initiative and organized diving expeditions. In the process, he qualified several of his buddies to dive, including Corder and his two sons. Bucko had gelled particularly well with Postai, the son of a World War II fighter pilot. "I was assigned to both the 64th FWS and 65th FWS," he recalled, "and immediately got on well with Mark, whose cover story lay with being assigned to the 65th FWS. At the beginning, a lot of the Air Force guys were a little stand-offish because I was a Marine, but not Mark." Living nearby each other meant that the two spent increasingly more time together socially; Bucko's girlfriend and Postai's wife Linda also shared the common bond of both studying to become nurses, further cementing the relationship.

One day, as Bucko sat talking about fishing and the two men drank beer at the edge of Lake Mead, Postai turned to him and said, "Hey! Let's buy a boat." Bucko agreed. "We bought a $2,000 fishing boat. We had a gentlemen's agreement that we shook on: 'If anything happens to one of us, the other gets the boat, no questions asked.' So, that was the agreement. We would tell the girls that we were off fishing, but often we would just go out there to the lake and talk shit, tell each other lies, and drink beer. Mark was a good guy, fun to be with, and without a chip on his shoulder."

When Heatley had left the Red Eagles in April, Bucko had arrived to find the unit without a photographer. Heatley, who later published two photo books showcasing the Navy and Marines' white world tactical fighters, was an avid photographer, and Bucko was of the same mold. "I would take photos at all of our parties and days out, and of the non-classified stuff that we did.[23] We would have a party every month or so, and I was the guy that organized the food and the entertainment." Such parties often took place at Lake Mead, just outside Las Vegas, and Mark and Bucko would often take their boat.

Bucko didn't stop there. He organized white-water river rafting, set up a camping trip, and trained more of the Red Eagles and their wives to scuba dive. Bucko played guitar and made songbooks for everyone to sing along once the alcoholic drinks came out in the evening, but his party piece was his 1950s Cadillac hearse, the "Nifty Fifty," which had been modified with the extendable roof of a campervan and which could accommodate up to nine people. Someone even gave Bucko a mannequin for his hearse. "I put a dress on it and used to leave it in the driver's seat when it was not in use." When he and the others were cruising downtown Las Vegas in it, the mannequin's legs were hung out of one of the windows. It was all good fun.

More traditional squadron functions also represented an opportunity for continued buffoonery. On one occasion, the men were marking the departure of one pilot, and celebrating the arrival of his replacement, at the Sunrise Cedars Bar in Las Vegas. The bar was the customary location for such "hail and farewell" parties, and this time Bucko decided to stuff chicken wings up his nose. The wings had been rolled in chili sauce, which "ranged from 'entry level' up to 'nuclear' hot," he winced. The problem was that someone had ordered the hottest ones without Bucko knowing. "I took these really, really hot ones and stuck them up my nose, trying to look like a walrus. At the time I had been drinking, so I didn't really feel it, but the next morning I woke up with blisters inside my nose. I knew I was going to have to go and see the flight surgeon, but I had these burns around my nose and up my nose and so it looked a lot like I had been inhaling chemicals." Unsure of what to make of it all, the flight surgeon assigned Bucko DNIF status until the blisters healed.

RED FLAG

In June, Whittenberg left the Red Eagles, to be replaced in August by a Navy pilot, Orville Prins, "Bandit 30." By this time, the Red Eagles had more fully incorporated CONSTANT PEG into Red Flag. They were still selecting pairs of pilots and exposing them first to a PP and then to some BFM, but now a third sortie would take the form of part of a larger Red Flag mission, according to Myers.

The Red Eagles were becoming a key element in Red Flag's simulation of an Integrated Air Defense System (IADS) – SAMs, AAA, GCI, and MiGs – of the kind seen in Russia and Soviet satellite states and foreign customers. Bucko added: "We would now choose a small number of visiting pilots from different squadrons. Say, two F-111 crews, two F-4 crews, and so on. We would give them their own little mini Red Flag within the two-week Red Flag deployment." This special strike package would break off from the main Red Flag force and make as if to attack Tonopah's runway and hangars. Red Air was provided by the Aggressor F-5s, the 4477th TES's T-38s and, of course, by the MiGs.

For Myers, one of the most impressive parts of this new exposure was the launch. Rather than waiting at the ends of the runway to get the nod from GCI that the strikers were inbound or to listen for the Blue Air pilots to check in, the Red Eagle pilot now sat in the hangar. Loudspeakers would instead broadcast a running commentary from the GCI. "You could hear the 'enemy forces' forming up, establish which elements of the strike force were taking which route, and which formation they were in," Myers recalled. "We'd open the hangar doors and push out all the airplanes that were going to go on that mission. In the winter there would be snow on the ground, and to make it feel even more like being in Russia, they'd play the Russian national anthem over the loudspeakers as we launched. It was just like being ready to go into combat with these airplanes. I was always enthralled by it."

Myers flew both the MiG-21 and MiG-23, and the latter made for some excellent flying in these mini engagements over the expansive Nellis ranges. "They have quite a few hills," he said, "so you could come in low using GCI to position you." Coming in from down low, the Flogger pilot was striving to perform a "stern conversion" – an attack from directly behind his target. "The limitations of the Russian Atoll missile meant that we needed to come from the beam [perpendicular to the Blue Air flight path] and then do a stern conversion. Because both the Fishbed and the Flogger had such small frontal profiles, it was very hard [for Blue Air] to see them, especially against a desert background."

The MiG-23 would also be flown in concert with the MiG-21 on occasion, Matheny recalled. "You would fly the Flogger up high so that you got everyone's attention – you got all of their radars looking at you. Then you would 'drag turn' or 'beam turn' away while the real threat to them [the MiG-21] came from down low. He then got into a stern weapons envelope and started morting out [killing] the players with unobserved shots."

Red Flag was the most impressive military exercise in the world, and it pushed those who participated to the limits. As the 4477th TES integrated into Red Flag, it was becoming increasingly common to send its pilots out on Aggressor road shows. Shervanick explained:

The Aggressors would sometimes take an FWS IP with them on their road shows. So, if they were going to go to an F-15 squadron, they took an F-15 Weapons School IP. The idea was that the F-15 guy from the Weapons School would be able to advise Blue Air on the best way to deal with the Aggressors. That way, these Blue Air guys wouldn't go into it "cold." Sometimes, the Aggressors would take a Red Eagle.

We maintained our cover as Aggressors and did not draw attention to ourselves, but we were able to give briefings on the enemy that were based not just on EM diagrams and photographs, but on our own personal exposures. We could say: "This is what the enemy sees, and this is what he feels when he is in his MiG." We were close to "the Man" as a result of what we were doing. I could add detail that I was unable to before. Until then, I could tell someone what guns and missiles the different MiGs had, but now I could tell them what had to be done mechanically to fire the guns, shoot a missile, or drop a bomb in the MiG-21 or MiG-23.

SENIOR TREND

In July 1982, Gibbs left the Red Eagles for the National War College. Although the assignment had been planned for some time, his successor had not been named when he left Nellis, and Corder, the ops officer, was temporarily in charge. Corder, I was told, had hoped he would gain command of the squadron, and was disappointed when Gibbs' successor was announced. His name was LtCol George "G2" Gennin, and he arrived at Tonopah on August 3. On August 23 the first F-117 stealth fighter, codenamed SENIOR TREND, also arrived at Tonopah.

Gennin was the only member of the 4477th TES to be briefed and read into the SENIOR TREND program at this time. Tonopah's stealth fighters would make use of 20 "barns" or hangars that had been purpose-built for them at the north end of the base – the opposite end from the Red Eagles – and to which more were constantly being added. The F-117 was being flown by the 4450th Test Group (TG), which was previously headquartered at Nellis, but was now being moved to Tonopah.

SENIOR TREND's flight operations at Tonopah were the responsibility of the Det 1 of the 4450th TG, and their cover story was that they flew the A-7D to conduct secret testing of atomic antiradar devices. Their cover, itself a "secret" that was deliberately leaked, was given credence by the historical testing that had been undertaken at Tonopah. The Soviets may have further believed the story because they knew about another of TTR's secrets: the Tolicha Peak Electronic Combat Range. Tolicha Peak is situated adjacent to

Tonopah and is home to captured or otherwise acquired radar emitters of Soviet design. It was, and remains, the electronic warfare equivalent of the Red Eagles, and the farm of Soviet radar dishes and search radars would have been clearly visible to Soviet satellites.

For some of the Red Eagles maintainers, the arrival of such an austere aircraft and the "real" Air Force, along with all its rules and regulations, was the beginning of the end of their participation in CONSTANT PEG. For most, though, the arrival resulted in severe restrictions on their movements as the hours of darkness approached and the F-117s came to life. Soon, a handful of additional Red Eagles (to include Scott, Corder, and McCloud) were read in on SENIOR TREND, but the vast majority of the pilots and maintainers were not permitted to see the aircraft. Air Force Security Police replaced the civilian patrolmen supplied by EG&G, and they roamed the ramp after dark and accosted any Red Eagle, maintainer or pilot, who had ventured out of either the hangars or the trailers. "I felt like a prisoner on my own base," Bucko said.

The arrival of the stealth fighter also prompted an increase in the number of flights undertaken by civilian transport aircraft operated by "Key Airlines." The shuttle service had started in order to help ferry 4450th TG and 4477th TES personnel between Las Vegas' civilian airport, Tonopah, and Groom Lake. This was in addition to the Red Eagles' MU-2s, for the moment at least.

G2

Gennin would prove to be the most influential of all the Red Eagle commanders, and for many, also the most controversial. He spoke with a thick southern accent that sounded more farmer than fighter pilot, but that was deceptive. He was a no-nonsense officer who was tough but charismatic when he needed to be. He had flown three tours in the F-4 over Vietnam, logging more than 450 combat missions, of which more than 100 had been over North Vietnam. Like Shervanick and Scott, Gennin had an air-to-air-oriented background, and had been one of the elite who flew pure air-to-air in the F-4E with the 4th TFW at Seymour Johnson. In 1973 he had attended the F-4 FWS, and had then worked for Frick at the TFWC.

While his primary responsibility at the TFWC had been to support the test and evaluation for the Lightweight Fighter competition's YF-16 and YF-17, he had also been exposed to HAVE IDEA and the assets at Groom Lake. He supported Frick on the Red Baron reports and began helping him put together the initial planning for the 4477th TES. "From about 1976 I supported him off and on. My job was to help put together the justification for the Red Eagles," he said succinctly.

After a brief staff tour in Germany between 1977 and 1978 that saw him in charge of F-15, F-16, and air-to-air requirements, Gennin returned to Hill AFB, Utah, where he became the commander of the F-16 Multinational Operational Test & Evaluation (MOT&E) team. The MOT&E consisted of personnel and resources from the United States, Belgium, Denmark, Norway, and the Netherlands. Upon completion of the F-16 MOT&E in 1981, Gennin returned to Nellis as chief of the Multi Command Manual 3-1, the classified "Bible" for fighter tactics. Simultaneously, he participated in numerous F-16 air-to-air operational tests and tactics development programs.

Then, out of the blue, he got a call from Col Richard "Dick" Guild, the 57th FWW Director of Tactics & Test. "He said, 'You are being considered for a squadron, and we want you over at the 4477th.' I asked him why, and he told me, 'Because it needs some help.' I told him, 'OK, but I am not an Aggressor, I am a Weapons School guy.' He said, 'That's exactly why we want you. We don't need more of the same.'"

Gennin interviewed with Gen Mike Kirby, the 57th FWW commander, and then with Gen Jack Gregory, the TFWC commander, before heading to Langley AFB, Virginia, to meet Gen Creech. "Creech made it clear that he was not happy with the way the squadron was going. He was satisfied it was now established and that it had come a long way, but he said it needed change. My tasking from him was to provide the leadership needed to make the Red Eagles a professional organization, to bring it into the mainstream Air Force, and to make him proud of it." In the years to come he would constantly be reminded of the personal interest that the TAC commander had in the program: "Creech would call often, and he would always remind me: 'Don't forget, George, this is *my* squadron.'"

Creech highlighted to Gennin three main areas that needed immediate improvement: the maintenance function, operations, and the close interaction between the enlisted and officer ranks – so-called "fraternization." "The main thing was they were a rag tag organization that were not performing up to his standards. Why he never jumped on the previous commanders and got them to change this, I don't know. He gave me my direction and told me to do whatever I needed to do to make it happen. Clearly, I had the support of Generals Kirby and Gregory." It is unlikely that Creech just suddenly took the view that the squadron was headed in the wrong direction. More likely, Gibbs' departure presented Creech with time to consider the future of the program; this would certainly explain why there was a delay between the outgoing and incoming commanders.

Gennin's appointment as the man to turn it all around was fitting: in recent years he had worked extensively in the operational test world, and while he was knowledgeable of Nellis he was not an Aggressor. This was important because Creech was becoming increasingly unhappy with the way the Nellis fighter community was handling itself, and in particular the Aggressors. Much of the humility that Henderson described as an essential ingredient had gone, and the mishap rate among the 64th and 65th FWS was so alarming to the TAC commander that he was advising his wing commanders to avoid the Aggressors altogether.[24] Gennin had no one in the Aggressor community to protect at Nellis, and would not be predisposed to toe the Aggressor line. His no-nonsense personality was going to seriously grate on some key squadron members. Trouble was brewing.

September saw the departure of Navy pilot Laughter. "Next to John Nathman, Sel was the smartest guy and the best pilot I have known," Bucko said. Matheny concurred: "Sel was the only guy who could routinely grease [land very smoothly] the MU-2 on the ground when landing. The rest of us tried in vain to match his skill."

CHAPTER 8

POSTAI'S CRASH

October 21, 1982, started as a normal Thursday for Linda Postai. A former enlisted troop who'd worked at Beale AFB, California, as a photographic technician handling highly classified intelligence photos taken by the Air Force's SR-71 Blackbird reconnaissance aircraft, she was now separated from the Air Force and attending nursing school. Early that morning, Mark kissed her goodbye as he set off to work. He was the youngest member of the 4477th TES, but was considered a talented fighter pilot with a promising future ahead of him. As he'd kissed her that morning, Linda had stirred from her slumber and enjoyed the intimacy and warmth of the fleeting moment. "Only, this time it felt different," she told me at a sleepy breakfast diner north of Albuquerque on a sunny February morning in 2007. "There was something special about that kiss."

Heading off to nursing college later that morning, her day was uneventful. She finished early in the afternoon and set off in her car to the condominium in the suburb of north Las Vegas that she and Mark called home. She wasn't sure if he would be home tonight; sometimes he stayed over wherever it was that he worked. She didn't actually know where that was, only that there was an emergency telephone number she could use if she needed to reach him urgently. The secrecy was no big deal – she'd worked on one of the most highly classified white world programs the Air Force fielded, and knew why it was so important simply to let Mark do his job. Nearing home, she was only a few streets away when she spotted a blue car with Air Force license plates. "I knew immediately. Even though they had parked on a different street from our house, I knew that they were here to see me." It was the moment that every Air Force wife dreads. Something had happened to Mark.

Linda's instincts were confirmed when she pulled up to her driveway and got out of her car. The blue car – containing the wing commander, his wife, a female Air Force officer, and the wing's chaplain – followed her. The car's four occupants got out, walking slowly towards her. There was no hysteria. "I was calm. I said to them: 'What's happened to him?' When they said nothing, I asked them again. 'Just tell me: what's happened to him?' That was when one of them suggested that I might want to go indoors with them and call a friend." Their response, unobliging as it was, told her all she needed to know. Mark was dead.

She'd met Mark at Nellis' photographic studio when he was a newly qualified Aggressor with the 65th FWS and she was still an Air Force sergeant. "He came in to have his photo taken. He had kind eyes and a warm smile, and there was instantly a spark there. He was handsome, too! In fact, there quite literally was a spark – as I touched him to position him for the photo a small spark of static electricity leapt from my fingers to his chin!" Linda knew instantly that Mark was the man for her: "Not love at first sight," she qualified, "but there was instant chemistry." And so she contrived to ensure that she would get to see the young captain again. She called the squadron and left a message for Capt Postai: "It said that his photos were ready for collection, but that he could only pick them up from me." Braving scorn from her supervisor, she took the captain's photos and locked them in her own locker. That way, no one else could assist the handsome Aggressor pilot if he called by the photo lab when she was off duty. The rest was history. They dated and eventually shared accommodation, but "not romantically." Linda separated from the Air Force and they finally wed in the ancient San Felipe de Neri church in Old Town, Albuquerque, in the spring of 1979.

It was now all just a memory. Sitting with the wife of another Aggressor pilot whom Linda had called to the house, the blue-suited Air Force officers told her what little they could. Mark had been killed earlier that afternoon. They didn't know exactly what had happened, but he had died instantly. It was all true, but it was not the complete picture.

Postai had been born the son of a World War II fighter pilot, and aviation was in his blood. Shervanick called him a great Aggressor and a great fighter pilot, and Tom Boma said that he had better SA (situational awareness) than anyone he ever flew with before or after: "He could go up there and fly these complicated flights, maneuvering and talking to the guy he was teaching. On the ground, he'd reconstruct the set-ups on the board and they would be perfect. I mean, there was no one I knew who could do that as well as Toast." Matheny was in complete agreement: "Toast was an exceptional Aggressor and pilot.

No one had better situational awareness and was better at recreating an air-to-air engagement than Toast. He could reconstruct and extract the significant learning objectives like none other I have known. He epitomized the Aggressor mantra; well read, informed, proficient at debriefing and humble. A total professional." Oberle recalled that "Mark was a great guy and a great Aggressor: a natural pick to come into the Red Eagles." And Henderson summed him up as "a happy, outgoing, upbeat guy, with a baby face, great hands, and a heart of gold." Bucko and Myers were closest to Mark, and the three men enjoyed the great outdoors and shared a passion for life. Mark's love for adventure and excitement had never diminished.

He had been killed at approximately 1330hrs that afternoon: he was 31 years old. Bucko had been reading in the squadron when he'd heard Postai's voice over the radio. "He said that he had a problem. That he was coming back, and that he was on fire." He'd been flying a MiG-23BN[25] against an Aggressor F-5E on a capabilities comparison sortie when he'd experienced an engine fire. Returning to Tonopah with great urgency, he shut down the Flogger's crippled motor and set up for a deadstick landing on Tonopah's 10,000ft runway. Myers, whom Postai considered his best friend along with Bucko, was debriefing an upgrading MiG-21 pilot at the time. "Someone came in and said, 'Mark's coming back engine-out,' to which I responded, 'OK, I'll finish up here and then I'll be right out.' It wasn't as though I could do anything brilliant sitting here on the ground while he's in the air with the engine stopped."

"The problem was a ruptured afterburner [AB] fuel line that caused a fire in the aft end of the aircraft – in actuality, except for the AB, the engine was fine," Scott explained. From Mark's perspective, Scott continued: "It was an 'unknown problem' and it appeared to be an engine fire. Our procedures called for engine shutdown in case of engine fire. He shut the engine down as he was trained to do." Matheny was in no doubt about how difficult the task at hand now was: "Landing the MiG-23 was hard enough with the motor working, but without it you really had a handful of airplane."

As Postai covered the last mile or two of the approach, Bucko listened aghast to the radio: "The Supervisor of Flying [SOF] was yelling at him to get out of the jet. We didn't have a major tower in those days, but we did have a jeep – the SOF jeep – that had all the radios and gave us full communication with the crash team. But Mark rode it in." Bucko continued, talking about that day for the first time:

> The SOF called me and told me to get to the end of the runway immediately to start taking pictures. He said, "We have a satellite coverage time coming up and I don't

know how long we've got." Satellite coverage pretty much ran our lives in those days and we were constantly hiding from them. With some of our previous mishaps we had used bulldozers to temporarily bury the MiGs, returning to them and digging them up when the satellites had passed. At the very least we would cover them with a tarpaulin. So, I jumped in another jeep and drove out to just short of the end of the runway where Mark's airplane had smashed into the ground. There were parts all over the place and there were cactus trees on fire all around. I found some big parts of the airplane, and then I found the nose section, but Mark was not in there.

It did not take him long to find his friend, but he did not instantly recognize him. "I saw the flight suit, but it was all rolled up in a ball. And then I saw his face. I shook him and tried to talk to him." It was no use, Postai was dead. It was all very surreal, and Bucko found himself paralyzed. "I couldn't take any pictures. I just puked." He forced himself to photograph the orientation of the wreckage thinking, "I don't want anyone to see these photos," and then he returned to the squadron. "There was nothing more I could do." Shervanick helped photograph and record the scene, taking measurements of impact marks.

Scott was immediately called from Nellis to be the investigating pilot officer for the mishap. He had been the pilot officer on the mishap investigation of Postai's previous MiG-17 deadstick landing in April, and was viewed as a good choice since he was already familiar with the ropes. There was little left by the time he arrived at Tonopah. Avionics technician Jerry Bickford joined a number of other maintainers moving the MiG's shattered pieces into a hangar on base. "It took all afternoon," Bickford said sorrowfully.

Scott and the other members of the mishap board concluded that Mark had been just short of Tonopah's runway overrun and had tried to gently raise the Flogger's nose to extend his glide, but had run out of speed. At a mere 200ft the plane's right wing dipped sharply as it gave up the last of its fickle grip of the air. The MiG yawed right and hit the ground.

In what would become a long-standing regret for Linda in the decades ahead, she asked the TFWC wing commander whether Mark was still "intact." While still enlisted in the Air Force, she'd been sent to photograph the scene of an aircraft crash as part of the mishap investigation that followed in its wake. "It was grim. I took photographs from the ground, and then from a helicopter as it hovered above." She was left in no doubt as to what the impact forces could do to the human body. But Mark was still "intact," she recalled them telling her, and it was instinctive to ask immediately to see his body. The response was negative – she would not be permitted to do so. "I was still in deep shock. I don't recall arguing with that decision. But in the years that followed it made me angry."

In reality, according to Bucko, Mark had not been "intact" when he had found him. The ejection seat had tumbled along the ground and a brief post-crash fire had worsened things further: "There was no hand left to see and Mark's face had been badly burned," Bucko said, after a moment of composure. The Air Force had done what it thought was in Linda's best interests. Mark had died of a broken neck, Linda was told. He had facial injuries consistent with impacting the canopy frame as his ejection seat left the Flogger. Scott could never ascertain whether or not Mark initiated the ejection; all that he could say for sure was that the ejection process was underway as the Flogger started to break up. Mark also had an impact wound to his skull – his helmet had been punctured by a blunt object. "Because the ejection sequence was not happening properly, his head hit the canopy, or the canopy hit his head," Scott said.

Being married to an Air Force pilot, "and particularly a fighter pilot," meant that Linda always knew in the back of her mind that one day her husband might not come home. Indeed, she knew that Mark had come close to death before. On one occasion, before they'd met, he'd punched out of an F-4 that began to fall apart seconds after take-off. But her closest brush with the grim consequences of "a bad day at the office" for Mark had come on April 8 that year. As Linda lay in bed late that night, there came a knock on the door. Mark had been carried home by two friends, drunk to the point of semi-consciousness, his flight boots caked in dust and sand, and his flight suit similarly soiled. "Normally, it was Mark carrying his buddies home, and not the other way around. I knew that he must have had something happen to him in the desert because of the state of his clothes and the fact that he was so drunk. I knew that whatever it was it must have scared him." Linda never asked Mark what had happened: "He was not the kind of man to talk a lot about the guys or the flying," she explained. It was a separate part of his life and Linda respected that.

April 8 had been the day his MiG-17's engine had failed on take-off. Getting drunk to the point of oblivion was the fighter pilots' way of dealing with these experiences, and Linda was well aware of this. Bucko had watched Postai overcome the trauma of the mishap, and when the Fresco had been retired and sorties in the squadron's six MiG-21s became scarce, it was the young captain who was earmarked to join Corder and the four Navy pilots in C Flight to fly the MiG-23. "Mark did not want to fly the MiG-23, no one did, he had some challenging flights like everyone," Bucko explained.

Mark was clearly a pragmatist: he had taken the time to discuss what would need to be done if one day he never came home. It was an element to flying that could not be avoided, and he had the forethought to ensure not only that all of his insurance, administration, and paperwork was squared away so that Linda would be taken care of, but also that she knew what was what. "He went through all of the documents with me. He told me what each one was, what I had to do with it if he died, and how it all worked. He had the entire table covered with papers so that I knew how things would work," she said. What he hadn't done was tell Linda about his agreement with Bucko regarding the fishing boat that they shared.

Mostly alone with her grief in the days that followed, brief visits by friends to offer their commiserations were little more than a blur, and throughout it all, the Air Force told Linda "nothing more." There was a blanket ban on letting specific details get out; Mark's pilot buddies from the 4477th TES couldn't say anything and had to maintain a professional and emotional distance to protect themselves and the Air Force's secret MiGs. What little information she learned came from the wives and girlfriends – Bucko had sped along the desert in a jeep and had been first to reach Mark, the Marine's girlfriend had told Linda, but even this small detail had come only because Bucko had shared his sadness with his partner and such "pillow talk," Bucko admitted, "was against the rules."

For the most part, though, Linda was simply left to wonder. But Mark had left her three major clues. "They were wooden model airplanes. When Mark flew the F-5 for the first time he bought an F-5 model on a stick and put it next to his F-4 model from his days flying the Phantom in England. One day he came in with a box of new models. They were MiGs. I asked him, 'What are those?' and he said, 'Oh, nothing.' But on the base of each was a Red Eagles sticker. It was the same as the patch he had started wearing only recently." Linda contemplated briefly the meaning of the models, but it was really only now, as the veil of secrecy enveloped her husband's death, that they told her what no one else would or could. Linda spent the next few weeks going through the inevitable and difficult stages of grief – shock, denial, and mourning. She had again asked the Air Force to see Mark's body, but the request was once again denied. Amid the turmoil, and understandably without the presence of mind to take a stand, she accepted their decision.

Still unaware of the extent of Mark's injuries even in early 2007, Linda repeated: "If I could have seen just a hand, it would have been better than nothing." But the Air Force resisted and Myers, who had been assigned as the Mortuary Affairs Officer, escorted the closed casket back to his friend's hometown of Pittsburg, Kansas, for burial. Gibbs, his former squadron commander, took time off from his posting at the National War College to attend the service. "It hurt my soul that Mark had been killed. He was a great pilot and I wanted to pay my respects." Bucko was there, too: "It was raining and the cloud was so low that it was right on the deck. Right on time the Kansas Air National Guard flew over. You couldn't see them, but you knew that there were three F-4s overhead and another pulling up into the vertical." Bucko just wanted to walk up to Linda and hug her, but such a display of emotion would not have been seen as appropriate, and all of the Red Eagle pilots were expected to maintain a professional distance.

When Mark had finally been laid to rest, Linda sought comfort from what was left behind at the house. "I didn't wash his clothes. I took a huge pile of them and laid in them. It was comforting to smell him. I didn't clear out his stuff for a long time. I kept things the same." Curiously, the .45-cal. revolver that she kept in her bedside table for self protection had gone missing. "Perhaps Buffalo [Myers] took it because he was worried about my state of mind?" she speculated. Linda approached Bucko to recover the $1,000 to cover her husband's share in the fishing boat, blissfully unaware that the two men had agreed that it would be gifted to the other in the event that one of them died. Bucko, the great friend that he was, said nothing to Linda and handed over the cash. After all, the agreement wasn't really about money, he told me, it was just a great example of the *esprit de corps* that he had shared with his friend: "It was about this band of brothers that we had going as fighter pilots. We were all invincible, and none of us was ever going to crash and die."

Without children and all alone at Nellis, Linda traveled to her parents' house in Albuquerque to get away from it all for a short while. She was exhausted. But a knock on the door one day brought with it a surprise. It was a lawyer. "He told me that it might be possible to show that the Air Force or Northrop was negligent or responsible for Mark's death. He asked if I wanted to sue them both." Linda's reaction was one of astonishment and anger: "Why would I want to sue the Air Force? Mark loved flying, he loved the Air Force, and his country. He died doing what he wanted to do." The lawyer's unsolicited approach was followed by a call from the popular TV news program *60 Minutes*. A researcher told Linda that they were putting together a show that would feature bereaved Air Force wives who were taking the government to court over their husbands' deaths. "They already had the wife of an F-15 pilot who was suing the government over her husband's death, but I had no interest in taking part," she said.

Although she cannot remember specifically being told that Mark was killed flying the F-5, several of the pilots flying MiGs with Mark at the time recall that this was their cover story. Whatever the exact truth of the cover, the lawyer's suggestion that Linda had a case for the Air Force to answer gave Northrop, the F-5's makers, a scare. They contacted the Air Force and demanded to know which F-5 had gone down, and what the cause of the accident was – they needed to prepare a defense in case a court notice was served against them. CONSTANT PEG's cover story was starting to crumble. The Air Force was left with little option but to modify their official line. They quietly told Northrop, and Linda, that Mark had been killed flying in a classified program. They could not divulge which aircraft type was involved, suffice to say that it wasn't an F-5.

The episodes with the lawyer and *60 Minutes* exacerbated Linda's grieving process. Combined, the two intrusions further fueled an uncontrollable reflex to deny what had happened. Linda started wondering whether Mark was actually still alive. Although she explained that overall she had felt "peaceful" about Mark's death, she also confided that: "I thought it possible that he was alive somewhere. That he was maybe some part of a witness relocation or protection program for a classified project." That niggling doubt would stay with her until Jack Manclark, the penultimate Red Eagles commander, called her from the Pentagon in October 2006 and told her he was going to visit her. He told her that he would finally be able to tell her what happened to Mark.

Before Manclark arrived, Linda asked one of Mark's buddies from pilot training, Doug Dildy, to sit with her. Dildy knew exactly what Mark had been doing at the time of his death, and had stayed in contact with Linda and Mark's three sisters and mother in the intervening years. But, like so many others who cared for her, he had no choice but to remain silent.

Dildy knew about Mark because, as a young F-15 pilot in 1981, he'd flown against the CONSTANT PEG program during a Red Flag deployment. In-briefed and familiar with what Mark's Red Eagles patch symbolized, he talked to his old friend about the MiGs. "Mark told me that maintaining multiple currency [in the F-5E, T-38, MU-2, and MiG-23] at the same time was challenging. It was a cause of concern to him. He also told me about his deadstick landing in the MiG-17. I think that he was worried that one day he might not be so lucky," Dildy explained. But Mark had largely kept his concerns to himself, and like all the CONSTANT PEG pilots before and after him, he carried on regardless of the risks. He was no different from any other pilot in that respect, and nor would he have wanted to have been singled out to receive special attention.

Manclark sat with Linda for three hours, explaining that the program had still not been declassified – although that was imminent – and provided her with the details of Mark's death and of the importance of CONSTANT PEG. It had been 24 years since Toast had been killed.

What should have been an ordinary Thursday that October in 1982 led Linda down a road that has been mercilessly long, at times lonely, and always devoid of answers or facts throughout. But in spite of this, she maintained that "this story is about Mark," when I spoke to her during a follow-up telephone call in March 2007. In truth, it is about them both. Mark gave up his life in defense of his country, and Linda quietly, and with dignity, braved the 25 years of silence that followed. The exact same is true of Linda Brown, who knew even less than Linda Hughes. Henderson summed it up best when he said, "I cannot think of a peacetime situation where a widow has been left with so many unanswered questions for so long a period of time." On the morning of my interview with her, Linda had tried on Mark's flight jacket. "I had forgotten how small he was. The jacket barely fit me," she laughed. And then she smiled: "But I'll never forget his humor, or his smile." On her desk at home is a striking photograph of a smiling, happy man with a 4477th TES patch on his right arm; and sitting incongruously atop her bookcase is a collection of curious wooden models: an F-4, an F-5, and three MiGs with a 4477th TES Red Eagle sticker at the base of each ... Mark "Toast" Postai's memory lives on.

CHANGE

Postai's crash had occurred barely eight weeks after Gennin's arrival at Tonopah. During that time he had watched and observed the Red Eagles' daily routine, forcing himself to be patient before he made changes, lest he settle on the wrong course of action. That had been easier to say than do. "My observations were twofold: the pilots were all great, some of the best; I knew most of them, but boy did they look rough. And the maintenance were obviously good and professional, but not in their appearance."

Postai's MiG-23 crash served as an eye-opener to him. "Suddenly, I have all these people [at TAC HQ] asking me: 'Where is the documentation? Where is that form? Where is your training program? Where are your aircraft records?' Well, we didn't have any of it. That realization was that I needed to move double quick to turn things around." He had seen all he needed to.

The first thing on his agenda was to bring his pilots and maintainers into line with TAC's dress codes. For the maintainers, that meant no more beards, mustaches, white overalls, jeans, or lumberjack shirts. "I put them into their fatigues, and they did not like it. I made it clear to them that if they were not wearing fatigues the next morning, they were not going to be in the squadron any more." For the pilots, it meant wearing flight suits with the correct patches and the 57th FWW's black and yellow checkered scarf. No longer would Gennin put up with pilots wearing scarves and patches that represented other organizations. "I called a meeting on a Friday and wore my flight suit and patches. I told them to look at me carefully. I then told them that if on Monday morning their flight suits did not look like mine, they were no longer going to be in the squadron." Times had changed, clearly. Gennin was the antithesis of CONSTANT PEG's first commander, Frick. He believed that if the maintainers and pilots wore proper uniforms, they would soon have a greater sense of belonging to a unit. "Up until then," he said, "every single one of them thought they were king of the hill. In a way, they were; but that amounted to an ego problem, and there was no room for that."

As an outsider coming into the Red Eagles, and as what effectively amounted to an outsider coming into an Aggressor-centric community, some of the pilots took exception to Gennin. "A particular individual told me that if I messed up his squadron, he would kick my ass. I advised him, 'I think you'll find this is my squadron now.'"

By far the most unpopular changes that Gennin started implementing were those on the maintenance front. "I sat down with maintenance, and I told them how I saw maintenance working in the future. And then I hired a new maintenance officer." That officer was Capt George Tittle, whom he knew from Nellis, where Tittle supported all logistics and maintenance requirements for the Nellis test program. "He was a very smart maintenance officer. I showed him my vision, and he took charge and made it happen." For the two officers to sequester the maintenance function from the enlisted maintainers represented a monumental task: "They had been working this way for at least seven years and we knew we would encounter resistance, especially from the senior individuals," Gennin explained, "but neither George Tittle or I came there to make friends. I told them that I hoped they liked me, but that it really wasn't that important to me that they did. I had a job to do. It was going to be done right and safely."

That was just as well, because there was considerable dissent among the men. Scott appealed directly to them in an attempt to douse the fire:

Gennin was not popular with the maintenance guys when he showed up here. I was probably the longest standing pilot in the squadron when he showed up, and I called all the maintenance guys together and had a meeting. I said, fairly tactfully, "Hey! You can fight this, but then you are going to be gone. It is not George Gennin who has thought all this up. It is the mandate he has been given by the bosses above him. If he doesn't get it done, then someone else will come in here and get it done. So, the bottom line is that we should stop worrying about fighting things we cannot control. This is bigger than any of us: salute, move on, and then worry about the important things, like making sure our airplanes fly properly and perform properly."

Matheny also supported the new commander:

The bottom line was that G2 was going to make the Red Eagles safer, more reliable, and more productive by increasing the Tactical Air Forces' exposure to the threat. I will always believe that part of the maintainers' resistance to change was based on the thought that if this change is necessary then the ways of the past must have reflected badly upon them. I think it was more a matter of natural growth and learning for the unit. Certainly, the unit could not have begun or even started without breaking a few rules, but as time went on we needed to learn how to do our jobs better and more safely.

EJECTION SEAT UNCERTAINTY

Gennin grounded the MiGs on a number of occasions soon after assuming command. Whatever the fault, when he imposed a grounding he would issue the instruction first, and then inform his chain of command. "They saw this sort of step as being positive. My job was to fly airplanes, but I wasn't going to fly them when they were unsafe."

On one occasion, Tittle had discovered that the SK-1 ejection seats in the MiG-21F-13s were not being inspected periodically as they should have been. Since Oberle had received the reverse-engineered pyrotechnic cartridges from the Navy labs, they had been largely neglected. "That meant that the seats were questionable. Would they work if we needed to use them? The bottom line was that we didn't know, so I grounded the fleet," said Gennin. He returned to the Navy and asked them to test the old carts and build new ones before he would allow the older Fishbed to fly again. The more recently acquired MiG-21s, with the newer MK-1 seats, were believed to be in good working order, Geisler recalled. With the Navy labs working quickly to test the carts, there was improved confidence in the SK-1 ejection seat of the Indonesian Fishbeds. It was just one example of the Red Eagles' commander "forcing 'scheduled' maintenance practices, versus some 'hit or miss' maintenance practices that had been ongoing until that time. It resulted in much better MiGs to fly in the long run," Geisler concluded.

There were more examples: "I walked out onto the ramp one day and saw this MiG-21 leaking fuel," Gennin recalled. "I asked the maintainers what was going on, and they told me that the fuel bladders on some of the MiGs routinely leaked. So, I grounded the fleet until we repaired it." Henderson, who investigated the leaks, explained: "The fuel bladders on the MiG-17 and MiG-21 were made of rubber and they rotted out easily. We had some reverse engineered and tried to replace most of the old Soviet bladders, but their shelf life was not very long."

These discoveries, "backed up by documentation," Gennin said, had led him to draw some scathing conclusions, all of which contributed to the eventual fall from grace of Ellis and some of the other senior maintainers: "I believed that the condition of the airplanes and the fact the seats had not been checked for years was definitely known to Bobby Ellis and his maintenance folks. Over the years, the level of maintenance on the seats had hit rock bottom." Despite this criticism, Gennin was certain that an emphasis on operations – being pressured to get the MiGs ready to fly each day – was at the root of it all. "Many aircraft were flown with known malfunctions, and these aircraft should have been fixed first. This practice, to produce sorties at the risk of safe operations, would cease." The brief groundings of the MiG-21s allowed the new commander to ensure that all of his pilots had their T-38 currencies up-to-date – they would fly instrument check rides in the Talon, for example.

While fixing MiG-21 fuel bladders took mere days, there were no quick fixes for the MiG-23's engine problems, which would often see the Flogger fleet grounded for several months at a time. The Flogger was already unpopular because it was so dangerous, and it was even less attractive when a Red Eagle considered its frequent groundings and how little time he would get to fly it. Part of the problem was that when one Flogger motor presented a fault, the whole fleet had to be grounded to check that the fault was not systemic but was instead peculiar to just one particular motor.

To remedy the situation, Gennin would transition his MiG-23 pilots back to the MiG-21. This was far from desirable, although ultimately the only recourse available. Shervanick recalled upgrading from the MiG-21 to the MiG-23 under the tutelage of his mentor Watley, only to be forced to return to the MiG-21 when the Floggers were grounded. Months later, he again went back to the MiG-23. Matheny explained: "Each of the MiGs had their own little idiosyncrasies, and you wanted to know what they were. Once you had moved to the MiG-23, you tended not to take much notice of what was happening with the Fishbed anymore, because you wanted to spend all your concentration getting to know the MiG-23." Having to return to the Fishbed meant re-learning some aircraft and systems knowledge that had been allowed to slip into the recesses of the mind.

Constant problems with the Floggers' wing carry-through boxes also meant that they were subject to austere G limitations that were often applied for long periods of time. "The MiG-23 carried fuel in the fuselage wing box for the swing wing," explained Henderson, who also investigated this problem as part of his role heading special projects for the 57th FWW. "They developed hairline cracks and fuel would seep out. We researched old intelligence reports and found that the Soviets had a similar problem eight years before, especially on older model Floggers that we were flying. They fixed the crack problem by putting a plate on the inside surface and a stiffener on the outer skin. We did not have that capability. The decision was made to weld on top of the crack on the outer skin and reduce the G-load allowed in flight."

The G limits that followed were prohibitive. "They turned us into little more than a baseball being swung around on a piece of string," said Bucko. "We would fly around in this circle and guys would come up to us and fly formation. We would show them the different wing positions: Alpha, the wings all the way forward; Bravo, the wings midway back; and Charlie, the wings all the way back. Then we would do a 'drag race' to show them our acceleration." But the Red Eagles never flew the Flogger on a "pitch rate demo," which was used in the MiG-17 and MiG-21 PPs to show the other pilot how rapidly the MiG could point its nose in a different direction. "In the MiG-23, doing a pitch rate demo would scare the shit out of you – you'd constantly be on the edge of departure," Bucko recalled. The Flogger's wing carry-through box problem regularly surfaced and was never fixed, so the self-imposed G limits were never removed, although they were eventually reduced enough that the Flogger could once again maneuver quite aggressively.

The MiG-23 was still viewed with distrust when it came to its ejection seat, though. Its MK-1 seat was big and heavy, and was not a "zero-zero" ejection seat: it would not work at zero airspeed and zero altitude. Bucko joked that to his mind, the MK-1 was a zero-zero seat in one sense: "There was zero chance that I would ever use it, because I felt there was zero chance of it working. They looked old, they smelled like an old baseball glove, and they had tubes and wires all over the place. To eject, you had to let go of the stick, lift both of your feet off the rudder pedals and place them in stirrups, grab two trigger handles, one with each hand, squeeze and lift. That can take a long time when you finally realize that it is time to go!"

The seat had been built with extreme altitude and airspeeds specifically in mind. Matheny explained: "It had leg stirrups, shoulder harness, pelvic D-rings, and a three-parachute system for stabilization, speed reduction, and personnel descent. The drogue system that stabilized the seat had been designed for high-speed ejection."

Myers said that there had been a general distrust of the MiG-23's seat that predated Postai's fatal mishap. "This wasn't like an F-15 squadron, where the ejection seat was looked at every day and had a proven track record, and the truth was that there was just not much of a supply of spares for the Flogger seats. By the same token, gliding an airplane that has those kinds of speed requirements, 200 knots plus, meant that you could not touch down unless you could make a dry lakebed or the runway."

In the immediate aftermath of Postai's death, a test sled at Holloman AFB, New Mexico, was used to trial the Flogger seat. "It was an outcropping from Mark Postai's fatal accident," Scott, who monitored the test, recalled. "The investigation revealed a general lack of confidence in the seat among our pilots – it was thought that this lack of confidence *may have* contributed to Mark's delay in initiating an ejection. I emphasize *may have* as opposed to *did*, because there were many other factors that were at work influencing his decision to bring the aircraft home. The test proved the seats, or at least that particular seat actually did work!" But in the years ahead, some of the pilots came to distrust even the sled test. It consisted of two ejections. Predictably, the first, with zero airspeed, had been a failure. The second, with the sled hurtling down the track at pace, had been successful. But this had only temporarily alleviated some of the pilots' confidence issues in the MK-1.

Each pilot had his own view on what he would do if faced with a carbon copy of Postai's mishap. When Press deadsticked the Flogger into TTR in 1980, following the spin and engine flameout on his third MiG-23 sortie, the choice had been clear: "I didn't want to eject when McCloud told me I was on fire and to get out. That was simply because I didn't trust the seat." Whether a successful MiG-17 deadstick influenced Postai's decision once again to attempt a deadstick landing when his Flogger lost power will never be known, but Matheny said that as the squadron's life support officer (in charge of everything pertaining to equipment and ejection seat training) he knew that "Toast had no confidence in the seats. None whatsoever." Given his experience with the MiG-17's seat earlier in the year, that was hardly surprising.

One way to fend off being put in the invidious position of deciding whether to trust the seat or not was to be aware of alternative locations to land. Shervanick was "constantly on the lookout for lakebeds I could land at if I couldn't make the airfield. There were geographical points that I would remember from which, at various different altitudes and airspeeds, I knew whether or not I could make it back to Tonopah. If I could not, then there would be a lakebed that I had physically gone out and walked along, as an alternate. From altitude, the beds look perfectly level, but as you drive over them in a jeep you see crevices that you know the undercarriage won't be able to handle." Distrust of the seats aside, he noted, "You would do almost whatever you could to save the airplane – it was a national asset."

When Myers had first started flying the Flogger, the Red Eagles would practice SFOs only in the MiG-17 and MiG-21, since even simulating the emergency was deemed too risky in the MiG-23. Flogger pilots instead flew a more sedate "precautionary landing" practice. Besides, with the exception of Press' exceptional feat of airmanship in 1980, it was accepted that gliding the Flogger was such an unattractive proposition that no one was actually going to attempt it again. The precautionary landing, Myers revealed, was a sort of SFO lite. "You would arrive overhead the airfield at 10,000ft with the engine at idle. The intent was to simulate a motor that wasn't running quite right, not a no-kidding flameout." The Floggers did eventually start flying SFO approaches some time later.

The inevitable question was whether Postai's death and the increased risks of flying the MiG-23 were actually worth it. Creech obviously believed so, as did those Red Eagles who flew what the Soviets had christened "the Crocodile." "The accident was a really big deal for the squadron. Toast was one of the best, and if it had happened to him, then ... After that, you saw a lot of people clearing out their desks and making out their wills," Matheny admitted. "Everybody grieved for Mark," Myers added, "but then a couple of days later you have to strap the jet back on and get back to work."

They had known all along that their work was dangerous, but for the most part the men compartmentalized such thoughts. The work they were doing was of tremendous importance to national security, after all. The MiG-23 represented an excellent tool to learn from, believed Matheny, if only to refute some of the claims that the Air Force's own intelligence community had previously made about the Flogger. "I ended up not believing a lot of what they told us. When the MiG-23 had first come out, they had told us that this was going to be a huge threat to American and Coalition airplanes. They told us it had tremendous capabilities and that we should all be scared to death of it." But since HAVE PAD commenced in the summer of 1977, the real truth trickled slowly into the vaults at tactical fighter squadrons around the world. TAC's findings from the Flogger's exploitation were covertly introduced into the 3-1 weapons and tactics manuals of the various fighter communities. The Red Eagles' exploitation of the Flogger built on that process, and of course gave other fighter pilots the chance to see the MiG's deficiencies first-hand. For Matheny, who had so keenly studied the Air Force's threat assessments on the Flogger, actually flying it was nothing short of a revelation. "From a tactical fighter pilot's point of view, the thing was a piece of junk." It was a lesson that had no price.

THE PETTING ZOO'S FLOGGER

1982 had seen 1,055 sorties and 575 exposures flown by CONSTANT PEG. In total, it now had eight MiG-21s – two up on the year before – and three MiG-23s.

The additional Fishbeds were reportedly the first two from a new batch.[26] That new batch is likely to have been some of a reported total of 16 MiG-21MFs that the United States had sourced from Egypt in 1978. That year, photographer John Lear had taken a panoramic photograph of Groom Lake whilst standing on public land, the resulting images clearly showing a later model MiG-21 outside the Red Hats' hangars.

The MiG-21MF Fishbed J was the non-Warsaw Pact export version of the improved MiG-21S. Instead of the more modern RP-22 radar, it featured the older RP-21 SPIN SCAN A radar that was less capable, but still an improvement over the SRD-5M Kvant in the Indonesian Fishbed C/Es. The new MiGs carried slightly more gas, resulting in an enlarged "spine" from the canopy to tail plane, and also had a slightly larger nose cone to accommodate the RP-21 radar dish. Another obvious difference was the installation of the KM-1 ejection seat found in the MiG-23.

The new Fishbeds were good news, but while they breathed fresh life into the 4477th TES's ability to expose TAF fighter pilots, the Air Force was putting certain individual MiGs out to pasture. One of them was a Flogger. This particular MiG-23 had arrived from Egypt with the aeronautical equivalent of a broken back. X-ray inspections had revealed a fractured "longeron," a strut that ran back from the cockpit section and into the MiG-23's fuselage, and the aircraft was deemed damaged beyond repair. It was gutted and cannibalized for spare parts, at which point Henderson was tasked with transporting it to the Petting Zoo at Nellis.[27]

The MiG was boxed up in a custom-built plywood container and driven from Tonopah to Nellis on a flatbed trailer, towed by the Red Eagles' Kenworth 18-wheeler. It arrived in the afternoon and was parked near the truck off-load ramp, near base operations. "We made the transfer in the early hours of the morning in the winter of 1982, and we had told the security police to shut down the main road running through Nellis. The funny thing was that they knew something was up and were all intrigued, and it seemed like every cop on the base had shown up to keep the area cordoned off," said Henderson.

Covered in a tarpaulin, the MiG emerged from the box to begin the final trip down the flight line. A large piece of lumber was placed horizontally across the nose and under the tarpaulin to break up the distinctive outline of the Flogger fuselage (the wings and tail were in a separate box). The aircraft was towed down the flight line and was slowly moved across Nellis' main thoroughfare to the Threat Training Facility's buildings. There, it was towed diagonally into a building with three walls and a ceiling. Once it was in place, the building's final wall was added, brick by brick. By the time the sun came up, the wall was complete and the secret was still safe. TTF had its very own Flogger.

Things were progressing nicely at Tonopah, too. Gennin was already seeing improvements in the operational, logistical, and maintenance sides of his squadron. For the first time in CONSTANT PEG's history, he had a sufficient inventory for the MiG-21 and was building one for the MiG-23.

CHAPTER 9

EXPOSING THE TAF, 1983

In January 1983, a new member of the Red Eagles became qualified to fly the MiG-21. Maj David F. "Blazo" Bland became "Bandit 32." As Bland got to know the ropes, Gennin continued to learn on a daily basis. Now five months into the job, there remained a number of core issues to address, but Gennin's main challenge was that some of them he had yet to discover. "I was always concerned about what new problem was going to present itself, or what problem I had yet to learn about," he said. To pre-empt as much of that worry as possible, he had ordered Tittle to perform no-notice inspections on the MiGs to keep the maintainers on their toes, but neither man was omnipresent or all-knowing, and some issues slipped through the net.

One of them was the matter of fatigued or failing canopies. This had first occurred before Gennin arrived, according to Matheny: "Toast had already had a canopy start to come apart on him in the MiG-21 before he was killed in the MiG-23, but on that occasion although the canopy had started to raise, he had managed to get the MiG back down again."

The problem wasn't that the canopy latches were failing, but rather that the Plexiglas itself was starting to come away from the framing in which it was mounted. In addition, recalled Bucko, "Some of the canopies were getting spider web or crazing cracks all on the front canopy wind blast panel. We were worried about the things imploding, but we each knew it would happen to someone else." That someone else was Matheny. It became standard to keep a close watch on the integrity of the canopy, but one day the former auto mechanic was involved in an incident that nearly killed him:

I was at about 18,000ft, in full afterburner, doing about 500 knots. I was doing a performance profile as an initial sortie for deployed pilots and was going to do a 180-degree turn in afterburner to show how much energy the MiG-21 bled in a turn. I was expecting to end up at about 200 knots, and the F-15 was to stay inside my turn circle to see how he could maintain it using military power while the MiG bled airspeed like crazy. I racked the jet into the turn, and the entire canopy imploded on me.

It broke my helmet and oxygen mask off, knocked me unconscious, and cut my head up real bad. I regained consciousness headed straight down at the ground. I started hauling back on the stick, and tried to pull the throttle back, but there was a piece of Plexiglas jamming it fully open. There's a lot of land coming up towards me and I am now supersonic heading straight down.

Thinking quickly, he reached over and pulled the Plexiglas from the throttle, and then managed to pull it to idle. He then pulled back hard on the stick to return to level flight, and started throwing the bigger pieces of canopy over the side.

Massively disorientated, unable to communicate because his flight helmet and mask were gone, covered in Plexiglas, and unable to see forward because the Fishbed's bulletproof forward canopy had shattered, Matheny was in trouble. "I was having to stick my head out to see where I was going, but the real problem was that now the air was rushing over this unclean surface of the cockpit, a harmonic frequency began to develop. It was like somebody had taken an ice pick and stabbed it into my shoulder and then started stirring it around. It was tremendously painful."

He decided to put the Fishbed down on a dry lakebed, and was setting up to land on "Mud Lake" in the northwest corner of the ranges. "I was concerned that I would pass out again. But then it dawned on me, 'I can see the runway from here. Why land on a lakebed?' So I flew on a little and landed at Tonopah. As I was on base to land, Billy Bayer, our GCI, was able to talk the F-15 pilot's eyes back on me. When he saw the missing canopy he communicated this to Billy who passed it on to our ops so they had a clue what the problem was. As soon as the nose wheel touched the runway, the pain in my shoulder stopped."

Bucko was about to take off in a MiG-23 just as Matheny landed:

He did an amazing job getting the plane on the ground and saved a very valuable asset. I was taxiing down the center of the runway to go to the far end and make a 180 turn and then take off when I see Thug's jet at the far end. I get there to find Jim lying on the runway with blood all over his face and people attending. Then I am cleared to make a 180, go up the runway a little and quickly take off because we had a satellite overfly time window that I had to make. It was not very comforting to see him on the ground and it was definitely in the back of my mind ten minutes later when I was doing 800 knots trying to show a couple of F-15s that they were not going to catch me. Once again, my mindset – like most successful fatalistic fighter pilots – is, "It ain't going to happen to me. I know this machine. I am in charge of it. It will do what I say. And if I fuck it up, I will fix it or at least look good as I hit the ground." Another pilot in a MiG-21 taxied past the broken jet and equally broken Matheny, took one look, turned around and taxied back to parking. "He decided it was not a good day to fly!" Matheny joked.

The implosion was simply the result of age, it was later determined. "They made superb canopies that were extremely clear, but we later learned that they replaced them quite often. At the time, we didn't know that, or if we did, we just blew it off as unimportant," Matheny explained.

Naturally, Henderson became involved in the research and reverse engineering process for MiG canopies. A static test program on the canopies followed, and the pilots were briefed in the interim to conduct daily visual checks for early indications that a failure might be about to occur. Eventually, Henderson and Nelson located a company in southern California, Swedlow Plastics, which specialized in transparent plastics for various engineering and domestic uses. A small number of its staff signed contracts committing them to silence, and were then sent the Perspex canopies from which to make molds. The reverse-engineered copies were shipped direct to Tonopah.

Matheny had been evacuated to Nellis in one of the MU-2s.

Gen Kirby met me at the aircraft, took one look, said thanks and told the guys in the ambulance: "Get him to the emergency room ASAP!" That night all the Red Eagles got very drunk. It took quite a bit of faith to get back into the MiG again. Even when the T-38's air conditioner would clog with ice and then clear with a sudden, loud "pop!" it would get my attention pretty quick – I found myself ducking, but I never told anyone. I think the guys all watched me closely to be sure I was OK. It was a big event – I had seen the cockpit as my office, my own personal space, and when you're at work and in your office you don't expect the world to cave in on you.

Matheny was awarded an Air Medal for recovering the aircraft. There was no let-up for him, though. In February, and with barely a year in the MiG-21, he was selected to start flying the MiG-23. The decision coincided with the arrival at Tonopah of Air Force Capt Stephen R. "Brownie" Brown, "Bandit 33."

THE VIP HANGAR AND ME

Gennin was concentrating his efforts across a range of areas. Maintenance and operations took up the bulk of that focus, but he also looked to develop further the unit's links with the various intelligence agencies. First, he shored up his own intelligence function by building an intelligence facility on site at Tonopah, moving his intelligence officers and enlisted personnel from Nellis to the remote airfield; then he hired additional personnel to support the intelligence mission. Next, he sent his intel officers into the intelligence communities to learn as much as they could about the MiGs. "These people didn't volunteer this information, you had to go out and get it. My intel folks would come back with as much information as they could about operating and keeping the MiGs flying, and we would work this information into our maintenance and flight manuals." Nelson recalled that one over-zealous intel captain had ordered new computers that not only turned out to be incompatible with each other, but also did not fit through the doorway of the purpose-built building in which they were destined to be homed.

On March 4, yet another distinguished visitor stepped out onto the Red Eagles' ramp for a tour of the MiGs. This time it was Secretary of Defense Casper Weinberger. Weinberger was just one of many, and since the arrival of the F-117 the number had increased dramatically. A VIP could now expect to tour not only the MiGs, but the mysterious-looking stealth fighter, too. It was the budget cycles, Gennin said, that determined who came out to see them, and the truth was that the F-117 was now the main attraction at TTR.

While most commanders believed that they spent too much of their time hosting such visits, the Red Eagles maintainers also spent time cleaning hangar floors and washing MiGs smeared with oil, grease, and hydraulic stains along their bellies and wings. Assigning a party of maintainers to clean the jets every time someone important was in town did nothing for the sortie rate of the squadron, and such distractions were unwelcome. However, Gennin whole-heartedly supported visits by these VIPs since it provided him an opportunity to show off his MiGs and obtain the support and funds needed for his vision of growth and mission expansion.

He and Tittle took action and established a VIP hangar in which one of each of the MiGs was permanently housed. They were the hangar queens that had been cannibalized internally for parts, or were otherwise not airworthy, and they were cleaned and re-sprayed to look brand new. They had no motors in them, but they were kept in such a condition that they could be connected to a power supply to make all of the cockpit lights come to life. That proved more than exciting enough for most of their visitors. The floor was coated in a smooth epoxy and painted a bright gloss white, making it reminiscent of the Thunderbirds' hangar back at Nellis, and a large red star was painted on the floor in front of the MiGs. Behind hung a massive American flag. It was a visual delight.

The visitors were often politicians, and senators from defense committees with oversight for the spending on black programs were among those who frequented the base. Other times, the VIP might be a high-ranking general. Bucko had spent some time flying Marine generals into Tonopah while he was a TOPGUN IP, before he had even joined the Red Eagles. His aim was to ensure that the top brass in the Marines realized how important it was that the Corps got to participate in the program. Gennin was now using the increasing frequency and number of VIPs to help secure additional funding and support for CONSTANT PEG, investing large quantities of his time giving tours to influential figures from all the armed services. Working closely with McCloud in the Pentagon, he was able to obtain support and funding for much-needed spare parts, the expansion of existing facilities and creation of new ones, GCI capability upgrades, and additional aircraft, all of which helped either to expand or consolidate operations at Tonopah.

As part of the public relations effort, Gennin also had all of the MiGs painted with red stars in place of the standard "stars and bars" insignia common to Air Force, Marine, and Navy aircraft. The stars did not have white borders, as was standard on Soviet aircraft, but had yellow borders as a small gesture of individuality. He also had several of his MiGs painted in camouflage representative of some of America's other enemies. This soon led to the new cover story that the 4477th TES was involved in classified tests of camouflage schemes.

The VIP hangar created the added benefit of freeing up the pilots' time for operational matters. With Gennin keen to increase the volume and diversity of the pilots being exposed to CONSTANT PEG, he revisited the Weapons Schools with a view to increasing their benefit from the MiGs. Henderson had started the process with a dedicated 1 v 1 sortie, but Gennin wanted to develop that. With that desire in mind, the Red Eagles conducted tests to evaluate the viability of routinely flying in the Weapons Schools' GAT phase, subsequently known as the Mission Employment (ME) phase. This was another step forward for the Red Eagles and for some, like Matheny, the tests were even more exciting than taking part in Red Flag.

ME was the last ride in an FWS student's syllabus, and it combined everything that had been taught into one sortie that they were expected to plan, brief, lead, and debrief to the exacting standards of their IPs. Crucially, there were few rules and once either Blue Air or Red Air was called "killed" it returned directly to base. Passing the course and becoming an FWS graduate depended on this sortie going well. "In those days, to fail one of these rides was a huge thing," Matheny noted.

The tests saw the FWS students and their IPs fly up to the range space near Tonopah to tangle with the MiGs. "In those early days the rules were simple: minimum altitude of 100ft, and don't hit each other or the ground. As I recall, the body count at the end of the tests was like 11: 27, not in their favor. I think that it was an eye opener for them to see what you could do with those airplanes if you used some advanced tactics and GCI," recalled Matheny.

At around this time, there was increasingly more emulation being flown by the Red Eagles during the early stages of their set-ups than there had been since the first CONSTANT PEG exposures in the summer of 1978. Prior to the merge, GCI directed the MiGs while the Blue Air fighters used their radars to seek them out at beyond visual range. Now the MiGs would be flown according to whichever nation they were supposed to be representing. "Russian tactics were different from some Soviet satellite tactics," Shervanick said by way of example. "So we would fly the appropriate tactics for the guys who were visiting. If they were from PACAF, USAFE, or TAC, we would fly the airplane according to how our enemies in those parts of the world flew theirs."

Once at the merge, the emulation ceased and the handcuffs came off. At that point, the CONSTANT PEG pilot metamorphosed into a fearsome adversary, as the Weapons Schools had learned so brutally. "We are here to show you what it will be like to employ your airplane against the best pilot that there can be in this airplane," Matheny would hammer home. Following the metamorphosis at the merge, ensuring that the exercise continued to offer learning points for the Blue Air pilot rested firmly with the Red Eagle. Matheny continued: "You had to know how to fly your aircraft, and know how to fly *his* aircraft, so well that you could make him do something that you wanted him to do. Whether that was a Yo-Yo [a maneuver into the vertical and then back down again] or a repositioning maneuver to fall into a weapons envelope, you wanted to talk to the guy and explain to him in real time over the radio exactly what was happening. If you could do that, the light would come on and he would understand what to do."

It took incredible skill to accomplish this – to have a three-dimensional picture of the battlespace, to be flying the MiG at the same time as mentally putting yourself in the shoes of the other pilot, and all the while to be transmitting a running commentary over the radio. Matheny elaborated:

Sometimes on an initial BFM sortie you would have to tell the guy, "OK, now's the time to get your nose down!" or to tell him when to counter the maneuver you were currently flying. It was often not a matter that the guy didn't have the BFM skills, but that they were just enamored with actually fighting a real MiG! We all wanted them to learn and get the most out of it; they could not just have their asses handed to them by the Red Eagles. Don't get me wrong, all the Red Eagles will admit that there were times when they got their asses kicked by a skilled pilot in a US jet, too.

Being this good was certainly made simpler by the fact that a Red Eagle pilot could sometimes fly as many as five BFM sorties a day. The permanent arrival of the T-38s meant that a pair of the Talons could fly up to Tonopah each morning, flying a quick BFM set-up on the way. "So, before you even landed to go to work you already had a BFM sortie under your belt," Matheny concluded.

SACRIFICES

While the deaths of Brown and Postai had created two widows and two fatherless children, CONSTANT PEG brought about less obvious sacrifices in other families, too. The secrecy surrounding the program was tough for the maintainers in particular, since they were away four nights a week and their wives could not be told where they were going. An emergency contact number at Nellis was provided in the early years, allowing a message to be left with an administrative officer in case one of the men was required to attend an emergency. Eventually, calls could be patched through to Tonopah via the Nellis switchboard, but TTR remained a secret and many men would simply refer to it as "up range" or "up north" in front of their families. Of course, much depended on the temperament of the wives in question, and while it is clear that some handled their husband's enigmatic work lives better than others, there is no doubt that sacrifices in the quality of relationships between husbands and wives, and fathers with their sons and daughters, were made.

For the pilots, things were a little different because they often returned home each evening. But other factors were at play that complicated matters, not least of all that the pilots actively had to deceive their wives and insist they were Aggressor pilots. Eventually, Nelson said, in 1981 the Air Force's Office of Special Investigations (OSI), a little like the USAF's version of the FBI, had called all the wives into a meeting in an auditorium at Nellis. "Your husbands are part of a classified program. You are not going to be told what that program is. If anyone asks what your husband does, you tell them he is an Aggressor." Nelson sympathized with his wife: "She didn't know who I was, where I was, or what I was doing! She was kind of pissed."

For some of the pilots, their egos wrecked or threatened to ruin their marriages. "Being picked as an Aggressor and then as a MiG pilot made you feel like you were the best," said one. "I became a person different from the one that my wife had married, and I wasn't the father or the husband that my family wanted in their lives. My wife tells me now that she hated me then. Despite this, she knew she was my rock, and that she would wait for the real me to return one day." Then there was the buzz, the addition of excitement, hits of adrenalin and the sense of importance in what they were doing: "It was so thrilling, and so exciting, that I couldn't say no to any of this. One part of you has doubts and fears, but my alter ego – the part of me with a call sign – is just so fucking excited about it that I don't care."

"DON'T CALL ME FRANK"

In March Bucko left the Red Eagles for his first ground tour since joining the Corps. He had accumulated 246 MiG sorties: "I would say that the split was about 100 in the MiG-23 and 146 in the MiG-21. Those are like dog years and should be multiplied by ten for all the challenges we lived with. I was really pissed off that they were going to send me to Japan for a ground tour. I was the most qualified pilot in the Marines: I had flown every airplane that the Navy, Marines, and Air Force had, plus I had flown two types of MiGs! But I had had three exchange tours and I had to pay my dues." He was replaced by Air Force pilot John B. Saxman, "Bandit 34."

Bucko's fini flight had angered Gennin. It had actually taken place sometime prior to March: given the Flogger's terrible serviceability, he had been advised to take the opportunity to mark his last sortie in the MiG-23 while there was still one that was actually flyable. Things had become so bad, Bucko said, that he had flown the MiG-23 hardly at all for the last six months of his time with the Red Eagles.

From a few miles out, he had descended to 100ft, swept the Flogger's wings all the way back and thundered over the base just below the speed of sound, ensuring that everyone who could would come out to celebrate his final flight with him. He circled the base, repeated the pass and this time pulled up and then put the wings forward to 45 degrees – their mid position – before tucking the nose back under in a 70-degree break to align with the runway. This maneuver was prohibited as the Flogger pilots had stopped "pitching out" in the circuit some time before. Bucko had landed and parked the MiG, and then proceeded to strip naked before being sprayed by foam and water in a manner that was traditional for the Air Force. As the fire trucks opened up their hoses, Bucko ran into the crowd to ensure they got soaked, too.

The display upset Gennin so much that he couldn't even look at the Marine for 30 minutes. "It was totally against all of TAC's regs. I had seen a young pilot kill himself performing a similar maneuver upon returning from his last mission over Vietnam. He pitched out too fast and lost control of the airplane. Those regs were there for a reason." The next morning, Gennin told his pilots: "If I hear about or see anyone doing that kind of thing again, you will be gone from this squadron. And I will do my best to take away your wings at the same time."

Upon leaving, Bucko was awarded an Air Force medal in recognition of his work at Tonopah and his prior participation in overland ACM work from Miramar. "It was presented to me later on by a Marine Corps general who said to me, 'I do not know what this is for and I know the Air Force gives everybody medals for just about anything, so here it is.' I wanted to choke the bastard because he had no clue what I had done for my country. He also gave me shit for being away from the Marine Corps for three years and said that it was time to come back to work and stop playing around. There were many, many times that I just wanted to tell somebody what I had done and how valuable it was but it just could not be done. I still have trouble talking about it but it is the most important thing that I have accomplished in my life."

As one big personality left, another came in. "Bandit 35," former Aggressor Maj Francis "Paco" Geisler, joined CONSTANT PEG in April. Geisler had been picked by the Red Eagles after Buffalo had recommended him as his eventual replacement. Myers checked him out in the MiG-21 and had explained to him how Gennin was changing the squadron. "He was looking to increase our exposure to the TAFs. We were going to start to pick two squadrons to come on TAC-directed TDYs to Nellis. They were going to arrive on a Sunday, and we were going to fly against them all week long. On Friday night we were going to have a big debrief, and then the next week we were going to start over with two new squadrons. We were going to train everybody." Like Myers, Geisler would fly the MiGs for four days a week, but would fly the Eagle and schedule the FWS students' exposures one day per week.

Geisler, who is loath to be addressed by any form of his Christian name, had joined the Air Force not because he had an enduring dream of flight since childhood, but as a last resort when he couldn't find employment as a football coach in his Florida hometown. With his major in physical education, he had been told that if he joined the Air Force he could well be assigned to coach the Air Force's football team. He agreed to join, ostensibly to go to UPT and become a pilot, but he had it in mind that he would expedite his transfer to the coaching bench of the "Falcons" by filing a "self-induced elimination" at UPT as soon as he arrived at Reece AFB, Texas. Luckily, his IP there, Capt Dwaine Hutchins, persuaded him to give it a shot. He agreed. A legendary fighter pilot and story-teller was in the making.

FORMALIZING

In May LtCdr Bud Taylor left the squadron at the same time as Capt Michael C. Roy, "Bandit 36," and Marine Corps Major George C. "Cajun" Tullos, "Bandit 37," were qualifying to fly the MiG-21. Tullos was the Marines' replacement for Bucko.

As the two new pilots went through the checkout process, C Flight in particular was singled out by Gennin for additional responsibilities. The gold wings had been largely left to their own devices by previous commanders, but Gennin recognized that the Navy and Marines could not afford to send anyone but their best and brightest, and that these men were valuable assets for the 4477th TES that should be utilized to their fullest potential.

Gennin used the men to help formalize the squadron's documentation, and thereby to improve safety in the process. He looked to C Flight and a number of Air Force pilots to rewrite the manuals for both the MiG-21 and MiG-23. "The Dash 1s, STAN/EVAL, and the formal training program needed to be documented to the standards TAC expected," Gennin explained. He assigned Prins and Green the responsibility of writing the flight and weapons manuals for the Fishbed, and Nathman and Matheny were ordered to take a rough translation of a Cyrillic version of the MiG-23 manual, and to make sense of it.

Until then, according to Matheny, a lot of learning was still being passed on by word of mouth. "We wrote manuals for how to employ the MiG-23 and how to take off and land. Before that, if you wanted to fly the MiG-23 you would climb up into the cockpit and I would sit on the canopy rail next to you, and we'd start talking about it. You'd spend the night before your checkout at the bar, talking about the academics and trying to understand how to interpret the Russian 'kumquat' gauges when you were used to English ones. Actually, it didn't really matter what system the gauge was calibrated in, so long as the needle was pointing where it was supposed to!"

The translation he and Nathman had to work with was peculiar because it had been done by computer, probably using the USAF's Air Technical Intelligence Center's (the predecessor to the National Air Intelligence Center) automated translation computer that had first been developed by the FTD. The latest FTD system at that time was an IBM 360 Systran mainframe computer. It analyzed the Russian text sentence-by-sentence to provide improved grammar and syntax. Integrated into the IBM 360 in October 1982 was an "optical character reader" that could read original documents and convert them into digital Cyrillic characters for translation. It was all very clever, but it wasn't perfect and the end product, that which Nathman and Matheny now had to work with, required more than a little human interpretation. Matheny revealed: "You would get sentences like: 'The pilot from when descending to earth from altitude.' It took some interpretation. So we did a lot of writing and re-writing of Dash 1s for the airplane. Nathman was superb at this with his test pilot background. I could barely spell 'performance' let alone explain it."

Gennin had a very organized personality and was never afraid to knock heads together or fire people if they underperformed or got in the way. Those traits made him ideally suited to bringing the unit back in line with TAC standards. "The previous commanders all did a great job and played their part in taking funny airplanes and a difficult maintenance function and creating what turned out to be a great squadron," Gennin applauded, but every commander of the Red Eagles would leave their mark, and reorganizing and firing were two of Gennin's. Scott explained: "The early commanders took the program forward, but some were required to stop, tighten the reins, and look at how things were done. Then there were guys who had to formalize, move it forward again, and keep it going. George Gennin was one of those: he knew what to do, and how to tell people how to do it. He was the one who made our program 'no-kidding formal.' Books done, manuals done in the correct Air Force- and TAC-approved methodology."

TACTICS MANUALS

As the Dash 1s and training manuals started more closely to resemble the TAC standard, Gennin put Shervanick to work on creating a tactics manual for the Flogger: "I wrote it in the same style as a US tactics manual. I took a compilation of many different tactics that we had seen, heard about, exploited, or obtained from other sources, and I put them into this manual with pictures and diagrams to explain them all. These were real world tactics that had been exploited from other countries." Shervanick had been to Germany to observe the GCI tapes, and had visited a number of intelligence agencies in order to compile the manual. This was by now a standard technique, and his source material included that gathered via ELINT (electronic intelligence) and COMMINT (communications intelligence). That meant he had detailed information on the Soviet use of electronic systems such as radars, radar modes, electronic jamming, and so on, and intercepted communications between the Soviet pilots and their GCI controllers. Shervanick was also able to call upon HUMINT (human intelligence) in the form of Soviet defectors. He also visited Scandinavia and Berlin on "cloak and dagger" trips that he cannot talk about to this day.

In the midst of this research effort, Shervanick had spent time in London, discussing Soviet tactics with intelligence experts from Britain's Ministry of Defence. The trip to England was actually part of a two-way exchange of information (organized by the CIA or DIA), and he would later return to London with another Red Eagle pilot to give "one-on-one briefings on the MiG-23 to two defense experts." Neither man was required to explain how they had such a good working knowledge of the jet – it was just "understood," he said. "They were asking questions that were very specific. They wanted to know about the human aspect of flying the MiG-23. You can get a lot of information through observation and electronic means, but sometimes it's important to understand what someone is actually doing when they operate the aircraft."

He had been involved in and exposed to HAVE IDEA as an Aggressor, and was one of a small handful of pilots like Press, Scott, McCloud, and Sheffield who were sent on special fact-gathering TDYs. When they returned with new intelligence, they would share it with the others, but they were not always permitted to tell even their fellow squadron mates how they knew. "It was just accepted. You would return and tell them: 'This is what I learned, and this is how they do things.' It was part of being in the black world and everybody in that world understands. It was all about being the best fighter pilot; how you got the information didn't matter." Most of these TDYs were organized by the CIA or DIA, and some even included sending maintainers to pick through MiG crash sites for parts, or pack up discarded MiGs in crates overnight. Then, of course, there were the TDYs that involved flying, like the Somalia trip in 1982.

A NAVY PERSPECTIVE

The "squids" often looked at the way the Air Force operated, and noted how rigid it was in the style it ran its flying operations. By comparison, Navy and Marine units were a great deal more relaxed. There was some truth in the old saying that the Air Force had a book for all the things you were allowed to do in the air, and anything not specifically written down was prohibited; whereas the Navy's rule book contained all the things you were not allowed to do, and anything not written down was perfectly legal.

The differences worked in the favor of the likes of Nathman, who was the Navy Officer in charge under Gennin. "I could make a phone call and get a jet up to Tonopah to fight a MiG the same day. So, we took advantage of the rigidity in the way they scheduled things. If they had a jet abort at Nellis, they couldn't replace it as quickly as I could call for a jet from Miramar or Yuma or Lemoore [Naval Air Stations]. I could get a new guy in a new jet within about three hours. We felt that we could leverage that system to take advantage for the Navy guys. We weren't trying to get ahead of the Air Force, but we wanted to maximize the opportunities. If there was a flyable MiG but no one to expose it to, then we lost a mission, and that was a waste."

To permit this sort of flexibility with such a highly classified program, the Navy had taken to pre-briefing its young fighter pilots – reading them into CONSTANT PEG before they were even diarized to fly up to TTR for their first exposure. "We were pretty liberal about it," explained Nathman. "These guys were all deserving of the experience, so we didn't limit it just to the guys who we knew were coming. We would lean forward and take advantage of the rules so that we briefed guys we thought were likely to get exposed in the future. We'd brief the greatest number of people in a squadron that we were permitted to. In doing this, we had these guys who were pre-alerted and all we had to do was call them up and tell them to jump in a jet."

Blue Air pilots of all three services were benefiting from Gennin's influence and the change in attitudes that he had instilled. Nathman explained that previously sorties would be canceled if the forecasted winds over TTR's runway were too high. Gennin had put an end to speculative practices such as that, and instead based his decision on actual winds and weather. That meant more sorties were flown, and therefore more exposures were created.

TAF EXPOSURES

Gennin's biggest priority was to get as many frontline TAF pilots exposed to CONSTANT PEG as he possibly could, and 1983 was the year in which that would happen. The biggest factor influencing the number of pilots that had so far been exposed was an administrative one. Pairs of pilots from a squadron visiting Red Flag might have been pulled aside each day and read in on the program for an exposure the next day, but in a squadron of 30 pilots, there were always some who would leave the exercise without having seen the MiGs. To resolve that, TAC started ordering entire squadrons on TDY to Nellis for seven days specifically to be exposed, as opposed to just six jets and eight pilots, which had typically been the case until now. "They would get a call telling them to go to Nellis to participate in a classified program, and that they would get more information when they arrived," Geisler explained. For these squadron-sized exposures, it become standard practice to pair up a visiting squadron with a Red Eagle whose background was in their jet fighter.

It became clear to Geisler that some things would never change. When the Aggressors and Weapons School aircrews had been exposed to IDEA in the 1970s, their IPs knew as they briefed their students throughout Monday that Tuesday "was going to suck," said Geisler. "Wednesday would get better, and Thursday and Friday they were going to be kicking their asses. It took time, and it didn't matter how well someone briefed you on the MiGs, or how much advice they gave you on how to beat it; the first time you went out there and flew against them, you would fuck it up."

That applied to everyone, including Geisler. Flying had come so naturally to him that he was shocked when a classmate was removed from flying training. "When a guy washed out, I looked at him and thought that he just didn't want to do it" – he could not get his head around the fact that some just did not have the innate talent that he did. His IP in T-37s, Capt Hutchins, had flown F-4s in Vietnam and roomed at Reece with another Phantom jockey from Vietnam, Capt John Alexander. Geisler was expected to graduate near the top of his class, and would almost certainly get to fly whatever he wanted. He sat down with two vets at the bar one evening and they asked him what he wanted to fly. "You know," he told them, "I have been looking at some books, and I *really* like that B-52. What a beautiful airplane." The two fighter jocks were aghast. "They told me, 'No, that is not going to happen. You are going to take an F-4 or an F-105, as we didn't spend this time teaching you for you to take something just because it looks good!'" A decade later, he had finished a tour with the F-15 Weapons School as their youngest ever IP and was now teaching TAF pilots how to fight real MiGs.

"The F-15 community had been just brutal: the rules, the briefings, and the debriefing. Those years in the Eagle would set the tone for the rest of my Air Force career," Geisler stated. Now he would apply that same honesty and candidness to his Red Eagle briefings.

> I would brief a visiting Eagle squadron when they arrived on a Sunday. I would tell them, "I have over 2,000 hours in the F-15 and I know what your airplane can do, and I know what my airplane can do. I am not going to give you any breaks, but I am going to tell you how to beat me in the MiG. This is how you do it …" They'd go out there on Monday and they'd fuck it up. At the debrief, they'd all have their heads held low. You'd tell them, "Yep, it was ugly." But then you start over again the next day and you would repeat what you had told them the day before. Now they started getting better.

As the week-long deployments for entire squadrons became more common, the operational tempo became so high that it was impossible to conduct face-to-face debriefs every time. When this was the case, the debriefings would occur over the phone. Eventually, Geisler said, it became the norm for the Red Eagles to conduct the welcome brief on the Sunday and then not meet the visiting pilots again until the big debrief the following Friday. Creech had mandated that the Red Eagles did face-to-face briefings with every pilot due to be exposed, and whilst a mass briefing at the start of the week was not what he'd had in mind, this briefing still satisfied the rule.

Individual sortie debriefs occurred on the phone after the sortie, as Geisler explained: "All of our sorties used the call sign 'Bandit,' followed by the sortie number for the day. A guy at Nellis could phone up and say, 'It's Nickel 22 calling to phone debrief with Bandit 5.' We would talk about the lessons learned within the limits of the unsecure area he was working in."

To ensure that the schedule remained synchronized, the Red Eagles would call the squadron at Nellis each morning to check for changes. Geisler clarified:

> Sometimes they would change the pilot for a particular sortie, and that could mean that he needed a different sortie from us, or to be exposed to a different type of asset. At Tonopah, we would then conduct our briefings – "Thug, you're flying against Nickel 21 and he needs a MiG-23 sortie with a defensive set-up. Wiley, you're going up against Nickel 22, and he needs a MiG-21 PP." It could be awkward for them at

first, because they were used to having face-to-face debriefs, but we just didn't have time. They would get a four-hour in brief on the Sunday, but we couldn't then spend another two hours face-to-face debriefing and briefing every 20-minute hop.

For the TAF pilots who had never been exposed before, the actual experience could be intimidating and some required a little coaxing before they would join up in close formation for the PP. The PP had changed only slightly over the years. It consisted of ten steps, as documented by the enigmatic kneeboard checklists that Geisler drew up for flying the MiG-21:

Sit Ht/Restraint Sys/SP Brakes
Blind Cone
Roll Rate
AB Acel [sic] – 550 Kts – 10K' 15K'
Sustained Turn – 15K'
Instantaneous Turn – AB 450 Kts
Pitch 60 [degrees] – Slow Speed Demo
Split "S" – 250 Kts 20K' – MIL
Lead-Lag-Lead
Tail Chase

Geisler explains more about how the exposure developed in the air:

I always had him join up, fly formation with me and get a good look at the MiG. I wanted him to know how low I sat in the cockpit, how restrained I was in the seat, and see the speed brakes deployed. Lead-lag-lead was where I would get behind him about 6,000ft and I would show him the "pursuit curves." I called out ranges as I closed and would show him when I was pure pursuit, nose pointed straight at him for a missile shot; lead pursuit, pulling my nose ahead of him for a gun solution; and lag pursuit, when I was nose-off and just trying to preserve energy and not immediately threatening to shoot something at him.

For the tail chase, the Blue Air pilot would be able to track the MiG in his gunsight, and use his AIM-9 Sidewinder to track the heat signature of the MiG's motor.

Day two of the week-long deployment would introduce BFM, defensive as well as offensive, followed the day after by a 2 v 2 ACM set-up. The ACM set-up was the only time that the Red Eagles would emulate Soviet tactics for this particular type of CONSTANT PEG exposure (they still emulated pre-merge for the FWS), and this sortie was all about allowing Blue Air to practice its two-ship tactics in a beyond-visual-range environment.

The deck was stacked in the two Red Eagles' favor, Geisler explained: "We knew F-15 tactics, so we knew what he was doing at 30 miles, and we knew that at 15 miles the two of them would be taking their final lock-ons. So, we would fly this very close formation, and at exactly the right times we would maneuver. One of us might turn one way while the other guy dived in an opposite direction. Then we would wait for GCI to tell us who they were going after. If it was me, I would drag them while the other Bandit came back into the fight."

Once these set-ups were complete, the four aircraft would split back into 1 v 1, and the real fun would begin, Geisler said. "We would then fly from 0 knots to 800 knots, maneuvering from very low altitude up to 50,000ft plus. We flew those airplanes as hard as we could. We gave them as difficult an opponent as we could." The rationale for such overt aggressiveness was understandable when you considered the threat, as Geisler pointed out:

> They made around 18,000 MiG-21s, of which about 15,000 were exported. In the mid-1980s there were 32 different countries flying it and they [the TAF] might have had to fight the MiG-21 anywhere in the world.
>
> Our charter was not to do things half assed, and we were going to give them the full spectrum. The two squadrons would turn up on a Sunday and you would stand in front of them, and you knew that some of them were assholes and that some were pretty good guys. But it didn't matter which one they were when we told them: "We are not here to emulate. We are going to try and give you the toughest fight we can." That resulted in wing commanders arriving at Nellis who did not want to participate in CONSTANT PEG. They thought it was dangerous. The commanders did not want to lose a jet and were terrified by the idea. Sometimes, they would even call us up and tell us they were not coming, and TAC had to call these people up and tell them: "You are going to do this shit whether you like it or not." But every single time they finished the program they would tell us it was the best training they had ever had.

The new computers that Gennin had bought were particularly useful for tracking the training records of the TAF pilots. The Red Eagles could peruse a database that contained the name of every pilot to have received an exposure, seeing instantly which types he had flown against, and which boxes had been ticked or remained blank for each type.

If a TAF pilot was lucky enough to be exposed to CONSTANT PEG twice (because he had changed squadrons, for example), then his training could be picked up right where it had left off. Automation and computerization like that is the norm today, but it wasn't for most Air Force units in 1983. Dedicated points of contact – usually wing weapons officers – in every TAF wing would keep a duplicate set of these records so that the CONSTANT PEG program manager at TAC HQ, or someone from within the 4477th TES, could work with them to plan future TDYs.

"I'M NO ETHIOPIAN"

Geisler and the other MiG-21 pilots had a number of tricks up their sleeves that probably exceeded anything that most Russian, Soviet, or Soviet-trained MiG pilots – usually tightly controlled by GCI and discouraged from exploring the full envelope of their jets – would attempt by a considerable margin. Getting slow with the MiG-21 when flying an F-5E may have been acceptable, but the same could not be said of the F-15. Geisler's 2,000 hours in the Eagle gave him a true appreciation of this. Slowing down the fight when he flew the MiG-21 was his first line of attack:

> The first thing I would do is try and get the fight below 150 knots. Even if I could get them in a position where they were below their corner velocity [the given speed at which a fighter can generate the maximum sustained turn rate], I was putting them in a position where they were not playing to their strength. I would use a lot of rudder, and sit there with my nose up at 70 knots. I would already have told them that trying to fight me below 250 knots was going to be like trying to fight a kite, and that I knew it even better than they did because I'd flown their airplane, too. Now, they might have been able to gun an Ethiopian MiG-21 pilot in a slow-speed fight, but I was no Ethiopian.

Getting slow in the MiG-21 was easy, he explained: "Its corner velocity was about 380 knots. If I was between that and 400 knots and I went to a max G turn, I would lose 70 knots per second. From 500 knots I could be down to 70 knots of airspeed in less than 90 degrees of turn. There was not another airplane in the world that could do that – the other guy is going to overshoot you with a great deal of speed, and with absolutely no warning that you are going to still be able to point at him for a tracking shot with the gun."

Next, he would feign a loss of pitch authority by allowing the Fishbed's nose suddenly to drop:

They would see that and think that even though they were low-speed, they now had the advantage. When they tried to point at me, I would wait until I got back up to 90 knots and then I would point the nose back up and disappear into the sun. They would fly right by, and I would then roll in right behind them. They knew all this stuff because I had told them it in the brief, but they still let it happen.

Then we would repeat the same thing every day until they quit doing it. I'd sit there with afterburner plugged in and flaps down, sitting on my tail and still able to pull my nose up. When I told them to get slow and bury the stick in their lap, their nose was just not going to come up.

Geisler explained to them that much of the difference in nose authority at slow speed was to do with the fact that the MiG-21's radar and nose cone weighed only 70lb, whereas the F-15's radar and nose cone came in at 325lb. It was a lesson of importance that could be taught only because America had the MiGs.

Blue Air F-15 pilots soon learned to "extend" out of the flight by flying away from the MiG, rather than being drawn into a series of speed-sapping turns known as the scissors. Extending from the fight meant that they could re-enter the fight with lots of airspeed and use the vertical maneuvering plane and their superior thrust-to-weight ratio. The Fishbed would be unable to follow them, and they would be able to gun it or shoot a missile at it.

Keeping the Blue Air pilots on their toes throughout the remaining few days of the week was important. As they gained confidence, the level of difficulty would increase accordingly. To help keep things unpredictable, sometimes Geisler would take off in the opposite direction than Blue Air was expecting, climb in afterburner to 50,000ft, and then make a 180-degree turn back towards his opponents. "Then you were really reliant on GCI to tell you where they were, but you would look down and see these F-15s the size of your fingernail. He doesn't know where you are, and you come down at him doing 800 knots. You were in his stuff before he had any idea what was happening. We'd also often tell them to turn up 'clean,' without any external fuel tanks. 'Come looking as though you are ready to do something! Don't come looking as though you're about to do a cross-country,' we would brief."

SCOTT, GEISLER, AND WILMOTH

In June 1983, Scott left the Red Eagles. The next month he started a staff tour at TAC HQ, Langley. "I became the Aggressor manager, and the manager of the

CONSTANT PEG program." He would stay in this role, helping to grease the Red Eagles' wheels, for 2½ years.

One of the things that Scott did at Langley was find money for the TAF exposures to CONSTANT PEG. He recalled that Dee Wilmoth was the civilian who looked after the black world money:

> He was the Tonopah money guy who was responsible for the money for us and the F-117. He was very helpful to me and to the Red Eagles program from both a training perspective and an operational perspective. In order for units to come out and participate in CONSTANT PEG, they had to utilize their own funds. Likewise, when the Aggressors needed these units to come in so that they could train their new F-5E pilots, and the Weapons School needed them to visit Nellis so that they could conduct their own syllabus [using the visiting units as Red Air], the units also had to use their own funds. Well, having been integrally involved in utilization of the Nellis ranges and scheduling while I was at Nellis, I had a big picture of the requirements of all these people. So, when a unit started blocking – a wing commander started saying he couldn't afford to spend money to come out and support the Aggressor and Weapons School syllabi, and how they should be paying him to turn up at Nellis – I would say, "Well, coming out to visit the Red Eagles would be in your interests, right?" I was then able to negotiate with Dee to get a little extra money to pay for folks to come out and fly against the Red Eagles and then stay an extra week to support the Aggressors or Weapons School.

Scott had managed to negotiate a solution that benefited both black and white worlds simultaneously. Dee was the prime player who provided the funds that enabled units to deploy to Nellis and participate in CONSTANT PEG, as well as support the Aggressor and FWIC syllabi. "He was always easy to deal with, and he always found the money."

Scott was also heavily involved in working with Geisler to put together a good schedule to take advantage of the extra money that Wilmoth had secured. "Paco would talk to the weapons officers at the different units and would create what he thought was a good plan. Then I would promulgate a message to all the different commands, including USAFE, saying that we had openings that we wanted to schedule for them to visit us. I'll always be proud of what Paco and I achieved while I was at Langley and he was out at TTR, in terms of providing training and getting people ready to employ their jets."

In September, LtCdr Jim "Rookie" Robb became "Bandit 38." He joined the 4477th TES off the back of three consecutive tours flying the F-14. His place on the Air Force squadron was sponsored by TOPGUN, which had by now fully incorporated CONSTANT PEG into its training program. The TOPGUN brief was still as mysterious as it had been when he had flown against HAVE IDEA some eight years earlier. "They told the student that they were going to go on an operational sortie, but not what they were going to come up against." By keeping the nature of the opponent a mystery, the Navy was further enhancing the "gee whiz" factor that caused Buck Fever.

Robb went through the same hoops as most of the other Navy and Marine pilots before he arrived at Tonopah; he arrived at the remote airstrip as a qualified TOPGUN IP and Air Force Aggressor. As an overachiever – first in his pilot training class, the first pilot to go straight to the F-14 from pilot training, and one of only two pilots in the first TOPGUN class for the F-14 – none of this posed him much of a problem. In fact, the Navy pilots being sent to the USAF's Aggressor IP school were so good that they were exempt from the internal gunnery and air-to-air competitions that the Aggressors used to encourage excellence. "Nathman was one of the causes for this: when they added up his gun kills, it was incredibly high. They just decided that it was unfair [on the Air Force Aggressors]," explained Robb.

Robb explained his feelings on entering the 4477th TES:

> Joining the Red Eagles was a great thrill for me. My job as the senior Navy guy was to manage the planning and execution of the flying we did against Navy and Marine Corps units, who would typically be allocated about one-third of the bandit sorties available to be flown. The 4477th TES bore some similarities to a Navy squadron in that it maintained its own aircraft – usually, a separate Air Force squadron would maintain the aircraft. Having Navy and Marine guys inside an Air Force squadron was a good thing: we were more than ready to challenge the Air Force's way of thinking, and we benefited from having a little more standardization put upon us. In the end, the "jointness" of this program helped all three services operate together.

Having qualified to fly the Fishbed, Robb spent another four weeks upgrading as an IP. He quickly became involved in helping to develop new threat emulations. "Since the enemy reacted to new capabilities that we had with new tactics of their own, that was an ongoing thing. It was most important to make sure that we were doing the right emulation of pre-merge tactics and so on. We were very strong at representing this pre-merge threat."

As Robb came in, out went the Air Force falconer. In October, Gennin terminated the military bird control program and contracted the responsibility for clearing the larks from the runway to REECo, which established a civilian bird control program "on a limited basis." Meanwhile, Corder was leaving the unit, to be replaced as ops officer by Myers. Corder's departure left a vacancy that was filled by Capt Robert J. "Z Man" Zettel, who became "Bandit 39" and the first of Gennin's hires to come from an organization other than Nellis – he was taken straight from the 26th TFTS at Clark.

Gennin had earlier visited the Military Personnel Center (MPC) at Randolph AFB, Texas, and had already given them a list of people that he wanted to work for him. He had also left them with instructions to be on the lookout for other good candidates, particularly from the FWS and other regular AF units. Meetings at the MPC became a regular event, and were essential in what he saw as a key move to balance CONSTANT PEG's pilots with talent from outside of Nellis. This, he said, "was a real uphill battle. It took time to get even the generals to agree to that."

More controversial was his decision to make it mandatory for "pilots to leave the squadron after three years, and for maintainers to leave after a similar time." Some of the maintainers had been on the squadron or working black projects like CONSTANT PEG and HAVE programs for more than eight years, but to Gennin's mind this was unhealthy. "It created great corporate knowledge," he said, "but I didn't want that. I wanted written procedures, written manuals, and maintenance checks."

Henderson shared Gennin's concerns over documenting the knowledge the maintainers had accrued, but he was just one of many who thought that his decision to limit a maintainer's tour to three years was a mistake:

> I could almost never get Bobby to write anything down, and there was a scary amount of information in his cranium – procedures, background data, points of contact, future plans, etc. I worried all the time about his "only man" control. If something ever happened to him we would have been left floundering in the dark for a considerable amount of time. But it was critical to hold onto the experience that had been gained by years of work on systems that had no tech orders, had no major aircraft company engineers to consult, and had very limited spare parts. Those assets – the maintainers – were priceless.

Gennin was ruling with a fist of iron, with no silk glove in sight. He had designated a number of "bad actors" in the maintenance department as *persona non grata,* and got rid of them by transferring them to other units. "The bad actors were the ones who told me how to do my job. Or that my selection of maintenance officer was not very good," he clarified. One of them was Ellis.

GOODBYE, DADDY

Of all of the changes that followed Gennin's arrival at TTR, the biggest was yet to come. Gennin got rid of Ellis. "He told me that he ran maintenance. Well, he didn't. I did. He was unwilling to conform to TAC standards, so I removed him." Ellis' departure had been on the cards for some time. When Gennin first arrived, he had attended a squadron function at Lake Mead. He had only been at Tonopah for a week, yet this party was enough to show him that the officers and enlisted were mixing together in a way that he believed was inappropriate – the maintainers were even calling the pilots by their first names. This, he explained, was a fundamental breach of military etiquette the world over. "You lose respect for the officer. If you go out and get drunk with the enlisted troops, you start to lose their respect. And respect is something you need to be an officer." It was also one of the three main issues that Creech had highlighted to the new commander when he had visited Langley for the TAC commander's approval.

The week after the party, Gennin had made it very clear that there would be no more fraternization. "Unless I said so, there were not to be any more mixed [officers and enlisted] parties. I met with the ops guys and told them, and then I met with the maintainers, and told them. They did not like it one little bit." The maintainers moaned collectively, but one voice was louder than the rest. "Bobby Ellis' wife called my wife and told her how I had screwed up the squadron. Then she came and visited me in my office at Nellis to tell me how I had messed it up. I told her, 'Mrs Ellis, I appreciate your input, but I want you to understand something: I am the commander of this outfit. Your husband is not.'" It was an absurd situation; Ellis and his wife had overstepped the mark, and Gennin ran out of what little patience remained.

Removing Ellis was probably the only way that he could ever have begun to turn the maintenance function around – "Daddy" was so highly revered that the maintainers answered only to him, and certainly not to the commander. Bucko had noted this fact early on, and it was obvious to him that whatever Gibbs or Gennin had instructed a maintainer to do was given a polite nod and a "Yes, sir," but the maintainer would check first with Ellis before actually carrying out the order. Brad Fisher, one of the maintainers, told the author that "Ellis, not anyone else, owned the MiGs" while he was there.

This intransigence and complete breakdown in the chain of command was not lost on the new commander: "When I turned up, the maintenance officer was Capt David Stringer. I was told by many that he wasn't really in charge; Bobby Ellis was running the show. That told me all I needed to know."

Gennin had given Ellis the choice of either being fired, or retiring from the Air Force. Ellis took the latter.

There were two sides to Ellis, Henderson revealed:

Bobby Ellis was a very complex man. He had a brilliant mind with incredible retention of voluminous information. He was a walking encyclopaedia of Soviet aircraft, and he was the equivalent of having ten Russian technical representatives on site to provide support. He could tell you that a hydraulic accumulator fitting on a Su-7 would fit a MiG-17 engine fuel supply line but not on a MiG-21. He knew all MiG-17 and MiG-21 engine variants and the differences in sight and sound. He knew every single MiG spare part we had on hand at Tonopah on first name basis. He knew everyone in the US who could reverse engineer everything from fuel bladders to disk brakes. All this without referring to a single written word; it was all in his head.

But Bobby was bull headed and nearly impossible to steer in any direction. He frustrated me more often and in more ways than any other squadron member with his independence. Even when he would appear to be compliant with a plan or proposal, I often was left with doubts about whether he truly did what I wanted. He was crafty and elusive enough to work the system and leave no visible trace.

This was Gennin's concern – that in many instances the chief was the sole knowledge available to resolve maintenance issues, and he was unwilling to document his knowledge and experiences. Gennin said, "'I wanted maintenance procedures formalized and written down. I was willing to take a chance on losing some of Ellis' knowledge to achieve that goal. The 4477th TES benefited in the long run by the departure of Ellis – a formal maintenance organization was established under Tittle that could withstand the trials of time."

In any case, "Ellis was approaching mandatory retirement after 30 years of service," Henderson concluded. "Tom Gibbs had asked me for help getting an Excepted Service (civilian) position approved for Ellis so he could stay on and work as the chief of maintenance. It took me several months to get it written and approved, but it never got implemented because Ellis went to work for IMI, owned by Bob Faye and Gerry Huff [who by now had presumably tempered his principles with the prospect of making great quantities of money]. Ellis went on to be a wheeling-dealing international arms dealer and was their main source of income." Although IMI was never awarded the maintenance contract, Henderson had thought it warranted discussion. "I thought the idea of outsourcing the maintenance for the MiGs was an excellent idea and I said so in my evaluation of IMI's unsolicited proposal. Gibbs had concurred and sent it forward to ACC manpower. It languished there well into the Gennin era and I never heard the final reason that was given for not pursuing it."

WEAPONS SCHOOL INFLUENCES

Gennin's personal vision for the Red Eagles was to make it a "mini Weapons School. I wanted the best instructors, and I wanted guys who knew everything about our airplanes. The best instructors were at the Weapons School and TOPGUN teaching about tactics and weapons. These guys, guys like Nathman, were the best placed to write weapons and tactics manuals."

The Red Eagles' longest-serving FWS influence was its new ops officer, Myers. By now, he had been the squadron's MiG-23 FCF pilot for some time, but would still marvel at its raw power every day he flew it: "Most American airplanes that I flew couldn't go faster than the placarded limits, but every single MiG-23 I flew could go faster than the top speed allowed simply because they had so much power. In fact, the limiting factor was not power, but that the canopies would implode if you allowed the airplane to get too fast."

Myers was an F-4 combat veteran who had been in several MiG engagements over North Vietnam, but had no confirmed kills. A graduate of the F-4 FWS, he was in the initial cadre of instructors for the F-15 FWS, and had also been in the very first F-15 Eagle class at Luke AFB, Arizona, in 1975. He had therefore built up a wealth of experience in the Eagle. Unsurprisingly, therefore, he was assigned from the 4477th TES direct to an F-15 squadron in Alaska. At Tonopah he had flown 317 MiG-21 sorties and 23 MiG-23 sorties. While Geisler had already been brought on board in advance of his former FWIC IP's departure, Gennin went straight to the F-15 FWS to further bolster the numbers, hiring Maj Paul "Stook" Stucky.

Stucky, whom Geisler called the brother he never had, was one of the Holloman Eagle pilots who had flown the AIM-9P tests against the 4477th TEF in 1978. The two had first met when they were both assigned to the 49th TFW, and he had followed Geisler to the Weapons School first as a student in May 1980, and then as an IP in June 1981. He arrived at the Weapons School in less than jovial circumstances, as the replacement for an IP and friend of Geisler, Bobby "Hostile Man" Ellis (no relation to the 4477th TES maintainer), who had been killed over the Nellis ranges following a mid-air collision with an F-5E.

Stucky had graduated from pilot training in 1975 and gone to the F-4E, first being stationed at Clark AB with the 90th TFS, where he'd met some of the original members of the 26th TFTS, including Henderson (who was attached to the unit), and had roomed with Mike Scott. He'd returned to America to be sent to the 49th TFW, and six months later the wing converted to the F-15 Eagle. This was great news for the young captain, not least of all because he already had his sights set on flying the Eagle.

As a student at the F-15 Weapons School, he had bumped into Henderson at Nellis, and had been invited to spend a day at Tonopah. He had agreed without hesitation, and Henderson had personally flown him to the base in one of the Cessnas. "It really got me pumped about the program and made me want to be part of it," Stucky recalled.

Stucky had later learned that Gennin was looking for more Weapons School IPs to come and fly with the Red Eagles: "He wanted guys who could come in and keep one foot in both worlds." He already knew Myers, since he had been a student of his, and the big man soon introduced him to Gennin. Before long, Stucky became "Bandit 40" and the third F-15 Eagle pilot to join CONSTANT PEG.

While Gennin looked to the Weapons Schools and further afield for fresh blood, he also started analyzing the make-up of CONSTANT PEG exposures. He was happy with the initial PP on the first sortie, but reached the conclusion that the second sortie was being flown with too much aggression and that there was room to introduce complex ACM and BFM maneuvers more gradually. "We were flying a limited number of national resources: we could not afford to be hotdogs when we flew these airplanes," he stated. To that end, he would regularly review the 4477th TES's GCI radar tapes to ensure his pilots were not showboating. He did so blatantly, in order that they knew he was not spying on them, but that he certainly was keeping a watchful eye out.

To bring the Red Eagles further in line with TAC standards, Gennin made two more important decisions early in 1983. He revoked permission for his Flogger pilots to revert to the MiG-21 when the MiG-23 was grounded and, later, put an end to the previous practice of Red Eagle pilots being attached to the Aggressors, although Myers and three other F-15 and F-16 FWS IPs who would later join were permitted to continue to fly with the Weapons Schools.[28]

Gennin took away the dual MiG currencies purely in the interest of safety: "I did not want my pilots getting confused and crashing and killing themselves." It was a decision that some of the MiG-23 pilots took badly, despite the dangers inherent in flipping back and forth between two foreign aircraft. The main consideration was the impact the decision would have on the quantity of Blue Air exposures, an impact Gennin had judged correctly to be minimal. This was the case because Gennin not only had an additional Fishbed and three new MiG-23s available (for a total of 15 MiGs), but also because his changes and new leadership were producing results: the 4477th TES was increasing the number of sorties it flew each month.

Eradicating his pilots' attachments to the Aggressors was motivated completely by his desire to instill a sense of unity and discipline that was commensurate with that found in almost any TAC fighter squadron. "The days of flying for the Aggressors and showing up at Tonopah whenever it suited you were over. From now on, you were to turn up at Tonopah whether you were flying or not, and when you weren't flying, you were to do normal squadron duties: training, STAN/EVAL, and so on."

At the very beginning, Creech had told Gennin that he was concerned about the risk of another MiG loss, but he had noticeably "lightened up" about the prospect, Gennin said, when he saw that the 4477th TES was beginning to conform to TAC standards. Yet he still continued to call regularly, Gennin recalled. "He would ask me if I needed anything and would check on the way things were going. Since I flew back to Nellis every night, Gregory would be waiting for me." "What in the hell have you been doing talking to Creech?" the TFWC commander would quiz him, to which he would respond, "Sir, he called me. I had to talk to him!" Later, Kirby, the 57th FWW commander, would accost him, asking, "What in the hell have you been doing talking to Creech and Gregory?" to which he would respond without a hint of a smile: "Sir, Gen Creech called me and Gen Gregory met me at the airplane, so I had to talk to them."

While he had to contend with the politics associated with his commanders, he also had to maintain a solid grip on his subordinates. On one occasion he awoke to find that his alarm clock had failed to go off and that he had missed the 0500hrs MU-2 flight out to Tonopah. No one from the squadron had called him, and the MU-2's pilot, his newly appointed ops officer, Watley, had left without him. "I was not amused. I called Monroe up at Tonopah and told him that I wanted to see him before the end of the day. I got word that he was more nervous than a cat on a hot tin roof. Needless to say, he didn't do it again! But Monroe was a great guy and an excellent ops officer."

As of December 1983, the 4477th TES had a complement of nine MiG-21s (six MiG-21F-13s, three MiG-21MFs), six MiG-23s (two MiG-23BN Flogger Fs, serial numbers 22 and 19; and four MiG-23MS Flogger Es, serial numbers 26, 28, 31, and 32, according to Shervanick) and had flown 1,198 sorties, generating 666 exposures. The arrival of more Floggers, presumably those

Egyptian examples that had been retained by the Red Hats for exploitation, had the welcome effect of helping to improve the availability of spares and an increased in-sortie ratio.

Bucko had watched two of the Floggers arrive. "I remember seeing them with their ventral fin ground off, and I wondered aloud, 'What kind of bad pilot would ever do that?' If you look at a picture of the Flogger in flight, you will see that the ventral fin underneath the fuselage sticks out almost like a reflection of the vertical tail. The fin helps reduce yaw, which in turn keeps the 'roll due to yaw issues' at a minimum. Above Mach 2, this can be a problem." The MiG-23's ventral fin was so large that it would prevent the pilot from landing unless it was hydraulically folded prior to touchdown. This was done via a cockpit switch, and it was for this reason that Bucko was critical of whoever had ground down the fins on the Red Eagles' "new" jets:

> Six months later, when landing the airplane in a high crosswind, I came in flat and fast and landed in a sort of three-point landing attitude. I bounced into the air a little, applied a little forward stick and got into a PIO [pilot-induced oscillation] that caused me to hit the tail on the ground and grind off the fin a little even though it had folded up like it was supposed to. During the landing and PIO, one wing came really close to hitting the ground also as the crosswind got underneath it. It was a real close call and I felt for a moment like I was going to ground loop the airplane, which is hard to do on a tricycle landing gear airplane doing 150 knots!

At least he now understood how the other two Floggers had ended up in the same condition. "The Flogger was a real handful and I always treated it like a tail dragger insofar as I always tried to stay on top of the situation: I flew it from chock to chock. It kept you on the edge of your seat with excitement."

CHAPTER 10

"THE AIR FORCE IS COMING," 1984

In January 1984, "Bandit 41," Maj John "Grunt" Skidmore, joined the Red Eagles as Nathman prepared to leave to take command of VFA-132 "Privateers," a squadron of F/A-18C Hornets aboard the aircraft carrier, USS *Coral Sea*. Stucky took responsibility for writing the MiG-23 flight manual once Nathman left.

Skidmore was the first F-16 FWS IP to join the Red Eagles, joining Watley, Stucky, and Geisler as Weapons School IPs assigned to fly the MiGs. "Myers had established a precedent for FWS guys to go to the Red Eagles," Stucky said, adding: "Getting people with experience of the primary weapons systems was a good idea because you had guys from the Aggressors who knew Soviet tactics really well, but didn't know much about what the other communities did. Guys like Monroe Watley, 'Buffalo' Myers, Paco Geisler, and John Skidmore came in with great experience of different weapons platforms. We did the same with the Navy, hiring guys like 'Rookie' Robb and Orville Prins from the F-14, and George Tullos and [later] Marty Macy from the F/A-18."

Stucky, by now the Red Eagles' training officer, recalled:

> Gennin had his way of doing things, but that's not necessarily an unflattering thing. I built the training records from the ground up that showed what each [4477th TES] pilot had been taught. It was an example of how Gennin was taking the squadron from a safety standpoint into a mode that was more standard for the Air Force. Until then, the way that things had been run was indicative of the black world – some general gives a group of guys a charter, and says, "Go fly these MiGs." He might

sign a document to make that happen, but there were not going to be the same documented processes in place like there would be in a normal squadron.

Gennin had also taken to personally approving the flying schedule for each day, and while viewed as increasingly autocratic, he was delivering tangible results. He spent time with Nelson, analyzing the resource requirements of the squadron and creating a vision of what he wanted. To make that happen, he worked with former Red Eagle, Maj Dave McCloud: "McCloud was running black world programs in the Pentagon, and he was instrumental in allowing me to do my job by loosening the purse strings. Without him we could not have done what we needed to do. He had good vision and knew where to find the money." From a facilities standpoint, Gennin used the increased budget from McCloud to invest in new technologies to help make the Red Eagles more efficient. He couldn't remember what the budget was, but he did recall that "money was not an issue."

One such change was the use of computers, whose introduction brought about a range of benefits. One of them, Scott recalled, was "the proper tracking of the pilot's qualifications on computer, making the grease board that I had used as head of STAN/EVAL look redundant and rather antiquated." Technology also allowed Gennin to source state-of-the-art command and control (C2) equipment for his GCI operators. He had already turned his attention to the GCI function within the squadron, hiring a new GCI flight commander in the form of Capt Billy Bayer. Now, Gennin ordered that the new C2 equipment be installed not at Nellis, but at Tonopah. It was logical, he reasoned, that the combination of a co-located GCI center and the best equipment available would allow him to create an IADS (Integrated Air Defense System) of the truest kind. The new site would take time to build and would not be ready before his departure, but with the help of McCloud in the Pentagon, he had sourced the equipment and got the ball rolling.

By May, two-star general Eugene Fischer had replaced Gregory as the TFWC commander. Fischer's remit from Creech was almost a carbon copy of Gennin's, only Creech had told Fischer to "clean up" the whole of Nellis and all its organizations. The real problem at Nellis was the Aggressors, who by now bore little resemblance to the initial cadre that Suter, Moody, and O'Neill had formed 11 years previously. When Fischer arrived, the Aggressors were experiencing 22.9 mishaps per 100,000 flying hours, whereas the TAC accident rate for the entire command was just 3.2 – without the Nellis stats to skew that figure, it fell to just 1.9.

Fischer later gathered the Aggressors in an auditorium at Nellis and minced none of his words. He told them that they were "a cancer on the side of TAC," and that even Creech had told his wing commanders to "treat them like the plague." He was there to cut the cancer out, he had told his packed audience, defying anyone to blame the 22.9 mishap statistic on emulating Soviet tactics and flying BFM. The mishap rate, he said, was down to "dumb shit pilots and dumb shit instructors."

He finished the talk, which became a rallying point for the Aggressors and later became known as the "Heart to Aggressor Talk," by promising them this: "Some of you are doing just an absolutely superb job and I couldn't be prouder of you. But as a group, you stink. And you gotta crawl out of the shit so you don't smell no more ... but I am not going to lose any more F-5s. I am not going to have any more F-5s go out of control. And if you do, you'd better have another God-damned career planned, because it's not going to be part of the Air Force. I'll do everything I can to run you out on a God-damned rail." Unsurprisingly, the Red Eagles were distancing themselves more and more from the Aggressors at Nellis.

THE MAN CAMP

At Tonopah, the number of F-117s and the operational tempo of the 4450th TG gradually increased. Since few of the 4477th TES had been read in on SENIOR TREND, the activity at the north end of the base was intriguing indeed – more hangars were being constructed and the buildings had started to receive the two-tone paint scheme so popular at the time. When Geisler had asked Gennin what was going on, his boss had responded evasively, "The Air Force is coming."

The Air Force's arrival resulted in the Red Eagles maintainers moving out of the Indian Village trailers behind the MiG hangars. The F-117's money had paid for the development of what was called the Man Camp, located about six miles north of the base and accessed via a single, straight asphalt road. Actually, the Air Staff had provided the funds for the Man Camp, but had routed it via Nelson (making it appear as though it was being paid for by the 4477th TES).

Man Camp was opulent by comparison to the trailers that had been home up until then. It had permanent accommodation, bars and chow halls and a bowling alley for the officers and enlisted men. It even had an Olympic-size swimming pool. While the maintainers spent some time at Man Camp, the pilots rarely stayed overnight unless the next day's schedule dictated it. When they did, they often left with more questions than answers, as Geisler revealed:

At the Man Camp, I would bump into guys that I knew who were now working for this other unit. They would tell me, "I can't talk about what I am doing," but they always wanted to come down and see our airplanes. I would say, "Fuck you! You can't tell me what you're doing; and even if you can see, I can't tell you what we are doing!" Eventually, one of them got a release for me to go down there one night. It was pretty impressive: I walked in the hangar and said, "Holy crap. Does the cover come off? Is there a fighter in there somewhere underneath?" They said, "Kiss my ass!" We then started letting them come down to our hangars for a look at the MiGs.

Operationally, the F-117 pilots had even taken to using the Bandit call sign associated with the Red Eagles, a measure designed to ensure that their radio transmissions, which could be intercepted by a basic handheld scanner, did not sound out of the ordinary. In fact, the SENIOR TREND pilots had started assigning Bandit numbers to newly qualified pilots, too.

Geisler devised an interim solution for those pilots on the squadron not yet briefed on SENIOR TREND to get a look at the strange aircraft. "We would get lawn chairs and go out there at midnight and sit in the corner of our ramp. They would be asking what the hell they were doing, but I would tell them to be patient. Then all of a sudden this big old 'Doober' [F-117] would go by and they would just about fall out of their chairs."

BOND'S MISHAP

In March 1984, "Bandit 42," Capt Thomas E. "Gabby" Drake, qualified in the MiG-21 and joined the Red Eagles, followed in April by two more new faces. Air Force Capt Robert E. Craig became "Bandit 43," and Navy pilot LtCdr Daniel R. "Bad Bob" McCort became "Bandit 44." As they went methodically and slowly through a carefully created TX syllabus with their Red Eagle IPs, another man was about to rush that process. It would cost him his life. The mishap report remains mostly classified, but several Red Eagles who have seen it or were given pertinent information from it at the time were highly critical of his actions. One of them said without sympathy, "He should have read the flight manual."

On April 26, LtGen Robert "Bobby" Bond, the vice commander of AFSC, was killed when he lost control of the MiG-23BN Flogger F he was flying. Bond was making a high-speed run, the second of two orientation flights, when the incident occurred over Area 25 of the Nevada Test Site. He was the same Bond who had ushered Peck into his office in 1976 and shown him the HAVE BLUE file. His orientation sorties were part of what appears to have been a farewell tour of AFSC's black world. In March he had visited Groom Lake for two orientation flights in the full-scale prototype of the stealth fighter, the YF-117A.

It is alleged that Bond had insisted on a simple briefing on the supersonic handling characteristics of the Flogger from a pilot sitting on the canopy rail. Compared to what was the official TX course at the time, that decision appears to be particularly ill advised. The MiG-23 TX course consisted of a taxi sortie to familiarize the pilot with ground handling, and then six flights – three for familiarization, two to become acquainted with the MiG-23's systems, and a sixth ride to be formally checked out in the jet. This syllabus was based on the TX course no doubt put together after the completion of HAVE PAD, and is dated November 1, 1979, according to the official Air Force Safety Center mishap report. Instead of in-depth academic classroom study and supervised sorties that had been created and approved by test pilots of his own command, Bond had opted for an expedited explanation of the MiG's operating procedures that was insufficient by the standards of the briefest of TX syllabi.

At 40,000ft, the Flogger's powerful motor pushed the aircraft beyond the sound barrier, leaving his T-38 chase lagging miles behind. The speed he was traveling at remains classified, but was presumably beyond Mach 2. As the aircraft continued to accelerate alarmingly quickly, a hydro-mechanical inhibitor became energized that prevented the motor from throttling back, even if the throttle in the cockpit was physically retarded. Bond could move the throttle back to halt the acceleration if he wished, but the motor was not going to respond, and would not even have come out of afterburner. The inhibitor was there to ensure that the pilot could not pull the throttle back and cause such tremendous deceleration that the R-29A motor would have torn free of its mountings, causing a catastrophic explosion. To make matters worse for Bond: "With the wings back at 72 degrees," Matheny had told me as part of his overview on the handling characteristics of the Flogger, "you would run out of stabilator authority to control the pitch of the nose. You just became the classic bullet. Above Mach 2 it didn't want to turn at all." Matheny said he'd flown the MiG-23 up to Mach 2.5, which may have been slightly faster than the target speed for Bond's test flight.[29] The difference was that Matheny had been extensively prepared for the experience.

Bond was now in real trouble. He was at more than twice the speed of sound, had very limited pitch authority, was accelerating to the placarded limits above which the canopy threatened to melt or implode, and was unable to get the MiG to slow. The solution lay in understanding that the inhibitor would gradually reduce the thrust output, and to decelerate the jet by pulling back on the stick and waiting for the nose to rise above the horizon, which would help the airspeed to decay sufficiently for the inhibitor to disconnect.

When the Flogger failed to stop decelerating, and no doubt with the throttle "jammed" in afterburner, the MiG's nose might also have started to sweep from side to side. This was another characteristic of the Flogger of which Bond may not have been adequately aware, but one which was known to occur not only as the aircraft accelerated into (and decelerated out of) Mach 1, but also above Mach 2. Disconcerting at the best of times, the yaw created a powerful sideslip that could rip the motor from its mountings or cause the compressor blades to catch the engine case. Worse still, the yaw at this speed also created a rolling movement that could worsen and lead to a departure from controlled flight. At that speed, such a departure would lead to instant and catastrophic structural failure. Having left his T-38 safety chase for dust, Bond transmitted that he had lost control. "I gotta get out of here," he exclaimed. Seconds later he ejected.

The supersonic slipstream caught the lip of his flight helmet, ripping it backwards violently, causing the chin strap to suddenly tug his head backwards. He died instantly from a broken neck and fell to earth beneath a tattered, shredded parachute. The MiG-23 impacted the ground at an angle of 60 degrees, apparently with the motor still running just below military RPM and with no other indications of flight control, structural, or systems failure evident to the mishap investigating team. So classified was this mishap that the subsequent investigation was chaired by none other than the commander of the Air Force's Inspection and Safety Center, Gen Gordon E. Williams. Several Red Eagles were angry about Bond's actions. He may have been a great pilot and commander, but flying the MiG-23 – a national asset – when he was about to retire was something that many felt he had no business doing. Unlike other mishaps, there was no fallout from this crash, probably because of Bond's rank; his boss was a four-star general.

FLOGGER MOMENTS

With the wing carry-through box problems recurring intermittently, the main issue affecting the Red Eagles' MiG-23s remained the continuing shortage of Tumansky R-29A motors. The maintainers did all that they could to keep the troublesome jet in the air. "They were a beast to work on, especially pulling an engine. We called them Javalinas, after the wild pig found in Texas," said Rick Wagner, a Red Eagle maintainer who replaced Jerry Bickford in the avionics shop in 1984. As more Floggers arrived the maintainers gave them nicknames that mocked their status as pigs but were also a term of endearment. "One was called 'Miss Piggy,' after the famous character in *The Muppet Show*, and another was christened 'Arnold,' the name of a pig owned by the Ziffle family on a popular 1960s US comedy show *Green Acres*," Wagner enlightened.

Postai's October 1982 crash resulted in a long grounding for the Flogger, said Matheny, but the unreliability and need for constant maintenance meant that little had changed. The MiG-23 Bond had been flying when he was killed had Air Force records dating back only three years (to 1981) that showed it had flown for only 98.2 hours in that time, and that in the three months leading up to the mishap, it had flown barely an hour a week.

Some of the problems arose from an unfamiliarity with the techniques employed by Tumansky, and the difficulty GE faced in reverse engineering them. "There were things about the motor in it that we just hadn't seen before," Shervanick pointed out. "For example, the turbine blades had tiny air passages running through them that allowed cooling air through to keep the motor cool. It ran so hot that this was important. We were also not used to the size of the compressor blades at the front of the motor, or the amount of twist that was on them."

While innovative, these techniques for keeping the motor cool were also its Achilles' heel. Whereas Western engine manufacturers used long-lasting coatings to prevent their turbine blades from melting in the extreme heat of the turbine section, the drilled Tumansky blades had a very limited life. "These motors had never been intended to fly this many hours," recalled Shervanick, who was by now an experienced Flogger pilot by 4477th TES standards, and the Red Eagles' MiG-23 FCF pilot. "They were good for a couple of hundred sorties at most, and it was part of Russia's way of making money that they would sell new engines to their export customers for hard currency." In addition, because the R-29A ran extremely hot, the fleet was plagued by false alarms when the temperature sensors in the engine bay of the gangly jet would reach a critical temperature, thus energizing fire warning lights in the cockpit. Such an indication resulted in an immediate "Knock it off!" call and return to TTR.

Each fire warning light activation was treated with the utmost caution and respect, and following a thorough inspection on the ground the aircraft in question would have to be flown on an FCF sortie before it could be released back onto the flying schedule. On one occasion, Shervanick had to fly three FCF sorties in a row on the same Flogger when the fire warning light illuminated on successive flights. "It felt like every day one of the MiG-23s had a fire warning light come on," Geisler reflected, "and so we ended up putting in a second fire warning system that was of American design. If the Russian one lit up and the American one didn't, then we knew it might be a false alarm."

A month after Bond's mishap, Watley left the Red Eagles, running naked from his MiG following his final flight as was now customary, according to Nelson. But like several other ex-Red Eagles, Watley wouldn't be away from CONSTANT PEG for too long. His immediate assignment was Air Command & Staff College, which would take a year or so, but he was then slated to become the Pentagon's program manager for the Red Eagles. He was a big character who would be missed. Nelson said, "When he'd meet you he'd say, 'Hi! I'm Monroe Watley, the world's greatest fighter pilot!' His smile was as big as Texas." Watley and Nathman had become close friends during their time on the squadron. "He was an incredible pilot, in the air and on the ground," Nathman said. "Just the way he prepared for missions showed you that. He was a joy to be around, and everyone looked at him as the consummate professional.

"At one time, Monroe and I were the only guys flying the Flogger. There was one experienced guy who had just left, leaving the two of us without a whole lot of time in the jet." Since Bucko's three-point landing in the MiG-23, the aircraft had been subject to a 23-knot crosswind landing limit. One day, Nathman and Watley tested that figure. Nathman recounted: "I landed with the crosswind right on the limit. It was gusty, but I decided to put the drag chute out anyway. One wing started lifting up under the crosswind, and the drag chute in the MiG-23 only aggravates that. So, I started being pulled across the runway and ended up running into all the runway lights with my nose gear. I was holding the stick all the way over to the right to keep the wing down, but the drag chute release handle is way over on the left, so I was having a problem reaching it. I eventually got it stopped, having scared the shit out of myself."

It turned out that none of the runway lights had broken, so there was no glass in the nose wheel tires of Nathman's jet that would serve as evidence for his embarrassing landing. "About four days later, Monroe and I were sitting down having a beer. He said to me, 'Hey! Black, you know that crosswind limit on the [MiG] -23? I think it should be lower!' It turned out that he had done the exact same thing as me the day before. He hadn't told me and I hadn't told him. We both looked at each other and started drinking heavily; we then knew that we would have to compare notes more frequently."

Watley's departure coincided with some good news, though. "Bandit 22," Marine Corps pilot Lenny Bucko, had by now returned from his ground tour to assume a three-year posting as executive officer (XO) to an F/A-18 Hornet squadron based at El Toro. He would once again be involved in CONSTANT PEG. "I made several trips to Tonopah in the Hornet, and I remained on the Clearance List for about eight years to help make it easy to coordinate short notice [exposure] flights with the Marines, and to be able to get the Corps more than their share of sorties."

Bucko's association with the 4477th TES had followed him to Japan, where it had stood him in good stead. He had arrived on the Japanese island of Okinawa for his ground tour to find that 18th TFW – which consisted of two squadrons of F-15s – was commanded by none other than Peck. The two had got on well, and Peck had arranged for Bucko to give tours of the MiG-23 in the classified Warrior Prep center on base. Bickford and some of the other Red Eagles maintainers had transferred the Flogger to Japan in great secrecy, flying with the disassembled MiG in the back of a C-141 Starlifter transporter, and then reassembling it once it had been transferred in secret to the inside of the facility (another MiG-23 had been transferred to the USAFE's Warrior Prep center at Einsiedlerhof AB, Germany).

Less pleasant were the problems he was now experiencing with the Internal Revenue Service (IRS), which queried his tax return from 1982 and insisted that he explain some of the more peculiar expenses that he had claimed. "They told me I either told them what they were for, or I would have to get a letter from the general." He got a letter explaining his expenses were bona fide, but the IRS paid him close attention for another two years nonetheless.

As spring gave way to summer, Gennin was reaching the end of his two-year command and prepared to hand over the squadron to his successor, LtCol Phil "Hound Dog" White. Gennin was off to the War College. He was pleased with what he had achieved and was ready to move on to the next challenge, but he was less than excited about going back to school. White arrived in June to learn to fly the MiG-21, along with Air Force Capt Timothy R. "Stretch" Kinney. Kinney qualified first, becoming "Bandit 45," followed shortly thereafter by the new commander, "Bandit 46."

"HOUND DOG" WHITE

In July Gennin handed over the reins to White. White was a charismatic man who was fond of the ladies and had been one of the initial cadre at the 26th TFTS at Clark. He had worked for Roger Wells, knew Scott, Shervanick, and Henderson from the Philippines, and had come to know most of the other Red Eagles, past and present, through his ongoing Aggressor work. He was a completely different leader from Gennin: more laid back, more willing to empower his pilots, and less autocratic. But he too would be controversial: there was still much change to bring about, and while Gennin had accomplished much during his two years at Tonopah, CONSTANT PEG still had untapped potential.

White was well connected at TAC, and was known even to Creech before he was given control of CONSTANT PEG. He had worked a staff tour at TAC HQ, Langley, in the summer of 1981. There he attained the rank of lieutenant colonel and was a division chief in the office of the Director of Requirements, but he had soon been promoted to XO for the two-star Director of Requirements:

> I was interviewed twice for squadron command while I was there, but one of the squadrons I was going to get was closed down and its F-4s given to the Turkish Air Force; and the other, an F-16 squadron, never happened because I got a call from the secretary of Gen Mike Kirby, the one-star wing commander for the 57th Fighter Weapons Wing at the time, asking if I could attend an interview.
>
> I was now confused, and I asked my boss what was going on. He told me he knew all about it: "Just shut your mouth, go to Nellis, and interview." He knew what unit it was, I did not. At that time, Mike Scott was doing the black world job for the two-star TAC DO, who was really the general who ran CONSTANT PEG. Mike [helped arrange my TDY to Nellis] and told me what was going on.

White interviewed first with Kirby and then with the TFWC commander, Fischer. He knew Fischer from his F-4 days, and the two-star told him that he would probably have to meet Creech for final approval. But since the TAC commander already knew White and had endorsed his last two performance reports, Creech waived the final interview and approved the position.

In August, James Green left the squadron as White began to make some initial changes. The first, which brought a sigh of relief to those who disagreed with Gennin's policy of curtailing the duration of maintenance tours, was the reversal of the three-year limit. The other was to hand back responsibility for the daily flight schedule to his ops officer, David Bland.

Before White had properly got his feet under the table, the 57th FWW's new commander, Gen Joe Ashy, took the decision to prohibit Skidmore, Stucky, and Geisler from flying any more Weapons School sorties. This angered both the pilots and the Weapons Schools, and resulted in Skidmore asking for reassignment, as Geisler explained: "When Ashy told us we couldn't maintain our duel currency in the school and 'up north,' 'Grunt' asked if he could instead go back to the Weapons School. It was a career decision, and they granted him that choice." He would be allowed to move back to the F-16 FWS in due course, but not immediately.

Ashy and White were friends who knew each other already and frequently drank together as members of the covert Air Force social club, "The Bar Stoolers," but this was the start of a turbulent working relationship between the two. White was a West Virginian who had joined the Air Force's ROTC program, graduated pilot training and had gone straight to the F-4. There, he'd had the misfortune to spend his first combat tour in Vietnam flying from the back seat of the F-4 – a policy that affected all of the pilots going to the F-4 straight from UPT at that time. After six months he had been upgraded to fly from the front cockpit, and had eventually flown the F-4E with the 4th TFW, Seymour Johnson. In January 1975, he had been picked out of a tour flying the F-4E in Japan to help stand up the 26th TFTS Aggressors. Two years later he was a flight commander with the 65th FWS at Nellis. He had progressed to the TFWC as the then wing commander, Chuck Cunningham's, XO. When Hugh Brown had died, White was assigned to the 64th FWS as its ops officer, replacing Henderson, who had gone to take over the Red Eagles.[30]

By the time White arrived at Tonopah, news of the decision to deny Scott a DFC for his recovery of the MiG-17 and MiG-21 had reached the vice commander of TAC, who happened to be the former TFWC commander and recently promoted three-star general, Robert Kelley. Fully aware of the details stripped from the unclassified write-up, Kelley called the board and personally recommended that they award the medal. Tim Kinnan, Kelley's XO, and John Jumper, Creech's XO, were also instrumental in helping push the award through, said Scott. The board agreed and Scott received the medal.

EXTRA-CURRICULAR TESTING

At various times in the Red Eagles' history, the squadron worked closely with AFSC's 6513th TS, Red Hats, and its test pilots at Edwards AFB to conduct testing that fell outside of CONSTANT PEG's original remit. "The airplanes were used not only to validate tactics, but also to do initial tests," Matheny explained.

Some 4477th TES commanders disliked such collaborative efforts, perhaps because they had little say in the matter and because the assets and their pilots were sometimes sequestered by Systems Command, but most probably because they took exposures away from the TAF – the frontline squadrons. However, these tests were usually of great value. Sometimes, AFSC wanted more, and "borrowed" assets from the 4477th TES when it needed them.

White recalled that Gen Fischer particularly disliked having to share the assets with the Red Hats. "He hated them with a passion. Several times, the only reason we did testing with them was because we were ordered to do it by HQ." Whether Bond's mishap had influenced Fischer's view is not clear, but White said this: "He thought that they were unprofessional, that their facilities were shabby, and that they didn't go by normal maintenance standards or practices. On one occasion they had asked for the use of one of our airplanes. The call had come to my home on a Saturday morning while Fischer was away on a cross-country trip in his F-15. I met with Gen Ashy and we agreed we'd meet him when he landed on Sunday. The next day, we met him after he put his gear away. Ashy told him what had happened. Fischer jumped out of his chair and almost screamed, 'Not only no! But, hell no!' and stormed out. Ashy looked at his chest and then looked at mine and said, "I didn't even feel that bullet go through.'"

The relationship between the 4477th TES and the 6513th TS did sometimes have benefits, and several Red Eagle pilots over the years flew Soviet MiGs and Sukhoi jet fighters and fighter-bombers belonging to AFSC that the Red Eagles did not have. Some of these were completely new types, and others were more advanced versions of the MiG-21 and MiG-23 operated at Tonopah. Such brief exposures gave the Red Eagle pilots an appreciation of what they needed to be teaching the frontline fighter pilot about more modern and capable threats, or illuminated the subtle changes between one marque of aircraft and another.

The Red Eagles occasionally flew against TAC's 422nd TES, "The Four-Two-Two," which was based at Nellis and developed tactics and procedures that would accompany the introduction to service of a new aircraft, weapons system, radar upgrade, or capability. Some of these tests brought the technical exploitation of the MiGs full circle. For example, HAVE GARDEN, an earlier program to profile the MiG-21's compressor and turbine blades, resulted in several US radars having their electronic identification (EID) libraries updated. These new updates were given their operational testing by the 422nd at Nellis, and to do so, the 422nd needed to fly against the actual MiG-21. The Red Eagles were therefore asked to help. The same process occurred with the Flogger. "The Tumansky R-29-300 in the MiG-23 would show up on our radars as a DC-10 because the compressor face was just so huge," said Matheny. He flew the MiG-23 against 422nd TES F-15s equipped with the latest radar modifications to ensure that the new computer algorithms could correctly identify the radar returns as being those of an R-29A, as opposed to the General Electric CF-6 motors of the commercial airliner.

The wing sweep lever in the MiG-23, with detents at the 16-, 45- and 72-degree positions. (Steve Davies, www.constantpeg.com)

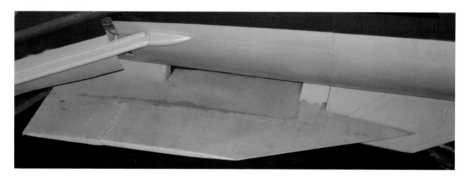

The MiG-23 featured a dorsal fin that folded upon lowering the undercarriage. Lenny Bucko had wondered how any pilot could manage to grind the fin off during landing, but all became clear when he managed to do exactly that months later! (Steve Davies, www.constantpeg.com)

1   2   3

The original 4477th TEF patch, designed by Navy pilot LtCdr Chuck "Heater" Heatley and approved as a result of Maj David "DL" Smith's efforts at TAC HQ, Langley AFB (1). When the Red Eagles were elevated to squadron status, the patch was changed to reflect the new "TES" status (2). Over the years, the patch was modified very slightly (compare the Eagle and the background colours with the 4477th TEF patch), and this is a scan of the last ever official batch. It was taken from the vault at Tonopah in March 1988 by Maj James "Tony" Mahoney and given to the author in mid-2007. When Col George "G2" Gennin ordered the maintainers to wear official Air Force uniforms, a revised copy of the 4477th TES patch was created to include a low-conspicuity black star (3). The officers continued wearing the version with the white star. (Steve Davies' collection)

The right side console of the Eglin MiG-21 shows the red and yellow striped handle of the Fishbed C/E SK-1 Canopy Capsule Seat. Another handle was installed on the other side of the seat, and both had to be squeezed and pulled upwards to initiate ejection. (Steve Davies, www.constantpeg.com)

There is strong evidence to suggest that "Red 85," the Fishbed C/E at Eglin, is the former 4477th TES VIP hangar MiG-21F-13 (USAF serial number 14) from Tonopah. This aircraft was repainted on arrival at Eglin, but I was told it was repainted identically. This aircraft simply "arrived at the museum overnight," and the curator was told not to ask any questions. (Steve Davies, www.constantpeg.com)

Adorned with the name of LtGen David McCloud, a former Red Eagle who was killed flying his aerobatic Yak-54 over Alaska in Jul 1998, this MiG-17F Fresco C is believed to be HAVE DRILL. It is now located outside the TTF at Nellis AFB. (Steve Davies, www.constantpeg.com)

A view through the cockpit glass of the MiG-21F-13 on display at the Eglin AFB Armament Museum, Florida. Note the US G-meter (far left). Many of the instruments carry English language placards. (Steve Davies, www.constantpeg.com)

The MiG-21 wasn't a "vertical" fighter, but its slow speed capabilities meant it could be looped at much lower airspeeds than any American fighter if the need arose. (USAF via Steve Davies)

When the US Air Force declassified a small selection of Red Eagles photographs, this image was inadvertently included. It shows the cockpit of a MiG-21MF, and its inclusion in the cache of images supports the possibility that the 4477th TES did indeed operate this marque of Fishbed. (USAF via Steve Davies)

"Red 96," a Chinese-built J-7B with the USAF serial 47 on the nose landing gear doors, was one of the last MiGs acquired by the 4477th TES before its closure in March 1988. (USAF via Steve Davies)

Now painted in silver and positioned outside the 64th FWS at Nellis, this MiG-21F-13 is a former 4477th TEF/TES example and can be seen in the middle photo on the previous page wearing a black and green camouflage scheme. It is rumored that this aircraft was the first of the Indonesian Fishbeds, and had USAF serial 004. (Neil Henderson via Steve Davies)

Returning to base meant flying over a number of roads and dirt tracks, but most of these fell within the controlled airspace of the Tonopah Test Range, and the MiGs maintained sufficient altitude in case of an engine flameout that they were very difficult to see in any case. (USAF via Steve Davies)

The Old and the New. A green, black and gray MiG-21F-13 (left) of Indonesian origin sits alongside a white Shenyang J-7B in late 1987. This particular F-13 was retired to the Threat Training Facility at Nellis, where it stayed for many years. (USAF via Steve Davies)

Photographed between 1987 and early 1988, a Chinese-built Shenyang J-7B Fishbed lands at Tonopah. (The scratch and attempts to touch it up were conducted before the image was released to the public.) (USAF via Steve Davies)

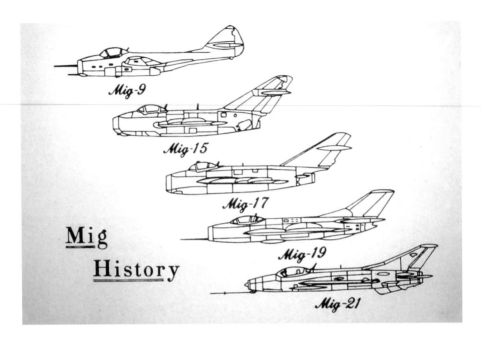

A 4477th TES briefing slide shown to visiting TAF pilots; it charts the progression of the MiG family of fighters. (USAF via Steve Davies)

LtCol Jack Manclark poses in the VIP hangar with the 4477th TES Red Eagles pilots, intel officer and GCI controllers in c.1986. The Fishbed, "Red 85," is an Indonesian MiG-21F-13 with a USAF serial 14. (USAF via Steve Davies)

The throttle in the MiG-23 had a mechanical lock (lever in front of the throttle grip) which prevented it from being retarded at high Mach numbers, thus averting sudden decelerations that could have ripped the motor from its mounts. (Steve Davies, www.constantpeg.com)

The MiG-23 front panel, with white stripe down the center to assist the pilot in neutralising the control stick during out-of-control flight. Even from an elevated angle, this photograph demonstrates how poor the visibility ahead was. (Steve Davies, www.constantpeg.com)

Photographed in the mid-1980s, a 4477th TES Indonesian Fishbed C/E poses for the camera. Note the intake cone fully retracted for subsonic flight. (USAF via Steve Davies)

Maj Thomas Drake's MiG-23MS Flogger E, "Red 49" (USAF serial 20). When he finally left the unit, Drake remarked that the MiG-23 had tried to kill him on every sortie. With 294 sorties in the interceptor, he was the 4477th TES's most experienced Flogger pilot of all time. Note the "battleship gray" gloss paint and the curious pentagon-shaped emblem on the nose. (USAF via Steve Davies)

LtCdr Cary "Dollar" Silvers unstraps from the front seat of his F-14 Tomcat during a visit with his parents at NAS Atlanta in 1982. Four years later he would be flying MiGs at a secret desert location. (Cary Silvers via Steve Davies)

An early photo, probably from the early 1980s, showing an FWIC F-16 and a MiG-21F-13 in flight. The Weapons School was one of the first to benefit from CONSTANT PEG. (USAF via Steve Davies)

A 4477th TES T-38 Talon sits on the ramp at Tonopah in the midday sun. The eventual acquisition of four Talons by the Red Eagles made life considerably easier. (USAF via Steve Davies)

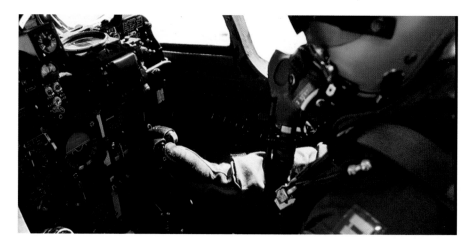

The white line down the instrument panel – so important when recovering from uncontrolled flight – is visible in this wide angle view of one of the Red Eagles' Indonesian Fishbeds. (USAF via Steve Davies)

4477th TES maintainers board one of the Red Eagles' Cessna 404s for the early morning flight from Nellis to Tonopah. (Lenny Bucko via Steve Davies)

MiG-21F-13 "Red 84" taxis past the tower at Tonopah. Dated approximately 1986, this was one of the last of the Indonesian F-13s retired by Manclark. It carries the USAF serial number 11 on the nose landing gear door. (USAF via Steve Davies)

The MiG-21F-13 cockpit left much to be desired from an ergonomic standpoint, but equally as alien to the American pilots were the "kumquat gauges," which measured parameters in unfamiliar units – kilograms, liters, etc. (USAF via Steve Davies)

Mark Postai's models and Aggressor flight helmet (left to right): MiG-21, MiG-17, F-5 and MiG-23. These models helped Linda Postai put together the pieces of the puzzle following her husband's tragic death. (Linda Hughes (Postai) via Steve Davies)

Maj Karl Whittenberg straps into the front seat of a T-38 at Tonopah. The T-38s were vital for the "clean and dry" checks that were performed on the MiGs immediately following take-off – an event that soon turned into a competition to see who could join formation the quickest and closest! (Lenny Bucko via Steve Davies)

Until the 4477th TES was able to acquire its own T-38 Talons, it borrowed examples such as this 57th FWW Aggressor jet. (Lenny Bucko via Steve Davies)

One of only two surviving contemporary photos of a 4477th TES MiG-23MS Flogger E. The enlarged spine of the vertical tail was intended to work in tandem with the extending dorsal spine (folded away in this photo) to help reduce the jet's tendency to yaw from left to right in high-speed flight. (USAF via Steve Davies)

Capt Mark "Toast" Postai's MiG-23 model. Custom made and painted to the last detail (note red stars with yellow boarders), it is poignant that the young fighter pilot chose "Red 23" to be painted on the nose – the very Flogger in which he was killed. (Linda Hughes (Postai) via Steve Davies)

LtCol Earl Henderson (in the cockpit of the F-5) formally takes command of the 4477th TEF following Gail Peck's dismissal. Prior to his new appointment, Henderson had been the 64th FWS operations officer. (Earl Henderson via Steve Davies)

Aileron rolls in the MiG-21 could be exciting if the pilot failed to blend in rudder inputs gently. IPs throughout the history of the 4477th TEF/TES would allow their students to learn this lesson the hard way! (USAF via Steve Davies)

Red Eagles maintainer Billy Lightfoot could fix anything with a motor and wheels. This c.1981 photograph at Tonopah showcases just a few of his improvised vehicles. (Lenny Bucko via Steve Davies)

The Red Eagles compiled a number of classified briefing slides to show visiting TAF pilots. This one compares the relative dimensions of the F-5 (red) with the MiG-21 (yellow). (USAF via Steve Davies)

In June 1979, TAC executed a counter cover operation in an attempt to hide the true purpose of the recent renovations at Tonopah from Soviet satellites. This F-86 Sabre was just one of the aircraft flown from the bare base as part of that effort. A month later the first MiGs arrived. (USAF via Steve Davies)

The Fishbed's two dorsal speed brakes and the starboard cannon port are clearly visible in this c.1987 image of a Red Eagle MiG-21. Less obvious is the black navigation aerial, which was one of the few external modifications made to the MiGs by the USAF. (USAF via Steve Davies)

Construction of the MiG-23 hangars commenced around 1982. This aerial photograph shows the ground north of the MiG-21/MiG-17 hangars being flattened and compacted before the structures were erected. (Lenny Bucko via Steve Davies)

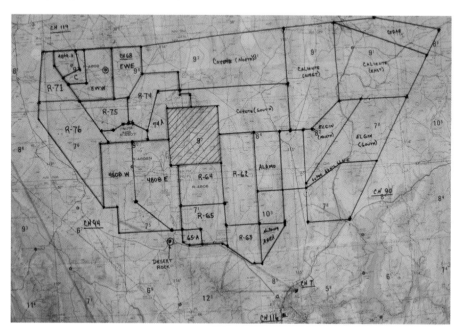

The Nellis and Tonopah ranges are shown clearly in this 1982 photograph of the 4477th TES's airspace chart. The red hatched mark in the middle is Area 51, while Tonopah is located in the far northwest of the map and is labeled 4809-A. Nellis. (Lenny Bucko via Steve Davies)

Two 64th FWS F-5s formate with a 4477th TEF MiG-17 (leading) and MiG-21 (trailing). The MiGs transferred from HAVE IDEA were all finished in a natural silver, but of note in this photograph from c.1979 is the TAC badge applied to the vertical fin of the MiG-21, clearly identifying its new owner! (USAF via Steve Davies)

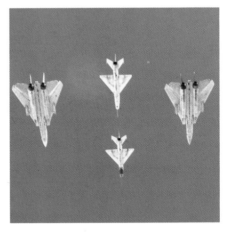

A 4477th TEF MiG-21 taxis back to parking at Tonopah. Presumably a still image taken from a cine film, the Fishbed is seen carrying a center line fuel tank – an unusual sight for a Red Eagles jet. (USAF via Steve Davies)

The US Navy had been a major proponent of MiG exploitations since HAVE DOUGHNUT in 1968. Here, two Navy F-14 Tomcats bracket a pair of smaller 4477th TEF MIG-21s in a photo dated c.1980. (USAF via Steve Davies)

Matheny also worked with the Nellis squadron to conduct AIM-9L and AIM-9M testing against the MiGs' motors. He flew his MiG in front of a fighter armed with a captive Sidewinder: "We wanted to see at what ranges, and under what conditions, the newer missiles could actually see the MiGs. 'Can you see me here at this range, this throttle position? If I go to idle here, can you see me?' That kind of stuff."

Although the Red Eagles never fired live missiles, some former pilots recall that they did carry inert AA-2 Atolls. Dating from the 1960s, the Atoll worked just like the Sidewinder in that it looked for the hot exhaust of an engine, emanating a warbling tone in the pilot's headset that varied in pitch according to how well its IR seeker head was locked on. When the tone reached a high-pitched shriek, the missile's seeker had achieved a lock-on and the missile could be launched at will.

The AA-2 was less sophisticated than the newest versions of the Sidewinder for which Matheny had provided a target, and was easily decoyed by flares dropped from an opponent, or even the sun or a heat source on the ground. Similarly, its seeker head needed to be positioned almost directly behind an opponent before it could lock on to the hot engine. By contrast, the newer Sidewinders had an "all aspect" capability – they could be fired from head-on or from the side, because their seekers were sensitive enough to track the aerodynamically heated skin of the target if its exhaust nozzle(s) was not in view. This imbalance was unfair on the Red Eagles, but it did represent the reality of America's technical advantage over the Soviet Union. Later, old versions of the AIM-9 were carried to simulate the AA-2.

In one test in 1985, Matheny flew the MiG-21 against AFSC test pilots assigned to fly the F-16XL, an advanced version of the Air Force's lightweight fighter competition winner featuring a highly swept cranked-arrow delta wing; and the concept demonstrator of what would become the F-15E Strike Eagle, a strike-fighter version of the air-to-air F-15 Eagle. At the time, the two were competing against each other for the Air Force's Dual Role Fighter competition. "The F-16XL was being flown by test pilots from Edwards," Matheny explained. "We briefed each other about our airplanes and they turned around to me and told me that they were going to be all over me – they had a roll rate of 800 degrees per second, which was the fastest rate in the inventory." Up until then, the record had been held by the T-38, which could be coaxed into a roll of 720 degrees per second.

"I got to thinking about that and it turned out that the roll rate meant nothing," he continued. "The problem with that airplane was that it was a big bleeder: it just bled airspeed like nothing else when it was forced to turn hard. I ate them alive in the MiG-21. The F-15 on the other hand, flown by 422nd TES pilots, was a pretty good performer – they resisted the urge to get slow and jump in a phone booth with the MiG. They flew all the way around the ranges at low level trying to burn off all this gas and he still needed to burn off more when we joined up on each other."

In November, two new pilots joined the squadron: Capt Edward D. "Hog" Phelan, "Bandit 47," and Navy Lt Guy A. Brubaker, "Bandit 48." Phelan was a surfer, UCLA graduate, and cheerleader who'd once interviewed for a sales position with IBM, but found the stuffy corporate image incongruent with his own. With a desire to drive either boats or aircraft, he looked to the Coast Guard first, but actually joined the Air Force when someone told him they wouldn't make him get his hair cut short. Since he saw his hair as crucial to his ability to chase skirt, that was a major consideration.

Following pilot training in 1973, he went to Torejon AB, Spain, to fly the F-4. There he had met David Bland, forming a friendship that ultimately resulted in his getting assigned to the Red Eagles. He had gone through the 414th FWS in 1981, and then been assigned to the F-4 RTU. "I was an IP, but my real task was to try and get the IP corps infused with some good air-to-air experience. As a Weapons School graduate, I was there to teach them some broader and deeper air-to-air skills." It was far from an exciting assignment, and few of the IPs wanted to hear what he had to say.

By 1983, he was interviewing at Nellis for a job at the 414th FWS. "The problem was that I had not been at the RTU for long enough, and they weren't willing to flex. Luckily, I had met Dave Bland at the bar at Nellis, and he told me that he might be hiring. Part of the thinking was that the 4477th TES was too Nellis inbred – all the people were coming from Nellis – and the program was moving from being super-Top Secret to something less." In order to join the Red Eagles, Phelan had first to go to the Air Force's flight safety school, since Bland was recommending Phelan to Gennin on the basis that he would join the squadron as a trained safety officer.

Gennin had agreed, and Phelan was hired. But he almost never made it to the Red Eagles. Before he could fly the MiGs, the squadron sent him to get his Federal Aviation Authority (FAA) commercial multi-engine rating. "My 400-hour check pilot tried to kill me a couple of times. In fact, on my last check ride we ended up in storms and 80-knot winds. We were in this little Cherokee and there was so much turbulence that he turned the airplane around on the airways. I took control and got us home. When we landed, he kneeled down

and kissed the ground. Then he hugged me and thanked me for saving his life."
Next he got rated in the T-38, and finally he started transitioning to the
MiG-21. The whole process took around one month.

In the fall of 1984 Gail Peck, the Red Eagles' creator and now a colonel,
would once again be briefed into the program. His dismissal by Kelley all those
years before had seen him "read out" of CONSTANT PEG, resulting in his
being totally in the dark about its progress. Fortunately, his career had not been
ruined, and he'd been promoted and assigned the position of vice wing
commander of the 18th TFW, the F-15 Eagle wing based at Kadena AB, Japan.
Peck had deployed six jets to Nellis to fly against CONSTANT PEG, and
himself flew a sortie against a MiG-23. With the deployment over, Peck was
once again read out of CONSTANT PEG.

Between November 26 and 30, the 4477th TES was the focus of a local
Management Effectiveness Inspection (MEI) that had been directed by 57th
FWW Deputy Commander, Tactics & Test, to prepare the Red Eagles for an
upcoming TAC MEI. This MEI was yet another sign that the Red Eagles were
being treated increasingly like other TAF units.

PRANKSTERS

While the 4477th TES had its fair share of brash, loud, outspoken, and eccentric
personalities, few could match the quirky nature of one particular technical
sergeant known universally as "Weird Harold." Harold's eccentricity wasn't
universally appreciated – particularly not at the squadron commander level – but
most thought him particularly entertaining. Harold was an ex-Thunderbirds
maintainer who hailed from one of the southern states, and with whom fellow
maintainer Brad Fisher had briefly shared a trailer at Indian Village – "He used
to bring back moonshine," he recalled approvingly. Bucko recalled that Harold
would often work the ramp area – servicing the MiGs and preparing them for
flight – wearing a dress. He sometimes waved the MiGs out from the ramp with
nothing on other than his belt and radio.

For Gennin, who had been unaware of who and what Harold was, his first
meeting went down like a lead balloon. As the new Red Eagles commander sat
at the bar in the Indian Village, Harold, wearing red lipstick, a blonde wig, and
a flowery dress, pulled up a chair next to his new boss and introduced himself.
Gennin, bystanders said, was not amused.

For new pilots, said Matheny, Harold reserved a vile but equally hilarious trick
known as his "baby chicken in a box." He would excitedly invite the pilot to

rummage through the straw to see his baby chicken. The poor victim would put his hand in the box to pull back the straw, only to discover Harold's genitalia stuffed through a hole in the side. Shervanick recalled that Harold would also occasionally wear a rubber chicken on his head. "He was like the character Corporal Klinger out of the TV show, MASH, but I tell you what, he could fix an airplane."

Geisler was present one day when US Navy Admiral Tom Cassidy, of HAVE DOUGHNUT fame, arrived in an F-5E for a VIP visit. "Hound Dog was stood at the ramp as the admiral shut down. From behind him, Harold ran out to the jet. He had his combat boots, a web belt, and a hat on. Nothing else. He ran up to the airplane, climbed up the ladder and kissed the admiral on the cheek. Then he ran back into the hangar! Phil just did not know what to do. We all knew that Weird Harold and Admiral Cassidy were good friends, but Phil did not."

While Harold may not have left Gennin with the sort of enduring impression from a first meeting that most people would have aimed for, since Ellis' departure Harold (whose experience probably went back as far as DOUGHNUT) had stepped up to the plate as one of the most senior maintainers and his colleagues and superiors respected him. Geisler was one of them:

> Gennin knew how the maintenance guys respected Harold. He walked a fine line and treated Harold with a degree of respect. I personally think Gennin was able to somewhat "win" Harold over, and that was one reason maintenance got on board with the changes he introduced. In turn, they became the best bunch of professional maintainers in the military. Harold never wanted anyone to get hurt and was very protective of "his" pilots and MiGs. Gennin and Weird had professional respect for each other. Never did I ever see or hear Gennin ever say anything negative to or about him.

However, Gennin told the author that he eventually ordered Tittle to have Harold reassigned.

There were also well-established pranks and traditions that the pilots would play on one another. One of them was called "Firsts," where a new pilot was told that the first time he did anything in the squadron he had to pay a fee to the bar fund. "If it was your first taxi, you paid $10. Your first take-off, $20. Your first landing, another $20, and so on," Matheny chuckled. "Some guys you could get $200 or $300 out of, and then of course you'd go and buy something for the squadron and show it to the guy, telling him, 'Hey! You bought this for us!'" Time and again the same name came up as the main protagonist behind many of the other pranks that characterized the lighter side of life at Tonopah in the 1980s: Geisler.

Geisler was the genius behind what became known as the "Boom Recovery." Initially it began because it was a useful bargaining tool, but later it seemed to be little more than a sport. He confirmed that it had all started when he had been talking to the F-117 pilots at the Man Camp:

> I asked them if we were keeping them awake during the day. They told me, "Hell, no, it'd take more than that to disturb our sleep." "Really?" I said. The next day I briefed the new Boom Recovery to all the guys: "These fuckers don't think that we can keep them awake. Save enough gas to descend from 30,000ft as fast as you can. Point directly at the Man Camp and make sure you're at 5,000ft when you pass over it supersonic – make it brutal! Then fly up the initial [the approach to the runway] and land." We end up booming them so bad that the hangars were shaking, pictures were falling off the walls, and we were even scaring the crap out of our own guys! Then the phone rang – the -117 guys said, "OK, we give up!" Those booms were scary and we had flattened that Man Camp!

Some of the booms to which the Red Eagles subjected the F-117 pilots and maintainers were far more innocent. In winter time particularly, the MiGs performed better in the cold Tonopah air, their jet engines deriving an additional performance boost the colder it became. This was not lost on Stucky who, one day, having recently converted to the Flogger under the tutelage of Saxman, was giving a pair of F-14s a PP:

> We did an acceleration profile, where I was going to show him how fast we could go. 860 knots was the red line on the Flogger's airspeed, so we would go right up to that speed. We were flying over the "Dog Bone" lake near Tonopah at about 0900. We ran up the Dog Bone and boomed the whole [TTR] complex because there were three of us. The commander of the other unit [4450th TG] was Col Mike Short, who I had flown F-4s with. He was having a staff meeting at the time and a bunch of his ceiling tiles had come loose and dropped onto his table.

Short was not amused.

Stucky and Geisler were soon operating as partners in crime, and their friends and fellow pilots learned quickly that neither man could be trusted where jokes were concerned. All of the Red Eagles were given a security badge that could only be worn at Tonopah and without which they could not disembark the MU-2. If they were already at TTR when they lost it, they would be detained until the squadron commander walked into the security police building and verified they were who they said they were. The badge policy offered Geisler and Stucky all sorts of opportunities for mischief. "You could bump into a new guy in the hallway and take his badge off him without him noticing," Geisler admitted. "You immediately went to the pisser and taped it inside the urinal. Then you'd go to the maintenance guys and tell them that so and so's badge was there, and they would line up to piss on it. Then we would announce on the loudspeaker that the pass had been found and was available to collect from the men's room."

One variation of the game included stealing a pilot's pass as he slept during the journey from Nellis to TTR in the MU-2. The Red Eagles' Marine at that time, Tullos, often fell foul of this trick, Geisler exclaimed. "He would never learn, and he always fell asleep. While he slept, we stole his pass. The cops would arrest him as he got off the plane, and we'd look over our shoulder and say, 'It's OK, I'll fly your hops today, Cajun!'"

When they grew bored with this, Stucky confessed, they concocted an even crueler trick. "We took Cajun's briefcase, changed the combination to the locks, and then put his pass inside it. We all get off the airplane but George won't because he knows he is in big trouble if he steps off without his pass. It was like the Samsonite suitcase commercial, where this big gorilla is trying to get into the suitcase. We were calling, 'Hey! Cajun! Come on, let's go!' Eventually, Cajun just threw the briefcase out of the airplane to the surprise of the cops. We opened it for him, but he was just beside himself."

Geisler's sense of humor sometimes got him into trouble with his commanders, particularly when it was for the benefit of the Russian satellites. Tonopah was a magnet for satellite interest as it was, with each exposure lasting in the order of 22 minutes. "I once had the maintenance guys go up and paint '*moya zopa*' – 'kiss my ass' in Russian – on the top of one of the hangars. On another occasion, I had them put a T-38 nose out of the front of a hangar, and an F-5's tail out of the back, so that from the air it looked like we had an airplane about 108ft long. In the end, it actually attracted more satellite attention, so the commander told me to quit doing shit like that."

Geisler explained more about Soviet intelligence efforts: "We knew that they [the Soviets] knew [about the MiGs], but we knew that they didn't know how many, how often we flew them, or to what degree we were using them – they had no idea how many pilots we were training against them." He added: "At around that time, some Soviet general officers and other dignitaries came to Nellis on a 'be good to each other' tour. Myself, the squadron commander, and some Aggressors were having dinner with them and everyone was being cordial.

Then, one of these Soviet Air Force generals interrupted one of our generals mid-speech: 'So, General, how many MiGs do you have at Tonopah?' Without batting an eye, he turned around and said, 'I don't know. Maybe 300, or 350?' and then went back to his conversation. It didn't phase him a bit. The Russian guy almost passed out."

RESULTS

At the end of 1984, the 4477th TES had 15 MiG-21s and nine MiG-23s on strength. While this represented a total of nine more aircraft than they had at the close of 1983, the most significant statistic was that CONSTANT PEG had flown 901 sorties more than the year before. This improvement was largely down to Gennin. When Nathman had joined CONSTANT PEG in April 1982, one of his initial observations had been that some of the pilots thought of themselves as being just a little too exclusive. "The mission was to expose Air Force, Marine, and Navy guys to the MiGs, but it seemed like sometimes the Air Force would find any excuse not to fly. We actually started calling it Constant Keg because that was how it felt [since they spent their time at the bar instead of flying]."

But as Nathman departed Tonopah for the last time, it was clear that CONSTANT PEG's operational footprint had deepened and widened significantly in the two years he had been there:

One of the things that Gennin did was to focus the squadron back on its mission – he made it act and breathe like an operational squadron. The Air Force was paying a lot of money, and there was a lot of talent. What we were seeing was us getting away from thinking that we were some kind of demigod out there in the desert, some sort of niche; and let's really start getting our product out there: the exposure. In my first year, we didn't fly that much, but by the time I was into my last year, we were flying our butts off. What I was most proud of, though, was that the experience – the exposure – had improved qualitatively, too.

The improvement in exposures is a fact evidenced, at least statistically, by the ratio of sorties to exposures in 1984: 2,099 sorties for 800 exposures, or 2.6 exposures per Blue Air pilot. In 1983, that figure stood at only 1.8 exposures per Blue Air pilot (1,198 sorties for 666 exposures). "Gennin had delivered exactly what the Air Force had asked of him," Nathman applauded.

CHAPTER 11

FROM BLACK TO GRAY, 1985

"George Gennin had done a lot with the unit, but when I had interviewed with Fischer he had sat me in his office for two hours and told me what else he thought needed doing," White recalled. "He did not favor George at that time because one of the maintenance guys had died servicing a fuel cell [at Tonopah].[31] Fischer blamed George and Tittle, the maintenance officer, for that. George and I had been friends a long time, and when I took the squadron, George told me: 'I only tell Fischer what I want him to know.' Fischer was aware of this.[32] It was clear that there were lots of people at TTR that were working for the two-star, which was how he knew what George was telling him, and what he was not."

Fischer had also told White that the continued growth of F-117 operations at TTR, and what he believed was an ambulatory change to some of the maintenance practices of the 4477th TES, despite Gennin's obvious successes, were reasons enough for him to be very clear: "He and Joe Ashy told me straight: 'We are tired of not getting straight answers. The first time we get what we consider not to be all of the answer, you are gone.'" It was also immediately obvious that White would be under significant pressure from Creech, via the general's XO and the two-star TAC DO, Gen Dugan. They, too, were clear: he was to increase sortie count and nail down the maintenance operation once and for all. If the results did not come quickly, he would be fired.

COMPETING DEMANDS

White was now in an unenviable position and under considerable pressure. He had to balance the demands of two hawk-eyed, no-nonsense generals at Nellis who had overtly threatened to fire him before he had even set foot at Tonopah with the needs of his squadron, the directives of the TAC commander and his DO (whose threats of dismissal were less direct but equally as real), and the demands of the TAF's Blue Air pilots, whom he had to expose to CONSTANT PEG in greater quantities than any previous commander. The balance he struck didn't make many of his pilots happy. Some already disliked the fact that he was going to perpetuate the culture of change that Gennin had started, and some thought that he would go on to spend too much time at Nellis "fire fighting," and not enough time actually at Tonopah.

But he was adamant that since "about 90 percent" of the pilots he was now in charge of had already worked either for or with him, he automatically had confidence in their ability to manage themselves when he was not there. "In the first week I was at Tonopah, I made Paco the assistant ops officer to Blazo. I understood the need to delegate – I had learned that as the ops officer with the 64th FWS and on my staff tours. I had seen guys try to do everything, and super-control their people, but it had not worked. Letting the operations run didn't mean that I lost any control; I could still look at the schedule and take out anything I didn't like, for example, but I wanted my ops officer to put it together each morning." Placing trust in Bland and Geisler was essential if he was going to be able to deliver results.

Flying more sorties was the first hurdle to overcome. "It seemed to me that the main thing stopping us was the availability of range space. We could fix that through manipulation of the range areas," White was sure. He also identified quickly that he needed more maintainers if the sortie count was to rise. He briefed Fischer, then Dugan, and finally, Creech. "Creech looked at me and said, 'Fine, it sounds like you're doing what we have asked you to do.' He looked at his generals and told them to give me what I needed."

A solution to the maintenance issue was more complex, though. He was sent on a commander's maintenance officer course:

It was the one they gave wing commanders and those who were independent of the normal wing structure. I talked with George [Gennin] about it and he was adamant about what he thought still needed doing. I went back to Langley and got permission to brief in the TAC head of logistics and some of his staff. They came to Tonopah and helped us get a proper maintenance organization going – until then it was loose and there was no real structure to it. For example, if you wanted some hydraulic tubing, you'd go into our supply hangar and try and find a bit of tubing that looked right among a mass of tubes hung on nails.

Gennin's early inventory had presumably fallen by the wayside, because White recalled: "We didn't know how much of anything we had. Parts would just turn up in the big crates, and guys would keep their passports on them so that they could fly at no notice to visit MiG crash sites. If they could reach the sites, they would come back with boxes of parts."

Having established what needed doing, White came up against the same sort of problems with a small contingent of maintainers that Gennin had faced, but this time it was much more severe:

> There were men who had been there since Tom Gibbs' days. They told me, "You can try and change it, but it is not going to happen. We are going to do things our own way." I would say, "OK," and a week later they would be reassigned to another unit. More than one threatened me with bodily harm and with ruining my career. For the most part, we had all the right people, but there were a few "old gang" guys that I had to get rid of who had told me that they were not going to do things my way. When people realized that I was firing people and that they were not coming back, they got the idea, and lots of the other old gang guys moved over to my side pretty easily.

While these men were good, they were not indispensable, as Gennin, and now White, made clear. The loss of their knowledge was certainly a short-term blow to the Red Eagles, but the MPC at Randolph quickly found replacements. "We called the people in Texas our 'Green Door' people, because we could get anyone we wanted." He credits a big airman, Chief M/Sgt Matt Mazzerati, as being his eyes and ears among the maintainers, and for being a crucial supporter of the changes that were being brought about. Gennin had hired Mazzerati to replace Ellis, and he was continuing to help ease the transition from Yosemite Sams to Air Force NCOs with a can-do attitude throughout. White liked the man: "I called him Maserati, and he stood about 6ft 7in. He had spent about eight years as an instructor NCO. He was the best. He was my first sergeant and I told him that anytime he needed to talk to me, he should just kick the door down. It took a good six months for the tension to ease, and Maserati would get right in people's faces if they got in the way."

In the meantime, the new boss spent considerable amounts of time at Nellis, working to keep Fischer and Ashy appraised of the latest developments.

Ashy in particular was an often awkward character. "We called him 'Screamin' Joe' because he would yell and throw things." The general was a hard-to-please task master who had a penchant for physical fitness and conditioning, and would quiz White on his officers and NCOs being overweight. The real problem was that he often failed to differentiate between a big man and a fat man. "Maserati had a big barrel chest and was just huge, but Ashy always complained that he was overweight. It was the same with Paul Stucky – this guy had been recruited by the Air Force to play football, to be a lineman; but Ashy now wanted him to go on the weight control program."

White was sometimes required to keep Ashy in the loop via the 57th FWW AT commander, Col Bob Lauderette, and this usually occurred when White attended the wing's weekly meeting at Nellis each Friday. At one such meeting, White said, Lauderette had tried to force him to check out an Aggressor pilot in the MiGs so that he could get the TAC DO's endorsement on his Officer Effectiveness Report (OER), and in doing so improve his career prospects:

> I told him that he didn't have the authority to order me to do it. "I am not going to do it. You don't even have the authority to get him up there [to Tonopah]! I tell you what, let's go and ask Ashy if it's OK." He said, "Hell, no! I know what Ashy will say!" Lauderette wouldn't tell Ashy anything that smelled of bad news, so I would tell the general direct. He'd want to know why I would tell him and Lauderette wouldn't, and I said, 'Because I am not afraid of you. You can fire me if you want.' And sometimes he did. In fact, I got fired by Ashy twice when I was there!

Fortunately for White, the number of reinstatements by Ashy equaled the number of firings.

THE WRONG BOYLES

White always personally hosted VIPs visiting the squadron, but despite his best intentions, things did not always go to plan. On one occasion, he'd mentioned to Geisler that a general by the name of Bobby Boyles was en route for a tour. Geisler had responded that he knew him and that the general had scored a MiG-21 kill in Vietnam:

> Hound Dog told me: "Great! You stand by the MiG-21 and I'll introduce you when he arrives." Anyway, the airplane arrives and this guy steps out, but it's not the same Bobby Boyles as I know. Hound Dog walks him over and points to me:

"I know you know Paco," he says. The general's looking kind of weird, and then he goes, "And here's the MiG-21. This is probably the closest you have been to one since you shot one down." The guy goes, "I'm not even rated."

Hound Dog had not even looked at the guy's jacket to see if he was rated. When the guy left, he turned to me and said, "What the hell did you tell me you knew him for?!" and I said, "Well, I do. But that's not the same guy! Couldn't you see he wasn't wearing any wings when he got out of the airplane?"[33] That was the kind of shit that Hound Dog did from time to time.

White's faux pas did not stop there. Since he was busy developing a maintenance model for the unit, he was not always up to speed on the rules and regulations on the operational side of things. That was sometimes a problem, as these formed part of the briefing for most VIPs. Geisler explained one particular incident:

When Gen Ashy was posted to Nellis from TAC, he visited for a briefing, and Phil was insistent that he gave it. Since Ashy is coming from TAC, he knows about the program. Right off the bat, Hound Dog starts talking about a sortie where we fly BFM with the MiG-23. Ashy turns around and says, "I didn't think you did BFM with the MiG-23?" Phil replied, 'Well, sir, that was not exactly what I meant. Paco, tell him what I am trying to say." I gave Ashy the correct information, that we only did a single defensive BFM set-up with the Flogger. He responded, "Well, that's not what your commander just said!" I responded by telling him that it must have been a slip of the tongue. Well, I'll be darned if Phil doesn't open his mouth and say another off-the-wall thing immediately, and Ashy calls him on this, too. Well, this went on for an hour-and-a-half.

Next, Ashy was briefed by Matheny: "I took over as the STAN/EVAL pilot after Scotty, and ran the program the whole time I was there. On the day of Ashy's visit my job was to brief the STAN/EVAL program. Gen Ashy was very upset when he found out we were rated in multiple aircraft. At the time, I was qualified in the T-38, F-5, MU-2, and a MiG, as I recall. In his mind, even a pilot qualified in only two aircraft was one too many. I don't think he listened to anything I said about testing, multiple evaluations, in-house self evaluations, proficiency, or professionalism."

As the day drew to a close, "Ashy jumped in his F-16 and returned to Nellis," Geisler recounted. "We were all standing there watching him take off when Hound Dog turns around and says, 'I think that went pretty well.'"

KEEPING THE SECRET

"Naturally, secrecy was a big deal for the 4477th," Robb explained. "No one was allowed at Tonopah without special permission. If a Blue Air aircraft had an emergency in the range and had to land there, we would meet the pilots at the aircraft, blindfold them, and take them into the hangar. They would receive a special briefing and be sworn to secrecy. Most of the time they had run low on fuel in the excitement of the fight and were filled up and launched home, probably not to take part in any more of that Red Flag: breaking the rules of engagement or running out of gas was dealt with pretty severely." Robb also revealed:

> There were occasions when small aircraft would fly through the ranges either by mistake – usually a lost private pilot – or even drug runners using our airspace on purpose. We flew the T-38s on patrol over the range while we were flying the MiGs. If an intruder showed up, we would intercept them and escort them from the range. On several occasions the drug [smuggler] guys would try to evade and fly really low and slow. We would work with the local police in an attempt to arrest them when they landed. If a private pilot intruded the range and later landed at a civilian airfield, he would be met by a security team who would sort out his intentions.

Geisler added that he once intercepted a private aeroplane and tried to give it hand signals to get it pointed away from Tonopah, but all to no avail:

> The guy turns out to be a dentist. He lands at Tonopah and is immediately surrounded by cops. He knows right then that he has really hosed this up. He's got his girlfriend with him and they are told to lie face down on the runway. I take a map and sit down next to him and say, "Where did you think you were going?" He points on the map to Tonopah Airport. I took his finger and dragged it over to the hash marks showing a restricted area on the map and he said, "Oh dear." I told him, "Yeah, you are in an ass load of trouble, buddy!"
>
> We put hoods on them and put them in a jeep. I told intel and the cops that use of deadly force was authorized, and I did not want them seeing anything or hearing anything. Then I asked them, "Y'all can't hear anything, can you?" to which they said from under their hoods, "No, sir!" The civilians were made to sign legal forms that bound them to secrecy, and were told that they would be under surveillance for the foreseeable future to ensure that they kept their word.

With TTR being a designated divert base for Blue Air and Aggressor Red Air pilots experiencing trouble, there were occasionally unexpected military visitors, too. Typically, these were single-engine aircraft – the A-7 and F-16, for example – who had serious engine problems that meant the journey back to Nellis was inadvisable. When they landed, they would be quizzed by the squadron's intelligence officer, and this gave the squadron even more room for entertainment. "We had a brand new intel guy we called Lt 'Flagg,' after the secretive intel officer in the TV show, MASH," recalled Stucky. "He adopted this persona when he interviewed these military pilots. He was a funny, perfect guy to do that job." It wasn't all bad, though: once the pilot had been debriefed, he would be given a guided tour of the MiGs. "It was ironic that it was so difficult to get into the program, but if you were a single-engine airplane with an engine problem and you diverted in, you got in pretty easily!" Stucky observed.

To ensure that foreign participants of Red Flag never got to see the MiGs, CONSTANT PEG operations ceased when foreign pilots were airborne in the Nellis ranges, and the MiGs were put back in the hangars. Geisler added: "If they had to divert into Tonopah, all it would have looked like was an airfield that had been locked up."

Phelan explained:

Tonopah was part of this incredibly protected airbase with stealth fighters on it, and part of an overall cosmic secret airspace. Everybody on that base had at least a Top Secret, Special Access security clearance. Once the sky cops found out we were giving tours to the military pilots who diverted in, they quickly put an end to it. To get into Tonopah from the Man Camp, you had to have your palm scanned. That was forever a nightmare because it never worked right. They would have people backed up down the road and would eventually just have to open the gate and let people in. It all felt a little bit James Bondish until you realized that it didn't work!

"There were rumors out in the press occasionally that the unit existed and press aircraft would fly the borders of the ranges to see if they could find out what was going on," Robb continued. "The magazine *Aviation Week & Space Technology* had a pretty detailed article on the operation in 1984 that directed a lot of attention to the program. The Air Force refused to comment and we continued to fly in spite of the press."

The 4450th TG was continuing to expand its operations, and the number of F-117s at Tonopah was growing steadily. Phelan recalled: "At this point, CONSTANT PEG was as much of a cover for that deployment as it was a secret program in and of itself. There were even stories of pilots that came to the base thinking they were going to fly MiGs and ended up in F-117s." Some of these pilots knew about the MiGs at Tonopah because they had flown against them, but others had heard whisperings about Soviet jet fighters flown in the desert within the vaults of the TAF, and had reached their own conclusions.

GOODBYE MU-2S

On February 8, the 4477th TES acquired two additional T-38s to make a total of four Talons. On the same day, the squadron flew its last MU-2 sorties. Shervanick was at the controls of one, "453MA," with five other Red Eagles on board. "We flew in formation with 452MA on the final flight from Tonopah, landing at McCarran International Airport, Las Vegas, at 1400 local."[34] Orville Prins left the squadron the same month. The MU-2s were no longer considered cost effective, and the increased volume of traffic going from Nellis to Tonopah had resulted in the Air Force detailing Det 5 of the 1400th Military Airlift Squadron at Nellis to provide four C-12F Hurons – eight-passenger, twin turboprop aircraft – as full-time shuttles for CONSTANT PEG personnel. The Red Eagles called it the "Teeny Weenie Airlines," or TWA.

Between March 5 and 19, the Red Eagles were subject to their first ever MEI, directed by the Inspector General, TAC HQ. Its purpose was to evaluate the management, organization, and mission capability of the squadron, and it passed with an overall management effectiveness rating of "excellent." White explained that:

> Up until then Creech had banned such inspections at Tonopah on the grounds of security. As soon as Creech retired, Dugan[35] brought in the MEI. It was not an operational inspection, but one that looked at the rules and administration and so on. A small team was set to come in for three weeks to inspect both us and the 4450th TG. For both units, this was the first ever inspection for both of us. It was led by the TAC Inspector General, who I already knew. In a way, the MEI was a good thing because it reinforced to the maintainers that this was how life was going to be in the future.

March's MEI led to the decision to award the squadron with a Joint Meritorious Unit Award (JMU). The official citation, signed on June 4 by Secretary of Defense Casper Weinberger, awarded the 4477th TES with the JMU for services to Navy, Marine, and Air Force fighter squadrons between February 1, 1979 (six months before the MiGs started to be flown out of Tonopah) and February 1, 1984.

March saw the departure of Skidmore, who returned to the F-16 Weapons School as an instructor and division ops officer. Tullos also left the squadron in the same month, to be followed in July by Robb, who had been promoted to commander, the equivalent of an Air Force lieutenant colonel. Tullos, Geisler recalled, was a source of amusement who would be missed. He had once experienced an IFE and struggled to communicate quickly the nature of the problem in terms that were vague enough to keep the identity of his aircraft secret from prying ears. "We would tell him to watch what he said on the radio, but he would say, 'Fuck it! If I am going down I am going to tell them [the Russians] on the radio exactly what I am doing! I am going to tell them who we are, where we are, exactly how many we've got. I am going to tell them everything, so by God you'd better make sure mine flies!' He was a great guy." Tullos' propensity to sleep on the MU-2 and C-12 meant that he had endured the shenanigans of Stucky and Geisler for most of his tour. By the time he was leaving, the duo had progressed to tying his bootlaces together as he slept on the journey to Tonopah. The effects of that as he tried to stand, still sleepy, are easy to imagine.

Robb was off early to assume command of F-14 Tomcat squadron, VF-51, "Screaming Eagles." He said that his last flight with CONSTANT PEG was the only time he came close to losing or damaging an aircraft:

> After a couple of engagements with an F-15, I returned to the field for my final landing and traditional hosing off from the fire truck. I snapped sharply into the landing pattern with the minimum fuel required and lowered the landing gear. At the final turn I noticed that my landing indicators were not green and asked the tower safety officer to check for all down. He confirmed that my right main gear had not left the well.
>
> The only option to a one main gear landing was to fly into the barrier at the approach end of the field; but with the MiG landing gear so close together, this would most likely have totaled the aircraft and probably me along with it. I decided to hop out of the pattern and accelerate to 300 knots and proceeded to yank as much G on the aircraft as I could get. Coming out of the turn ... still no gear down indication on the panel. I accelerated again to a slightly higher speed and pulled once again. About half way through the turn I could feel the gear release from the wheel well and go down and lock.

A successful landing ensued. "I had almost no gas but was at least in one piece. And I still got hosed down."

Robb described himself as "lucky to fly the MiG 21 for the entire time" he was in the unit. "The MiG-23 was not popular with the pilots. When you transitioned to MiG-23s your knife fight days were over. As for the Fishbed, it was a terrific maneuvering aircraft that was fast and hard to see. I routinely marveled at its simple design and exceptional slow-speed handling qualities. Although the aircraft was very low tech, it was very reliable; it was really just the single engine which was a concern considering we were jerking the aircraft around pretty good."

He was leaving Red Eagles with a real appreciation for the MiG-21's capabilities when compared to those of the F-14:

> The F-14 was underpowered, but it had magnificent aerodynamic qualities and if you flew it well it was the equal of the MiG-21 in a dogfight. The MiG's strengths were its small size and very slow-speed handling characteristics. You had to fight just to keep sight of a MiG, especially in the vertical, to the extent that sometimes the F-14 would be maneuvered sub-optimally. You really wanted to fight the MiG using a series of loops, and that meant that you would spend a lot of time upside down looking for a small, camouflaged adversary against a desert background. That was very difficult to do. The MiG always turned hard, slowed down, and kept his nose pointed at you. The later variants of the F-14 had new engines that were tremendously powerful, and in that model I would be able to turn with a MiG-21 and fight him in a phone booth. The smart thing, though, was to shoot the guy with missiles before he turned inside your turn circle and got behind you.

Robb recalled a number of memorable sorties in the MiG-21:

> The first was against Col Manfred Reich, who was flying a Marine F/A-18 Hornet. Manfred had been one of my TOPGUN instructors when I went through the school in F-14s and was a legend in his own time as a skilled aviator and aggressive dogfighter. He brought a Marine squadron that was under his command to Nellis to fly against the MiGs, and I made sure we were paired up for one of the afternoon 1 v 1s.
>
> Manfred brought his best game with him that day and had a knife in his teeth for sure. We were both dedicated to an aggressive game plan and jumped into the "phone booth" fairly quickly. This is slang for a tight rolling scissors fight that tested the slow-speed maneuvering skills of the pilots. We rolled and twisted our way to a stalemate after jousting for over five minutes. I think we may have broken a few of the altitude rules on that flight, but I will never tell.

The second memorable flight was against Capt Dale Snodgrass. Dale and I grew up in F-14s together and also flew A-4s against our students in VF-101, the East Coast F-14 training squadron in 1978–80. Dale is one of the best natural pilots I have ever seen and a legend for his aviation skills and leadership of the Tomcat community throughout his career.

Dale and I squared off in a battle to the death one afternoon in 1984 with him in an F-14A and me in the MiG-21. I committed to my usual aggressive game plan and turned hard into him at the merge. We went several turns vying for position, with the MiG trading altitude for energy in an attempt to hot-nose the F-14. Dale kept his airspeed up and lost some angles in doing so, but was max-performing the jet as I was slowly losing energy. On the third pass or so he exploded into the vertical, doing a looping maneuver high above me. I extended to gain energy knowing I would have to bait him back into a turning fight to stay alive. [By extending, Robb had lowered the MiG's nose to create weightlessness, and was accelerating the MiG as fast as he could.]

As Dale came down from his loop I pulled up and into him, trying to get him to overshoot below me. This allowed me to high-G barrel roll over the top in an attempt to get him to flush out in front of me as he headed back up. As I came out of the high-G maneuver he should have been in front of me, but he was nowhere to be found. I put the MiG's flaps down and slowed to about 70 knots, thinking he must still be below me. In several hundred previous engagements I had not found any aircraft that could fly slower than the MiG-21. After 20 seconds or so Dale pulls up behind me at 1,000ft and calls a gun shot. He had the landing flaps down [a prohibited maneuver for air combat in the F-14] which allowed him the advantage. As they say in the fighter business, "No rules in a gunfight!"

July also saw the departure of Michael Roy and the arrival of Tullos' Marine replacement, Martin S. Macy, "Bandit 49." Macy was the son of a World War II B-24 bomber pilot who had become an IP at the age of only 19. When Macy Jr was a boy, his father had started a crop dusting business, but it had taken a visit to an air show at Klamath Falls, Oregon, when he was 17 years old, to really make aviation capture his imagination. "I saw the Air Force Thunderbirds, and they really impressed me. I met their leader and shook his hand. And that's when I knew that I wanted to fly." Aged 23, he went first to the Air Force and then the Navy to join up, but both had a two-year backlog for pilot training in 1974, so he joined the Marines. By 1976 he had graduated and been assigned to fly the F-4J, and by 1982 he was experienced enough to be assigned as a new IP with the MAWTS 1. In fact, he had been a student of Bucko.

While at MAWTS 1, he had deployed to Nellis for one week of CONSTANT PEG exposures, flying against MiGs piloted by Scott and Shean. The draw of the MiGs was considerable, and he made a beeline to join the enigmatic unit operating them. He worked hard and lobbied the MAWTS 1 XO, Randy "Dragon" Brinkly, and his commander, Jake "Big Jake" Vermilya, to make it happen. He had to prove himself not only by flying extremely well, but also by becoming a leading authority on air-to-air instruction, a challenge that he devoured, becoming the unit's "many v many" and low-altitude tactics expert. In 1984 Macy arrived at Miramar to become a TOPGUN qualified IP. It was the last hurdle that he needed to jump and he soon found himself being promoted to major to ensure that he was of the right seniority to fit the 4477th TES's stringent standards. A quick trip to the 64th FWS at Nellis to get Aggressor qualified was all that stood in his way.

In July 1985, Capt Frederick H. "T-Bear" Thompson joined the Red Eagles. Matheny taught Thompson academics throughout July. "One day he tested me. 'You are taking off and you have an engine failure. What do you do?' he asked. 'I will apply the correct procedures and then turn around and try and make the runway,' I responded. 'You can't make the runway,' he told me. 'OK, then I guess I will have to eject.' 'How do you know that the seat is going to work?' he threw back at me. There wasn't a correct answer. He was telling me that this was not the same kind of flying that I was used to." Thompson became "Bandit 50" in August.

Thompson had an F-4, F-15, and Aggressor background, and had flown against a MiG-17 piloted by Scott as part of his check out with the 64th FWS in 1980. "I did a very quick PP and then we did a BFM set-up. I got into his phone booth and he beat me!" As an Aggressor, Thompson had been an academic expert on emerging fighters like the MiG-29 "Fulcrum" and Su-27 "Flanker" and on "the Man": "There were actually two men. One did everything by the book, didn't do much experimentation and didn't fly very often. The other man was someone who scoffed at the regulations and broke them. He went his own way. This was the guy we were concerned about because he was just like us – he was going to find out the limits of his airplane, and he was also going to find out his own limits, and then he was going to learn from this. There were only a few of these guys, but they could be very aggressive and difficult to deal with."

Unusually, Thompson had left the Aggressors in 1983 to join the 48th Fighter Interceptor Squadron (FIS), an ADC unit that had just transitioned from the F-106 to the F-15. "It was a little ironic. I was hired because I was an Aggressor to help turn the 48th FIS at Langley AFB from an interceptor squadron to an air superiority squadron. Ten years earlier, the likes of Dave McCloud and Earl Henderson had been coming from ADC to TAC to help them get some tactical expertise. Now ADC were looking to TAC to help them do the same."

White, who had been Thompson's ops officer in the 64th FWS, had turned up at Langley one day looking to hire the 48th FIS's maintenance officer. "I asked him if he needed any pilots," Thompson recalled, "and he said, 'Sure. When can you start?' He invited me out for an interview with Gen Ashy." Thompson was hired.

SHADES OF BLACK

Thompson arrived at Tonopah at a time when CONSTANT PEG was undergoing even more changes. Most obvious was the fact that the runway had been closed for resurfacing, resulting in the temporary relocation of the assets back to Groom Lake and an almost complete cessation of flying operations. The other change was less obvious: it was clear that CONSTANT PEG was moving from the deep, jet-black abyss of secrecy to a world of gray shadows that blurred the join between the white and the black. There had even been some discussion among the TAC generals about turning the 4477th TES into a wing consisting of two MiG squadrons, making CONSTANT PEG "white" in the process to allow mass exposures. That white concept had never materialized, and CONSTANT PEG remained a highly classified program.

However, because so many people were now read in on the MiGs, the reporting structure and direct chain of command were subject to changes that reflected the reduced sensitivity of the program. The Red Eagles had begun life effectively reporting directly to the air staff at the Pentagon, then to the 57th FWW Deputy Commander of Tactics & Test, which had been something of the wing's black division since it stood up; and as of September 9, 1985, it would be reassigned under the command and control of the Deputy Commander, Adversary Tactics, 57th FWW.

Administratively, things were changing too. Phelan recalled that whereas the pilots' OER reports were once reviewed by the vice commander or DO of TAC, a three-star or two-star general (respectively), now they were handled by the 57th FWW at Nellis. The OER could make or break a career, and until now it had been a courtesy and privilege that all the Red Eagles had their reports endorsed by at least a two-star.

None of this was of any real consequence to the Red Eagle pilots, though; it was inevitable that there would be murmurings about the MiGs, but they remained tight-lipped regardless. When Nathman had taken command of his Hornet squadron onboard the *Corral Sea*, he never explicitly divulged the source of the intelligence and advice that he gave his pilots: "They all knew I had just spent two years at Nellis and they could connect the dots – it was left unstated, but they knew. And guys generally didn't ask; I had a broad background in air-to-air and guys knew that I wasn't going to make shit up in front of them. But there were some things we didn't want anyone to know about, like where we got our intelligence and where the MiGs actually came from. If that had started to get out, our sources would have dried up."

The rumor mill inevitably produced some "intel" that was wide of the mark. Some ideas were even funny. Because the visiting squadrons were briefed at the beginning of the week by a Red Eagle previously from their airframe and community (i.e. a Red Eagle from the F-15 would brief a visiting F-15 squadron), the remaining Red Eagle pilots were little more to the Blue Air pilots than enigmatic faces hidden behind oxygen masks, visors, and helmets. At the end of the week, the Red Eagles would fly into Nellis for the Friday afternoon mass debrief, marking the first time the Blue Air pilots had set eyes on the majority of the men who had been instructing them all week. Being a friendly bunch of aviators, the Red Eagles would walk up and introduce themselves, sometimes prompting remarkable reactions, as Geisler recounts: "One evening I walked up to this guy and said, 'Hi! My name is Paco Geisler, and I flew three MiG-21 sorties against you this week.'" Perhaps it was the Czechoslovakian national flag painted on Geisler's MiG-21 that fooled him, but the Blue Air pilot responded, "You speak just like an American." He was flabbergasted, but not quite as much as Geisler now was: "'I am an American, you asshole. What the hell are you thinking?' He said, 'I thought that you all had guys who you contracted to come out and fly these things.' I told him to get his head out of his ass." The Red Eagles were apparently still unfathomable even to those read in on CONSTANT PEG.

Sometimes the challenge was to keep the Red Eagles' ancillary missions secret from the TAF. Stucky, for example, worked with Henderson to garner information on the MiGs from other intelligence sources, and spent time trying to insert as much new data into the Air Force's classified 3-1 tactics manuals as possible without revealing the identity of a source, or making it apparent that some of the information came from very specific sources. "These things were written at Nellis, so it was easy to migrate information into them. But we did it subtly, so there was no big announcement that we had provided the information. We passed it to our contacts in the different services," ensuring that writers of the Navy, Marine, and Air Force tactics manuals had the same data to work with.

The information eventually made it to the frontline squadrons, but it did sometimes take time. "I remember being amazed that we had the MiG-23 and knew all about it, but that we weren't even telling our own crews about it," Phelan admitted. "[In the early 1980s] we were still using DIA estimates on the Flogger's capabilities that were based on engineering documents. We were all worrying about having to face the MiG-23 because we were told it was like a mini Tomcat, but the reality was that we would have waxed the Floggers without any problems."

THAT FLY-BY

In September 1985, Ashy fired White for the first time when he made Geisler the ops officer ahead of Bland's scheduled November departure. "If that's the best God-damned decision that you can make, then you're fired!" he had told White. White explained: "Paco had a reputation from his days in the F-15 as being non-conformist, and Ashy knew all about that. Ashy paced up and down and jangled his keys in his pockets and said, 'OK, but the first time I see him do anything [wrong], you're both fired!' Eventually, on a visit to Tonopah, he saw Paco chewing out one of the pilots and he turned to me and said, 'I knew Paco would be great.' I had an excellent relationship with Ashy and Fischer because I was prepared to go down there and talk to them."

October saw Shervanick fly his last MiG sortie. He prepared to leave Nellis to replace Scott at TAC, running the Red Eagles and other black projects. As was customary, he marked the occasion with flair: flying his MiG-23 between two of the Red Eagles' hangars and then pulling up into the vertical. Like Bucko and Watley before him, he then stripped naked as he sat at the end of the runway. He dismounted the MiG-23 wearing only his flight helmet and boots and saluted White, who had been waiting to congratulate him on a successful assignment. Meanwhile, around 70 highly entertained maintainers watched in fits of laughter.

In November Matheny and Bland left CONSTANT PEG, and LtCol John "Mad Jack" Manclark and Navy pilot Evan M. Chanik Jr, Bandits "51" and "52" respectively, joined. Manclark arrived to prepare to take over from White early in the next year, and Matheny was leaving for MacDill AFB to fly the F-16. He'd left the Phantom in April 1979 and flown nothing but the F-5, T-38, MU-2, and the two MiGs since then. "I was sad to leave the Red Eagles, but there was the realization after spending so long flying VFR and BFM that there was a whole new world of technology out there in the form of the F-16 that I was going to get to experience."

Bland's departure, like Shervanick's the month before, was marked by an impressive fini flight, but whereas Shervanick's had been flown on what was just a normal day at Tonopah, Bland's sortie coincided with a visit from Gen Ashy and was less of a celebration and more of a protestation. Bland marked his final sortie in the MiG-23 with a fly-by that would go down in the record books. Ashy had been personally invited up to Tonopah for Bland's final sortie, much to the bewilderment of Geisler:

> We were standing between two MiG hangars about 30 yards apart. We're looking out towards the runway and I am thinking, "This is a bad idea." GCI called on the "Big Voice" speakers across the compound, "Hey, Blazo's coming back!" and the maintenance guys all came out. We are all waiting, but Blazo doesn't show. I called the tower on my little radio and asked quietly if they had seen him. They told me they hadn't, and now I really am thinking that this is not good.
>
> All of a sudden this Flogger goes over the top of the three of us between the two hangars at about the same height as the hangar roofs. I don't hear anything, I just see it go over the top. I thought I could reach up and touch the burner can. He goes over the top of me, Ashy and White … and then the fucking noise just *hits* us. Then there is the heat from the afterburner.
>
> To my left I see Ashy and White have both jumped into the air in shock and then gone flying for the deck, and Ashy's hat has rolled off. Meanwhile, Blazo is trying to turn this MiG-23 and is ripping right beside the tower. He lands and as he taxies back in Ashy is pissed, as you can imagine. "That's his last damned flight. He is not flying up here again," he said. Everyone turned around and said, "Well, yes, it is his last flight!"

White told the author that he had personally approved Bland's fly-by and knew that it was going to be spectacular when he had invited the general to watch, but several people maintain that Bland had deliberately pushed the limits as a defiant gesture to White and Ashy, neither of whom he cared for. "There had rumblings among even the senior pilots about how it wasn't like the good old days any more," one person said.

"Later," White continued, "Ashy asked me if I had approved it and I told him I had. Blazo hadn't broken any rules and there were no other airplanes flying. Instead of flying initial up the runway, he had flown initial across it. He told me, 'Next time it happens I am going to fire you!'"

"Bland's fly-by marked the end of most of the shenanigans," one pilot told me. "It generated even more high-level interest on the south side of Tonopah's ramp, as if there was not already enough. Ashy had threatened administrative punishment over the incident, allegedly letting Bland twist in the wind. In the end, the edict came down that there were not going to be any more "Tonopah fini flights."

While Ashy eventually cooled down, Lauderette, who had been on a tour of the facilities at Tonopah with Manclark and had also witnessed the fly-by, did not. White believes: "He wanted it to look like he was in control, and he wanted me to report to him everyday. I wasn't going to, so he took even more of a disliking to me." As for Manclark, the incoming commander explained that he was far from impressed: "Lauderette was so angry that he could not speak for a number of minutes. And it looked to me that if Blazo had crashed he could have taken out half of the F-117s with him." Blazo's point had been made, but some thought his actions were reckless and irresponsible.

CLEVER THINKING

With relations with Lauderette strained, and Fischer being equally as awkward at times, White began using Scott at the TAC DO's office to bypass Nellis when he wanted something. "I started sending things to Scotty to pass to Gen Dugan. I would do this when I couldn't get what I wanted out of Fischer. Dugan would then send a message to Fischer telling him that he had an idea. Sure enough, I would get a call from Ashy's office and he would tell me that the TAC DO had an idea. 'See this message? Do you think you can make this idea happen?' Ashy would ask me. 'Well, sir,' I would reply, 'Give me till tomorrow to see what I can do.'"

The year 1985 had seen the Red Eagles fly 1,779 sorties and 688 exposures, slightly fewer than the year before, despite having an additional two MiG-21s (17 in total) and one additional MiG-23 (ten in total). Nelson, who was preparing to leave the squadron for his next assignment to Holloman AFB, estimated that his annual budget by this time was close to $80 million.

The dip in the figures for 1985 was not indicative of White's effectiveness or the changes he was making to Tonopah – he had actually increased the weekly and monthly sortie figures for the MiG-21s. But for at least six to eight weeks of the summer (starting in July), Tonopah had been closed to allow the runway to be resurfaced. Only a handful of MiGs were moved to Groom Lake while the work was underway. During that time the Red Eagles flew a number of test sorties with the 422nd TES and worked with the Red Hats, but there were very few tactical exposures. In fact, according to Phelan: "Most of the pilots would turn up and fly one sortie every two weeks, while only a small handful flew more often. Most of the sorties were just 'transition sorties,' flown single-ship wherever there was an open range, or they were in the pattern to keep our currencies."

The year had also been one of continued pranks. Stucky and Geisler had taken to putting a generous smear of black shoe polish on the earpieces of the squadron's black telephones, with predictable results. Stucky revealed other pranks:

Paco also started removing the rank insignia from your Air Force cap and putting it on the back of the cap. He even did it to Phil White. He'd be out there giving a VIP tour and he would have his rank on the back of his hat. It was hilarious – we would just howl with laughter. Paco would do it to anyone; even a visiting colonel. If anyone left their cap lying around, Paco would mess with it.

We were now doing a 30-minute briefing every morning to cover all the admin for the flying that was going to happen that day. It saved about two hours of admin that would happen in a normal squadron, and allowed us to just fly our butts off. During that time, we had normally had two or three cups of coffee, and when the meeting finished, there was often a rush to the bathroom. Our men's room had no windows and only one light switch by the door. I would rush to the first stall – by the light switch – and wait for the other two to fill up, and then I'd run out and turn the light switch as I left. You'd hear shouting and hollering, because with the lights out you could see nothing. It was totally dark. That became a running joke, even after I left the squadron.

The boss was known to have a self-deprecating sense of humor; there was a line, but Geisler, Stucky and the others knew where it was drawn. White recalled:

One day, I went to fly and turned up at my locker to find that my G-suit had been frozen solid in ice – they had put it in the freezer. On another occasion, we were hosting a dignitary. I would put one of the guys who flew the MiG-21 and one who flew the MiG-23 next to the aircraft in the VIP hangar, and I would let them talk to the visitor about the MiGs. I recall that I was receiving a group of about five four-star generals from all three services. It was winter and it was really cold. We had different uniforms – one to work on the airplanes in, one for day-to-day operations, and one that we called the "show" or "VIP" uniform for when we were showing visitors around.

I was sitting in my office waiting for them to arrive when the call came in that the car was heading south [from the F-117s]. I grabbed my jacket and walked out with Paco. I start to put my arm in my sleeve, but it won't go. He's had the machine shop sew up my sleeves at the end. He's doing the typical Paco innocence routine, asking me, 'What's the matter? We gotta go. They're coming!' I just threw my jacket on the chair and followed him out to the car. He's there in his winter jacket, and I am standing in my flight suit. Just as the car pulls up he said, "Damn, Boss! It sure is cold out here!" and we both started chuckling.

Some of the jokes were on Geisler. For a start, Stucky used to remove the microphone from the telephone on his friend's desk. "When he would pick up the phone he would be talking, but no one could hear him. He would be screaming down this phone thinking that he had a bad connection." But worse was to come. "He would leave his can of chewing tobacco on his desk when he went to fly. Once, I cut the bottom out with a razor blade and then slid the can back onto the desk. When he walked in and picked up the can, the tobacco went everywhere. On another occasion, I found this big, meaty, house fly. I caught it and then put it in the can. Paco came along and grabbed a pinch of tobacco, and came away with this huge fly between his fingers. That put him off tobacco for a while!"

For many, these bouts of humor served a purpose: "The antics of Paco, Stucky, Lenny, and others made life interesting and at times served to relieve the tension," Matheny admitted. "Nothing got a laugh like flying against Paco and finding out, after you were all strapped in the cockpit with your helmet on, that he had smeared butter all over the inside surface of your visor. But, to a man, all were professionals with unique qualities and the tightness of the unit served to make us all better instructors. I know I learned from every person I knew in the Red Eagles."

PART 4

THE FINAL YEARS, 1986–88

CHAPTER 12

INCREASING BLUE AIR EXPOSURES, 1986

The advent of 1986 at Tonopah brought a change of command, as White departed and Manclark came in. Two new Air Force pilots also arrived at the desert base, Capt Brian E. McCoy, "Bandit 53," and Capt Herbert J. "Hawk" Carlisle, "Bandit 54." During the traditional handover ceremony, where the outgoing commander formally relinquished command of the squadron to the incoming commander, Gen Ashy took the 4477th TES flag from White and fixed him with a slight grin, as White recounts: "He said quietly, 'You've been going behind our backs all of this time, haven't you?' to which I said, 'Yes, sir.' 'Good job,' he said, 'we'd never have got it done without you.'" Despite their often turbulent relationship, and the fact that the general had twice fired White, the two had remained on good terms. Indeed, Ashy had looked after White, and ensured that he had been promoted to full colonel early.

Ashy was himself preparing to move on from Nellis to become the Inspector General of the Deputy Chief of Staff for Plans at TAC HQ. Some time before he had departed, he had made it known to Manclark that he wanted to speak with Geisler, since he was personally involved in deciding what the ops officer's next assignment should be. Manclark recalled:

> I sent him to see Ashy in a T-38. Before I left, I said, "Be nice, Paco." After the interview my hotline rang. It was Ashy. He said, "You tell that fucking Geisler to quit looking at me like I am the stupidest man in the world!" and he slammed the phone down.

So, I am sitting in my office when about an hour later Paco walks by with his parachute. I said, "Paco, how did it go?" "Really good, I think," he replied. "No, Paco, it went really bad!" Paco had a way of doing things! Ashy was always screaming and hollering, though, and in the end he did help Paco get a good follow-on assignment.

While Ashy and White had been preparing to move on, Geisler, who had become a MiG-21 IP in November 1984, had been checking out some of the new pilots in the Fishbed. Carlisle was just one of several new pilots the prankster taught, joining White, Brubaker, Macy, Chanik, Phelan, and Craig. Macy said of Geisler: "Paco was a good instructor who had been the youngest IP at the Weapons School. He had a wit about him and he had this gift for making things seem really easy; he was a great instructor who made it easy to learn."

Some of his instructional techniques were less than orthodox, but they had been handed down the generations and always related to an important learning point. Geisler gives one example:

Take Herb Carlisle for example. He was then a slick-winged captain who had never flown an airplane that he really needed to actually fly. Now all of a sudden he's out there in this MiG-21 and I am chasing him in a T-38 at 14,000ft. I said, "Herb, why don't you just slap that stick to the side and make that thing roll, just for the hell of it?" Well, in the MiG-21, if you didn't use rudder, you went out of control. And that's exactly what he did. He's screaming on the radio, and I just told him to let the stick go and the jet will recover. That's when I said, "There is a third flight control in your airplane. It's called a rudder!" We did it to every new guy, and it had been done to us in the F-4. We knew that guys coming from the F-15 would probably not have flown the airplane with all three flight controls.

Carlisle was an FWIC graduate who had joined the Red Eagles from the 9th TFS at Holloman, where he had been the F-15 squadron's chief of weapons and tactics.

In February, Geisler got two more new Bandits qualified in the MiG: Capt Shelley S. "Scotty" Rogers, "Bandit 55," and Capt John C. "Flash" Mann, "Bandit 56." Mann was hired after Geisler put in a by-name request for him. "I was eligible, as I had graduated from the F-15 Fighter Weapons School in 1981. Paco and I had been stationed together at Holloman flying the F-15, but at the time of his by-name request I was flying the Eagle with the 1st TFW at Langley. Paco and I ran into each other at the bar at Nellis when I was TDY to a Red Flag, and he asked if I wanted to come and work for him. Needless to say, I jumped at the chance."

The T-38s were crucial in the instruction of the squadron's new pilots. Without the luxury of training a new Red Eagle in BFM by flying one MiG against another, the Talon was used instead. But in an improvement over previous years, the MiG-21 TX now consisted of four rides before the new pilot even left the ground – it was a far cry from the days of IDEA, where a complete checkout was comprised of two rides. Geisler detailed how: "A guy got two rides just to learn how to taxi it. You'd follow him around in a jeep telling him what to do. Then he'd get another two rides for high-speed taxi tests. He'd light the burner and then abort by popping the [brake para]chute at about 130 knots. The next day he would take off for the first time." Stucky added: "The first taxi in the MiG-21 was always traumatic, because you never knew if you would make it out to the runway without running out of air. It was such an unnatural thing that the entire squadron would turn out to watch."

Some of the Red Eagles formed the habit of taxiing very fast, between 30 and 60 knots, where the rudder became effective and the awkward pneumatic differential braking was redundant. It became so normal to transit between apron, taxiway, and runway with such pace that when some of the pilots left for their next flying assignment they had difficulty reverting to the usual Air Force taxi speeds of 15–20 knots. Like driving down the motorway significantly above the speed limit and then slowing down to the legal maximum, it felt like little more than a crawl. The MiG-23 offered nose wheel steering and was therefore less of a handful on the ground.

Although a new pilot would learn to fly the Fishbed based as much on feel, intuition, and experience as on academics, at various points it was necessary to reference the cockpit instrumentation – take-off and landing being the most obvious. Geisler was critical of the Soviet design:

> The instrumentation was basic, and when you got in and found that the biggest light in the cockpit is the fire warning light, you had to wonder about it. They [the Soviets] had no idea about cockpit ergonomics or human factors engineering. It became pretty obvious that this thing was built for someone who today is behind a buffalo ploughing a muddy field somewhere, and tomorrow is being asked to be a pilot. There were hardly any lights to tell you if something was working or not – you would flip a switch, and either it worked or it did not. We also had no AoA [Angle of Attack] gauge, so we flew the landing circuit based on speeds: fly up the initial at least 300 knots; break onto downwind with no more or less than 215 knots; gear down and flaps down and then the final turn at 195 knots; into the final at 175 knots with power on, because it took eight seconds to go from idle to military power; and then touch down at 155 knots.

It was very mechanical and you spent a lot of time with the student training him how to land it. You could not afford to get behind the power curve with this thing.

In a change from earlier times, completing the TX course and becoming a fully qualified MiG-21 driver no longer involved qualifying to fly BFM in the MiG. Five sorties were set aside to master basic handling before the new pilot would be permitted to conduct a Blue Air exposure, but it was limited to just flying a PP. Getting qualified to fly BFM took a couple of months and required additional formal instruction, said Geisler. "We would take him out and teach him the really high-speed characteristics and the really low-speed handling. We would walk him through it while we were in the T-38 doing loops around him because you couldn't follow him." The MiG-21s had an 8G limit, but the squadron policy was to try not to exceed 6.5G.

LOGBOOKS AND ADMINISTRATION

In the very early years of the HAVE MiG exploitations, flight time in the assets was usually logged in the Air Force logbooks as: A-4 Skyhawk for the MiG-17; F-5 Tiger II for the MiG-21; and F-4 Phantom for the MiG-23. This allowed the true identity of the MiGs to remain hidden. The Navy and Marines used the same system.

The Air Force had also established a series of "experimental type" designations that were unclassified and which utilized the prefix "YF." This system was actually more descriptive without compromising security, and allowed the MiG pilots to identify not only the types of MiG that they had flown, but also the specific airframes. This was necessary because, at that time, the Air Force's "Form 5" flight record carried no space to record the serial number of the airframe in question. Thus, the first two MiG-17s and the single MiG-21 from Israel had their own specific YF designations: YF-110B for the HAVE DOUGHNUT MiG-21F-13 Fishbed E; YF-113A for the MiG-17F Fresco C used in HAVE DRILL; and YF-114C for the MiG-17F Fresco C used in HAVE FERRY. The Chinese-built "MiG-17F" J-5 Fresco C used in the HAVE PRIVILEGE program, and flown by Wendell Shawler, also used the YF-113C designation.

The Air Force eventually modified its Form 5 to allow a serial number to be recorded, and as more and more MiGs became available to both Red Hats and Red Eagles, the prefix and suffix for each type were largely standardized. The MiG-17PF Fresco D that Peck had flown was designated the YF-114D. The Red Eagles' other MiG-17F Fresco Cs were all logged using the YF-114C designation.

For the MiG-21, YF-110B was used for the MiG-21F-13 Fishbed C/E, YF-110C for the Chinese-built J-7Bs, and YF-110D for the MiG-21MF Fishbed J. Finally, for the two MiG-23s, YF-113B was assigned to the flat-nosed MiG-23BN Flogger F bomber, and YF-113E to the MiG-23MS Flogger E interceptor. The Navy and Marine pilots did not always use this nomenclature, as Macy said that his logbook referred to the MiGs only by the earlier F-5 and F-4 designations.

When talking over an unsecure line or in the squadron bar, the accepted nomenclature had been to refer to the assets by "Type": Type 1 (MiG-17), Type 2 (MiG-21), and Type 3 (MiG-23),[36] just like they had during the HAVE programs. But by the time Bucko joined the Red Eagles in 1981: "That system was drawing too much attention and we decided it was far easier to substitute it for the names of American airplanes. If you were in the bar, you'd talk about A-4s, F-5s, and F-4s, because everyone knew what they were."

The names weren't intended to pigeonhole the performance capabilities of the MiGs, as some people came to believe. According to Bucko: "We had A-4s in the Marine Aggressor program that had the newer, bigger engines and would perform up to the top of the subsonic limits just as well as the MiG-21. And if you wanted to simulate the turn capability of the MiG-17, the T-2C Buckeye trainer was a closer match than the A-4 if you stayed in a 400-knot or slower flight."

Actually keeping track of flight time in the MiGs was something that not everyone did, and those who kept logbooks measured their experience by the number of sorties, in much the same way as the Navy measures experience and credibility by carrier landings – "traps" – as opposed to flight hours. Robb recalled: "I flew over 200 flights over two years with the squadron but probably only had 70 total hours in the aircraft when I left." Scott clarified:

The normal Air Force philosophy was to add five minutes to your logbook for taxi time. If our MiG-17 sortie was only a .3 [18 minutes],[37] then that extra five minutes would have added another 25 percent to our total time, and we couldn't afford to do that. So, we didn't count taxi time on our totals; that way we could get more flying time out of the jets and the engines between maintenance inspections. Our sorties were short. I flew mostly .3s and .4s [24 minutes] in the MiG-17 and MiG-21.

"We would take off in afterburner," Manclark offered, "and would stay in afterburner until we hit 'high key,' where we knew we could safely land the jet if the motor shit itself. By that time, you were at 12,000ft and were pointing at the guys you were going to fight, who were just behind a hill ahead of you. You would call, 'Fight's on!' and stay in afterburner until the end of the first set-up.

Then, for the first time since taking off, you would come out of afterburner. That meant that a .5 was a long sortie!"

The MiG-23 offered better endurance than even a "clean" F-4, i.e. one carrying no external stores, and represented a significant improvement over the MiG-21 and MiG-17, so its sorties were often longer. Matheny said that the MiG-23's endurance speed of about 230 knots could be used to stretch a sortie to about an hour if the mission objectives dictated it, but that on a sortie where he had used a lot of afterburner, he would still usually find himself logging .7 or .8 in his logbook.

MANCLARK

Manclark had joined the Air Force because he wanted to fly fighters in Vietnam, but he had missed the war by just three months. He had flown the F-4 before being assigned to the USAFE's 527th TFTS Aggressors at RAF Alconbury in 1979. After three years in England, he had been assigned to TAC Headquarters at Langley AFB for a staff tour that was cut short when Ashy hired him to be the ops officer with the 64th FWS in 1985. "I was in that job for about eight months when Ashy called me in and asked me if I would rather command one of the Aggressor squadrons or the 4477th. I told him that I wanted the 4477th. I figured it would be more of a challenge."

Manclark had first learned of the MiGs as an Aggressor student at Nellis in winter 1978, but it was not an official briefing that he had received: "It was not the best-kept secret," he admitted. He first actually saw the MiGs the month he was officially told that he would indeed be taking over the Red Eagles, flying up to Tonopah with Lauderette (whom he knew from his days flying F-4s at Hahn AB, Germany) for the informal introduction that ended with Bland's fly-by. "By the time I got there, it was pretty much an Air Force squadron. People were in uniforms and there were some Dash 1s written," he confirmed. He had inherited a staff of 200 maintainers. Now, having already checked out in the Fishbed the previous November, he immediately turned his focus to the maintenance function and to the assets.

"I had a solid ops officer in Paco. He was a good guy," and the qualifications of all of the squadron's pilots were so exceptional that they inspired a great sense of confidence. "I didn't worry much about the flying of the airplanes – we had a few captains, but mostly it was majors and above and they were all extremely well qualified. My big concern was that we were still flying a bunch of the older MiG-21s. Nobody had confidence in the seat, so everyone's plan was to deadstick it into the desert. That was not a good plan, because the desert was not a runway

---

by any standards. We had changed the parachutes and carts as required over the years, but by the time I got there, no one was going to use that seat."

Manclark was a well-respected leader who flew frequently and looked after his men. He ordered a new building at Tonopah that became the envy of the 4450th TG. "It was actually a series of trailers placed together, but you would never have guessed it. We had big flags of the Navy, Marines, and Air Force, and we had Soviet missiles sitting in painted racks. It looked pretty good."

He also occasionally allowed his men to leave the Man Camp and go into Tonopah proper. By this time, written permission from the squadron commander was required to exit the confines of the TTR complex. "I didn't really like signing it, but I did every couple of months," he said. "The problem was that you would have to drive 40 miles along this dirt road back to the airfield. Since the cattle men always left their cattle out to graze, there was a fear that they might crash into a cow or one of the wild horses that roamed out there." It was a valid concern. The 4450th TG had now taken over Tonopah, with the 4477th TES being assigned as a tenant unit, and Mike Short, the F-117 wing commander, had already called a meeting to address the matter of mustangs and cows. "He said, 'I am going to asshole the next person who hits a horse!' Of course, the very next day it's his red pickup that is in the ditch from hitting a horse!" Manclark laughed.

INCREASING THE THREAT LEVEL

Lulls in week-long dedicated TAF deployments for CONSTANT PEG freed the Red Eagles up to spend more time participating in Red Flag. This was still limited to US-only Red Flags, where there was no chance that a foreign pilot participating in the exercise might somehow learn about the MiGs. And, says Geisler, there were even occasions when every single participant of these Red Flags was briefed in on CONSTANT PEG. "This happened very rarely, perhaps only once or twice a year, but when it did we were able to expose them to a more advanced level of threat. We would orchestrate with the Aggressors to cover a two-hour period to protect the ground targets south of Tonopah."

This wasn't an accident, according to Macy. Indeed, the objective was to increase the threat level by incorporating the MiGs into Red Flag more fully: "We had all these F-15s, F-16s, and F/A-18s that were dominating the exercise. They needed more assets to fly in it to make it more realistic, but they also wanted us to make it more challenging – these Blue Air guys could sit back and have everything sorted by the time we had closed to 20 miles. We wanted to make it as dynamic as we could right to the merge."

As was the norm, the MiGs would launch on cue from GCI as the Blue Air forces got close, but their small fuel fraction meant that there was no way that they would be able to cover a 90- or 120-minute "vulnerability" period, so they would take off, fight, land at Tonopah, and refuel with the pilots remaining in the cockpits, and then repeat the process until the time was up. With it being unlawful for the Blue Air players to enter Tonopah's airspace, there was some gaming involved, Geisler admitted: "You would turn around and run into Tonopah's airspace and GCI would scream at the other guy that he was about to enter restricted airspace. Once GCI told you he'd turned around, you'd do the same and chase after him. In one respect that pissed them off, but we explained to them that there are country borders where exactly that kind of situation would be encountered."

Non-critical equipment failures in the MiGs occurred from time to time, altering the dynamics of the sortie somewhat, and forcing the use of revised tactics. Geisler remarked: "Sometimes you couldn't find anyone and the radios didn't work. When that happened, you had no radar and no GCI, so you got low to try and find guys. Sometimes you found no one, and other times you flew over a ridge and holy shit! they were all there in front of you. If you did that, you called everyone and told them where you were, and they then all converged in on you in clusters."

Knowing who had killed whom in these massive Red Flags relied not on GCI to validate kills as was normally the case, but instead used computers that combined the GCI radar tapes and audio with the unique IFF [Identify Friend or Foe] squawk that every aircraft in the exercise was assigned. Back at Nellis, the computers would crunch the numbers and later on in the day a list of results was available. For the MiGs, once the initial GCI-vectored intercept and Soviet tactics emulation was over, a degree of luck was involved to stay alive at the merge. Prior to that, with no radar or long-range weapons, and a radar warning receiver that was extremely basic, garnering really good SA about the Blue Air opposition force was almost impossible. Geisler explained: "You were therefore often surprised in the debrief about how many times the computer said you had died, compared to how many times you thought you had died when you were actually up there. When you were flying you felt invincible and like no one had seen you." The reality was very different.

THE FIRST WING

Back at TAC HQ Mike Scott, now a lieutenant colonel, was preparing to leave his role as program manager for CONSTANT PEG and the Aggressors, to be replaced by Shervanick. Shervanick's career was almost identical to Scott's – the two had served together at Seymour Johnson, Nellis, Clark, and the Red Eagles before now. Scott's next assignment was a tour flying the F-15 Eagle as the Chief of Safety with the 1st TFW at Langley. He was attached to the 71st TFS, and it should have been a good posting for him, but it was not to be. "Prior to my assignment, the Chief of Safety was the sort of posting where you put people out to pasture. But Gen Bob Russ, the TAC commander, had decided that in order to reduce accident rates the Chief of Safety was going to be a 'good job' where the Air Force would put ex-squadron commanders or people that were destined to be squadron commanders. I was on that track, so under that philosophy I was hired by the wing commander at the time, Col Billy McCoy." Scott showed up at Langley for his new job in April 1986 on the same day that McCoy handed over command of the 1st TFW to Col Buster Glosson. Unfortunately for Scott, Glosson was a less than popular leader who many considered to be an egotist who rated himself too highly.

This had been true as far back as August 1979 when the then Major Glosson had been assigned as the XO to the commander of the TFWC, working for two-star general Robert Kelley. The XO was a role used to groom future Air Force leaders, and when in the spring of 1980 Henderson was diagnosed with heart disease, Glosson assumed he would be selected to pick up the reins of the 4477th TES. It was a belief he was confident enough in to share freely with anyone who would listen, and one supported by Gen Cunningham and Gen Kelley at Nellis. But despite their high-level support, Creech had vetoed his appointment to the squadron. Glosson was perceived by others at Nellis as an outsider, and it is alleged that in the eyes of most of the TAF his lack of credible fighter experience made him ill suited to be a commander of any of the Nellis flying units. When Gibbs, who had been expected to get command of the 414th FWS, was selected to command the 4477th TES instead, Glosson was reportedly left hugely embarrassed. Cunningham and Kelley gave him command of the 414th FWS as a consolation, much to the chagrin of the FWIC instructors.

On Scott's first day of work, the vice wing commander, Col Hugh Morland, formally introduced Scott to Glosson in the wing commander's office. "Hey, sir! I'd like you to meet our new wing Chief of Safety. You may know each other, because you were out at Nellis together," Morland told Glosson. Glosson responded, "Well, he looks familiar. What did he do?" to which Morland replied, "He was in the 4477th, the Red Eagles." Glosson's reaction was plain according to Scott: "It could have been just me, but he was less than thrilled that I was the guy that was in a job that was en route to becoming a squadron commander in his wing." The room had turned cold, and Scott's prospects as TAC's Chief of Safety at Langley suddenly took a nose dive.

It didn't take long for Glosson to start pushing Scott out into the cold, as Scott recounts:

> Later, we had an inspection that the previous guy in my job had not done a good job of preparing for. We got through it, and I felt like I did a good job getting us through it. Anyone that knows me knows that I am aggressive about getting a job done that needs doing, and that sometimes I forget to back-brief my bosses about how I did it, or even that I did it. I had done a couple of things that I thought needed to be done, and I think that that, combined with the Red Eagles issue, led Glosson to conclude that I was not suitable material to be a squadron commander in his wing.

At the next reshuffle of wing personnel Glosson replaced Scott as the Chief of Safety, prompting the 1st TFW's Director of Operations, Col Dick Bethurem, to ask what was going on. Scott explained as best he could, to which Bethurem responded: "Don't worry. We'll find you a job someplace. In the meantime, you can come and work for me as head of scheduling." Downtrodden, Scott agreed.

CREDIBILITY

There was no doubt that being selected for the Red Eagles was a huge ego boost, but it was always tempered by the realization that the only thing that mattered was to deliver great exposures to the TAF. Macy said that he often reminded himself of his purpose. "I was there to be an IP for a new squadron every week of the year. I knew that I had to be very impressive if I wanted any of these guys to listen to what I was telling them. The MiG-21 was an easy airplane to instruct from, and from which to earn that credibility; because it was so predictable and we knew it so well, we could concentrate on teaching these really vital learning points. We ended up getting so good that we could see the guy was going to make a mistake before it even happened." Macy, now a MiG-21 IP, was also training the likes of Capt Michael G. Simmons, "Bandit 57," who joined in April.

Meanwhile, in the Mediterranean Sea, "Bandit 29" Nathman was leading his Hornet squadron in operations against Libya. America was preparing to launch a punitive strike against targets on the Libyan mainland, and Nathman's squadron was intercepting marauding Libyan Air Force MiGs and Sukhois in the run-up to the strike. On the actual evening of the raids – flown by USAF F-111s based in England and a host of Navy aircraft – his squadron helped ensure that no Libyan fighters threatened the strikers. Nathman's ability to impart so much information about the MiGs – how they were flown, what they would look like at different ranges and angles, and how they could be defeated most readily – was a tremendous boost for the young pilots of the Privateers.

Back at Tonopah in March, Stephen Brown was preparing to leave, followed in June by John Saxman. They were replaced by Maj Thomas "Boomer" Boma, "Bandit 59," in June, and Maj Charles E. "Smokey" Sundell, "Bandit 58," in July. Boma had grown up 100 miles south of Chicago with six brothers and sisters. He was a product of ROTC, and had a grand plan to learn to fly with the Air Force and eventually become an airline pilot like his uncle. "When I started flying contact at UPT, which was the visual phase, that plan changed. I knew then I wanted to fly fighters." He had received an F-4 assignment on graduation from pilot training in late 1976, and from there had flown nearly every version of the Phantom – the F-4C, D, E, S, J, and RF-4B – thanks in part to an exchange tour with the Marines.

Boma had been exposed to the Red Eagles while he attended the F-4 FWIC in 1983. But he was on his exchange tour, flying out of Yuma Marine Corps Air Station (MCAS), when he was called to interview to join them. Boma actually took the slot of Aggressor pilot Spence Roberts. Roberts and Manclark had been stationed together and Manclark thought he made for a good hire. But Lauderette disagreed: Roberts had once punched out of an F-5 when it twice became uncontrollable during a FCF. It was not Spence's fault – mechanical failure was eventually blamed – but the AT commander was now vetoing his selection on the strength that he had once lost an aircraft. It was a patently absurd view, but one that ultimately worked in Boma's favor.

Sundell had been an Alconbury Aggressor who had first been exposed to the MiG-17 in 1980, and had actually been invited to Tonopah to see the MiG-23 during the same TDY to Nellis. "It was very, very hush-hush. I flew an F-5 against the MiG-17, landed at Tonopah and then climbed all over the MiG-23 to help me put together my Aggressor Flogger briefing. Then I returned to Alconbury. I couldn't tell anyone that I had seen it; I could only tell them what I had learned." He had gone on to fly the F-15 with the 48th FIS, becoming friends with Thompson in the process. It was while he was at Langley in late 1985 (Thompson was already a Red Eagle by then), that Scott had phoned him and asked if he wanted to take some jets to fly against CONSTANT PEG. "I had a really good commander, but he did not know about the program. So, Mike Scott cleared me to brief him. He liked it, so we took six jets to Nellis and I got to fly against the MiGs for the second time. I thought it was really shit hot, so I went up to Paco and asked him what I needed to do to get a job." Sundell put together a package, interviewed with Kempf and White, and was hired.

While Sundell had actually been hired by White, by the time he arrived at Tonopah it was Manclark who was in charge. The two knew each other well – they had flown F-4s together at Hahn AB, Germany and had then flown F-5s together at Alconbury during back-to-back tours. Macy had been his IP as he went through the TX course, taking him aside and advising him that it was not necessary to pre-flight the jet. He landed from his first solo to be handed a beer. "The guys said to me, 'Congratulations, you're number 58.' That's when it really dawned on me that this was something unique."

While all of the Aggressors-turned-Red Eagles brought with them a wealth of general and specialist knowledge, Sundell's time as a USAFE Aggressor, working in close proximity to the divide between NATO and the Warsaw Pact, meant that he was particularly well briefed on East German MiG-23 operations. "We had done a lot of the research into the Soviet Forces in Germany," and they had also spent time working with the Air Force's European Tactics Analysis Team (ETAT), the authority on such intelligence matters.

On August 4, the 4477th TES flew its first mission under the control of the new GCI facility located at Tonopah. Gennin had initiated the construction of the facility on the airfield, but it had taken the continued stewardship of White and then Manclark to ensure its success. The centralized facility meant that the squadron was now almost completely Tonopah-centric, with only a few administrative functions remaining at Nellis.

Later in the month, Zettel left and was replaced by Maj Dudley A. Larsen, "Bandit 60." Navy LtCdr Cary "Dollar" Silvers, who became "Bandit 61," also arrived ahead of the planned departure of both Brubaker and McCort.

Larsen had always had his eye on flying. When he was just eight years old a T-33 had flown over his head while he walked with his father. Immediately, he had turned around and told his dad that he was going to be a pilot when he grew up. "Making that happen was another matter," though. He had gone through ROTC at a college in Wisconsin and graduated pilot training just high enough to get an F-4. But he missed being sent to Vietnam, and was assigned instead to RAF Bentwaters, England, in 1973. There he had flown Phantoms, first F-4Cs and then F-4Ds, and he would continue flying the "Rhino" next in Korea, then as a FWIC student. Of the notoriously tough FWIC course he said, "I barely survived that. It was a bit like – 'What do you call the last man in his physicians' class at Harvard? Doctor!' I just scraped through."

An exchange tour with the Royal Canadian Air Force (RCAF) ensued, giving him the opportunity to fly the Lockheed CF-104 Starfighter for almost four years. The Canadian exchange was invaluable in preparing him for the speeds of the MiG-21 that he was now learning to fly. The F-104 was better known as the Zipper, on account of its incredible speed, and Larsen was now the first CONSTANT PEG pilot to have flown both. "It was exciting to fly the MiG-21. I had flown the F-104 and now I was going to fly its parallel from behind the Iron Curtain. But it was also intimidating. Intimidating because everyone in that squadron was a superb aviator; some of them were unbelievably talented. People like Chanik and Geisler – incredibly good fighter pilots who you knew about by reputation before you even arrived at Tonopah. When you are an average kind of guy, those are some big shoes to step into." As a Weapons School graduate, Larsen is almost certainly being modest about his skills as a fighter pilot, but his extensive background flying the F-4 and CF-104 in a multirole environment and lack of Aggressor background meant that when he arrived at the remote airfield his air-to-air skills, so paramount in the Red Eagles, were lacking.

Larsen set about rectifying that situation. He was well aware of the MiGs' strengths and weaknesses, and their dangers, long before he had ever joined the unit. In 1979, America sold 35 F-4Es to Egypt under PEACE PHARAOH, a foreign military sales program that sought to re-equip the Egyptian Air Force and was no doubt heavily influenced by Egypt's earlier sale of MiGs to the US. As part of PEACE PHARAOH, Egyptian pilots had been trained to fly the Phantom in the United States, and Larsen was one of the IPs:

> We checked them out in the F-4E, and one of the guys I checked out had flown the MiG-21 and MiG-23. He had told me about how he hated the MiG-23 because it went out of control so easily, but that he loved the MiG-21. He was a very talented pilot who had been the first MiG into Gaza during the 1973 war with Israel. He also had multiple air-to-air kills in the MiG-21 against Israeli F-4s, and he had once bailed out of a MiG-23 when it had got into an unrecoverable spin. One day we went out and, as part of some F-4 advanced handling sorties, I showed him slow loops, entered from only 350 knots when the usual minimum entry speed was 500 knots. The F-4 would flop about at the top, and the maneuver was kind of prohibited. I asked him what he thought. He told me he could do the same maneuver in the MiG-21 with only 275 knots of entry speed.

Learning how to employ the MiG-21 to the same level of expertise as the other Red Eagles was a challenge for Larsen:

> I remember flying against Marty Macy on one of my TX rides. I went out in the MiG-21 and he in a T-38, and he beat me up like some kind of red-headed step-child. I just did not understand air-to-air as well as any of them – Ted Thompson,

for example, had more fighter sorties than he had fighter hours for a long time. It took me a long time to learn how to knife-fight the Fishbed in a phone booth, and it was all down to familiarity. The learning curve was very steep, and when someone handed me my ass, I would come back and look at exactly how they had done it.

Like all the Bandits, he was flying sorties at a prodigious rate. "On some days I would walk out to an aircraft, fly a 22-minute BFM hop and then land, run into maintenance to sign out the next jet, hop into it, and then repeat the process twice more. I could fly three BFM sorties in the space of two hours." With that sort of productivity, Larsen soon honed his air-to-air skills, and when he did he found himself able to offer some useful tips to his Blue Air opponents:

> The MiG's slow-speed capability was incredible, but not as good as that of the F/A-18. I had been lucky enough to get a few orientation rides in the Hornet before I had joined the Red Eagles, so I knew what it could do. Against the Marine and Navy Hornet guys I would try and "tree" them [see below]. Then, as we were both really slow and they were behind my 3-9 line, I would tell them, "OK, pull the stick all the way back, plug in the afterburners, and run the trim all the way back," and they would be able to settle in behind me and gun me.

Phelan explained what "treeing" someone meant:

> You treed someone by getting them to run out of airspeed so that they could no longer pull a loop. If they tried to, you knew they would fall off to either side, or they would bob their noses up and down. The Soviets had a terrific airplane in the MiG-21. Hands-down, I could kill anyone other than an F-16 or an F/A-18 in that airplane. The F-16 could fly over the top of me and get in behind, and the F/A-18 had even better low-speed handling. As for the others, I would do the tree. Taking the F-14 as an example, I would try and get them to go vertical a couple of times and then park right behind them.

Becoming a respected teacher of air-to-air combat was not without its psychological set-backs, though. Larsen once flew against one of his old FWIC IPs, Joe Bob Phillips. "I thought it would be an opportunity for the student to teach the teacher. It turned out that actually the teacher was going to teach the student yet another lesson! He was incredible when he was a major and I was going through the Weapons School, and now he was a lieutenant colonel and coming back to be the DO of Red Flag, he was still incredible. I just about held my own, but I did not win anywhere near as much as I wanted to."

Larsen was joining the ranks of the best MiG-21 pilots in the world. Once there, the microcassette tape recorders, used to record the radio calls during the engagements, almost became redundant. "You got so good that you could just write it all down on your kneeboard: 'Started north … F-15 at left 7 o'clock, 9,000ft, break turn … nose high reversal … intimidated with nose position … got slow … got into knife fight.' Then you could listen to the commentary on the tape to fill in the small details."

Every day offered the opportunity to learn something new, and sometimes that something new came as a shock:

I was flying against a TOPGUN F-14 one day. They were vertical fighters – they kept going fast like you did in the F-4, and they used the vertical plane to beat you. Anyway, I hear this call, "TOPGUN zero two is ballistic," and I had no idea what it meant. It turned out he no longer had any control of the airplane. He had turned into a big arrow, and I was chasing it uphill as it flopped onto its back and started downhill towards me. I knew that this was not a good place to be and suddenly understood what the ballistic call meant. I dumped the controls and only just got out of his way in time.

On another occasion, Larsen had induced a compressor stall and subsequent flameout by failing to observe a simple rule: "You had to let the afterburner in the MiG-21 stay lit for at least four seconds before you put a lot of AoA on the airplane. I had seen this F-15 coming at me and I broke into him without waiting. We both got pretty excited when flames shot out of both ends of my airplane, but I got the engine restarted and returned safely."

Macy was also teaching Silvers to fly the Fishbed. The affable Navy pilot had caused trouble on his first ever sortie up at Tonopah:

I was with Rob "Z-Man" Zettle in a T-38, and he was showing me the area. "OK, here's the base. We'll take off, look at the ranges and check out all the landmarks," he told me. So, we did all this and then he gave me the jet to fly for a while, but I wasn't as knowledgeable about where we were as he was. I went screaming down to the ground at about 500ft and then I pulled the nose straight up. Unfortunately, I was right off the extended centerline of the runway, and the SOF in the tower saw. Well, Rob got grounded for two weeks for flat hatting. Z-Man just took it, and he didn't tell anyone it was actually me flying.

Silvers had originally wanted to join the Air Force, but when there had been no pilot slots available for him to apply for, he had gone immediately to the Navy.

Graduating from flight school in 1978, he'd first spent three years as an IP on the TA-4 Skyhawk as what the Navy called a "selectively retained graduate." "One of the benefits of that job was that I got my first choice of airplane when it was over. So, in 1981 I went to the F-14 Tomcat." He flew a number of carrier tours with VF-143, the "Pukin' Dogs," before being offered a choice of joining either VF-43, or becoming an IP at TOPGUN. He chose VF-43, the Navy East Coast Adversary squadron; because he was newly married it offered him what he saw as the most rewarding work, as it would give him more time to be with his new wife, and was also a challenge. It was a good decision, and in short order Silvers was sent to Israel to learn how to fly the F-21 Kfir, a modified Mirage III being leased from Israel by the US Navy for use as a MiG-23 simulator.

Prior to joining VF-43, he had actually gone through TOPGUN as a student, but bad weather had resulted in the cancellation of his exposure to CONSTANT PEG. He'd been due to fly against Taylor, a man he described as "very professional. Very sharp. He almost looked like a Marine." The canceled sortie left Silvers and his RIO "heartbroken." His performance years later on in VF-43 resulted in his being given a second chance, though. "I became the East Coast liaison officer for the 4477th TES. I was a point of contact for any time an East Coast Air Wing visited Fallon NAS for training. Part of their training, whenever possible, was to get them exposed to CONSTANT PEG. So, I would go up there and get them read in." Interestingly, exposure to the MiGs was not a part of the syllabus for VF-43's IPs.

By early 1986, Silvers had been hired to join the Red Eagles. "In my career, I was always lucky to fall into great assignments. And this was one of them: it was a 'pearl' job that could result in a squadron command and built careers. Technically, all the Navy guys formed the Navy Fighter Weapon School's Nellis Detachment, which meant our immediate boss was the commanding officer of 'TOPGUN Fighter Weapons School, Detachment Nellis.'"

"ARE YOU SAD THAT PACO IS LEAVING?"

October and November saw a flurry of personnel changes as Geisler left the Red Eagles, followed weeks later by Brubaker, Stucky, and McCort. Maj Rick "Caz" Cazessus, one of only a handful of pilots Air Force-wide who was qualified as an Aggressor and a FWIC graduate, crossed paths with the four men as he arrived to become "Bandit 63" in November.

Geisler had racked up exactly 500 sorties (286 hours) in the MiG-21 – more than anyone before or since. "For my 500th sortie they had painted a big 500 on the nose of my jet in red and yellow Soviet-style numbers." His record can be attributed to the fact that not only did he fly a lot, but that he also never flew the MiG-23. "The deal had been that you would fly the MiG-21 for half your tour, and then the MiG-23 for the other half. But as the ops officer, sometimes you just had to be a dick about that sort of thing. They would say, 'OK, Paco, now it's your turn to fly it,' and I would respond, 'Fuck! I ain't flying that piece of shit! You can't do anything but intercepts in it!' It was kind of an ego thing for me, but there was no one there who could make me do it." In truth, Geisler was burned out and was keen to return to the Eagle. Ashy had helped secure him a flying position as the wing weapons officer at the 33rd TFW at Eglin AFB, Florida, and he was now chomping at the bit. He had been fond of the MiG-21, but he was clear about one thing. "I wouldn't have flown the thing within a mile of a combat zone!"

As a going-away present, Geisler was presented with a video made by the squadron. Filmed in the style of an investigative piece by TV show *60 Minutes*, it plays on Geisler's ego, his enthusiasm for weight training, and an apparent fear of going bald. The spoof documentary involves secret filming of Geisler, as well as interviews with his wife and children and a number of Red Eagles. The reporter, Brubaker, goes out onto the streets of Las Vegas and asks the general public what they make of Geisler's departure. "Who's Paco?" ask some, to which Brubaker responds, "Why, he's a world famous body builder!" Even more funny are the staged interviews with various prostitutes in towns surrounding Tonopah. In one segment Brubaker asks, "Are you sad that Paco is leaving?" to which the two women in a bed with another Red Eagle, his face hidden beneath the covers, respond, "Paco's leaving? We love Paco!" before presenting Brubaker with a fake check that they claim Paco must settle before he departs. It is quite a piece of investigative journalism.

A month later, Stucky also left the Red Eagles, but unlike his best friend, Geisler, the big man did not want to leave: "Least of all because they were sending me to Air Command and Staff college, where instead of flying I was going to spend a year in a classroom," he scoffed. The two pranksters had provided hours of entertainment over the years, with Stucky pulling off the most revolting, and ultimately the winning, prank: "He had cut off a bunch of his pubic hair and put it in Paco's box of chewing tobacco. Then he told Paco about it the next day in front of the entire squadron!," Manclark revealed.

The end of 1986 may have signaled the end of an era, but the squadron had cause to celebrate: it had flown a staggering 2,792 sorties – more than any year to date – for 982 exposures. That equated to 2.8 exposures per Blue Air pilot. This had been achieved despite a reduction in the number of MiG-21s (down from 17 to 14), and the continued problems of CONSTANT PEG's ten MiG-23s.

CHAPTER 13

"RED COUNTRY," 1987

In January 1987, "Stretch" Kinney left the Red Eagles and was replaced by Maj James D. "Tony" Mahoney, "Bandit 62."[38] Mahoney was soon joined by LtCdr Robert E. "Sundance" Davis, "Bandit 64." "I caught the flying bug early, and I naturally leaned towards fighters since they were cool," said Mahoney, who enrolled in the Air Force Academy and started UPT in 1975. Graduating first in his class in 1976, he got his first choice – the F-15 – and was sent on his first operational Eagle tour at Bitburg AB, Germany. By the end of 1980 he was en route to Nellis to go through the F-15 Weapons School, and he then flew the Eagle on two more consecutive tours, the first at Langley and the next at Holloman. "A fourth tour in the F-15 was not on the cards, so Paco, who I knew from Holloman, called me up and invited me to apply to the Red Eagles. I thought it sounded a lot better than flying a desk, so I agreed!"

Mahoney knew that Tonopah was home to something even more classified than CONSTANT PEG, but he was still surprised when he was given a tour of the F-117 facilities a few days after arriving in Nevada. "While assigned to Holloman, I had flown into the Nellis ranges on an exercise one night and had noted these IFF returns on the edge of my radar scope, right over Tonopah. When we landed at dawn and had our whisky and coffee breakfasts, a couple of guys mentioned them. 'Did you see all those friendlies up in the corner of the ranges? What were they doing?' No one had any idea." It was clearly something that the Air Force wanted kept quiet.

Back at Langley, Mike Scott was working at the 1 TFW's scheduling shop when one evening he had made his way down to the 71st TFS bar for a beer. The squadron commander there was LtCol Jon Goldenbaum, whom Scott knew from the Aggressors, and the two were talking when another former Aggressor walked into the bar. "It was John T. Manclark, who was very good friends with Goldenbaum. Both were also very good friends of mine. Manclark said to me, 'Hey! I need an ops officer. Are you interested in coming back out to Nellis?'"

It was a no-brainer decision; the only question was how soon he could leave Langley. Scott went to Dick Bethurem and asked him to sponsor his transfer. Bethurem quizzed him on the move, but having flown every frontline air-to-air jet fighter in the Air Force inventory (bar the F-16), being an IP, handling the Red Eagles' money and business whilst at TAC HQ, and his previous experience in the MiGs, there was no better qualified candidate anywhere else in the Air Force. Bethurem agreed, and took the request to Glosson. An hour later, Bethurem called him on the phone: "OK, Buster says that he doesn't think you can make it happen since you have been in the F-15 for less than a year and the personnel people are not going to release you, but if you think you can, he says go for it." Scott called Manclark and told him he had the green light to apply. Within a week Manclark had secured him orders to report to Nellis in April. He was to be the 4477th TES's new ops officer.

NEAR HITS

Some of the more aggressive sorties now being flown by the Red Eagles included 1 v 1s with the US Navy's Adversary A-4s. "They would fly in from Fallon for a one-on-one 'special' against the MiG-21," Phelan explained:

One of the start-ups was a 1,000ft line abreast, and the fight was on when you turned into each other. Now, remember that we had an RoE [rules of engagement] of 500ft around the airplane. So, you were not supposed to get any closer than that. One day I went out against a Navy guy, and all I can assume is that he just did not want to be beaten. Every time I turned to get a little more separation, he pointed right back at me. He must have passed me with less than 100ft separation. I called, "Knock it off! Knock it off! Go home!" and was just a little bit shaken.

When I landed, he called on the phone in a huff. I told him, "Man, you are lucky I am not calling your commander, because you tried to hit me." He said, "I was just trying to take your turning room away." I told him that he had certainly done that! Then he admitted that he may have got a bit carried away. "Actually," he confessed, "there was a time when I wasn't sure we were going to clear!"

Treeing an opponent would sometimes cause some pretty hairy situations to develop, despite the fact that the RoE called not just for a minimum separation distance to be maintained, but also for minimum airspeeds to be maintained. "On one occasion," recounts Phelan, "I had just treed this F-15 and am pulling up right behind this guy with less than 100 knots of airspeed. All of a sudden, this huge F-15 just starts falling back down towards me, out of control. He had completely run out of airspeed. I turned my head and said to myself: 'This is it. I am going to die.' A big shadow cast over the cockpit, but the Eagle went past me without hitting." Back on the ground, the Eagle pilot told Phelan: "I got lost in myself. For a minute I thought I was fighting a real MiG."

Many of the kills on Blue Air were directly attributable to the quality of the 4477th TES GCI controllers. Tom Boma used them to navigate very precisely around "The Box" – the restricted airspace of Area 51, which covered Groom Lake and was prohibited to even the Red Eagles without prior arrangement or in case of an emergency:

I once had these Air National Guard F-4 guys come in to do their ME. The squadron commander was a friend of mine and at the bar the night before, I told him I was going to get him. The next day I took off in the MiG-21 and climbed to 40,000ft. I had GCI direct me to the northern edge of the box and then down the side of it. I sneaked up on the four Phantoms and was killing the third one before they even knew I was there. They turned around and said, "We knew you were there! We just ignored you because we saw you flying into The Box!" We had great controllers.

Discipline among the Red Eagle pilots had improved since Bland's fly-by, but Manclark still had to send one or two of his pilots to spend a week in the control tower as the SOF when they misbehaved. "I kept my radio on in my jeep when I drove around, and the Flogger guys in particular would stop talking about their exploits when I walked into a room, but that was natural in any squadron. We had a hat with turds and a sign that read "Shit Head" glued to it, and anyone who goofed up or just screwed around had to wear that hat for a day. Some of the guys were actually proud to wear it, and the maintainers all liked the pilots walking around wearing it."

Fighter pilot buffoonery on the ground was still the norm, though. Boma recalled that the two side-by-side security turnstiles the men now had to go through once they arrived at Tonopah required a code to be entered into a keypad, and was followed by the palm scanner. Between the stile and the scanner was a laser beam at ground level that sounded an alarm when broken, and which was turned off by entering the correct code into the turnstile. "You would throw your bag onto their side, the alarm would sound, and they would get taken away to the clank. Then you would steal their sortie while they were busy trying to get out of jail."

FLYING THE MIG-23

Since its introduction to the 4477th TES in 1980, the MiG-23 had developed a reputation among the Red Eagles that made it infamous. Press was most blunt of all about it: "It was a piece of shit."

Some, like Geisler, actively sought to avoid flying it, and many thought that it represented all that was bad about Soviet engineering and safety. Scott, the only Red Eagle to fly the MiG-17, MiG-21, MiG-23, F-4, F-5, F-16, and F-15 in operational environments, summed it up best: "Of all those airplanes, the MiG-23 ranked bottom. The MiG-23 just was not a fun airplane to fly." Matheny was even more scathing: "The best thing we could have done was buy as many as we could afford and then give them all to our enemies so that they could all kill themselves flying it." Bucko was equally as weary: "It was a status symbol to fly, but I got to tell you, every flight in that thing was a major concern to me."

The Flogger had many quirks, some more problematic than others, recalled Myers, and they started from the moment you taxied the aircraft: The MiG-23 felt like it was "wallowing" on the ground most of the time. In the air, it got no better. "Whereas the MiG-21 had a light stick, the MiG-23 had a heavy stick," an undesirable quality according to Shervanick. Myers also recalled: "On both sides of the Mach, going up past it and coming back down below it, the Flogger had this yawing movement that caused the nose to hunt back and forth and you just had to sit there and wait while it did it. It was very uncomfortable for us F-4 and F-15 guys, and it would just abruptly stop. Most of us felt quite nervous about flying it, including myself, whereas the MiG-21 was a very comfortable and stable airplane by contrast." "I found the air-to-ground model to be a little more unstable pushing through the Mach," Matheny added.

In slow or maneuvering flight, "it was also squirrelly at high angles of attack," reported Press. "In fact, it had a 'knuckle rapper' on the stick that came on when you hit 17 units (degrees AoA). It was a plate that would rap your knuckles until you stopped pulling on the stick." Silvers called this a "dummy switch": "It was there to tell you, 'Hey! Stop pulling back on the stick so hard, dummy!' That was literally what it was for. The MiG-23 departed very suddenly, so guys were always wary of putting too much AoA on it."

The poor visibility and ergonomics of the cockpit meant that the Flogger pilot was always either busy manipulating switches, trying to visually acquire the enemy, or preoccupied with his fuel state. "The fuel gauges were funny," Matheny explained. "They measured fuel in a pipe, not what was in the actual fuel tanks. You filled up the airplane and then set the fuel gauges for around 400 liters. When the motor started, the fuel ran through the pipe and the gauge started going down. You had to be a little concerned that it was measuring it right, because it wasn't always the same as what you actually had in the tank." As a back-up, the pilots applied common sense: "You always tried to time the mission so that you weren't doing any low-altitude work towards the end, and so you were always in a position that if you did run out of gas you could make it back to Tonopah." On the rare occasions when there was a lull in the action, the Flogger at least gave the pilot the chance to listen to some rock and roll music, since the original Soviet UHF radio had been retained in some of the jets. "If you weren't too busy, you could tune it into some of the Las Vegas radio stations!" recalled Matheny.

In the landing pattern the Flogger was especially prone to bite. "I never tried to shine my ass in the pattern," Phelan stated. "Once that airplane departed, you were dead. We had big, wide, sweeping patterns; it was one of the things that we made the biggest deal out of as we chased new Flogger pilots in the T-38." Just getting to the point where landing the Flogger was possible could be exciting, according to Silvers: "On the F-14, your flaps and slats come down in a synchronized fashion, but if one came out and the other did not, or if there was more than a couple of degrees of difference between one side and the other, the system would lock out." This prevented one wing from generating more lift and decelerating faster than the other, which was critical because such forces could cause a yawing, rolling departure from flight. At low altitude, this would be fatal. The problem was that the Flogger had no such protection: "The flaps and slats would just deploy, regardless. They came down at different rates, so the aircraft would wobble and it was a bit like flying your downwind leg on a bowling ball. You knew it was going to happen, but you always wondered, 'OK, what's it going to do today?'"

Bucko concurred, going on to explain:

The landing attitude of the airplane is very critical. Landing it was like driving a World War II submarine: there were gauges and switches being thrown, and moving parts getting into position all over the place. When you finally touched down you were hoping that the drag chute came out when you pulled the handle. The "go around" capability was marginal because of the slow spool-up time for the engine to produce the thrust you needed to get airborne. I was lucky that my take-off numbers equaled my number of full stop landings, and people always came out to see our landings in the MIG-23; it was always a good show. Every landing was an adventure and not always a thing of beauty.

FIGHTING THE MIG-23

"The MiG-23 was the best trick the Soviets ever played on themselves," said Phelan. "They wanted this complex, sophisticated airplane, and what they got was what I called the Widow Maker. I interviewed a MiG-23 pilot from the Eastern Bloc and one from Cuba, at Wright-Patterson, where the DIA has all their engineering know-how. We were interested in how they flew the airplane and what their tactics were. What they told us only reinforced what we already knew."

"The MiG-23 was a terrible maneuvering aircraft that used speed to win but could be frustrating to fight because it refused to stay and turn," Robb said. "You didn't want to get into any kind of turning fight in it," Myers concurred, and added: "There had initially been some rumors that if it got into a turning fight, the wings would be swept full forward, at which point it would turn quite well. That turned out not to be true: it wallowed and bucked, particularly at high angles of attack. Unlike the F-15, where you could change weapons and radar modes without taking your hands off the stick and throttles, you had to reach all over the place to do the same in the Flogger."

Geisler talked about the rationale behind only ever doing defensive BFM set-ups with the Flogger during the BFM phase of a standard Blue Air exposure. "We taught guys that if you were defensive with a Flogger right behind you, then you were automatically offensive, because even the worst pilot in the world would be able to deny him the shot. You would turn, he would try and turn with you, but he would never be able to turn the same corner as you."

"You were a fool if you stayed and tried to maneuver against someone if you were in the -23," Bucko said. The MiG-23 could outrun the Hornet, "but if he tried to do that, you'd just shoot him with an AIM-9 Sidewinder." It might not always be that clear cut, though, as Geisler pointed out: "He would sweep his wings back and accelerate out of the fight, and sometimes by the time you had reversed your turn to point at him, he was already three miles away and the gap was increasing. What do you do then?"

In a 2 v 2 scenario, the MiG-23 could impress if flown properly, Bucko recalled. "One of the MiG-23s would retreat while the other guy would come in behind you. In the training environment the Blue Air pilots would do their intercepts at 350 to 400 knots, so when they all of a sudden get this Flogger coming at Mach 1.5, it really changes the geometry of things. It blows your mind because you are not used to seeing that kind of speed."

Geisler and Stucky teamed up to perform their own version of this maneuver. They called it the "Gorgeous George" routine, after the professional wrestler of the day. Stucky explained:

I was the sacrificial lamb who would turn my Flogger out in front of the Blue Air guys in a 2 v 2. I would turn just far enough ahead of them that they could see me but not shoot me. I would sweep the wings back and accelerate in afterburner so they would chase me. Paco would then convert on the two of them in his MiG-21. I was the decoy, Paco was the clean-up guy who was going to embarrass them. In the Gorgeous George routine, you had to be very careful with your speed because the MiG-23 would go through 900 knots easily.

Shervanick agreed:

I opened the eyes of several F-15 pilots with the MiG-23's speed and ability to take shots of opportunity at high speed. I would also use the vertical to climb up four miles [21,000ft] – if I had the speed. I would pull back on that very heavy stick and fly this huge loop. If anyone wanted to try and turn inside me or intimidate me, I would fly this huge loop in the vertical that they could not follow, cut back inside them at the bottom of the loop, fly a couple of miles outside their visual range, then cut back in and fly through their formation again.

Bucko explained another aspect of the Flogger in combat:

One of the things that you looked to show guys was how small the Flogger was. You looked at it in a museum and thought it was pretty big, but when you flew against it you thought that it was no bigger than the tail of an F-14. When you were looking at it nose-on, it looked like it was two miles away. In reality, it was only 2,000ft away and the guy was sitting there getting ready to shoot you.

Another thing that I would do when guys joined up on me was to put them behind me and show them the blind cone behind me. The MiG-23 had the worst visibility – forward and back – of any airplane I have ever flown. You couldn't see about 40 degrees back. The periscope above your head gave you a good view of straight behind you, but it did not have a wide field of view. Looking forward, your visibility was restricted to the point that it was pretty uncomfortable, particularly in the landing pattern.

There were two key areas where the MiG-23 was a very useful teaching aid: at low altitude, where the Soviets in Eastern Europe would use it to run down nuclear-armed NATO and American strike fighters heading east at 200ft; and at high altitude, where its speed could cause all sorts of problems for a Blue Air pilot who had taken his eye off the ball. "At low level," recalled Matheny, "in full afterburner, it would run the airspeed right off the charts. The only thing that had a chance of keeping up with it was the F-model F-111, which had powerful motors. In fact, we had a guy who oversped it without realizing as he was trying to run someone down." This event was similar to a story Geisler related of a Red pilot who had exceeded 900 knots in a MiG-23 attempting a stern conversion on two F-111s. The Flogger pilot was low and fast, and GCI asked him to briefly pop up so that he could be seen on radar, allowing them to give him a vector to intercept the F-111s. He had done so and followed the heading GCI had given him, learning that he was only five miles behind his quarry in the process. Moments later he had still not visually acquired the F-111s and so called GCI for an update. They requested he once again climb briefly, and as he did so they informed him that he was now two miles ahead of the F-111s. Such was the Flogger's impressive dash capability, he had actually overtaken his targets, both of which were already transonic. "He looked into the cockpit, saw 900 knots and still accelerating, and scared the shit out of himself," Geisler stated.

The MiG-23 was very useful at simulating what was known as the high, fast flyer, or HFF. The Soviets used the immense speed of the MiG-25 Foxbat to attack aircraft of great value, so-called high value asset (HVA) targets. In wartime, HVAs would be specifically targeted by Foxbats that would fly at Mach 3 at an altitude of around 65,000ft. The most obvious HVA was the American and NATO E-3 Sentry airborne warning and control system (AWACS), which is the airborne equivalent of a GCI station.[39] To kill an AWACS, or an air refueling tanker – another HVA target – the Foxbat would have to make a sudden or unseen maneuver. To thwart the attack, the US or NATO pilot would have to react with speed and precision, since the MiG-25 had a dash speed of Mach 3.2. In layman's terms, that equates to 2,385mph, or 40 miles per minute. Simulating that sort of attack at the more leisurely pace of Mach 2 in the MiG-23 still required some careful use of the TTR range space if the Red Eagle pilot didn't want to spill out into civilian air traffic corridors. "We would start from the southern boundary, the bottom of the range, and try to be just supersonic as we turned north," Matheny explained. "You accelerated as you came out of the turn, but by the time you got to Mach 2 you were in a situation where you needed to do your tactic pretty quickly before you ran into and out of the northern boundary."

In a head-on engagement against an F-15 carrying the radar-guided AIM-7 Sparrow missile, Matheny revealed that there was a tactic that would work:

> As you passed him, you'd go nose low and turn into him. You'd unload the nose so that you were weightless, plug in the afterburner, and sweep the wings all the way back. By the time he was pointing at you and had a lock for his AIM-7 shot he would be just in range. His simulated AIM-7 missile is streaking towards you and so you begin a supersonic climb. Well, that missile says to itself, "Oh my God, I now have to get him in a supersonic climb. I am not going to make it." Meanwhile, you're shooting out into the ionosphere, supersonic, and roaring in full blower. The R-29-300 was one hell of a motor for thrust.

While some of the Red Eagles' newer MiG-21s had the basic Sapfir RP-21 "Spin Scan A" radar to assist in acquiring range data for an Atoll shot, the Flogger E had a Sapfir RP-22SM "Jaybird" air intercept radar that displayed contacts on a scope in the cockpit. The Jaybird had first been fielded in later variants on the MiG-21,[40] and was installed in Flogger Es sold by Russia to allies outside the Eastern Bloc. It lacked the sophistication of the Sapfir RP-23 "HIGH Lark" that equipped newer Floggers, but it did mean that in theory the Red Eagle pilot could detect the Blue Air forces before he could visually pick them out against the desert or the sky.

In practice, the Jaybird was a confusing and clumsy radar that was a generation behind equipment found even in the old Phantom, and two generations behind that of the new F-15, F-16, and F/A-18. Matheny resigned himself simply to making use of its so-called "bore sight" mode: "I would put it into bore sight, align the other guy with the gun sight, and the radar would automatically lock on. Fiddling around with the radar was a waste of time, especially since we had good GCI." Shervanick added: "You could see a guy out to about 30km, and although it wasn't useful in anything other than bore sight mode, it would light up the warning equipment in the other guy's cockpit, which added to the immersion of the exposure." On which note, Phelan explained that he would only momentarily lock the Blue Air pilot: "I knew I was going to get killed anyway, so why did I want to make it easy for him by giving a good look at my azimuth from him? In the MiG-23 you could fantasize about dogfighting in it, but we were pretty much going to stick to Soviet tactics and not do any Nevada freestyle."

The Red Eagles' MiG-23s also had working "Serena 3" radar warning receivers (RWRs) and SRO 2 "Odd Rods" IFF systems. While both systems had already been exploited by AFSC during DRILL/FERRY/DOUGHNUT, Serena at least put the pilot in the Flogger's cockpit even more firmly into Ivan's shoes, as Matheny explained: "Serena consisted of a round display at the top of the instrument panel that had a little airplane on it with lights circling around it that would illuminate when sensors on the airplane detected a radar source. It would tell you which quadrant the radar was in and you could sometimes tell whether they were just in search or actually locked onto you. At times that was beneficial." Shervanick learned to glean even more information from the basic little display: "By watching the sectors light up, I learned to tell about how far away from me they were if I couldn't see them visually. It was only four little lights and was even more basic than our oldest RWRs, but it was still somewhat useful."

Some of the MiG-21s also had Serena equipment installed, but according to Geisler, it was mostly unserviceable. He and the others had gone out and purchased "Fuzz Busters," the radar detectors for drivers who wanted to know when the police were checking their speed with their handheld speed guns. "You'd stick it on your lap or wedge it in between the canopy and the instrument panel and when the other guy painted you with his radar, it would light up. We had used these in the Aggressors, and they were quite effective."

Like Shervanick's Egyptian friend, many pilots around the world had recognized the inherent limitations and weaknesses of the Flogger. Macy recalled:

> I spent a lot of time in Berlin watching the GCI tapes to verify that we were flying the right tactics, and it became clear to me that the East Germans knew exactly what the MiG-23's limitations were. They knew that since it was unmaneuverable, they had to attack from many different directions as fast as possible. It was sophisticated, and they were going to overwhelm us if we ever went up against them. I sat down with some analysts and linguists and listened to what the pilots were saying to their GCI controllers and I actually started to respect them for what they were doing with a very limited asset.

NEW PODS

In March, "Bandit 65," Capt Nickie J. Fuerst, arrived at Tonopah. He was followed in April by Maj Sam Therrien, "Bandit 66," and Scott too had finally returned, becoming the only person to serve with the 4477th TES twice. Therrien was a farm boy from south of Chicago. He had enlisted in the Air Force in 1972 and become a Russian linguist before he'd secured his commission and slot in UPT in 1978:

> I had been determined that I would get a college education and fly fighter jets. I had seen them scream over my head as a boy, and people always told me I was lucky that by high school I knew exactly what I wanted to do. I went to the Air Force Academy,

and as soon as I graduated I started flying. Flying came naturally to me, and I was the top graduate in T-37s. It was a fun and easy thing to me. I was in the top five out of a class of 35 in T-38s, and I knew that I was going to get a fighter, but I also knew that I was not going to get the one F-15 that was going to be offered to my class.

He got the F-4E, and was soon flying Bear intercepts over Alaska like Matheny had before him.

Two years later, he finally got to convert from the Phantom to the coveted F-15 Eagle when his squadron, the 43rd TFS, converted to the new type. Simultaneously, Myers arrived in Alaska and became the squadron's ops officer direct from his 4477th TES assignment. It was during this time that he had flown the Eagle down to Nellis for a Red Flag exposure to CONSTANT PEG, flying against both the MiG-21 and the MiG-23 in the process.

Two years later, in June 1984, he joined the 64th FWS at Nellis, where Manclark was his new ops officer. "I had my eye on the Red Eagles by now. I wanted to stay at Nellis as long as I could anyway, and when the opportunity came up to go for it, I was going to apply." Therrien and Manclark had got along well: "I told him that if there was an opportunity to go up to Tonopah, I was interested. I had been promoted to major two years early, and he just said, 'OK. I'll make it happen.'"

The squadron that Therrien was joining now was very different from that which Scott had left more than three years back. One of the most significant differences was the increased sophistication of the maintenance program: "In my first four-year tour," Scott reflected, "we would fly the assets and then be grounded for a while, then repeat the process. Now, as a function of the program maturing, we were measuring the maintenance operation just as the mainstream Air Force did," and that translated into fewer groundings. Much else had changed. The entire outfit was more formal, and each morning a briefing would be given outlining the status of the MiGs and their motors.

Another obvious change was the installation of new real-time air combat maneuvering instrumentation pods on the MiGs. The system was known as the Red Flag Measurement and Debriefing System (RFMDS). Scott described its function: "It was hooked into the systems of the MiG, as well as the rest of the Red and the Blue Force airplanes, and it sent everything back down to a big TV screen at the Red Flag building, where they could monitor what was happening."

The Red Eagles now had real-time "kill removal," as Scott further explained:

It had started to be trialed when I first left the squadron, but was fully in place when I came back the second time – they data-linked all the pertinent data back to Red Flag, and these guys could see a simulated version of what was going on. We didn't have a radar to tell us what our parameters were, and although we would carry AIM-9s that gave us a tone, it was all very much, 'That looks about right.' So, when we hit the pickle switch to simulate the missile launch, it would send a signal to the pod, which would then send a signal to the computers on the ground. Those computers would determine whether we had been in the correct parameters and would then register a kill or no-kill. The GCI controllers would then make the appropriate call: "Bandit 12, you're dead," which meant he had to do an aileron roll and leave the fight.

CLOSE CALL

The arrival of a new batch of 12 brand new MiG-21s – Chinese-built Shenyang F-7Bs, designated YF-110C [41] and purchased direct from China [42] – shortly after Therrien's arrival gave Manclark a solution to the distrust in the YF-110B ejection seats. "I retired the older MiGs. I flew the last sortie of the older models and turned around to the maintenance folks and said, 'Cut that stick off!' They mounted it on a plaque for me, which I still have today in my office. The plaque says, 'Aircraft #12. Last YF-110B sortie.'"[43] It was not a popular move, he admitted, but from a safety perspective it was the best decision he could make. The retired Fishbeds languished at Tonopah for some months, but Manclark did not know where they went from there.

The decision to retire the Indonesian Fishbeds in the early summer of 1987 was unpopular because, by and large, these were the favorite airframes among the Red Eagle pilots. Geisler elucidated: "I preferred the older MiGs because they were more maneuverable and the maintainers knew them better. The newer ones may have had more power, but they looked like they weren't as good as the old ones, and I didn't feel as confident pulling a load of G in them. The old ones you would walk up to and bang and they were like concrete, but the new ones were like hitting an old Pontiac."

That additional maneuverability, said Macy, came because the old MiGs had a "lighter nose." Phelan explained further: "The older ones were more maneuverable, but they had less power because they had a slightly smaller engine in them," adding, "I did like flying the new ones [J-7B], as these would always outfly their placard airspeed limit. I could hang in a straight ahead drag race longer and faster than our intelligence folks were telling the frontline squadrons that a MiG-21 could."

In June, Col James C. "Bear" Evans, the 57th FWW Adversary Tactics Commander, became "Bandit 67." Over the years a number of non-Red Eagles had visited first Groom Lake and then Tonopah to fly CONSTANT PEG aircraft, but he was the first full colonel from Nellis to do so, and was only the second non-Red Eagle to be allocated a Bandit number.

June also saw the departure of Thomas Drake and Robert Craig. John Mann recalled how Drake left the unit offering words from the wise:

I replaced Ted Drake in the MiG-23. His parting words to me were something of an admonishment to stop, as I put my foot on the ladder for every sortie, and tell myself that "This son of a bitch is gonna try to kill me today," and if I did that, I would be okay in the aircraft. "Yeah, Ted, right." However, his words turned out to be ever so accurate. During my third sortie in the MiG-23, while I was still in transition, the engine flamed out. We all knew the engines were flaky, and others had had flameouts, but a flameout on your third sortie is rather silly. And I went through a few long seconds of denial. But I was high enough, and close enough to the field, that it went into the glide just fine. As it turns out, it was a throttle linkage problem and the engine started back up on short final, and the landing was uneventful. When I got out of the MiG that day, I remember thinking that Ted's words might just be something to remember each time I put my foot on the ladder.

Until now, CONSTANT PEG had experienced relatively few mishaps since the death of Postai in 1982. There had certainly been some close calls. Phelan, who had converted to the Flogger in November 1986, had spun a MiG-23 and not only lived to tell the tale, but also recovered the Flogger back to Tonopah:

Our manuals told us to eject if you ever spun the Flogger, because of the arcing of the airframe and the turbine blades rubbing against the case. I had been flying the MiG on a 1 v 1 intercept ride against a Marine F/A-18 Hornet. We had started 20 miles apart in opposite directions. This guy was pretty good, and he was at the end of his week of training. So, I took a huge altitude advantage, putting him at about 20,000ft with me at about 30,000ft. I didn't lock onto him because the radar picked up such bad ground clutter.

I am expecting to be shot in the face by an AIM-7, but it never happened. As we close to about five miles I am starting to get excited, because I see him down there but he doesn't look like he sees me. I am finally going to get to sneak up behind someone in this thing! I started a slicing lead turn to the left, and had taken an offset from him to enable me to do that. In the Flogger, you had to really be careful of your speed in such maneuvers, so I was back in idle and even had the speed brakes out to stop me getting too fast. I got about 6,000ft behind him without him seeing me, and

I was doing fine. I just needed to pull my nose up 10 or 15 degrees more. I pulled back, not even to the AoA limit so that the ring knocker was not activated, but all of a sudden the aircraft started righting itself and started doing a very slow, large barrel roll. It completed the roll before I even knew I had lost control, and as it came through its second barrel roll, this Hornet still had no idea I was there!

Phelan pushed the stick forward – the standard recovery procedure for the Flogger – but it simply made matters worse:

The barrel roll tightened and then the aircraft spun to the left. I called "Knock it off! Knock it off!" to which he replied, "Copy, say reason?" I told him I was in a spin, and that's when GCI came on the radio and said, "Confirm you are in a spin!" I told him I was and that I was passing 18,000ft. I knew it was bad because I got this temporal distortion and I just watched as this altimeter wound down.

I didn't want to eject because the seat in that airplane kept you curled in the seat even after the parachute deploys, and the wind that day was gusting to 50mph. It was very windy. In my head as I am in this spin, I think that if I do eject, that seat is going to hit the ground and drag me along, breaking every bone in my body; I would end up paraplegic. So, I violated the Dash 1 and the GCI controller was calling, "Check altitude, check altitude." I knew it was going to be close. By now, the Hornet pilot had turned around, "My God! He really is in a spin!" he said.

Phelan deployed the drag parachute to try and stop the spin. "Not long after, the nose started to point down and the spinning started to slow. Then I have a face full of an Electronic Warfare (EW) site – one of many on the Nellis ranges to simulate you are in an enemy radar environment – and I pulled out somewhere between 300ft and 500ft over the top of that thing. Now my dilemma is whether the engine will work; I nudged the throttle forward a little bit and the power came back on without any problems."

Phelan landed the Flogger at Tonopah to find that the EW site had complained about an aircraft that had buzzed its facilities. It didn't phase Manclark, though: "As a commander I never worried the pilots. They were all top notch. I spent my day in maintenance. That's where the business was really done. The evening of Hog's spin we all went to Miramar and he got very, very drunk. When Denny got drunk he almost always took his clothes off. And when he did that, his wife would run out, jump in the car, and then drive home out of embarrassment. At one St Patrick's party he took his clothes off and he had painted it green. But he was a seriously smart guy."

Manclark was himself well respected. Boma and Silvers both recalled that he had a good sense of humor and commanded respect from all quarters, including the maintenance troops. But it was best to keep on his good side: Silvers had once been told to straighten up his act when he walked around the squadron one day with the black and yellow checkered scarf of the 57th FWW trailing along the ground from one of his flight suit legs. "The Air Force was very particular about this stuff and wanted us to wear these 'neckties,' but us Navy guys used to shove them down our flight suits. I hadn't realized that it was now dragging on the ground. Manclark was a very, very smart guy who was also extremely intense. He and Mike Scott sometimes got a little aggravated with the Navy guys, but he was a good squadron skipper who did a lot of good for the squadron and took good care of us and it."

MISHAPS

On June 25, 1987, CONSTANT PEG's luck ran out. Cazessus was flying a 1 v 1 exposure when his MiG-21, a J-7B with the USAF serial "045," experienced a flameout and refused to restart. The dual-qualified Aggressor and FWIC grad already had experience of losing the engine in a single-engine, high-performance fighter, having deadsticked an F-16 before he came to Tonopah. But this time he would not be so successful. Thompson had been his instructor pilot for his MiG-21 transition, and the two had also served as Aggressors in the 64th FWS together. "He was a great pilot," he told me.

Phelan was sitting on the apron in a MiG-23 when Cazessus experienced the engine failure. "He set up to do a flameout approach. It was going well until the last turn to final when you have to gauge between keeping enough airspeed by lowering the nose, and making sure you reach the runway. It turned out that he arrived a little too high and a little too fast – he would have landed long, maybe in the last 1,000ft of the runway, had he tried to touch down."

With his back now to Cazessus, Phelan leaned out of the side of the Flogger to catch a glimpse of where he thought the MiG would touch down. "All I saw was this airplane go past with no noise whatsoever, at 500ft and going pretty fast." Another MiG-21, flying chase for Cazessus, called on the radio, "You got to get the gear down!" That other MiG-21 was being flown by Manclark. Cazessus had failed to follow the SFO checklist and had not lowered his undercarriage. The tower called: "Go around. Gear not down." "Then," Macy continued, "Rick just laughed, pulled up for altitude, and punched out."

The tower called for the Red Eagles on the ramp to shut down as Cazessus drifted to earth beneath a blooming parachute. But much of this had been missed by Therrien, who was shutting down and climbing out of his MiG-21 unaware of the drama unfolding around him:

> As I got out I looked up and saw this parachute coming down to earth. My first thought was that someone had dropped out of a Cessna to try and take pictures. We had little Cessnas try and do stuff like that all the time. So, I walked into the squadron nonchalantly, and I said to Macy, "Hey, who have we got here parachuting?" to which he said, "Quit fucking around! We got an emergency going on!" We walked out and sure enough there is smoke at the end of the runway and Rick is trying to gather up his parachute.

The seat had worked, and Cazessus had survived. Phelan and Thompson, the squadron's safety officers, immediately began a mishap investigation. Col Joe Lee Burns, original Aggressor and HAVE IDEA pilot, was called in to head the board. "General Kempf, the TFWC commander at the time, met with me and broke every rule and convention ever written for an investigation: he told me to hang Manclark and the pilot out to dry – he thought it was too dangerous, and he wanted the unit shut down."

As the investigation got underway, Secretary of Defense Casper Weinberger signed a letter granting the 4477th TES its second Joint Meritorious Unit award – the so-called first Oak Leaf Cluster. This was for the exceptional service it had provided the TAF between February 2, 1984, and February 1, 1987.

The cause of the Cazessus mishap was never definitively identified, but Burns concluded that the engine had been starved of fuel, perhaps during a negative G condition. Given the large fireball that erupted as the MiG hit the ground, Burns' suspicion fell on the fuel pumps, one of which was found to have been wired differently than the others. Maintenance refuted this claim vehemently, showing Manclark that the wiring could not have been a factor, but he told them: "I am not getting blamed, you are not getting blamed, so let's just go with this theory." Indeed, Burns had refused to be intimidated by Kempf, and nothing more was said about the matter by the TFWC commander.

Phelan had spent a considerable amount of July sleeping over at Tonopah's Man Camp while he investigated Cazessus' mishap. In August he returned to Las Vegas and spent a long weekend away with his family to make up for his protracted absence. "When I got back, I had three messages on my answer machine from Tom Boma telling me to call Manclark right away because we had lost another jet. I thought he was kidding me because he knew how I had not enjoyed spending 30 days of my life locked on that damned base!" But it was no joke. On August 28, just over two months since the loss of Cazessus' Fishbed, Carlisle had successfully ejected from a MiG-23.

Phelan spoke to Manclark, who confirmed that he was once again to pack his bags and head out to Tonopah to participate in the investigation:

> I packed my bags and my wife thought I was kidding. It turned out that Hawk [Carlisle] had been flying what we called an "in-house" sortie in a MiG-23BN against a T-38. He was a low-time Flogger guy, and that version of the Flogger was more unstable than the intercept model because it had this slim nose that provided less drag for departures in yaw. In my mind, they had been flying an engagement that was a little too long – it was one continuous maneuver that amounted to what I called a "close fight." Bearing in mind that you didn't close fight the Flogger, in this case they had extended the engagement to the order of 1 minute, 30 seconds. They had flown a number of semi-vertical figure eights, with the T-38 eventually chasing the Flogger around, which was inevitable.

Carlisle's Flogger had departed controlled flight on one of these figure of eight turns as he pulled the nose above the horizon and started rolling the wings at the same time.

"Hawk did the right thing," Phelan continued. "He punched out at around 10,000ft above the ground." Manclark recalled that despite a successful ejection from the MiG itself, Carlisle had been lucky to survive: "The seats have a barometer on them and at a certain altitude it kicks you out of the seat and your chute deploys. When I went and picked him up, Hawk says, 'You've got to turn the barometers up. I was below the mountain before it kicked me out!' He was lucky that he had been over a valley."

In the aftermath of this second accident, Phelan and Manclark briefed not only the one-star commander of the 57th FWW, but also the two-star TFWC commander and the four-star TAC commander. "We briefed that the pilot had not broken off the maneuver because he did not recognize the signs of an impending departure," Phelan recalled.

The current TFWC commander, Gen Kempf,[44] had ordered Manclark to establish what the mishap rate of the 4477th TES was before he briefed the TAC commander. "TAC's accident rate was around four mishaps per 100,000 hours flown. That's a good number, and if it got up to six, everybody got excited. Ours was about 100 per 100,000 hours." It was a staggering statistic that reinforced just how much the Bandits were putting on the line. "Flying a single-engine airplane with no confidence in the seat made it a high-risk program," Manclark knew.

Phelan had left his mishap briefing with Kempf with a gut feeling that the writing was on the wall for the Red Eagles:

The general, who personally knew Hawk, said this: "What you guys are doing is way too dangerous. And I don't think that the pay-off is worth the price. I am not going to be the one that phones up someone's wife and tells her we have lost her husband." I could tell there and then that this guy was opposed to the program. When I got back to Tonopah I ranted and raved, mostly at Manclark. I thought the pay-off *was* worth the risk. We understood that we were going to lose people. Maybe we were cavalier about it, but we had all lost a lot of friends. They were dead. So what?

Death was part and parcel of the fighter business.

Manclark briefed the TAC commander with the TFWC commander in the room. "Kempf had turned around to me afterwards and said, 'Manclark, I am getting tired of traveling with you.' I knew that if someone ended up being killed, he was going to shut us down."

Tonopah had been plagued by problems. The 4450th TG had lost two F-117s and two pilots; crashed an A-7 into a Ramada Inn, killing some civilians; and run over and killed one of their personnel on the ramp at Tonopah, all within a short space of time. These had been followed quickly by the two 4477th TES losses. The result was that Gen Kempf was now flying into the air base once a week to keep a close eye on things.

Risk was a relative thing. Larsen, for example, had few qualms about flying the MiGs. "There had been more mishaps in flying F-104s in Canada than there had been since I got to Nellis." But Manclark believed that the risk now was not about losing a jet, but about losing a pilot: he assembled the Bandits in a room. "I told them, I did not want anyone staying with the aircraft to try and save it just because we had now had two accidents. My worry was that someone might ride one in trying to save it." It was surely ironic that now the squadron knew the seats worked perfectly well, there was concern that they might not be used for an altogether different reason.

Safety could even be compromised during standard operations, such as recovery of the MiGs back to the airfield. Silvers had once provided a moment of light relief during one particularly tense recovery, Manclark said:

An A-10 had fragged itself by dropping a bomb when it was on a strafing pass. It was on fire and came in to land at Tonopah, blocking the runway. Dollar was the SOF and there were about four Bandits airborne, including me. We were getting low on fuel and were about ready to divert [45] when he comes on the radio. "Do you want me to push him over the side, Boss?" He was about ready to go out there with a bulldozer to push it out of the way like they pushed airplanes over the side of the carrier in the Navy! I told him to leave it, the two-star at Nellis would have killed me! Eventually they got a tow truck out there and we all landed safely.

While humorous, the matter underpinned an important point. Silvers added: "There had been trouble getting a tow truck fast enough, so Manclark told me to take control of the tower. I did so, cleared him to land, and created quite a stink with the tower supervisor. We later had a meeting where Col Manclark made it very clear that the safety of his pilots and aircraft was the number one priority."

REVERSE ENGINEERING

Losing another Flogger undoubtedly put a strain on the program, Manclark said:

> We never had a good supply of engines, and I don't think we ever got more than about 30 hours on a motor before we had to pull it and rebuild it. We operated ten Floggers, and on our best day we probably had six running; it was usually three or four. The problem with the Flogger was also that you had to pull the plane in half to get the engine in or out. I would walk into a hangar and see up to seven of our ten broken in half, and I would ask myself, how many more times are we going to be able to put them together without someone making a mistake? Luckily, the maintainers put them back together right every time.

Keeping the Red Eagles' tactics up-to-date continued to require the ongoing support of a number of agencies. "The Systems Command people had an important role," Manclark pointed out. "I think they had some mock-ups of our equipment and the real stuff. They instructed the pilots on how to run the radar; they did all the analysis; and they gave us our performance data. They were a key part of the team, and any new MiG model we had they got their hands on it first and went through [exploited] it."

Reverse engineering continued to be an ongoing effort, too, despite the fact that the Air Force had been operating the MiG-21 on and off for more than 15 years by now: "I remember the maintainers came in one day and said they were running out of MiG-21 brakes. I said go out and get some MiG-21 brakes made. They came back probably six weeks later and said, 'We have a problem. We took the set of worn-out MiG-21 brakes and they [Good Year] made them exactly like the worn-out brakes.' We had $200,000 of brake pads that were no good," explained Manclark.

The ongoing effort to reverse engineer parts was now well developed. Prior to his departure in 1984, Nelson had negotiated with suppliers, looked at their processes, and scheduled manufacturing runs of new parts and materials in advance of when they would be needed. He had even developed contacts at the FAA to allow him to travel back and forth on commercial flights with MiG parts in his personal luggage: "I would call my contact up, tell them what flight I was going to be on and who I was bringing with me. They would meet me at the curb of the airport, take us to the ticket counter. They would take our tickets, pass them to the ticket checker, carry our luggage through security, and then escort us onto the airplane. We bypassed all of the security checks as a result. We would also have a letter stating that the contents of our bags were exempt from examination." Incredibly, Nelson and his team were even able to carry the pyrotechnic cartridges for the MiG seats in their personal hand luggage. On occasions, the parts were too numerous or bulky to load into a crate and fly home by airliner. One shipment of brake pads was so voluminous that Nelson had to buy a new truck to get it home.

Manclark acknowledged that others continued to support the flying operations. "One of them was Mike Coyle. At the time I was commander he was at FTD and he was the MiG-21 expert. So we would come to him to talk to him about everything to do with that airplane. If we had a question about the flight manual, if we had a question that our guys couldn't answer, we relied very heavily upon the community up here who had been studying that airplane for maybe ten years." Henderson was similarly impressed by the man:

I dealt with him when I was an Aggressor and again after I left the 4477th TES. Throughout that time frame, the MiG-21 was the most significant fighter threat around and Mike was the center of attention when queries came to FTD from the field. He was a fighter pilot's analyst. He was straightforward, exuberant, and always a pleasure to deal with. When you visited him the session was always a two-way street. He asked as many questions as he answered. He was always trying to gain a fighter pilot's perspective of the information that he was privy to, and he quickly began to speak the lingo – "nose authority," "pitch rate," "slice back," and so on. Somewhere along the line he got promoted to a division chief in charge of Soviet Advanced Threat and it never was the same dealing with the fighter analysts at FTD.

Other pilots also continued to trawl the classified channels for intelligence, including Thompson and Phelan, who were particularly interested in any information that would assist them in their capacity as the squadron's safety officers. Phelan could turn up at the DIA, CIA, and other agencies whenever he wanted:

> I had a pass that allowed me to go anywhere I wanted to get information. The DIA wouldn't even share information within their own building. It was always a one-sided conversation because they did not know about the airplanes or about what we did. There was some resentment because I could walk between offices and floors and talk to people that you still can't mention. All they knew was that we had clearance to get whatever information we wanted. As the safety officer and the weapons officer, one of my original tasks had been to write the weapons manuals and Dash 1s for the airplanes.

Keeping the manuals current required frequent visits, and when the Red Eagles started simulating the newer Molnyla R-60 (NATO: AA-8 Aphid) IR-guided missile instead of the AA-2 Atoll, Phelan was dispatched to get the latest data for his manuals:

> I went to Wright-Patterson to see what they had. Generally, the information was good, but sometimes it was just humorous, and that was because some of their assessments were based on photos. A two-man cell might be assigned to assess the performance of an Aphid based on some pictures, for example. These guys had engineering degrees, but that was all. So they were sometimes wide of the mark.
>
> On one occasion, a lady from one organization briefed me on how good the Soviet logistics system was, despite the fact that they had to stock ten engines for every airframe. She didn't know who I was, and continued to brief me about a level of efficiency that made the West look like we were bumbling idiots. She was talking about this great pipeline that spanned Western Europe and about how good their engines were. I knew this was patently BS, so I asked her, "What are your qualifications to do this assessment?" She said, "Well, we don't really have any logistics analysts, and I was only assigned to this role because there is no one else. Oh, and I have a private pilot's license." It was incredible!

The Red Eagles, who always dressed in civilian clothes on these visits, were even able to walk unchallenged between the two sides of the CIA, said one. "There were those in the CIA who drove to work, parked their car and went into the building; then there were those who drove to another location that was a cover, and were then driven to their real work." Being able to step between sources in these white and black worlds was unheard of.

Sam Therrien had been brought deep into the intelligence-gathering activities of the CIA and the Air Force's ETAT while he was an Aggressor, and continued to be involved as a Red Eagle. He explained that for all the glamour of the intelligence business, his job brought about some blunt realizations.

> I had often wondered where various pieces of information had come from, but now it was becoming clear why the sources were so well protected. Sometimes bad things happened. I would go to the CIA before visiting Berlin and seeing what our listening post had to tell us about the East Germans [and Russians]. [Back in the squadron] we would use this information at a SECRET security level, when it had actually come from sources that were much more than just SECRET. The problem was that when we used that information, the Russians sometimes found out about it, and they could then trace it back to the source. We would then lose a human [intelligence] resource … permanently.

Russia's policy with spies was to execute them. The Red Eagles always had to ask for information; it was rarely offered – no doubt partly because some of these agencies resented having to share their information, and no doubt because they didn't know who these plain clothed men were, or what they did for a living.

Sourcing engines and refurbished engines continued to be the biggest problem Manclark faced, but others often surfaced. When one MiG-21 experienced a gearbox failure, Manclark found this out first-hand. "I happened to be back at DIA the following week and they had their MiG-21 expert there. I said, 'Do you know anything about gears failing in the gearbox?' He was this older gentleman, and he went over to his card catalogue with 6,000 records, pulled out a card, and said, 'Yeah, they have that problem. They beefed up the gear.' No one had told us." The pilot in question was Shelley Rogers, Thompson told me. "There was no way he should have got that MiG-21 back to Tonopah. It was an outstanding piece of airmanship. I wrote him up for a DFC for that one." It was all the more remarkable given that Rogers was only attached to the Red Eagles, flying with them only a few times a week. His permanent position was actually as an XO at Nellis, according to Thompson.

LARGE FORCE EXERCISES AND MASS LAUNCHES

It had taken time to get permission to launch the MiGs in greater numbers than just single two-ship flights, but CONSTANT PEG was finally starting to get there. By allowing the MiGs to launch in greater numbers, the training potential of the assets was dramatically increased. The Flogger's utility was particularly improved, for example. It was not a dogfighter, and during PP demonstrations it was limited to training defensive BFM tactics, and to showing off its acceleration. But when employed as part of a four- or eight-ship of MiGs, it was a more credible adversary. No one could remember exactly when the mass launches were approved, but Sundell told me that they were first started in late 1987 and early 1988 to help the FWIC with its ME graduation exercises. Scott explained: "We would launch in groups of four airplanes at a time as Blue Air would come in." Thompson reckoned: "In our last year of operations, I would guess that we flew in every single Weapons School ME phase."

The ME sorties were invariably the most aggressive that the Red Eagles flew. One stands out in Thompson's mind: "We were a two-ship against two clean F-15s – they had no external stores or fuel tanks. They were flying a set-up where they had to visually ID us before they could shoot." The two MiGs were flying a trail formation – one leading, the other about 1½ miles behind – and both were supersonic.

> We were at 20,000ft, and the MiG-21 was not a great turning airplane at that speed and altitude. The MiG did its best turning below 400 knots, but at this speed and altitude we were essentially stealthy, because we were so difficult to see. And that's exactly what happened: the F-15 flight lead had tried to convert behind me, knowing that my flight lead was in front. He took his eyes off me to find his wingman, and I saw him just at the time he was doing that. I am looking for his wingman and go to full afterburner while I look for him. He's now lost sight of me, and I can't see him any more. I realize it's time to leave the fight. I look down at my airspeed and I am faster than the airplane is supposed to go – I was at 700 knots indicated airspeed, and the limit was 600. In the debrief, the F-15 pilot told me that by the time his radar had found me, I was 3½ miles away with 350 knots of opening velocity.

In this sortie, Thompson committed the cardinal sin of crossing the horizon, allowing the F-15s to acquire him visually. A tail chase ensued. "I got to ten miles from Tonopah when they called me dead. He let me look at his tape in the debrief and he had shot me with 150 knots of overtake. I had been doing 600 knots and he had been doing 750 knots. How much gas did he land with? Don't ask!"

Eventually, the Red Eagles started flying in Red Flag "Large Force Exercises." This meant that two four-ships would launch to meet waves of Red Flag participants either as they arrived for their two-week deployment, or at some point towards the end of the deployment. The limiting factor in the 4477th

TES's ability to get the MiGs airborne was, Scott recalled, "just a matter of bodies: even though we had a lot of airplanes, we were one of those squadrons that was not manned one-to-one: one pilot for every airplane. We always had fewer pilots than airplanes. If we got lucky and the maintainers had them all working at the same time, we could not get them all airborne at the same time."

As a large package of Blue Air fighters and strikers approached Tonopah, the MiGs would scramble. "The F-15s were always the first to go in to clean out the area," Therrien revealed, "so we would do various things – double pincers, single pincers – and other tactics straight from the Russians' sheets of music, and would drag them back to a CAP [Combat Air Patrol] area and wait for other guys [Red Eagles] to come in and try to kill them."

To compensate for their short fuel fractions, the MiGs were surged – "You would land, refuel and then take off immediately to get back into the action," Mahoney said, adding, "That was a realistic scenario for the Blue Air guys coming towards us, who were going to encounter waves of MiGs. For us it was a lot of fun, but it was also challenging. We couldn't just wander around single-ship, we had to stay paired up with our wingman so we could execute our tactics."

Another change that occurred in 1987 was the introduction of exposures to SAC's (Strategic Air Command's) nuclear bomber and tanker fleet. For SAC's FB-111 fighter-bomber crews, CONSTANT PEG was a rude awakening. These fighter-bombers, tasked with carrying nuclear weapons to targets deep in Eastern Europe, were going to rely on speed. The F-111 was the second fastest aircraft in the Air Force inventory (second only to the SR-71 Blackbird), after all. "They had planned to simply out-accelerate the Flogger, but on the first acceleration check they flew with us the Flogger disappeared out onto the horizon. Their plan was not going to work that well," Phelan revealed.

Phelan was sent to Barksdale AFB to brief the B-52 Stratofortress bomber crews and their KC-135 tanker brethren. "We didn't do any 1 v 1 missions with these guys, but we would chase them down when they were incorporated into the large Red Flag packages," he confirmed. "We also started completely integrating with the Aggressor F-5s, even to the point of briefing with them. Tonopah became the heart of 'Red Country.' That gave us more flying time than even an Aggressor F-5, which had to go back to Nellis for gas," he added.

Working with the F-5s, Phelan said, the MiG-23s were sometimes used as the clean-up team, with the bait being played by the F-5s:

They would get to just within AIM-7 range and then do this hook turn. We hoped that the Blue Air sweep guys would attach themselves to the Red Air F-5s, and we would then come in at Mach 2, get to the merge and take pot shots at the unprotected bombers. If you got really lucky, you'd find a B-52, which meant that there were another two around because they always flew in a cell of three. They would be so low that the cant of their wings hid their exhausts from our missiles. That, combined with the hot desert floor, meant that it was really difficult to get a lock on them with your IR missile. The Flogger's "nose hunting" was especially pronounced down low while chasing the B-52s. You were really supposed to reduce the throttle and climb when this happened down low, but sometimes I would just power through it.

Even more impressive than all of this was that the squadron was now doing the occasional Red Flag "Arrival Show." TAF and SAC squadrons set to deploy to Nellis for a Red Flag would already have been briefed by a visiting Red Eagle, and the arrivals always happened on a Saturday. Manclark explained further:

The aircraft coming in for Red Flag would rendezvous and then fly in as a complete package. The F-15s might come from Langley and the F-16s from Hill, and they would merge together and arrive as a package. We would meet these guys and give them some training. On one occasion my boss at Nellis phoned up and said he didn't want me to launch because since the strikers were inbound, the air-to-air F-15s had been delayed. I told him that we had briefed the mission and I now had guys in the MiGs ready to go; so I was going to launch anyway. He didn't like that, and of course we went out there and killed all these strikers, but my point was that if you were going to go to war you had better do it as a package or bad things would happen to you.

On November 20, Manclark handed over the 4477th TES to Scott. Manclark had received early promotion to full colonel by virtue of being the commander of the 4477th TES. "I left about three months early, which meant that I had to give up the squadron. I had just started to transition to the Flogger at that time, but we cancelled that once I got promoted. We were flying a lot of sorties towards the end, and even though I was away in Washington or at TAC HQ a lot, in 20 months I still managed to get 321 sorties in the MiG-21."

Manclark's departure coincided with that of Evans, the 57th FWW Adversary Tactics commander. His successor was Col Douglas M. Melson, who became "Bandit 68." Thompson liked Melson: "Having Doug fly with us was good for him and good for us. Whereas 'Bear' Evans had not flown with us much, Doug flew with us a lot. Having an O6 [full colonel] flying with us meant that the big guys took their eye off us a little bit." The year ended with a tally of 2,793 sorties for 905 exposures. The Red Eagles had a complement of 14 MiG-21s and ten MiG-23s.

CHAPTER 14

ARRIVAL SHOWS, 1988

In January 1988, Denny Phelan took off from TTR for the last time. He had been assigned a follow-on job on a staff position in Japan, much to his chagrin. Later, when he complained to his wife how much he hated his time in Japan, she rebuked him: "I don't have to worry about a blue staff car turning up at my door telling me you are dead." It was a brief glimpse of the effect that his time at Tonopah had had. What he probably did not tell her was that he was just as relieved as she. Manclark told me that when Phelan landed from his fini flight in the Flogger, "he walked up to the ops desk and said, 'It feels like someone just took 200 pounds of shit off my back.'" He had flown 135 MiG-23 sorties and 268 MiG-21 sorties.

As Phelan departed, the last ever Red Eagle pilot arrived, Navy Lt Stanley R. "Swish" O'Connor, "Bandit 69." Boma explained that O'Connor's call sign had been "Steamer" when he arrived, "but during his high-speed taxi test, he had had been at 120 knots and was supposed to release the drag chute. This was a switch that was close to another switch for the cannons. The cannon button used the same air as the brakes. As the chute should be coming out, he screams past and all you can hear is, pow! pow-pow! pow! pow! pow-pow! as the gun is cycling. He went fucking flying into the net [rabbit catcher], so we called him, 'Nothing but Net – Swish!' He was adamant that he had been pressing the drag chute button." By this time the rabbit catchers had been treated with camouflaged webbing to help hide the shape of an ensnared MiG should one make use of the barrier during one of the numerous 22-minute satellite overhead times.

Bar Carlisle and Cazessus' mishaps in 1987, all was going well with CONSTANT PEG, and Shervanick was making good progress in his efforts to run the program from his office at Langley. In early 1988, he had even sourced an additional MiG-23. "Don't ask me how, and don't ask me from where," he cautioned. He had all sorts of contacts not only within TAC, but across the entire Air Force. He could call up Military Airlift Command (MAC), and arrange a C-141 Starlifter or C-5 to support a visit to Nellis by any Air Force squadron in the world; and he could equally secure a MAC airlifter in order to ferry classified cargo from one country to another, or one secret airfield in Nevada to another.

Then, one Saturday morning early in 1988, he got a call. "I lived on base at Langley, and my house was across the street from HQ TAC, where the four-star commander-in-chief of TAC and two-star TAC DO had their offices. I got a call from Gen Dugan, the DO, and he said, 'Shy, I need you in my office. Can you come over here in about an hour?' I said, 'Sure.' He said, 'OK, wear your blues.' I got there and he told me I had to go up to the office of the four-star, the TAC CINC."

The head of TAC was Gen Bob Russ, whom Shervanick knew from as far back as 1975, when he had been a fresh lieutenant flying F-4Es with the 4th TFW at Seymour Johnson, and Russ had been 4th TFW commander. "He said, 'Shy, I want you to close the program down.' I was stunned. I said, 'Sir, can I respond? Can I answer any questions?' To which he said, 'No. There will be no more discussion about this. Close it down.' I walked down to the DO's office and asked him what was going on. 'You heard what I heard,' was all that Dugan could say."

Blindsided, Shervanick got straight on a secure line to the Pentagon to find that no one there had any idea that the order was on its way. "In fact, they started questioning me. 'Hey, wait a minute. *We* fund *you*. *We* decide when to close you down,' they said. I responded that I could only pass on what I had been told." Next he called Nellis and passed the news on to them. The next call he placed was to the squadron itself. "I nearly baulked, but then what do you do? The boss had told me to shut it down. I canceled a number of deployments that were due, and since I did all the scheduling, that was it."

The Red Eagles' imminent closure was all part of the funding drawdown that the Air Force was experiencing. Mike Scott had no idea that CONSTANT PEG was about to be shut down, but explained that it was just a part of a massive downsizing of the entire Aggressor program. "When it was announced that the 4477th was going to close, it was simultaneously announced that the Aggressors at Clark and Alconbury were going to lose their airplanes, and that the 64th and 65th were going to move from the F-5 to the F-16. It all occurred in the same time frame." Alarm bells had started to ring for him when he had received a call the previous December from TAC, quizzing him on his budget and the areas on which he spent his money, but he was shocked nonetheless at the finality of the decision.

While Shervanick knew that the generals at TAC HQ had been meeting, and that a budget cut was imminent, he had never expected that the Red Eagles would suffer, because they were funded directly through the Pentagon and were not on TAC's books. "The fact that they were being cut regardless suggested to my mentality as a major at the time that this was bigger than even a four-star. At that time, the F-22 Raptor was in the black world and that's where people were looking for the future. At the end of the day, it doesn't matter if the money for the Red Eagles was coming from TAC or the Pentagon, it all still came from one source – the Department of Defense. The four-stars were making cuts that were being made at the DoD level." The generals could either have fewer F-15s and F-16s, or they could reduce their training assets. With the Cold War still on, the choice was simple.

The news hit the Red Eagles like a train. Some believed that it was down to money, and others that the two recent mishaps had led the Air Force to lose its nerve. Mann summed it up:

It was hard to believe they were shutting it down, as it was such a great training program for our pilots. It was one of those situations where the guys in the squadrons, both the Red Eagles and the US squadrons that deployed to train with us, seriously believed and had the faith, but the headquarters weenies had lost that faith. An active aggressor program, complete with the other guy's toys, is one of the most important training programs we could possibly have. Every Sunday, a unit would arrive to participate in CONSTANT PEG for what was likely each pilot's first and only opportunity to train against the MiGs. The faces would have a serious "gee whiz" look on them, each guy really pumped up for the program. By the end of the week, those same faces were now the picture of confidence. Without fail, each guy left CONSTANT PEG full of confidence, and with the skills he would need to win if ever he was confronted in a real war. CONSTANT PEG was one of the best training programs TAC ever fielded.

Mahoney explained that there was a last-ditch effort to save CONSTANT PEG:

We mobilized a survey operation. It asked, "Which of the following programs are/were the most beneficial to you as a tactical fighter pilot?" We had listed about 10–12 programs, including Red Flag, CONSTANT PEG, and others (including a bogus one or two to disguise our intent). We had a free week somehow and dispatched most of the rank and file to tactical units across the US. We sanitized our flight suits so squadrons would not know who was doing the questioning and instructed pilots to rank these programs. If they hadn't participated in one or more of the programs they were to leave that line blank. At the end of the drill we assembled close to 1,000 responses back at the squadron. We tossed the ones that didn't have a response for CONSTANT PEG because the respondent had not been exposed to us, and of the remaining surveys our program ended up way out in front. In the end it didn't make a difference to the higher-ups with the purse strings, but it did give us a good feeling that what we accomplished had a very positive effect on the combat skills of US forces.

In February, Chanik departed to Staff School. Phelan had quizzed the Navy pilot on his next assignment, expecting to hear that he was going to be sent to command a Navy squadron somewhere. "When I found out that they were sending him to school, I thought that it sucked because for the Navy that was a career-ending assignment. As it turned out, that was not at all the case."

SAVING THE BEST UNTIL LAST

On Friday March 4, 1988, the 4477th TES flew its last ever sorties – a massive Red Flag [46] arrival show. Manclark returned to Tonopah to act as SOF so that the current Red Eagle pilots could all fly, and was one of several distinguished visitors who attended the last launch. Also present was Col George Muellner, then vice commander of the 57th FWW, in the capacity of Special Duty Officer. Muellner was an exceptionally interesting character who had an extensive AFSC and test pilot background that included being first the ops officer, and then commander, of the 6513th Test Squadron, the Red Hats, in the late 1970s and early 1980s (he became commander in April 1981). He was described as being very important in the story of the MiGs. Gen Peter Kempf, the TFWC boss, also attended in the capacity of squadron supervisor.

Thompson was the overall Red Air Mission Commander and McCoy the assistant Mission Commander, and the two planned and briefed the exercise to the Aggressor pilots, while Scott planned and led the overall 4477th TES portion of the mission. It was, he said, "a great final hurrah. A testament to what the program was really all about. We launched 13 MiG-21s, 4 MiG-23s, and a T-38: the largest mass launch we ever got up at one single time."

Five MiG-23s and a single MiG-21 remained on the ground, some ready in case a spare was needed. Scott explained the exercise:

We were listening on the radio for them. It was a simulation of a deployment into some forward area, some place where the Blue Force, our American forces, were going to have to fight their way into a target area, drop their bombs, and then fight their way back out. They hit tankers as they were coming across the United States, then when they got close, we launched Stan O'Connor in the T-38, and sent him out to be our recce so he could tell us exactly when Blue Air was crossing the battle area lines. Then we launched all the airplanes."

Blue Air consisted of F-15s and F-16s as well as F-4, F-15E, and F-111 strikers deployed from multiple Air Force bases around the country. It was a Red Flag arrival show, or "contingency arrival operation," of an unprecedented scale.

Scott's Red Air force was equally as unprecedented in scale: "We had what I would think is about as close to actual combat that any American pilot could aspire to or participate in without really being in an actual conflict." Silvers, who was flying as Bandit 44 in a MiG-23, concurred: "The sky was full of MiGs." The other Floggers were manned by ops officer Mann as Bandit 41; Carlisle, Bandit 42; and Macy, Bandit 43. The MiG-21s were led by Scott, Bandit 11. "We lost our share of MiGs, which is what was supposed to happen," said Scott.

At one point, Scott explained, "I led Doug Melson in a two-ship of MiG-21s towards a pair of F-15s, keeping them on the edge of their missile range. As they locked onto us and chased us, two MiG-23s snuck in behind them. John Mann was flying a Flogger E, the air-to-air version, because he got a radar lock on one of the F-15s and shot one of them down. Unfortunately, Doug didn't hang with me when we turned. He fell back and the Eagles got him in a weapons parameter and shot him down."

Melson became a statistic in the kill removal system linked into the RFMDS. On the ground at Nellis, controllers were calling the MiGs dead, forcing them to leave the fight. But to keep the fight going, Scott had negotiated with Red Flag DO, Col Joe Bob Phillips, for a new policy of regeneration. The new policy, approved only for this last mission, allowed a dead MiG to re-enter the fight much more quickly: "Now we would go back and fly a low approach as if to land at Tonopah, and then regenerate, effectively simulating the launch of another MiG." It was a very effective way of sustaining the training experience for the Blue Air pilots. Scott continued: "There were waves of fighters and bombers coming in. We wanted to get the escorts, the F-15 sweep, away from the bombers. We used some of the MiGs to do that, while the others went looking for the strikers. It was one big mass tactic."

"We had an incredible GCI controller, Maj Dan "Truck" Futryk, and we were just taking 'snap vectors' from him," recalled Larsen. "Dan would try and get our eyes onto the adversary and we would just jump into the fray. We wanted to disrupt their flow into and out of the target. It was an incredible air show to watch. It was a great learning tool for those guys coming in against us."

With that phase of the exercise completed, the strikers, escorts, and Red Eagles paired off for 2 v 2 fights in pre-designated areas of the Nellis range complex, Scott confirmed. "We also had altitudes that we picked. We were all on the same frequency, so I could hear when someone called bingo fuel and left their area. I would know then that that area was free and that I could spill guys over into it. It was all about situational awareness, and that's exactly why you had to hire great pilots."

"We never flew the aircraft in weather, but that day there was a scattered deck just west of the field where we made our recoveries," Mahoney recalled. "I distinctly remember coming in over those clouds, rolling inverted, looking 'up' and seeing the shadow of the airplane outlined on the clouds, complete with a rainbow around the canopy. I was thinking that it was a cool way to go out and that the 4477th had been a really great ride."

"I used every last bit of gas," Scott admitted, but the end of the 4477th TES was now inevitable, and as the last pair of Fishbeds – Larsen and his wingman Therrien – greased their wheels onto the rubber-streaked Tonopah runway, it was all over. CONSTANT PEG was no more. For all of those standing on the ramp that day, the declining whine of Tumansky turbojets was a sad moment. More was the pity considering the incredible learning that had been imparted for arriving Blue Air pilots and WSOs that morning – it was as though the program was being cut off in the prime of its life.

For Scott, one minor irritation remained: "I had wanted to fly 499 sorties in the MiG-21 and then phone Paco and tell him that I was about to fly the 500th! And then I was never going to do it. I already had more total MiG sorties than anyone else, but he and I liked to yank each other's chains a lot." Excluding his Third World visit, which was so secret that he could not even record his flying time on his flight records, he would finish his time at the Red Eagles with 569 MiG sorties: 106 in the MiG-17, 388 in the MiG-21, and 75 in the MiG-23.

On April 8, 1988, all T-38 flying operations ceased, and on April 11 the 4477th TES's five T-38s [47] were transferred to the 65th Aircraft Maintenance Unit at Nellis. Mahoney and Therrien were the last of the pilots to leave the unit formally, returning to Tonopah daily to fill out paperwork associated with getting awards and decorations for the enlisted maintainers. "They deserved recognition, and we wanted to make sure that their contribution was going to be recognized."

Therrien had managed to cram in 148 Fishbed sorties into his short tenure at Tonopah, and Mahoney just shy of 200 by the time the squadron closed.

Therrien had even been scheduled to fly more advanced versions of the MiG-21, perhaps with the Red Hats at Groom Lake, in order to bring back additional MiG-21 expertise to the Red Eagles, but that had been canceled when news of CONSTANT PEG's demise had reached Tonopah.

Neither man had experienced any major emergencies in their short time with the squadron, but Mahoney had just qualified on the MiG-23 and was not particularly enjoying the experience, and Therrien had put a MiG-21 out of control on one of his earliest exposures:

> The MiG-21 cockpit was not very user friendly, and since it bled speed so quickly in the turn, before you started the turn you put your left hand behind you to locate the flap switch and then pulled back on the stick. The idea was that when you decelerated to 250 knots you were ready to put the flaps out. If you didn't do that, the airplane would completely depart controlled flight. On this occasion the guy behind me was doing really well and I pressed the wrong button. The flaps stayed in, and I can't even tell you what happened, it was so sudden and out of control. The only good thing was that all I had to do was center the stick to recover the jet. In the debrief afterwards he was frustrated that he had been doing so well and I had then suddenly pulled off this maneuver he had never seen before!

While creating new paperwork for awards and decorations, the two pilots were simultaneously destroying and shredding excessive amounts of old paperwork – the squadron's classified material. "I am not sure what happened to the individual aircraft records, but I was shredding flight manuals, flight records, and that sort of thing. We spent days shredding," Mahoney explained. "We did keep some copies of some of the documents," Therrien added, "and most of what we were shredding were duplicates." Mahoney estimated that there were as many as 52 drawer safes to empty.

Among the more interesting items to be destroyed were video tapes from the Blue Air gun cameras. "These were classified SECRET, NOFORN [No disclosure to Foreign Nationals], CONSTANT PEG EYES ONLY, and so they had to submit them to us when they had finished their debriefs," Mahoney stated. "We had accumulated a lot of tapes over the years. After we bagged the formerly classified paper confetti we had to dispose of these big bags also. I took a few bags home to use as mulch in the vegetable garden and each spring for the next couple of years, when I turned the ground to plant tomatoes, squash, etc, I would notice lots of little snips of video tape that had gotten into the shredder bags. Good for a laugh and annual reminder!"

Mahoney went on:

> We had loads of other stuff that had accumulated over the years, too: tables, desks, chairs and about 45 or 50 safes – and part of my job was to consolidate all of this. We would load up Big Red, the unit's 18-wheeler truck, and transport this stuff around the country to other Air Force units that wanted it. One time we transported some of the safes to Florida for some weapons program down there. I later got a call in the middle of the night saying that there was good news and bad news. The bad news was that one of the safes had "escaped" to Florida with stuff still in the drawer; the good news was that the guy who opened it was a former Red Eagles enlisted guy! I took a lot of heat for that!

As for the aircraft and spares, Shervanick recalled that the spare motors were "pickled": lubricated and stored with fresh oil in their tubing and hoses to prevent corrosion and keep them flyable. From then on, the motors would periodically have their lubricants changed at predefined intervals to ensure that they remained airworthy. The MiGs were towed into the Red Eagles' hangars and left in flyable storage. "Every time I walked into one of the hangars," Mahoney admitted, "I couldn't help but think, 'What a waste.'" As Mahoney boarded the C-12 for the flight back to Nellis for the last time, he turned the keys to the buildings and hangars over to Maj Bob Belt, an Aggressor who had been tasked as the key holder when the 4477th TES finally closed.

In the last year of CONSTANT PEG, the 4477th TES had flown 1,342 sorties and exposed 412 pilots and aircrew to the assets. The unit shut down with 14 MiG-21s and 9 MiG-23s stored away in its hangars.

MOVING ON

The pilots all now needed to find jobs, which was easier said than done for some. Scott moved to take command of the 64th Aggressor squadron and was tasked with replacing the Aggressors' F-5Es with the newer F-16, which better replicated the maneuvering capability of the newer series of Soviet-made threats – the MiG-29 Fulcrum and Su-27 Flanker. He was joined by Cazessus, whose previous Aggressor and F-16 FWIC IP background made him an ideal candidate. Mann was an automatic choice to become an IP at the F-15 FWS, having graduated from there in 1981, and now became the ops officer. He had 257 MiG-21 sorties and 59 MiG-23 sorties.

Thompson had accumulated 470 MiG-21 sorties (second only to Geisler's 500) when the unit was closed down. He went to the 4484th Test Squadron at

Tyndall AFB, Florida, where he flew the F-15 and was also responsible for testing F-15 and F-16 avionics suites and software. Boma went to the Pentagon, and Carlisle stayed at Nellis, working at the TFWC as the director of the F-15 Multi Stage Improvement Program. Therrien had learned in March that his next assignment was going to be at the Pentagon, where he would manage aspects of the Advanced Tactical Fighter program, which would spawn the F-22A Raptor.

Larsen, who had 201 MiG-21 sorties, was faced with more of a challenge: by now a lieutenant colonel, he was not F-5 qualified and had not been an Aggressor. And while he was an F-4 FWS graduate, the 414th FWS had long ago deactivated. Initially he ended up flying a desk for the range group at the Indian Springs training grounds, but an old contact eventually pulled through for him and got him a flying job as an IP at the F-4 school at George AFB.

Macy left the Red Eagles for a ground tour in Japan with the 9th Marine Expeditionary Brigade, and returned to El Toro a year later to fly the F/A-18. Silvers left the unit with 160 MiG-21 sorties and 22 MiG-23 sorties, "which I tell people was 21 too many!" He had been good friends with many of the Red Eagle pilots and admitted that his last day on the squadron had been bittersweet. Before his departure from Tonopah and return to an East Coast Tomcat squadron, he and the rest of C Flight had carefully prepared folders containing information on how they had run the flight in case the Air Force or Navy started up the program again in the future.

Mike Simmons and Charles Sundell decided to leave the Air Force. Sundell was less than impressed by the way that the Air Force had handled the assignments in the aftermath of the unit's closure. He handed Mike Scott his resignation when the MPC told him that his next assignment would be in a staff position. He had accrued 240 sorties in the MiG-21 and his recent experience was of interest to a civilian contract company, Classic Aviation, which was staffed by senior ex-Air Force officers who were seeking to secure a contract to supply MiGs for test and evaluation sorties for the DoD. For about six months he and Simmons flew MiG-15s and MiG-17s, but the contract was never awarded. Sundell joined the Air Force Reserve, flying the F-4 and then the F-16. Simmons, "one of the funniest guys I ever met, a great stick, but often in trouble for being rebellious," according to Sundell, went to fly the F-15 with the US Air National Guard.

Since July 1979, CONSTANT PEG had generated 15,264 MiG sorties, exposing 5,930 aircrews to the assets in the process.

POSTSCRIPT

On November 13, 2006, the US Air Force officially declassified CONSTANT PEG at a press conference attended by former commanders Peck, Henderson, Manclark, and Scott. Sitting anonymously in the audience was Mike Coyle, the former MiG-21 expert from the FTD from whom the Red Eagles had learned so much. CONSTANT PEG was anything but a secret by this time, having been outed publicly first by *Aviation Week & Space Technology* in the mid-1980s, and then by author Robert Wilcox in 1994. A flurry of articles in the aviation press followed, but none that I read attempted to delve below the surface to find the real secrets that had been hidden all along – who, how, and why. During my interview with Gail Peck, he told me that CONSTANT PEG had been a well-kept secret, and in a sense he was actually right – the presence of MiGs at Tonopah was well known by the time the 4477th TES shut down, but who formed the unit, how it had sourced the assets, and why the idea had even come to fruition from the start had remained cloaked in secrecy.

For some of the pilots, the secret of what they had done was allowed to slip gently in the years that followed the closure of the 4477th TES. In 1992, Denny Phelan received an email from an Aggressor he did not know, asking him if he had seen his "F-5" recently. He ignored the email initially, but when several more came through, he responded. The sender instructed him to check out the MiG-21 on display at Offutt AFB, where the SAC museum was located. Two years later, Phelan, his two children, and his wife visited the museum:

> I was on a mission to find this MiG-21, but I told my family that we were going to drop by the museum on the way to visit one of my daughter's friends – that was my cover story. As we walked around, I spotted this tired old MiG among a group of other fighters. On one side was my name, and on the other was my crew chief's! Someone had not sanitized this airplane. I asked my family, "Do you notice anything

special about this airplane?" They said, "No, it's just an airplane." "OK, what about the names on the side?" Then my daughter said, "Oh my God! It says 'Major Phelan' on the side. Is that you, Daddy?" I sort of shrugged, smiled, and said, "Hmmm. Maybe!" Later my wife said to me, "You knew that airplane was there all along, didn't you? Is that what you were doing all those years?" I shrugged and smiled, "Hmmm. Maybe!"

What happened to most of the Red Eagles' assets remains unclear. At least five of the Indonesian YF-110B Fishbeds have found their way to museums or as gate guards around the world (one in Florida, one in New Mexico, one in Ohio, another in Nevada, and one in Belgium), but none of the YF-110Cs have surfaced and there are persistent rumors that these Chinese-supplied J-7Bs were buried at Tonopah a few years after the squadron closed. This had been an ongoing practice, according to Nelson, who recollected that broken wings, engines, and even whole airframes had been buried up to 40ft deep in the desert surrounding the airfield. Finally, the fate of the MiG-23s is also unclear. At least one of them now resides in a museum in Europe, and another has been confirmed as being used for target practice on an Air Force weapons range.

The decision to shut down CONSTANT PEG remains controversial, even today. Some believe that the MiG-21 and MiG-23 were simply not representative of a modern threat, while almost all of the Red Eagles agree that any MiG was enough to prompt Buck Fever in a Blue Air pilot – the point was always to make sure that Buck Fever was experienced first in a training environment, and for that you don't need a MiG-29 or Su-27.

Operating a more modern air threat proved impossible in a world of shrinking defense budgets, where every cent counted. In 1992, Thompson had worked on an FME program tasked with sourcing a squadron of Su-27 Flankers to be based at Nellis as a white world Aggressor program. He'd found the Flankers, but the funds for the program were never released. When he sourced later model MiG-23s from the former East Germany for static exploitation, he was permitted to do so only if Germany paid for the cost of shipping and supplied the Floggers for free. He was successful, but it was an indication of how strapped the Air Force was for cash. The Air Force did later buy a batch of MiG-29Cs from Moldova that would otherwise have been destined for Iran, but there was never any intention of operating these as Aggressors.

While CONSTANT PEG closed down in March 1988, the 4477th TES was not officially inactivated until as late as July 1990, according to one official Air Force history. What remained of CONSTANT PEG's infrastructure was absorbed by the 57th FW (formerly the 57th FWW), which eventually became Det 3 of the 53rd Test & Evaluation Group (TEG).

The USAF describes Det 3 thus:

> [It is a] representative for Air Combat Command's [formerly TAC] interest in USAF Foreign Materiel Exploitation, and training opportunities with Air Force Materiel Command [formerly AFSC]. The Detachment's primary mission is to ensure USAF combat aircrew personnel are prepared to fight with the latest knowledge available through FME. DET 3 maintains an active involvement with AFMC and other services ensuring all testing is planned, executed, and reported with combat aircrew in mind. In addition, DET 3 acts as liaison for all training opportunities conducted on the Nevada Test & Training Range (the Nellis Range Complex), providing procedures and acting as subject matter experts on key systems.

In 2004 I interviewed the commander of the 53rd TEG. As I sat in his office awaiting his arrival, I noted three control sticks – all of the kind found in the latest Soviet fighters – mounted on a wooden base and displayed proudly on his wall. When I asked about them, he brushed aside my question with practiced nonchalance. On another occasion, an Air Force pilot told me that one of the senior pilots in his squadron displayed a wooden model of a Flanker on his desk. When I asked him why he thought he would do so he responded, "Well, it's not because he thinks it's pretty or any good!"

While little anecdotal bits of evidence can lead to false conclusions, what cannot be refuted so easily is photographic evidence that has come to light that shows the US Air Force is operating MiG-29 Fulcrum and Su-27 Flanker aircraft out of Groom Lake. With AFMC almost certainly the lead organization exploiting these aircraft on a technical basis, it seems reasonable to conclude that ACC – the new name given to TAC in 1992 – occasionally gets to perform operational exploitation of the Flanker and Fulcrum, perhaps flying only against Weapons School instructors, 422 TES aircrew, and selected pilots from the newly formed F-16 and F-15 Aggressors, as was the case with HAVE IDEA in the early 1970s. Assuming that these are valid conclusions, then history has come full circle: the exploitation pecking order of the early HAVE programs has reasserted itself. For its share of playtime with the newest assets, ACC relies on Det 3. And Det 3's unofficial name? The Red Eagles.

ENDNOTES

1. TOPGUN was the US Navy's fighter weapons school, established in March 1969 in response to abysmal performances in the air combat arena in Vietnam by Navy fighter crews. It taught the Navy's best fighter aircrew advanced tactics, and expected these men to return to the fleet to disseminate their newfound wisdom.

2. Olds had concocted a devious plan that resulted in his Phantoms ambushing and pummeling NVAF MiGs that had been tricked into thinking the Phantoms were vulnerable Republic F-105 Thunderchief fighter-bombers.

3. Henderson returned to Wiesbaden in the summer of 1973 to interview an East German MiG pilot who had defected to the West.

4. The following have been attributed to Indonesia: 10 MiG-21F-13s, serial numbers 2151, 2152, 2153, 2155, 2156, 2157, 2159, 2162, 2166, 2170; 1 MiG-21U, serial number 2172; and 2 MiG-17Fs, serial numbers 1184 and 1187.

5. Peck did not know where the MiGs were coming from, and remained unaware of their source even when he later commanded CONSTANT PEG.

6. This claim directly contradicts Iverson's carefully worded 1995 Air Force biography, which suggests that Iverson was the ops officer. However, the timeline on Iverson's biography shows that this was impossible, especially as Mayo has paperwork that proves that he was ops officer at the time, not Iverson.

7. In his November 2003 article "Gone With the Wind," aviation historian Tom Cooper cites that, in total, the US received the following from Egypt: 16 MiG-21MF Fishbeds, 2 Su-20 Fitters, 2 MiG-21U Fishbeds, 6 MiG-23MS Floggers, and 6 MiG-23BN Floggers. The Flogger details do not match those put forth by Merlin.

8. Mayo never discussed the operating location for the time period he flew the assets, but since Tonopah was not ready, Groom Lake is the obvious alternative.

9. Peck did not mention or even allude to Groom Lake during the course of my 90-minute interview with him. I have surmised that he first learned to fly the MiGs at Groom Lake. There is a possibility that he and Suter may have already flown the MiGs during HAVE IDEA, during which time the 414th FWS had a small cadre of pilots involved (without the knowledge of the Aggressors) in the program.

10. I was unable to establish exactly when these Bandit numbers first started to be assigned, but they had certainly not been introduced at the very early stages. Some individuals I interviewed from this phase were unaware that the numbering system was even in existence, and others believed the early numbers erroneous. Since they

are taken from the only official roster surviving today, I have used them throughout the book as the definitive authority on full-time 4477th pilots (with three of the 69 pilots being "attached" part-time to the unit).

11. Drabant told me he could not discuss what he had been hired to work on for Iverson, but his résumé states: "Apr 1978–Sep 1979. Air-to-Air Analyst 4477th Test & Evaluation Flight, Nellis AFB, NV. HAVE PAD FME and establishment of Red Eagle operations at TTR." Given that he had been hired as an air-to-air analyst and was working on HAVE PAD, it is reasonable to conclude that he was assisting Iverson with early tactical evaluations of the MiG-23. Since Drabant stated categorically that he was hired by, and worked for, Iverson (as opposed to Frick), it also seems reasonable to conclude that Iverson headed the TAC HAVE PAD effort.

12. AFSC was plowing ahead with its FME programs. HAVE GARDEN, for example, involved the evaluation of the MiG-21's R-13-300 motor. Specifically, this 1978 project involved engine manufacturer Pratt & Whitney profiling the turbine and compressor blades of the foreign motor.

13. In May the following year, Iverson was working at TAC HQ when one enterprising Aggressor pilot tracked him down. "I was trying to build a better Flogger brief for road shows to include the aircraft and tactics that it might realistically use. Much of the 1 v 1 maneuvering we were doing seemed inappropriate when we were supposed to emulate the Flogger, but we didn't have hands-on knowledge. I found out that Iverson did. I managed to catch up with him one night at the Langley Officers' Club. I was prepared to do whatever it took to get the information I wanted. He was so cool and understood exactly what I needed and why. Without ever saying he had actually flown it, he spent about an hour in a private room with me explaining everything I needed to give the Flogger brief life."

14. The official 4477th TES history lists the lease of three Cessna 404 aircraft as commencing in October 1979, but Oberle maintains that he leased the first 404 at least 9–12 months prior to that. He also recalled that the second and third aircraft were added only later as the need dictated. Scott agrees: "I concur with Jose's recollection – when I arrived at the 4477th in August, we were flying a C-404. By the time the C-404s went away, we were flying four of them." In addition, Peck maintains that Huff, not Oberle, leased the Cessnas.

15. In November 2007, after the official declassification of CONSTANT PEG, V/Adm James M. Zortman, Commander, Naval Air Forces, US Pacific Fleet, and Capt (ret.) Chuck Heatley, visited Linda and explained everything about Hugh's death to her and her two sons.

16. Although Henderson joined the 4477th TEF in September 1979, one month after Scott, he checked out in the MiGs sooner than Scott. As such, Henderson's Bandit number is 13, and Scott's is 14.

17. Peck does not recall ever having a T-38 on his watch, but Henderson and Oberle are adamant that there was one.

18. These figures are actually based on Fiscal Year (FY) data, which is to say that the figures presented here relate to activities from October 30, 1978, to September 1, 1979. In this book, for clarity and structure, all of the FY data are incorporated into the text relevant to the end of each calendar year.

19.   Gibbs was pictured on the front cover of the October 1966 issue of *Air Force Magazine*.

20.   Scott declined to discuss either the identity of the nation involved, or the names of the two other Red Eagles. He simply stated: "A third-world nation that flew MiG-21s." I have deduced that the country concerned was Somalia, and Sheffield confirmed that he was the second pilot in question. Noriega's name was confirmed by other means.

21.   T-38s had become hard to come by at Nellis since the move to the F-5, and since the Thunderbirds were based at Nellis, they would borrow the 4477th TES's Talons when they needed additional aircraft to help check out prospective pilots for the next season.

22.   Mike Scott observed: "The general was BrigGen Mike Dugan, at that time the Air Division Commander at Luke AFB, and ultimately the USAF Chief of Staff!"

23.   Bucko also photographed the classified assets in-flight with visiting units, but these images were processed by the DoE's Sandia Labs at Tonopah, and were then stored in the squadron vaults. He also filmed with a 16mm movie camera that was used to give the classified briefings to visiting pilots at Nellis.

24.   TFWC Commander Gen Fischer said in a speech to the Aggressors on September 7, 1984: "I can tell you that two years ago as a W/CC, the TAC/CC [Creech] stood up in front of every TAC W/CC at a commanders' conference and said that when the Aggressors came to town, you ought to treat it, at your wing, you ought to treat it like the plague."

25.   Assigned the USAF serial number 023. Hugh Brown's MiG was serialled 002.

26.   This suggests that the Red Eagles only ever flew six of the ten MiG-21F-13s supplied by Indonesia, with the rest of them, plus the single two-seat MiG-21U, being either non-flyable or used only by the Red Hats.

27.   Peck had been involved in a similar exercise to get the first MiGs into the Petting Zoo many years before.

28.   Gennin maintains that this is not true, but it is claimed by Myers, Geisler, and Stucky.

29.   While the altitude of Bond's test flight has been declassified, curiously, the Mach number he was intending to fly up to, and the Mach number he actually reached, have been redacted from the report. One could infer from this that Bond had exceeded the speed he had set out to attain. One source has indicated that the MiG-23 in question was one of two secretly loaned to the United States by India.

30.   Henderson said, "I thought it was LtCol Paul W. 'Skip' Harbison who replaced me. [But] it doesn't really make any difference which squadron Phil became the ops officer of. I am sure Phil made his mark there."

31.   Geisler explained, "He was not following regulations when purging a MiG-21 fuel cell – he did not wear a mask or respirator. They were always supposed to have a partner too, but he was preoccupied. It was senseless."

32.   Gennin denies this: "I always kept my bosses informed."

33.   Scott explained: "The one-star was actually Bobby Boles, TAC's non-rated Chief of Personnel."

34.   454 and 479 were the serials of the other two MU-2s.

35.   General Michael J Dugan was TAC's assistant deputy chief of staff for operations, inspector general and deputy chief of staff for operations at the time. Creech was

succeeded as Commander TAC in 1984 by General Jerome F. O'Malley, who was succeeded in 1985 by General Robert D. Russ. Russ stayed in the post until 1991.

36. The Red Hats continued to use the Type designations for the duration of their history. Merlin told me: "In the late 1970s and 1980s, Red Hats flew aircraft Type IIB (HAVE COAT), Type IIIA (HAVE BOXER), Type IIIB (HAVE LIGHTER), Type IIID (HAVE LIGHTER – Modified), Type IIIT (HAVE FIREMAN). I have also seen a somewhat humorous document that mentioned 'geriatric Type 6 aircraft.'"

37. For the purposes of logging flight time, all pilots record fractions of one or more tenths of an hour. Each tenth of an hour equates to six minutes: thus a .3 sortie is 18 minutes; a 1.0 sortie is 60 minutes; and a 1.6 sortie is 96 minutes.

38. The official roster assigns Mahoney the status of Bandit 62, qualifying to fly the MiG-21 in January 1987. Cazessus, who joined in November 1986, is for some reason assigned the status of Bandit 63. It is likely that while Cazessus arrived earlier, his checkout in the MiG-21 was for some reason delayed, resulting in Mahoney being one Bandit number ahead of him.

39. The AWACS' big rotating radar mounted high above the fuselage provides a picture of the battlespace that covers several hundred miles, and is used by fighter controllers directing individual flights of F-15s, F-16s, and other fighters to the location of enemy fighters or bombers.

40. This may explain why several pilots referred to the Flogger E radar as being the Jaybird, but others referred to it as a Spin Scan.

41. All of the YF-110 suffixes described in the main text are based on general consensus, having polled as many of the Red Eagles as possible.

42. The MiGs were brand new on arrival at Tonopah, with fewer than three hours on each airframe. It is reasonable to conclude that they came direct from China, since at that time the United States and China shared a healthy relationship that included cooperation on defense projects, and the transfer of defense technology. It would seem odd that the DoD would source the MiGs through a third party when the two nations were sharing defense secrets – sourcing them direct would offer America the most clandestine means of acquisition.

43. Of the declassified photos from CONSTANT PEG, the #14 is the highest serial number visible on the undercarriage doors of the older MiG-21F-13 Fishbed C/Es. The lowest number visible on the J-7Bs is #47. Manclark went on to state that he also had other "newer" MiG-21s, presumably the MiG-21MFs (YF-110Ds) from Egypt, "towed out onto the range and shot up, because of where we got them." It is all very vague, and the official MiG-21 figures for the 4477th TES don't quite add up correctly against this version of events. Manclark declined to comment further on the matter when pressed.

44. Thompson recalls that Kempf had told the Red Eagles, "the days of the TAC vice or DO doing the OERs are over. If my endorsement isn't good enough, then neither are you. And I won't be endorsing anyone who is not a member of the Officers' Club."

45. The 4477th TES's divert base can only have been Groom Lake.

46. This Red Flag was actually a "Green Flag" exercise that used the Red Flag framework and concept, but had an added emphasis on electronic warfare.

47. Their serial numbers were 60-0553, 60-0572, 61-0851, 61-0870, and 68-8106.

APPENDICES

APPENDIX A

4477TH TES CLASS A MISHAPS

Date	Aircraft/USAF serial	Remarks
Aug 23, 79	MiG-17/002	Loss of control (fatality) (Pilot induced)
Mar 11, 81	MiG-17/008	Hydraulic accumulator blowout (Design deficiency corrected)
Oct 21, 82	MiG-23/023	Inflight fire (fatality) (Design deficiency corrected)
Jun 25, 87	MiG-21/045	Engine failure (ejection) (Design deficiency corrected)
Aug 28, 87	MiG-23/022	Loss of control (ejection) (Pilot induced)

Note:
Postai's April 8, 1982, mishap is not listed. The USAF definition of a Class A Mishap is: "A mishap resulting in one or more of the following: Total mishap cost of $1,000,000 or more; a fatality or permanent total disability; destruction of an Air Force aircraft."

The March 11, 1981, mishap actually relates to a 6513th TS Red Hats mishap and has been included in the 4477th TES history in error.

APPENDIX B

BANDIT NUMBERS AND SORTIE NUMBERS

This list is taken from a classified official history that has not survived. This was the only unclassified page in the document. It is reproduced here word for word, which means that there are inconsistencies in the spelling of some names included in the main text. Where a difference occurs, the main text should be used as the definitive source.

Bandit #	Name	Sorties		
#1	Robert Mayo			
#2	Ronald Iverson			
#3	Alvin D. Muller			
#4	Glenn F. Frick			
#5	Joseph L. Oberle			
#6	Gerrald D. Huff			
#7	Thomas A. Morgenfeld			
#8	Charles J. Heatley	MiG-17 (47)	MiG-21 (229)	
#9	Gaillard R. Peck			
#10	David J. McCloud	MiG-17 (150)	MiG-21 (2)	MiG-23 (120)
#11	Karl F. Whittenberg	MiG-17 (85)	MiG-21 (137)	MiG-23 (13)
#12	Melvin H. Brown	MiG-17 (9)		
#13	Earl J. Henderson	MiG-17 (12)		
#14	Michael R. Scott	MiG-17 (110)	MiG-21 (386)	MiG-23 (79)
#15	Charles T. Corder		MiG-21 (131)	MiG-23 (233)
#16	Robert Sheffield		MiG-21 (236)	
#17	Keith E. Shean	MiG-17 (169)		MiG-23 (125)
#18	Selvyn S. Laughter		MiG-21 (215)	MiG-23 (102)
#19	Clem B. Myers		MiG-21 (318)	MiG-23 (24)
#20	Michael C. Press	MiG-17 (102)	MiG-21 (82)	MiG-23 (5)
#21	Thomas A. Gibbs		MiG-21 (178)	
#22	Leonard J. Bucko		MiG-21 (131)	MiG-23 (94)
#23	Russell M. Taylor		MiG-21 (126)	MiG-23 (29)
#24	James M. Watley		MiG-21 (200)	MiG-23 (78)
#25	Mark F. Postai	MiG-17 (76)	MiG-21 (12)	MiG-23 (24)
#26	James W. Green		MiG-21 (243)	MiG-23 (16)
#27	James D. Matheny		MiG-21 (240)	MiG-23 (142)
#28	Larry T. Shervanick		MiG-21 (125)	MiG-23 (149)
#29	John B. Nathman		MiG-21 (61)	MiG-23 (52)
#30	Orville Prins		MiG-21 (168)	MiG-23 (90)

#31	George S. Gennin	MiG-21 (177)	
#32	David F. Bland	MiG-21 (241)	MiG-23 (124)
#33	Stephen R. Brown	MiG-21 (344)	MiG-23 (51)
#34	John B. Saxman	MiG-21 (182)	MiG-23 (116)
#35	Francis K. Geisler	MiG-21 (500)	
#36	Michael C. Roy	MiG-21 (230)	
#37	George C. Tullus	MiG-21 (234)	
#38	James A. Robb	MiG-21 (213)	
#39	Robert J. Zettel	MiG-21 (338)	MiG-23 (138)
#40	Paul R. Stucky	MiG-21 (230)	MiG-23 (96)
#41	John Skidmore	MiG-21 (175)	
#42	Thomas E. Drake	MiG-21 (147)	MiG-23 (294)
#43	Robert G. Craig	MiG-21 (355)	MiG-23 (105)
#44	Daniel R. McCort	MiG-21 (119)	MiG-23 (160)
#45	Timothy R. Kinney	MiG-21 (223)	MiG-23 (162)
#46	Philip W. White	MiG-21 (131)	
#47	Edward D. Phelan	MiG-21 (268)	MiG-23 (135)
#48	Guy A. Brubaker	MiG-21 (278)	
#49	Martin S. Macy	MiG-21 (360)	MiG-23 (66)
#50	Frederick H. Thompson	MiG-21 (470)	
#51	John T. Manclark	MiG-21 (301)	
#52	Evan M. Chanik Jr	MiG-21 (166)	MiG-23 (190)
#53	Brian E. McCoy	MiG-21 (287)	
#54	Herbert J. Carlisle	MiG-21 (146)	MiG-23 (170)
#55	Shelley S. Rogers	MiG-21 (237)	
#56	John C. Mann	MiG-21 (271)	MiG-23 (61)
#57	Michael G. Simmons	MiG-21 (254)	
#58	Charles E. Sundell	MiG-21 (234)	
#59	Thomas V. Boma	MiG-21 (265)	
#60	Dudley A. Larsen	MiG-21 (200)	
#61	Cary A. Silvers	MiG-21 (160)	MiG-23 (22)
#62	James D. Mahoney	MiG-21 (155)	
#63	Ricardo M. Cazessus	MiG-21 (174)	
#64	Robert E. Davis	MiG-21 (133)	
#65	Nickie J. Fuerst	MiG-21 (153)	
#66	Sam C. Therrien	MiG-21 (149)	
#67	James B. Evans	MiG-21 (4)	
#68	Douglas M. Melson	MiG-21 (31)	
#69	Stanley R. O'Connor	MiG-21 (9)	

APPENDIX C

MIG EXPLOITATIONS

HAVE BOAT
: Analysis of a Shenyang F-6 (MiG-19) in Pakistan in 1978.

HAVE DOUGHNUT
: Exploitation of MiG-21F-13 Fishbed E between January 23, 1968, and April 8, 1968.

HAVE DRILL
: Exploitation of two MiG-17F Fresco C aircraft between February 3, 1969, and May 3, 1969.

HAVE FERRY
: Exploitation of two MiG-17F Fresco C aircraft between February 3, 1969, and May 3, 1969.

HAVE GARDEN
: Evaluation of Soviet R-13-300 turbojet engine, including blade profiling and compressor maps, by Pratt & Whitney in 1978.

HAVE IDEA
: Formalized exploitation of MiGs starting in the spring of 1973 and led by AFSC, with TAC and the US Navy also participating. It was the follow-on from HAVE DRILL, FERRY, and DOUGHNUT, and precursor to CONSTANT PEG.

HAVE PAD
: Exploitation of the MiG-23 Flogger aircraft between summer 1977 and summer 1978.

HAVE PRIVILEGE
: Exploitation of Cambodian Air Force MiG-17F in November 1970.

APPENDIX D

RED EAGLES' DOCUMENTS

ASSIGNMENT/PERSONNEL ACTION			
LAST NAME · FIRST NAME · MIDDLE INITIAL	GRADE	SSAN	PERSONNEL ACTION NO.
MAYO, ROBERT E.	Maj		

TO: (Organization, Office Symbol, Location)	FROM: (Organization, Office Symbol, Location)
57CSG/DPME Nellis AFB NV 89191	4477TEF/DA Nellis AFB NV 89191

SECTION I   DUTY ASSIGNMENT/PERSONNEL DATA CHANGES

CAFSC FROM _____ TO _____
DATE DEPARTED LAST DY STN _____
DATE ARRIVED STATION _____
ASGN AVAL _____ DOA _____
INTERIM ASGN AVAL _____ DOA _____
ODSD/DEROS _____ STRD _____
OVERSEA TOUR STATUS _____
ACC STAT _____ REASON UNACC _____
ASGN LIMIT 1 ST _____ EXP DATE _____
ASGN LIMIT 2D _____ EXP DATE _____
ASGN LIMIT 3D _____ EXP DATE _____
FUNCTIONAL CATEGORY _____
ADSC DATE _____ REASON FOR ADSC _____
DIRECTED DUTY AFSC _____ REASON FOR _____
DDA _____
DDA - TVL - RESTRICT - EXP DATE _____
OFF-PROJ CLASN UPGRADE DATE _____
DUTY AFSC **N1115Z** EFF **1 Apr 77** DUTY TITLE **Operations Officer, FLT**

OJT: EFFECTIVE _____
ENTER/CONTINUE AFSC _____ TS CODE _____
WITHDRAW AFSC _____ TS CODE _____
SPECIAL EXPERIENCE IDENTIFIER (S)
     AIRMAN   OFFICER
CAFSC _____ LAST _____
PAFSC-1ST _____ SECOND _____
PAFSC-2D _____ THIRD _____
2 AFSC-1ST _____ FOURTH _____
2 AFSC-2D _____ FIFTH _____
DATE OF SEPARATION _____
REASON FOR ESTB. EXT. CURTAILMENT OF OFF
DOS _____
FLYING CATEGORY _____
SUSPENSION FR FLYING/EXCUSAL FR FLT
REQUIREMENT _____
INDIV FLT CONDITION STATUS _____ DATE _____

WPNS SYS ID _____ POSITION NO. **0289 588**

MEMBER'S REPORTING OFFICIAL IS (Grade, Last Name, SSAN, Date supervision begins)	MEMBER RATES (Grade, Last Name, SSAN, Date supervision begins)
N/C	N/C

OTHER

AUTHORITY

SECTION II

DATE	TYPED NAME, GRADE, TITLE OF SUPERVISOR/REQUESTING OFFICIAL	SIGNATURE
27 Jun 77	ALVIN D. MULLER, Capt, USAF Administrative Officer	*Alvin D. Muller*

CONCURRENCE OF MEMBER

I ☒ DO ☐ DO NOT CONCUR   SIGNATURE OF MEMBER

SECTION III   INTRA-BASE ASSIGNMENT ACTION

EDCSA _____ ASSIGNMENT ACTION NUMBER _____ REPT NLT _____
ASSIGN FR **64FWS** TO **4477TEF/DO**

SECTION IV   REMARKS

Resubmitted due to mismatch problems with current UDL.
Duty Phone: 5495   Office Symbol: DO   APPROVED PTI 443 ON 21 Jul 77

SECTION V   APPROVAL BY COMMANDER OR AUTHORIZED REPRESENTATIVE   DATE 27 June 77

FOR THE COMMANDER	TYPED NAME, GRADE, AND TITLE	SIGNATURE
	GLENN E. FRICK, Lt Col, USAF Commander, 4477TEF	*Glenn E. Frick*

SECTION VI   ACTION BY CBPO OFFICIAL

☒☒ APPROVED ☐ DISAPPROVED ☐ BOARD ACTION REQUIRED   DATE 21 Jul 77
HEADQUARTERS 57 CSGp/DPMUM-OFF
NELLIS AFB NV 89191

FOR THE COMMANDER	TYPED/PRINTED NAME, GRADE, AND TITLE	SIGNATURE
	C. E. BELL, SSGT, USAF NCOIC OFFICER MANNING	*Charles E. Bell*

SECTION VII.   CBPO COORDINATION RECORD

CH	ADMIN	PSM/MA	CC	ACDM		FT	OJT	QC	ER/PR	SA	
CAC	CIAC	R&S	PROC/DC	DC	IAO	RR E P/OR - AR	RREV	RP	PA		

AF FORM 2095 NOV 71   REPLACES AF FORM 1098, DEC 69, WHICH IS OBSOLETE.   AF FORM 4/10 COPY

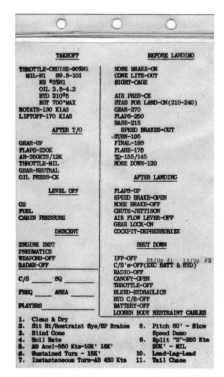

ABOVE AND RIGHT

Stained yellow with sweat and age, these three pages are the sanitized and enigmatic checklist for the MiG-21 that Geisler carried with him on each of his 500 Fishbed sorties. (Paco Geisler via Steve Davies)

OPPOSITE PAGE

Air Force Form 2095 – the orders signed by Frick that made Mayo the first CONSTANT PEG ops officer. (Kobe Mayo via Steve Davies)

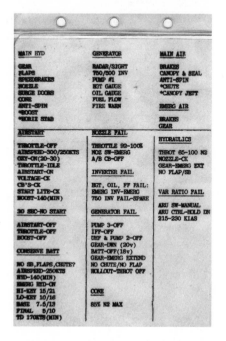

DATE: 5 MAR 88 (SAT)   4477 TES DAILY FLYING SCHEDULE   SCHEDULER: MAJ MAHONEY

LINE NR	TAIL NR	TYPE ACFT	TYPE MSN	CREW	CALL SIGN	TAKE OFF	LAND	FREQ SQWK	RANGE	ADVERSARY DATA POD #	CALL SIGN	TYPE ACFT	UNIT
		C-12	OPS		MAC 1	0900	1000	LSV TNX	PAX:	COL MELSON, LTC SCOTT, LTC HENDERSON, THOMPSON, MCCOY, DAVIS, ROGERS			
		C-12	OPS		MAC 2	0900	1000	LSV TNX	PAX:	LTC LARSEN, SUNDELL, SIMMONS, MAHONEY, FUERST, THERRIEN, NEWTON			
		C-12	OPS		MAC 3	0900	1000	LSV TNX	PAX:	LTC MANCLARK, MANN, CARLISLE, MACY, SILVERS, BOMA, WRIGHT			
										POD #			
151	19	F-4	CAO	MANN	BANDIT 41	1215	1300	6141		504			
152	28	F-4	CAO	CARLISLE	BANDIT 42	1215	1300	6142		560			
153	30	F-4	CAO	MACY	BANDIT 43	1215	1300	6143		418			
154	31	F-4	CAO	SILVERS	BANDIT 44	1215	1300	6144		556			
101	49	F-5	CAO	LTC SCOTT	BANDIT 11	1215	1245	6111		355			
102	52	F-5	CAO	COL MELSON	BANDIT 12	1215	1245	6112		430			
103	46	F-5	CAO	THOMPSON	BANDIT 13	1215	1245	6113		551			
104	53	F-5	CAO	MCCOY	BANDIT 14	1215	1245	6114		581			
105	59	F-5	CAO	SUNDELL	BANDIT 21	1215	1245	6121		499			
106	48	F-5	CAO	SIMMONS	BANDIT 22	1215	1245	6122		557			
107	47	F-5	CAO	MAHONEY	BANDIT 23	1215	1245	6123		548			
108	60	F-5	CAO	FUERST	BANDIT 24	1215	1245	6124		540			
109	50	F-5	CAO	DAVIS	BANDIT 31	1215	1245	6131		503			
110	58	F-5	CAO	ROGERS	BANDIT 32	1215	1245	6132		500			

DATE: 5 MAR 88 (SAT)   4477 TES DAILY FLYING SCHEDULE   SCHEDULER: MAJ MAHONEY

LINE NR	TAIL NR	TYPE ACFT	TYPE MSN	CREW	CALL SIGN	TAKE OFF	LAND	FREQ SQWK	RANGE	ADVERSARY DATA POD #	CALL SIGN	TYPE ACFT	UNIT
111	51	F-5	CAO	LTC LARSEN	BANDIT 33	1215	1245	6133		550			
112	62	F-5	CAO	THERRIEN	BANDIT 34	1215	1245	6134		289			
113	57	F-5	CAO	BOMA	BANDIT 35	1215	1245	6135		546			
601		T-38	CAO	O'CONNOR	BARON 71	1200	1245	6171		578			
		C-12	OPS		MAC 1	1300	1400	TNX LSV	PAX:	LTC SCOTT, MANN, SUNDELL, DAVIS, BOMA, THOMPSON, MAHONEY			
		C-12	OPS		MAC 2	1300	1400	TNX LSV	PAX:	COL MELSON, LTC MANCLARK, LTC HENDERSON, MACY, SILVERS, CARLISLE, MCCOY, NEWTON			
		C-12	OPS		MAC 3	1300	1400	TNX LSV	PAX:	COL MUELLNER, LTC LARSEN, O'CONNOR, WRIGHT, ROGERS, SIMMONS, FUERST, THERRIEN			

SDO	SOF	SQ SUPV
COL MUELLNER	LTC MANCLARK	MG KEMPF

NOTES
1. CLOSURES: 0716-0733/1415-1432
2. DEBRIEF AT RED FLAG AUDITORIUM/

John Mann

JOHN C. MANN, Maj, USAF
Operations Officer

The final 4477th TES flying schedule. (Mike Scott via Steve Davies)

1. (U) Visits of distinguished persons:

   a. (U) The 4477TES staff had the pleasure of entertaining over 450 distinguished visitors throughout its history. The visitors included Vice President Bush, members of the President's cabinet, Senators and Congressmen, Corporate executives, and senior military officials. The list of distinguished visitors is highlighted by:

      1. 27 Jun 80 Gen Allen, Chief of Staff of the Air Force
      2. 10 Sep 81 Gen Creech, TAC Commander
      3. 23 Nov 81 Gen Mathis, Vice Chief of Staff of the Air Force
      4. 18 May 82 Mr. Bush, Vice President of the United States
      5. 4 Mar 83 Mr. Weinberger, Secretary of Defense
      6. 20 May 83 Mr. Lehman, Secretary of the Navy
      7. 24 May 83 Mr. Orr, Secretary of the Air Force
      8. 3 July 84 Gen Creech, TAC Commander
      9. 10 Dec 84 Gen O'Malley, TAC Commander
      10. 18 Dec 84 Mr. McFarland, President's Advisor for National Security
      11. 21 Feb 85 Adm Watkins, Chief of Naval Operations
      12. 25 Feb 85 Mr. Schultz, Secretary of State
      13. 26 Mar 85 CMSgt Parrish, Chief Master Sergeant of the Air Force
      14. 17 Oct 85 Gen Russ, TAC Commander
      15. 4 Nov 86 Adm Crowe, Chairman of the Joint Chief of Staff
      16. 10 Jan 87 Gen Welch, Chief of Staff of the Air Force

A condensed list of some of the VIPs to visit CONSTANT PEG over the years. It is an unclassified portion of a still-classified history of the 4477th TES held by Det 3, 53rd Wing, Nellis AFB. (Earl Henderson via Steve Davies)

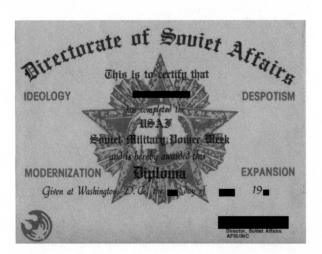

The FTD ran a Soviet Indoctrination week at Bolling AFB, Washington, for Air Force pilots. As part of that course, the pilots could enter a secure hangar in which was stored a static MiG-21F-13 from Indonesia. Noteworthy is the use of the Red Eagles' logo on the bottom left of the certificate. (Author's collection)

GLOSSARY

ACRONYM DEFINITION

AAA	Antiaircraft Artillery
AAM	Air-to-Air Missile
AB	Air Base (a USAF base on foreign soil); *also* Afterburner
ACC	Air Combat Command (formerly TAC)
ACEVAL	Air Combat Evaluation
ACM	Air Combat Maneuvers
ACMI	Air Combat Maneuvering Instrumentation
ACT	Air Combat Training
ADC	Air Defense Command, USAF
AFA	Air Force Academy
AFB	Air Force Base
AFFTC	Air Force Flight Test Center
AFIA	Air Force Intelligence Agency
AFMC	Air Force Materiel Command (formerly AFSC)
AFSC	Air Force Systems Command
AF/XO	Air Force Plans and Operations Officer
AGE	Aircraft Ground Equipment
AGL	Above Ground Level
AIMVAL	Air Intercept Missile Evaluation
AoA	Angles of Attack
ASI	Airspeed Indicator
ATC	Air Training Command
ATIC	Aggressor Tactics Instructor Course
AWACS	Airborne Warning and Control System
BFM	Basic Fighter Maneuvers
C2	Command and Control
CAP	Combat Air Patrol
CC	Commander
CIA	Central Intelligence Agency

CINC	Commander-in-Chief
COMMINT	Communications Intelligence
CVBG	US Navy Carrier Battle Group
DACT	Dissimilar Air Combat Training
DCS	Deputy Chief of Staff
DFC	Distinguished Flying Cross
DIA	Defense Intelligence Agency
DNIF	Duties Not Including Flying
DO	Director of Operations
DoD	US Department of Defense
DoE	US Department of Energy
DRMO	Defense Reutilization and Management Office
DT	Director of Test
ECM	Electronic Countermeasures
EID	Electronic Identification
ELINT	Electronic Intelligence
EM	Energy Maneuverability
ETAT	European Tactics Analysis Team, USAF
EW	Electronic Warfare; *also* Early Warning
FA	Frontovaya Aviatsiya (Frontal Aviation, Russian Air Force)
FAA	Federal Aviation Authority
FAC	Forward Air Controller
FCF	Functional Check Flight
FIS	Fighter Interceptor Squadron
FME	Foreign Military Exploitation
FTD	Foreign Technology Division
FWIC	Fighter Weapons Instructor Course
FWS	Fighter Weapons School; *also* Fighter Weapons Squadron
FWW	Fighter Weapons Wing
FW	Fighter Wing
GAT	Ground Attack Tactics
GCI	Ground Control Intercept
GE	General Electric
H&N	Holmes & Narver
HAVE	Codename given to AFSC program
HFF	High Fast Flyer
HUMINT	Human Intelligence
HVA	High Value Asset
IADS	Integrated Air Defense System
IAF	Israeli Air Force
IDF	Israel Defense Forces
IFE	In Flight Emergency
IFF	Identify Friend or Foe

IG	Inspectorate General, USAF
IMI	Information Management Inc
IP	Instructor Pilot
IR	Infrared
IRS	Internal Revenue Service
JMU	Joint Meritorious Unit
LARAF	Libyan Arab Republic Air Force
LFE	Large Force Exercise
LGB	Laser-Guided Bomb
MAC	Military Airlift Command
MAWTS	Marine Air Weapons Tactics Squadron
MCAS	Marine Corps Air Station
MCM 3-1	Classified Air Force tactics manual
ME	Mission Employment phase for the FWS
MEI	Management Effectiveness Inspection
MOT&E	Multinational Operational Test & Evaluation
MPC	Military Personnel Center
NCO	Noncommissioned Officer
NAS	Naval Air Station
NATO	North Atlantic Treaty Organization
NSA	National Security Agency
NVAF	North Vietnamese Air Force
OER	Officer Effectiveness Report
OSD	Office of the Secretary of Defense
OSI	Office of Special Investigations, USAF
PACAF	Pacific Air Force, USAF
PIO	Pilot-Induced Oscillation
PO	Purchase Order
POL	Petroleum, Oil, and Lubricant
PP	Performance Profile
PVO	Protivo-Vozdushnaya Oborona (Soviet Air Defense Command)
RAF	Royal Air Force
RCAF	Royal Canadian Air Force
REECo	Reynolds Engineering & Electrical Company
RFMDS	Red Flag Measurement and Debriefing System
RIO	Radar Intercept Officer
RoE	Rules of Engagement
ROTC	Reserve Officer Training College
RSU	Runway Service Unit
RTU	Replacement Training Unit
RWR	Radar Warning Receiver
SA	Situational Awareness
SAC	Strategic Air Command, USAF

SAM	Surface-to-Air Missile
SFO	Simulated Flameout
SOF	Supervisor of Flying
STAN/EVAL	Standardization & Evaluation
TAC	Tactical Air Command, USAF
TAF	Tactical Air Forces
TDY	Temporary Duty
TEF	Test & Evaluation Flight
TEG	Test & Evaluation Group
TES	Test & Evaluation Squadron
TFS	Tactical Fighter Squadron
TFTS	Tactical Fighter Training Squadron
TFW	Tactical Fighter Wing
TFWC	Tactical Fighter Weapons Center
TG	Test Group
TTF	Threat Training Facility
TTR	Tonopah Test Range
TX	Conversion course for experienced pilots
UHF	Ultra High Frequency
UPT	Undergraduate Pilot Training
USAF	United States Air Force
USAFE	USAF Europe
USN	United States Navy
VFR	Visual Flight Rules
VVS	Voenno-Vozdushnye Sily (Russian Air Force)
WSEG	Weapon Systems Evaluation Group
WSO	Weapons Systems Officer
XO	Executive Officer
XOO	Director of Operations and Readiness
XOX	Deputy Director of Plans

INDEX

CP stands for CONSTANT PEG;
RE stands for Red Eagles.

Figures in **bold** refer to illustrations.

A

Aggressors (64th and 65th FWS) **107**
    accidents and fatalities 151–152, 222–223
    command and control 132
    mentality 98–99, 175, 222–223
    RE relationship with 80, 125, 145, 218–219, 316–317
    start-up 26–34, 37–46
Air Force Systems Command (AFSC): tests and programs 17–18, 43–44, 54–55, 62, 135, 331
aircraft
    Cessna 404 **239**
    F-4 Phantom II 21, 22–23, 39–40, 167
    F-5E Tiger II 38–39, 42, 168, **233**, **235**, **236**, **238**
    F-8 Crusader 47
    F-14 Tomcat 12, 14, 163–164, **233**, **241**, 265–266
    F-15 Eagle 41–42, 249–250
    F-16 Viper 41–42, **111**, 174, **240**, 289
    F-86 Sabre **235**
    F-117 Nighthawk 54–55, 156, 172–173, 196, 223–224, 262
    F/A-18 Hornet 168, 289
    T-2 Buckeye 126, 280
    T-38 Talon 38–39, 40, **238**, **240**
    T-39A Sabreliner 18
    see also MiGs
Alconbury, RAF 37, 38, 39, 40, 319
Ashy, Gen Joe 230–231, 232, 256, 258–259, 260, 270, 271–272, 276–277, 281, 292
AWACs 300, 333

B

Bandit numbers 64, 335–336
Bland, Maj David F. "Blazo" 193, 230, 250, 257, 270, 271
Boma, Maj Thomas "Boomer" 177, 286, 295–296, 307, 308, 318, 326
Bond, Col Robert "Bobby" 54–55, 86, 224–226
Boothby, LtCol Lloyd "Boots" 25, 26, 28, 29, **106**, **117**
Brown, LtCdr Hugh "Bandit" **6**
    accident and death 86–89, 95–96, 99, 121, 331
    background 79–80, 87–88, 126
Brown, Linda 80, 87–89, 331
Brown, Capt Stephen R. "Brownie" 195, 286
Brubaker, Lt Guy A. 250, 291, 292
Bucko, Maj Lenny **115**
    background 141–143
    on colleagues 175, 215, 251
    leaves RE 200–201
    leisure 169–170
    on MiGs 163–164, 168, 188–189, 193, 220, 280, 296, 297–298, 299
    as RE 144–146, 158, 173, 178–179, 180, 181, 182, 194–195, 197
    after RE 228–229
    and White 230
Burns, Capt Joe Lee 43, 45, 46, **107**, 308
Bush, George Sr 168

C

Carlisle, Capt Herbert J. "Hawk" **116**, 276, 277, 309, 322, 326
Cazessus, Maj Rick "Caz" **116**, 291, 307–308, 325
Chanik, Evan M. Jr 270, 321
China 304, 333

Clark AB 37, 38, 40, 319
Clements, Capt Ed 45, 57, **106**, **107**
Cobleigh, Maj Ed "Fast Eddie" 34–36, 44
COLLEGE DART 29–30
CONSTANT PEG
   Blue Air briefings 269
   documentation 66–67, 95–96, 97–99,
      202–203, 221, 313
   exposure procedures 82–85, 98–99, 122,
      131–132, 198–199, 206–211, 218–219,
      282–283, 294–295, 314–317
   fooling Russian satellites 158–159, 254
   killer identification 283, 303–304
   secrecy and rumors 261–263, 268–70,
      279–280, 325–327
   set-up 50–56
   shut down 319–325
   see also Red Eagles
Corder, Maj Charles "Chuck" **111**, **114**, **115**
   background 124
   leisure 169
   as RE 136, 153, 158, 163, 173, 214
   as temporary commander 172
Corder, Maj John 26–27
Coyle, Mike 312, 327
Craig, Capt Robert E. 224, 305
Crawley, Ike **113**
Creech, Gen
   aims for RE 98–99, 131–132, 174–175,
      190, 207, 219, 222, 263
   attitude to dress 60
   and Bush's visit 168
   recruitment and briefing of RE commanders
      90, 133, 174–175, 256, 257, 284
   and tactics 131–132
   and Thunderbirds 151
Cunningham, Gen Charles J. Jr 131, 144,
   153–154, 284
Cuthill, LtCol Fred **105**

East Germany 32–33, 302
Egypt 61–62, 191, 288
Ellis, Senior M/Sgt Robert O. "Bobby" **108**, **119**
   background and skills 56, 80–81, 94, 134

leaves RE 187, 214–216, 258
and Postai's accident 162
recruitment methods 93
relationship with RE commanders 92, 133,
   187, 214–216
Energy Maneuverability (EM) theory 74
Evans, Col James C. "Bear" 304–305, 317

family life sacrifices 199–200
Fighter Weapons School (FWS) 22, 23–24,
   197–198, 217–220, 230–231
   see also Aggressors
fini flights 130–131, 200–201, 270, 271–272
Fischer, Gen Eugene 222–223, 230, 232,
   256, 272
formations 23, 24
Frick, LtCol Glenn "Pappy" **117**
   background and contacts 29, 31, 44, 45
   Cairo posting 61, 77
   character and interests 59–60
   and CP 53, 55, 56–57, 57–58, 60–61, 62,
      69–70, 73, 76–77
Fuerst, Capt Nickie J. 302
functional check flights (FCFs) 67–68
Futryk, Maj Dan "Truck" 322–323

Gaulker, Dell **109**
GCI 40, 85–86, 171, 222, 287, 295,
   322–323
Geisler, Maj Francis "Paco"
   and admin 212
   background 46, 202, 206–207
   on Bland's fini flight 271
   and Buck Fever 51–52
   on colleagues 186–187, 217, 252,
      259–260, 264
   documents **339**
   on HAVE IDEA 278
   joins RE 201–202
   leaves RE 276–277, 291–292
   and Mahoney 293
   on maintaining secrecy 261, 262
   on maintenance guy's death 332
   on MiGs 227–228, 278–279, 296, 298,
      300, 304
   as ops officer 257, 270, 281
   as prankster 252–255, 264, 273–274
   as RE IP and pilot 130, 206, 207–211, 230,
      269, 277, 279, 282, 283, 299
   and Scott 323
   and SENIOR TREND 223–224
Gennin, LtCol George "G2"
   background 173–175

D

Davis, LtCdr Robert E. "Sundance" 293
Donnelly, Gen Charles "Chuck" Jr 51, 52, 53
Drabant, Capt Bob 56, 74–75, 98, 124
Drake, Capt Thomas E. "Gabby" 224, **241**,
   305
Dugan, BrigGen Mike 154, 256, 263, 272,
   319, 322
Dugway Proving Grounds Range 69

E

F

G

and bird invasions 213–214
changes to flying practices 200–201, 205, 218–219, 221–222
changes to maintenance 184–187, 193, 214–217, 257, 258
changes to technology 222
and documentation 202
leaves RE 229
performance assessed 203, 255, 256
and SENIOR TREND 223
staffing practices and recruitment 214, 217–218, 250
takes over RE 172
and VIP tours 196, 197
and Weird Harold 251, 252
Gibbs, LtCol Tom **112, 114, 116**
background 129–130, 132–133
as RE commander 133–134, 137, 153–154, 158
after RE 172, 182
Gilbert, Col William W. 19
Glosson, Col Buster 284–285, 294
Gold Water Ranges 69
Graham, LtCol Rich 96, 151–152
Green, Capt James W. "Wiley" **115**, 160, 162, 202, 230
Green Flag 333
Gregory, Gen Jack 174, 219, 222
Groom Lake 12, 16–17, 268, 272, 295, 329, 333

H

Harold (Weird Harold) 251–252
HAVE BLUE 54–55
HAVE BOAT 337
HAVE DOUGHNUT 18, 20, 43–44, 63, 83, **105, 117, 118**, 279, 337
HAVE DRILL 19, 20, 43, 99, **118, 246**, 279, 337
HAVE FERRY 19, 20, 43–44, 99, **118**, 279, 337
HAVE GARDEN 232, 331, 337
HAVE IDEA 42–48, 104, 278, 337
HAVE PAD 73–74, 337
HAVE PRIVILEGE 19, 279, 337
Heatley, Lt Chuck "Heater" 67, 78, 89, 99, 126, 129, 169, 331
Henderson, Maj Earl "Obi Wan" **105, 107, 109, 110, 116, 117, 236**
and Aggressor program 29–30, 32–33, 37, 38–39, 40–42
background 29, 218
on colleagues 27, 28, 147–148, 178, 216
on Coyle 312
on exposure procedures 122

fini flight 130–131
on fooling Russian satellites 159
on maintenance 214, 216–217
on MiGs 99, 100, 101, 103–104, 127, 163
as RE commander 89–92, 93–99, 123–124, 127–129, 134, 143
as RE pilot 126
on RE STAN/EVAL 150
after RE 144, 153, 187, 191–192, 195, 216–217, 269, 327
Holden, Chuck 58, 69, 70, **117**
Huff, Maj Gerry "Huffer" **109**
background 58
as RE 62, 63, 72, 73, 74–75, 96, 124
after RE 153, 216

I

Indonesia 48, 51
intelligence 32–33, 196, 204, 269, 302, 312–314
Israel 17, 19
Iverson, Maj Ron **108**
background 45
and CP 57, 62, 63, 67, 73, 330
and HAVE IDEA 45, 47
and HAVE PAD 73–74

J

Jackson, Capt Gene 45, 57, **107**
Japan 229

K

Karnes, Tommy **110**
Kelley, Gen Robert 90–91, 93, 153, 231, 284
Kempf, Gen Peter 308, 309, 310, 321
Kinney, Capt Timothy R. "Stretch" 229, 293
Kirby, Gen Mike 174, 195, 219, 230

L

Larsen, Maj Dudley A. 287–290, 310, 322–323, 326
Larsen, Maj Jerry **105**
Lauderette, Col Bob 259, 272, 281, 286
Laughter, Selvyn "Sel" **115**, 129, 145, 163, 175
Libya 146–147, 285–286
Lightfoot, Billy 92, 236
Lyons, M/Sgt Don 64

M

Macy, Martin S.
background 266–267
on Cazessus' accident 307, 308

on colleagues 277
and intelligence 302
on MiGs 304
as RE IP and pilot 282, 285, 287, 288,
290, 322
after RE 326
Mahoney, LtCdr James D. "Tony" 293, 316,
320–321, 323–325
maintenance and maintainers **114**, **119**, **239**
changes and development 133–134,
184–187, 193, 214–217, 230, 257–258,
303
dress 92, 184–185
and F-117 173
family life sacrifices 199
fatal accident 256
proposal to outsource 153, 169, 216–217
protectiveness of assets 63, 64
recruitment 55–56, 93, 258
resourcefulness 80–81, 311–312, 314
see also Ellis, Senior M/Sgt Robert O. "Bobby";
MiGs
Manclark, LtCol John "Mad Jack" **243**
and accidents and safety 306, 308, 309,
310–311
aims and priorities 281–282, 306
background 281
and Bland's fini flight 272
changes made 282, 287, 304, 333
colleagues' views of 307
discipline 295
leaves RE 317
and maintenance 306, 311–312, 314
on Phelan's departure 318
and Postai's death 183, 184
on pranks 292
after RE 321, 327
recruitment 286, 294
on sortie length 280–281
takes over RE 270, 276
and Therrien 303
maneuvers see tactics and maneuvers
Mann, Capt John C. "Flash" 277, 305, 320,
322, 325
Matheny, James "Thug"
accidents 193–195
background 160
on collaborative testing 231, 249–250
on colleagues 175, 177–178, 251–252, 274
and documentation 202–203
on Gennin's changes 186
leaves RE 270
on MiGs 187–188, 189, 190–191, 225,
296, 297, 300–301, 302
and Postai 163, 177–178, 190, 193
on pranks 252

as RE IP and pilot 171, 197–198, 198–199,
267
and STAN/EVAL 260
Mayo, LtCol Robert "Kobe" **106**
and Aggressor program 40
and CP 57, 64–66
documents **338**
on Frick 59
and HAVE IDEA 45–46
learning to fly MiGs 62–63, 64
after RE 72–73, 141
Mazzerati, Chief M/Sgt Matt 258, 259
McCloud, Capt David "Marshall" **108**
background 79
as RE 97, 103, 126, 136, 143, 173
after RE 152, 163, 197, 222, 246
McCort, LtCdr Daniel R. "Bad Bob" 224, 291
McCoy, Capt Brian E. 276, 321
McHenry, Bill **110**
Melson, Col Douglas M. 317, 322
Merlin, Peter 43–44, 62, 68, 135, 333
MiGs
braking systems **120**
canopies 193–195
after CP 327–328
effect on US airmen 11, 13–14, 51–52,
65–66, 85
ejection seats 58–59, 101–102, 127, 163,
165, 186, 188–190, **247**, 281–282, 309
engines 58, 86, 94–95, 100, 165, 187,
226–228, 311, 331
instrument panels: white line 104, **240**, **242**
learning to fly 62–64, 277–279
logbook designations 279–280
RE markings 197
shape and dimensions 12–13, 39, **235**
US modifications to 79
US sources of supply 19, 48, 51, 61–62,
304, 333
USAF academics 42–43
MiG 17 Fresco **118**, **120**, **233**, **238**, **243**, **246**
accidents 156–158, 162–163
flying and fighting 12–14, 76, 95–96,
99–122
US acquisition 19
MiG-21 Fishbed **233**, **235**, **236**, **240**, **243**
accidents 138–139
Chinese **244**, **245**
cockpits **119**, **120**, **239**, **245**, **246**
flying and fighting 164–168, 210–211,
265, 277–279, 290, 324
HAVE DOUGHNUT **105**, **117**, **118**
Indonesian 48, 51, **239**, **241**, **244**,
245, 304
maintenance 187
US acquisition 17–18, 191, 304

MiG-23 Flogger **237, 238, 241**
  accidents 178–179, 224–228
  flying and fighting 163–164, 171, 187–191,
    217, 220, 270, 278, 281, 296–302
  internal features and controls **242, 248**
  maintenance 191–192
  overview 134–137
MiG-25 Foxbat 300
missiles 18, 22–23, 75–76, 233, 313
Mission Employment (ME) 197–198, 315
Morgenfeld, LtCdr Tom 47, 78, 79–80, 86,
  89, 105, **112**
Muellner, Col George 321
Muller, Capt Alvin "Devil" 45, 46, 57, 62, 72,
  73, **107**
Myers, Maj Burt "Buffalo" **115**
  background 129, 130, 217
  on MiGs 167, 190, 217, 296, 298
  as RE 130, 146, 153, 158, 178, 181–182,
    190, 201, 214
  after RE 217, 302
  on Red Flag 171

N

Nathman, John "Black" 160, 161–162,
  202–203, 205, 221, 228, 255, 269,
  285–286
Nellis AFB 22, 24, 36, **234**
Nelson, Maj John "Admiral" 148–150, 153,
  154, 195, 199–200, 202, 228, 272, 312, 328

O

Oberle, Capt Joe "Jose" **111, 112, 113**
  and Aggressor program 30–34, 37
  and Brown's death 89, 90, 95
  on colleagues 81, 124, 133, 152, 178
  and ejection seats 127
  on exposure procedures 83, 84
  on FCFs 67–68
  and Henderson's appointment 90, 91, 92
  and Henderson's fini flight 131
  on integration with Aggressors 80
  learning to fly MiGs 62, 63
  leaves RE 134
  on MiGs 100–101, 102–103, 121, 165–166
  RE career 57–58, 73
  on RE command and control 132
  as RE pilot 82, 126, 143
  and RE set-up 55, 58–59, 69, 73, 76
  on Red Baron reports 25
  on USAF performance in Vietnam 21, 22–23
O'Connor, Lt Stanley R. "Swish" 318, 322
Olds, Col Robin 21, 330
O'Neill, Maj Randy 26, 28, 31, 42, 44–45,
  117

P

Payne, Ralph **113**
Peck, Maj Gaillard "Evil" **109**
  background 35, 50–51
  and Brown's death 88, 89, 95
  dismissal and colleagues' reaction to 89–91,
    124, 151
  on exposure procedures 82, 83–84
  learning to fly MiGs 44, 63, 64
  on MiGs 101, 102, 104, 122, 166, 167
  as RE commander 61, 77, 80–81, 81–82,
    85–86, 96–97, 125
  as RE pilot 82
  and RE set-up 52–56, 61, 69–70, 71–72, 76
  after RE 229, 251, 327
  and Red Flag 34–36
Peck, Peggy 51, 52, 88, 89
Phelan, Capt Edward D. "Hog"
  as accident investigator 308–309, 310
  background 250–251
  and Cazessus' accident 307–308
  and Chanik's departure 321
  leaves RE 318
  on MiGs 297, 298, 301, 304
  near-accident 305–306
  on OER system 268
  as RE pilot 289, 294–295, 316–317
  after RE 327–328
  as safety officer 312–313
  on security and secrecy 262, 270
  on Tonopah runway closure 272–273
Postai, Linda 169, 176–177, 179–184
Postai, Capt Mark "Toast" **6, 115**
  accidents 162–163, 193
  background 143–144
  death 176–184, 189, 190
  leisure 169, 170
  models **237, 238**
pranks 60, 128, 251–255, 264, 273–274,
  295–296
Press, Capt Mike "Bat" **107, 113**
  background 42–43, 45, 57, 129–130
  leaves RE 143
  on MiG-23 296
  party for 60
  as RE 45, 52, 136–137, 143, 139, 189
Prins, Orville 170, 202, 263

R

radar 18, 232, 300, 301–302
Red Baron reports 24–25
Red Eagles (4477th TEF/TES)
  accidents and fatalities 86–89, 138–139,
    156–158, 162–163, 176–184, 224–226,
    305–310, 334

activation 56–61
admin and support 147–150, 268
awards 263, 308
documents 338–341
first ops room **119**
funding 71–72, 81, 212, 222
mishap rate 309
organization 129, 132, 144, 268
origin of names 61, 78
patches **248**
relations with Blue Air pilots 269
sortie length 280–281
sortie stats 125, 137, 154, 191, 219–220,
    255, 272, 292, 317, 326, 335–336
typical day for pilots 85
see also CONSTANT PEG
Red Flag 34–35, 64–66, 85, 170–172,
    282–283, 315–317, 321–323
Red Hats (6513th TS) 44–45, 68, 135,
    231–232
Reich, Col Manfred 265
Robb, LtCdr Jim "Rookie" 12–14, 48,
    212–213, 261, 262, 264–265, 280, 298
Roberts, Spence 286
Rogers, Capt Shelley S. "Scotty" 277, 314
Roy, Capt Michael C. 202, 266

S

Saxman, John B. 200, 286
Scott, Capt Mike "Scotty"
    background 37–38, 218
    on colleagues 203
    after CP shut down 325, 327
    on exposure procedures 131–132
    and Gennin's changes 185–186, 222
    joins RE 96–98
    on measuring flight time 280
    medal 231
    on MiGs 122, 136, 137, 163, 166, 296
    and Navy pilots 307
    near-accidents 138–139, 156–158
    and Postai's accidents and death 162, 178,
        179, 180, 189
    as RE pilot 126, 128
    second RE posting 293–294, 302,
        303–304, 315, 316, 317, 319–320,
        321–322, 323
    and SENIOR TREND 173
    in Somalia 139–141
    on STAN/EVAL 150
    at TAC HQ 211–212, 230, 270, 272,
        283–285, 286
    on TAC's relationship with RE 98–99
SENIOR TREND 172–173, 223–224,
    262, 310
Shawler, Col Wendell 19, 279

Shean, LtCdr Keith **113**, 126, 145, 163, 169
Sheffield, Capt Robert "Catfish"
    background 124–125
    leaves RE 152, 159–160
    and McCloud 152
    on MiGs 166–167, 167–168
    on pranks 128
    as RE pilot 126
    on Smith's death 151
    in Somalia 139–141
    on sortie stats 137
Shervanick, Capt Larry "Shy"
    background 36–37, 160–161
    on colleagues 177, 252
    and CP shut down 318–319, 320, 325
    on MiGs 227, 296, 299, 301, 302
    as RE 171–172, 179, 187, 190, 198,
        203–204, 263
    after RE 270, 283–284, 318–319, 320
Sidra, Gulf of 146–147
Silvers, LtCdr Cary "Dollar" **241**, 287,
    290–291, 296, 307, 310–311, 322, 326
Simmons, Capt Michael G. 285, 326
Skidmore, Maj John "Grunt" 221, 230–231,
    264
Smith, Maj David DL **106, 107**
    and Aggressor program 39
    background 43
    and CP 53, 57–58, 70
    death 151
    and HAVE IDEA 43, 45
    and Thunderbirds 78–79, 151
Smith, Mary Jane 71, 81
Snodgrass, Capt Dale 266
social lives 60, **110, 111, 115**, 129, 145,
    169–170, 306
Somalia 139–141
spin testing 126
STAN/EVAL procedures 150, 260
Strategic Air Command (SAC) 18, 316–317
Stucky, Maj Paul "Stook"
    background 217–218
    leaves RE 291, 299
    physique 259
    as prankster 253–254, 273–274, 292
    as RE 221, 230, 262, 269, 299
Sundell, Maj Charles E. "Smokey" 286–287,
    315, 326
Suter, Maj Richard "Moody" 26, 28, 34–36,
    50, 63
Swalm, Gen Tom 89–90, 93, 126

T

Tactical Air Command (TAC)
    caution 29–30, 34, 97–99, 127–128, 163
    and Red Flag 36

tactics 22
testing interests 18
training entry requirements 40
unhappiness with RE and Aggressors
    174–175
see also Creech, Gen
tactics and maneuvers
    Aggressor program 40–42
    Fishbeds 166, 167, 265–266
    Floggers 188
    high Yo-Yos 152
    manuals 203–204, 269
    NVAF 21
    phone booth 265
    pitching out 200–201
    treeing 289
    USAF in Vietnam 21–26
    see also CONSTANT PEG: exposure
        procedures; MiG-17: flying and fighting;
        MiG-21: flying and fighting; MiG-23:
        flying and fighting
Taylor, Lt Russell M. "Bud" 143–144, 145,
    163, 202, 291
Therrien, Maj Sam 302–303, 308, 314, 316,
    323–324, 326
Thompson, Capt Frederick H. "T-Bear"
    background 267–268
    on colleagues 317
    on OER system 333
    as RE 288–289, 307, 308, 312–313, 315, 321
    after RE 325–326, 328
    and Sundell 286
Threat Training Facility (TTF) 63, 192
Thunderbirds 78–79, 151, 158, 332
Tittle, Capt George 185, 186, 193, 196,
    252, 256
Tolicha Peak 172–173
Tonopah 119, **120**, **234**
    bird invasions 123–124, 213–214
    chosen as site 69–70
    GCI facility 287
    Indian Village 81, 223
    initial development and security 72–73,
        74-75, 76, 81, 86, 93–94
    later development 132, 134, 156, 196–197,
        282
    maintaining secrecy 261–262
    Man Camp 223–224
    runway closure 268, 272–273
    terrain around **244**
    transporting personnel to 76, 173, **239**, 263
TOPGUN 12, 19, 142–143, 212–213
Tullos, Maj George C. "Cajun" 202, 254, 264
TX course 82, 95–96, 103, 225, 278–279

U

US Air Force units
    18th TFW 229
    26th TFTS 37
    49th TFW 65, 75
    53rd TEG Det 3 329
    57th FWW 44–45
    90th TFS 217–218
    414th TFS 44
    422nd TES 232–249
    527th TFTS 39
    4450th TG 172–173, 223–224, 262, 310
    6512th Test Squadron 43–44
    see also Aggressors; Red Eagles; Red Hats
US Marine Corps 142, 144–146
US Navy
    A-4 1 v 1s with RE 194
    and DACT 29–30, 30–31
    funding for CP 71
    MiG exposures 46–48
    original pilots in CP 66, 78
    preparation of pilots for CP 205
    VX-4 47, 66

V

Vandenberg, Gen Hoyt Jr 51, 52, 71–72
VIP tours 127, 168, 196–197, 259–260,
    341

W

Warren, Eunice 147–148
Watley, Maj Monroe 143–144, 187,
    219, 228
Weinberger, Casper 196
Wells, Capt Roger G. 26, 27–28, 37, 38
White, LtCol Phil "Hound Dog" **110**
    background 229–230, 231
    faux pas 259–260
    on first MEI 263
    leaves RE 270, 276
    and pranks 252, 273–274
    as RE commander 229–231, 256,
        257–259, 268, 270, 271, 272, 287
    on working with Red Hats 232
Whittenberg, Karl "Harpo" 79, **111**, 124,
    126, 157, 170, **238**
Wilmoth, Dee 212
wing-loading 34

Z

Zettel, Capt Robert J. "Z Man" 214, 287, 290